HALF THE
HUMAN
EXPERIENCE

HALF THE HUMAN EXPERIENCE

The Psychology of Women

Second Edition

Janet Shibley Hyde
Denison University

B. G. Rosenberg
Antioch University

D. C. Heath and Company   Lexington, Massachusetts   Toronto

ACKNOWLEDGMENTS

p. 1	Dorothy Sayers, "The Human Not-Quite-Human," *Unpopular Opinions* (London: Victor Gollancz, 1946), p. 116.
p. 17	Sigmund Freud, "Some Psychical Consequences of the Anatomical Distinction Between the Sexes," *Collected Papers* (London: Hogarth Press, 1948), vol. 5, p. 190.
pp. 73, 229	Simone de Beauvoir, *The Second Sex*, trans. Parshley (New York: Knopf, 1952), pp. 391, 572.
pp. 89, 185	Boston Women's Health Book Collective, *Our Bodies, Ourselves*, 2d ed. (New York: Simon & Schuster, 1976), p. 63.
p. 113	Quote from Victoria in Phyllis Chesler, *Women and Madness*, Copyright © 1972 by Phyllis Chesler. Reprinted by permission of Doubleday & Co., Inc. and Penguin Books Ltd.
p. 149	Matina Horner, "Fail: Bright Women." Reprinted by permission of *Psychology Today*, Copyright © 1969, Ziff-Davis Publishing Company.
p. 205	Quote from woman respondent in Seymour Fisher, *Understanding the Female Orgasm: Psychology, Physiology, Fantasy*, Copyright © 1973 by Basic Books, Inc., Publishers, New York. Reprinted by permission of Basic Books and Penguin Books Ltd.
p. 220	Barbara Hariton, "The Sexual Fantasies of Women." Reprinted by permission of *Psychology Today*, Copyright © 1973, Ziff-Davis Publishing Company.
p. 249	Deena Metzger, "It Is Always the Woman Who Is Raped." In D. R. Nass, ed., *The Rape Victim* (Dubuque, Iowa: Kendall/Hunt, 1977), p. 6.
p. 271	Abbey Lincoln, "Who Will Revere the Black Woman?" *Negro Digest*, September 1966.
p. 293	Margaret Mead, *Male and Female* (New York: William Morrow, 1949), pp. 38–39.
p. 313	John Stewart Mill, "The Subjection of Women," 1869. Reprinted in *Three Essays by J. S. Mill* (London: Oxford University Press, 1966).

Preface

Our basic goal in preparing a second edition of *Half The Human Experience* is to provide a textbook on the psychology of women for undergraduates who have little or no prior exposure to psychology. While the book is designed as a core text for psychology of women courses, it has been kept relatively brief so that it may also serve as one of several texts in a women's studies course or as a supplementary text in a variety of psychology courses. We have covered the topics that we feel should be included in a comprehensive course on the psychology of women. Some of these are taken from the traditional gender-differences approach: for example, gender differences in personality and abilities. Others are not from the gender-differences tradition, but belong to the psychology of women proper: for example, work on menstrual cycle fluctuations in mood and on lesbianism.

In the first edition, many of the studies addressed rather simple problems and used relatively simple research methods. The new research that we reviewed for this edition seems, in contrast, far more sophisticated in conceptualization and design. Parts of this research have been incorporated into several new chapters. Chapter 7, "Problems of Adjustment and Psychotherapy," reviews evidence on adjustment problems in women, the evidence on sexism in psychotherapy, how traditional therapies work for women, and some new therapies — such as assertiveness training and consciousness-raising — that have been proposed for women. Chapter 9, "Women and Language," focuses on verbal and nonverbal communication and gender differences, along with the feminist analyses of power relations that have been conducted in this area. Chapter 14, "Violence Against Women," reviews psychological research on rape and wife-battering. The brief discussion of masculinity, femininity, and androgyny in the first edition is now expanded to an entire chapter (Chapter 4).

We have also added major new sections to some chapters. Foremost among these is a section on research methods and sources of sex bias in research in Chapter 1. This theme is carried through in later chapters in the interest of stimulating critical thinking. Emphasis on the positive valuation of the female represents another recent trend in woman's and feminist studies. We have developed this theme by pointing out alternative interpretations of the outcomes of many studies. Examples are found particularly in Chapters 1 and 9.

Throughout we have added more feminist scholarship and interpretations. Feminist analyses are becoming increasingly sophisticated and certainly constitute a major perspective in the field. We have included particularly the power, dominance, and status interpretations from feminist thought. With a "truth in labeling" motto in mind, however, we have tried carefully to label feminist interpretations as such, so that those who feel persuaded by the arguments will recognize what they are accepting, and those who are not will recognize what they are rejecting. Our intention is not to brainwash any unsuspecting victims but rather to present a major area of highly relevant scholarship.

To compensate for the additional chapters, we deleted the chapter on sex differences in animal behavior. Users of the first edition commented that faculty had found it interesting but that students often failed to see its relevance, and it did not seem to be in the mainstream of psychology of women research. Some sections — in particular, those on sex-linkage of spatial ability and on blood serum uric acid and achievement motivation — were deleted in light of recent contradicting evidence.

Of course, not everything has changed. In particular, we have tried to maintain the clear, simple writing style that was well received in the first edition. We have tried for solid scholarship explained so that students can readily understand it.

Many reviewers made valuable contributions by their critical comments on the manuscript. Special thanks go to Rhoda Unger and Bonnie Kind for reviewing the entire manuscript, to Cathy Spatz Widom and Bonnie Kind for developmental reviews, and to the reviewers of individual chapters: Annette Brodsky, Florence Denmark, Nancy Henley, Maria Roy, and Rita James Simon.

Janet Shibley Hyde
B. G. Rosenberg

Contents

5
GENDER DIFFERENCES IN
PERSONALITY AND BEHAVIOR   73

6
FROM INFANCY TO OLD AGE:
DEVELOPMENT ACROSS THE LIFESPAN   89

7
PROBLEMS OF ADJUSTMENT
AND PSYCHOTHERAPY   113

8
ABILITIES, ACHIEVEMENT,
AND MOTIVATION   131

HALF THE
HUMAN
EXPERIENCE

1
INTRODUCTION

The first thing that strikes the careless observer is that women are unlike men. They are "the opposite sex" — (Though why "opposite" I do not know; what is the "neighboring sex"?). But the fundamental thing is that women are more like men than anything else in the world.

DOROTHY SAYERS, Unpopular Opinions

The topic of "women" has been in the news a great deal recently. Women's groups strive for equal political and economic treatment, abortion on demand, day care centers, and other causes. Books with titles like *Sexual Politics* and *The Female Eunuch* have become best-sellers. *Time* magazine has added a news section on "The Sexes." And that sensitive barometer of public attention to the news, the cartoon, frequently focuses on women, satirizing the humorous side of gender role stereotypes or highlighting some of the absurdities in modern women's lives.

Much of the emphasis has been on the inequality of power relations between the sexes, women's lack of political equality, the scarcity of women in high-status, powerful occupations. According to this approach, women are second-class citizens, members of what Simone de Beauvoir, one of the great French existential philosophers of the twentieth century, calls "The Second Sex." While the political approach is important and certainly highlights one aspect of reality, we hope in this book to focus more on the psychological nature of women's situation.

SEX, GENDER, AND SEXISM

Before proceeding, some terms need to be defined. First, it is worth noting that in our language the term "sex" is sometimes used ambiguously. That is, sometimes it is used to refer to sexual behaviors such as sexual intercourse, while other times it is used to refer to males and females. Usually, of course, the meaning is clear from the context. For example, if an employment application says "Sex: ——," you don't write "As often as possible." It is clear here that the question is about whether you are a female or a male. On the other hand, what is the topic of a book entitled *Sex and Temperament in Three Primitive Societies*? Is it about female roles and male roles in those societies, or is it about the sexual behavior of primitive people?

To reduce this ambiguity, we are going to use the term "sex" to refer to sexual behaviors and the term "gender" to refer to males and females (Hyde, 1979). "Gender differences," then, refers to differences between females and males. Other scholars have adopted other conventions in this regard. For example, some scholars prefer to use the term "sex differences" to refer to innate or biologically-produced differences between females and males, and "gender differences" to refer to male-female differences that result from learning and the social roles of females and males (e.g., Unger, 1979). The problem with this terminology is that studies will often document a female-male difference without being at all clear as to what causes it—biology, society, or both. Therefore, we are simply going to use the term "gender differences" for male-female psychological differences, and leave their causation as a separate question.

"Sexism" is another term that will be relevant to some of the discussions in this book. The *American Heritage School Dictionary* defines sexism as "discrimination by members of one sex against the other, especially by males against females." That is a reasonable basic definition for our purposes. There has been a recent trend toward using the term "reverse sexism" for discrimination against males, although it would seem preferable to use the term "sexism" for discrimination against either females or males on the basis of their gender. (Actually, using our terminology, the term should probably be "genderism," but it will not be used because sexism and sex bias are the standard terms.) Here we will be concerned with sexism as discrimination against women. Some people feel uncomfortable using the term "sexism," because they think of it as a nasty label to hurl at someone or something. Actually, however, it is a good, legitimate term that describes a particular phenomenon, namely discrimination on the basis of gender, particularly discrimination against women. It will be used in that spirit in this book, not as a form of name-calling. Finally, it is important to recognize that men are not the only sexists; women can also be prejudiced against women.

One final term that needs to be defined in this context is "feminist." A feminist is a person who favors political, economic, and social equality of women and men, and therefore favors the legal and social changes that will be necessary to achieve that equality. Feminists generally consider this term preferable to others such as "women's libber" or "libber," which are often used in a derogatory manner.

Let us turn now to the topic at hand.

FIGURE 1.1

DOONESBURY   **by Garry Trudeau**

Source: Copyright, 1974 G. B. Trudeau / Distributed by Universal Press Syndicate.

IS THERE A PSYCHOLOGY
OF WOMEN?

Depending on the inflection, the above question has different meanings, and therefore requires different answers. Is there a *psychology* of women? Thus emphasized, the question refers to whether a psychological approach to understanding women, as compared with, say, a political or economic one, is valuable. We will leave this question unanswered for the present, but we hope to demonstrate in the course of this book that the psychological approach is both interesting and important, and that attempts to remedy women's political status, by themselves, may leave a host of psychological ills still present and in need of attention.

Is there a psychology of women? The second variation of inflection raises the issue of whether the psychology of women actually exists, whether it is a legitimate area of specialization within the field of psychology. Does the area contain sufficient content, research, and theory to be considered a subdiscipline of psychology? Or is it just a fad, another kind of "pop psych" (as some of our colleagues have suggested) that will produce a few paperbacks and then be forgotten, a field with which no "respectable" psychologist would want to be associated?

In fact, the psychology of women has quite respectable ancestry in a traditional field of psychology known as *differential psychology*. That people differ, one from another, in their behavior has probably been obvious ever since humans have been capable of self-awareness. For the last century these individual differences in behavior have been the subject of scientific study. One particular dimension of individual differences is the differences between males and females, and these have received their due — perhaps more than their due — attention, both in research and in theories. Developmental theorists, from Freud to the modern role theorists, have given considerable attention to the observed gender differences in behavior. Generally their theories have had the problem (to which we will return later) of viewing the male as normative and the female as a deviation from this norm.

More recently, the psychology of women has emerged as a distinct area, which already has to its credit the discovery of some phenomena — the motive to avoid success, menstrual-cycle changes in mood, and, largely through the research of Masters and Johnson, a better understanding of female sexuality. There is no doubt, then, that there *is* a psychology of women, with a long history of theory and research and with a present of new and important discoveries. Recognizing this, there is now a division of the American Psychological Association on the psychology of women.

Finally, Is there a psychology of *women*? This inflection raises the question of whether women have a special psychology different from that of men. Certainly there are abundant stereotypes implying that women differ psychologically from men — they are reputed to be less rational and logical, and to have different attitudes toward and motivations for sex. Psychological research indicates that some of these stereotypes have a basis in reality, and that some simply do not. It is this research — showing when men and women differ psychologically and when they don't, and what this tells us about women's psychology — that is the topic of this book.

There is a paradox inherent in trying to understand the psychology of women, a paradox that is captured in the quote at the beginning of this chapter. Women are at once different from men and very similar to men. While gender differences are important in defining women's psychology, gender similarities are also important. Both scientific and nonscientific views of women have concentrated on how they differ from men; we hope to pay attention to the similarities. This paradoxical tension between gender differences and gender similarities will be a continuing theme throughout the book.

WHY STUDY THE PSYCHOLOGY OF WOMEN?

Most textbooks include an introductory section on why people should study that particular topic; the idea is, presumably, to motivate people to continue with the course and with reading the book. Such a section does not seem quite so necessary in a book on the psychology of women. The main reason for studying it is obvious: it is interesting. Many women, for example, take such a course because they want to understand themselves better, a goal they may feel was not met by their other psychology courses. Men may take such a course wanting to understand women better. Therefore, many good personal reasons exist for wanting to study the psychology of women.

There are also some good academic reasons for studying the psychology of women. Many of the traditional psychological theories have literally been theories about man. They have treated woman, at best, as a variation from the norm. Perhaps the best example is psychoanalytic theory, to be discussed in Chapter 3. Similarly, a sex bias has existed in many aspects of psychological research, a point to be discussed later in this chapter. As a result, traditional psychology has often been about men, and it has often operated from very traditional assumptions about gender roles. One way of correcting these biases is by developing a psychology of women. Psychology of women thus provides information about a group that has often been overlooked in research and theory, and it opens up new perspectives on gender roles and ways they might be changed.

Finally, one other reason for studying the psychology of women is that the female experience differs *qualitatively* from the male experience in some ways. Only women experience menstruation, pregnancy, childbirth, and breastfeeding. In addition to these biologically-produced experiences, there are culturally-produced uniquenesses to women's experience produced by the gender roles in our culture. For example, walking down the street and being whistled at is an experience nearly unique to women in our culture. One of the points of the feminist movement, and particularly of consciousness-raising groups, is that women need to communicate more with each other about these female experiences. It is therefore worthwhile to have a course that provides information on these topics, and that also gives people a chance to express their feelings about their experiences. Such communication should help women cope better with the female experience, or change the aspects of it that need to be changed.

SHOULD MEN STUDY THE PSYCHOLOGY OF WOMEN?

Some men express a hesitancy about studying the psychology of women, as if somehow the secrets of women's psychology should be known only to women. Yet it would seem to be of the utmost interest, not to mention practical value, to be able to understand one's spouse, girl friend, boss, or co-worker better. It is a rare male who is exempt from interactions with females, and certainly there is value in having a better understanding of such a large part of humanity.

In addition, recent research suggests that some of the phenomena discovered in women's psychology may also, in this time of social change, be in the process of becoming common for men. For example, in 1946, the sociologist Mirra Komarovsky documented the stresses of conflicting role expectations for college women — academic competence and career orientation are expected, yet these are in conflict with traditional femininity, which is also expected. More recently, Komarovsky (1973) has documented the appearance of a similar phenomenon for college men, who now seem to be caught in a conflict between the norms of intellectual superiority for men versus intellectual equality of women and men. With the current upheaval in gender roles, the psychology of women studied by men today may be their own psychology in a few years.

SOURCES OF SEX BIAS IN PSYCHOLOGICAL RESEARCH

Although research in psychology of women is really in its infancy, it is progressing at a rapid pace. Certainly we will be able to provide you with much important information about the psychology of women in this book, but there are still more questions yet to be answered than have been already answered. With research on psychology of women expanding so rapidly, many important discoveries will be made in the next 10 or 20 years. Therefore, someone who takes a course on the psychology of women should do more than just learn what is currently known about women. It is probably even more profitable to gain some skills so as to become a "sophisticated consumer" of psychological research. That is, it is very important that you be able to read intelligently and to evaluate future studies of women that you may find in newspapers, magazines, or scholarly journals. To do this, you need to develop at least three skills: (1) know how psychologists go about doing research; (2) be aware of ways in which sex bias may affect research; and (3) be aware of problems that may exist in research on gender roles or psychology of women. The following discussion is designed to help you develop these skills.

How psychologists do research   Figure 1.2 is a diagram of the process that psychologists go through in doing research. The diagram also shows some of the points at which bias may enter (to be discussed in more detail below).

The process, in brief, is generally this: the scientist starts with some theoretical model, whether a formal model such as psychoanalytic theory, or merely a set of personal assumptions. Based on the model or assumptions, the scientist then formulates a question. The purpose of the research is to answer that question. Next, she or he designs the research, which involves several substeps: a behavior must be chosen; a way to measure the behavior must be devised; a group of appropriate subjects must be chosen; and a research design must be developed. One of these substeps — finding a way to *measure* the behavior — is probably the most fundamental aspect of psychological research. Two interesting examples of measuring behavior relevant to psychology of women are the tests to measure androgyny (to be discussed further in Chapter 4) and the motive to avoid success (to be discussed further in Chapter 8).

The next step is for the scientist to collect the data. The data are then analyzed statistically and the results are interpreted. Next, the scientist publishes the results, which are read by other scientists and incorporated into the body of scientific knowledge (and also are put into textbooks). Finally, the system comes full circle, because the results are fed into the theoretical models that other scientists will use in formulating new research.

Now let us consider some of the ways in which sex bias — bias that may affect our understanding of the psychology of women or of gender roles — may enter into this process.

Biased theoretical model   The theoretical model or set of assumptions the scientist begins with has a profound effect on the outcome of the research. Sex bias may enter if the scientist begins with a biased theoretical model. Perhaps the best example of a biased theoretical model is psychoanalytic theory. A person with a psychoanalytic orientation might design

FIGURE 1.2

The process of psychological research, and ways in which sex bias may enter.

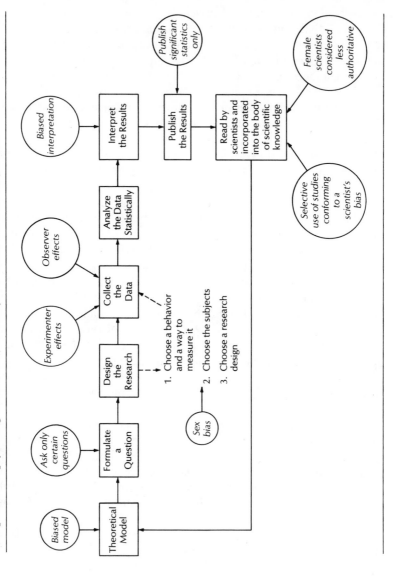

research to document the presence of penis envy, or masochism, or immature superego in women; someone with a different theoretical orientation wouldn't even think to ask such questions. It is very important for you to become sensitive to the theoretical orientation of a scientist reporting a piece of research— and sometimes the theoretical orientation isn't stated, it just has to be inferred — because that orientation affects the rest of the research and the conclusions that are drawn.

What questions are asked   The questions a scientist asks are shaped not only by a theoretical model but also by gender-role stereotypes. Bias may enter when only certain questions are asked and others ignored, partly as a result of stereotypes. For example, there are many studies of fluctuations in women's moods over monthly cycles. However, until quite recently no one has thought to ask whether men also might experience monthly mood fluctuations. Reading the research, one might get the impression that women are moody and men are not; but the research appears to indicate this only because no one has investigated men's mood shifts. Stereotypes about women and men have thus influenced the kinds of questions that have been investigated scientifically.

Sex bias in choice of subjects   There is good evidence that bias exists in choosing subjects for psychological research. In particular, males are used more frequently as subjects than females are. Not only is this true in research with humans (Carlson, 1971a; Dan and Beekman, 1972) but it is also true in research with animals. In a survey of studies of animal behavior, we found that 62 percent of the studies used one gender only, and of those, 75 percent used males only (Hyde and Rosenberg, 1976). Therefore, nearly half of all studies were based on male subjects only.

In research with humans, some entire areas of research have been conducted using male subjects only. A good example is the classic research on achievement motivation, which was based on males only (McClelland et al., 1953).

It seems likely that the choice of subjects is influenced in part by the kind of behavior the psychologist is studying, as well as by gender-role stereotypes. For example, in social psychologists' research on aggression — a "masculine" behavior — nearly 50 percent of the studies were done using male subjects only as compared with about 10 percent using females only and 40 percent using both genders. This 50 percent is higher than the percentage of male-only research in psychology in general (McKenna and Kessler, 1977). Therefore, it seems that when psychologists study a stereotyped "masculine" behavior — aggression — they are not likely to include female subjects.

The problem with this kind of bias is that it leads us to have not a psychology of human behavior, but rather a psychology of male behavior.

Experimenter effects   In the step of research in which the data are collected, two important kinds of bias may enter: experimenter effects and observer effects.

Experimenter effects occur when some characteristic of the experimenter affects the way subjects behave, and thus affects the outcome of the experiment (Rosenthal, 1966). In particular, it has been demonstrated that the gender of the experimenter may affect subjects' behavior. For example, in sex research, subjects report more sexual feelings to an experimenter of the same gender than to one of the opposite gender (Walters et al., 1962). The evidence indicates that with children, female experimenters get better performance, while with adult subjects, male experimenters get better performance (Rumenik et al., 1977; see also Harris, 1971).

It is rather disturbing to realize that an experiment might have quite different outcomes, depending on whether the experimenter was a man or a woman. Moreover, since the majority of psychological research, at least until recently, has been conducted by men, it seems possible that the results might have been quite different had it been conducted by women.

Incidentally, the problem of sex bias from experimenter effects is not an unsolvable one. The situation can be handled by having several experimenters — half of them female, half of them male — collect the data. This should balance out any effects due to the gender of the experimenter, and demonstrate whether the gender of the experimenter did have an effect on the subjects' behavior. Unfortunately this procedure is seldom used, mostly because it is rather inconvenient.

Observer effects   Another important bias that may enter at the stage of data collection is observer effects.

Observer effects occur when the experimenter's expectations for the outcome of the research influence his or her observations and recording of the data. For example, in one study observers (really the subjects) were to count the number of turning movements by planaria (flatworms); half of the observers had been led to expect a great deal of turning, the other half very little. The observers who expected a great deal of turning reported twice as many turns as the observers who expected little (Cordaro and Ison, 1963). To paraphrase Flip Wilson, what you expect is what you get.

Observer effects may be a source of bias in gender role research and psychology of women research. In particular, scientists are no more immune than lay people are to having stereotyped expectations for the behavior of females and males. These stereotyped expectations might lead scientists to find stereotyped gender differences in behavior where there are none. As an example, consider research on gender differences in aggression of nursery school children. If observers expect more aggression from boys, that may be just what they get, even though the boys and girls behaved identically. This is analogous to the observers who expected more turns from the planaria and found just that.

The technical procedure that is generally used to guard against observer effects is the "double-blind." It simply means that observers are kept unaware of (blind to) which experimental group subjects are in, so that the observers' expectations cannot affect the outcome. Unfortunately, the double-blind method is virtually impossible in gender differences research, as the gender of a subject is almost always obvious from appearance, and therefore the observer cannot be "blind" to it or unaware of it.

One exception is infants and small children, whose gender is notoriously difficult to determine, at least when clothed. This fact was used in a clever study that provides some information on whether observer effects do influence gender roles research. Adults rated the behavior of 17-month-old children on videotape (Meyer and Sobieszek, 1972). For a given child, half the observers were told it was a male, and half were told it was a female. Although the results were not conclusive, there was some suggestion that observers rated the behavior of a child differently depending on what gender they thought the child was.

Unfortunately, there are no other studies available documenting whether observer effects influence the outcomes of gender-role research. It remains to be demonstrated, for example, whether trained scientists would have the same bias as the adults in the study described above. Therefore we cannot make any firm statements about how much of a problem observer effects are. At the very least, though, we should be aware of them, and certainly they deserve further research.

Bias in interpretations   Once the scientist has collected the data and analyzed them statistically, the results must be interpreted. Often the interpretation a scientist makes is at best a large leap of faith away from the results. Therefore this is also a stage at which bias may enter.

As an example, let us consider a fairly well-documented phenomenon of psychological gender differences. A class of students takes its first exam in Introductory Psychology. Immediately after taking the exam, but before getting the results back, the students are asked to estimate how many points (out of a possible 100 points) they got on the exam. On the average, males will estimate that they got higher scores than females will estimate they got (see Chapter 8). At this point, the data have been collected and analyzed statistically. It can be stated (neutrally) that there are statistically significant gender differences, with men estimating more points than women. The next question is, how do we interpret that result? The standard interpretation is that it indicates that women lack self-confidence or have low confidence in their abilities. The interpretation that is not made, although it is just as logical, is that men have unrealistically high expectations for their own performance.

The point is that, given a statistically significant gender difference, it can often be interpreted in two opposite ways, one of which is favorable to men, one of which is favorable to women. Sometimes there is no way of verifying which interpretation is right. As it happens in the example above, there is a way, since we can find out how the students actually did on the exam. Those results indicate that women estimate their scores fairly accurately, while men make fairly large overestimates. Thus the second interpretation is probably more accurate than the first.

It is important to become sensitive to the point at which scientists go beyond their data to interpret them, and to become aware of when those interpretations may be biased. Other good examples of bias in interpretations are the research on gender differences in rod-and-frame test performance (to be discussed in Chapter 8) and gender differences in language (Chapter 9).

Publishing significant results only   Once the data have been analyzed and interpreted, the next step is to publish the results. There seems to be a tendency in psychological research to publish "significant" results only. This does not mean significant in the sense of "important" necessarily; it means significant in the sense of being the result of a statistical test that reaches the .05 level of significance.

What are the implications of this tendency for our understanding of gender roles and psychology of women? It means that there is a tendency to report statistically significant gender differences and to omit mention of nonsignificant gender differences. That is, we tend to hear about it when males and females differ, but we tend not to hear about it when males and females are the same. Thus there would be a bias toward emphasizing gender differences, and ignoring *gender similarities.*

This bias may also enter into psychology of women research such as menstrual cycle studies (a point to be discussed in detail in Chapter 11).

Other biases   The final two biases shown in Figure 1.2 are fairly self-explanatory and require little discussion here. If there is a tendency for reports by female scientists to be considered less authoritative than reports by male scientists, this would introduce bias, particularly when combined with bias due to experimenter effects as discussed previously. Also, another kind of bias is introduced if scientists have a tendency to remember and use in their work studies that conform to their own biases or ideas, and to ignore those that do not.

Conclusion   We have discussed a number of problems with research that may affect our understanding of women — and men. Of course, they probably are not present in every study in the area, and certainly we don't mean to suggest that all psychological research is worthless. The point is to become sensitive to biases that may — or may not — be present when one is reading reports of research. It is particularly important for you to become sensitive to the theoretical orientation of a writer and to biased interpretations of results.

LOOKING AHEAD

In the next chapter we shall consider the antecedents to the psychology of women by looking at the images of women in mythology and religion — at the "pre-scientific" view of women. These images are an expression both of reality and of the superstitions regarding women among primitive, less "civilized" people. They are also a source of many of the stereotypes and unquestioned assumptions held about women in this "scientific" age. In Chapter 3 we shall look at the contributions to the understanding of female development by some of the major theoretical systems of psychology — psychoanalytic theory, social learning theory, and cognitive-developmental theory.

Following these theoretical views, later chapters will focus on research about what women are actually like psychologically. Chapter 4 is about the traditional personality characteristics called femininity and masculinity, and a more contemporary concept, androgyny. Chapter 5 reviews evidence on gender differences in personality to see the ways in which women and men differ and the ways in which they are similar. In Chapter 6 we shall discuss female experiences, adjustment, and roles across the lifespan, from birth to old age. Following this, in Chapter 7, we shall consider various problems that may occur in female adjustment, what happens to women when they seek psychotherapy for their problems, and what new therapies are being developed for women. Following these chapters on female personality, we discuss women and achievement in Chapter 8, by considering research on gender differences in intellectual abilities, research on achievement in women, and several psychological factors (achievement motivation, motive to avoid success, and attribution patterns) that may contribute to women's success or lack of it. Chapter 9 is about women and language — whether there are gender differences in language use, how the structure of the English language treats women, and how women and men communicate nonverbally.

Chapters 10 to 14 are about women in relation to their bodies. Chapter 10 considers the evidence on whether there are biological influences — such as hormone effects — on gender differences and female behavior. Chapter 11 is about psychological research on several women's health issues — menstruation, menopause, pregnancy and childbirth, abortion, and mastectomy. Chapter 12 explores female sexuality, including Masters and Johnson's research on the physiology of female sexual response, research on the psychology of female sexuality, and sexual dysfunction and therapy for women. Chapter 13 is about lesbianism — a variation in female sexuality that has been prominent in the women's movement debate — and bisexuality. Chapter 14 is about violence against women as seen in rape and wife-battering.

An attempt is made in Chapters 15 and 16 to widen our perspective and to see to what extent the psychology of women, as described in the rest of the book, is limited to middle-class, white American women. Chapter 15 considers the psychology of black American women. It also examines the notion that psychologically, women are a minority group. In Chapter 16 we shall look at the large variations in women's roles cross-culturally, from primitive to modern, advanced societies. In the final chapter, we summarize some of the major themes of the book and suggest important questions for the future.

A number of important themes will recur throughout the book. One is *gender similarities*, the phenomenon that females and males are psychologically more similar than they are different. Another is the difference between *theory* and *empirical evidence*. Many theories of women's behavior have been proposed. Some have solid data (empirical evidence) backing them, while others do not. Not every theory is true, nor is every one a good description or explanation of behavior. Just because Freud said something does not make it true (or false). Readers need to become sensitive to the difference between statements based on theory and statements based on empirical evidence. Another important distinction is *traits* versus *situational determinants* of behavior. A continuing controversy in psychology is whether behavior is determined more by a person's enduring traits (such as a personality trait), or whether behavior is determined more by the particular situation the person is in. Advocates of the latter position point out how inconsistent people's behavior can be from one situation to another — for example, a man may be aggressive toward a business competitor, but passive or nurturant toward his wife. This suggests that his behavior is not determined by an enduring personality trait (aggressiveness), but rather by the particular situation he is in. Later in the book we will also refer to this trait as a distinction between intrapsychic or internal factors (traits) versus external (situational) factors. Applied to the psychology of women, the question becomes whether women are more influenced by personality traits that distinguish them from men, or whether their behavior is more determined by the situations they find themselves in. For example, is the lack of professional accomplishments by women due to some trait such as the motive to avoid success (Chapter 8), or to situational factors such as job discrimination? This distinction also has practical implications. In trying to improve women's lives, if we decide that the problem is personality traits, then we would try to change the early experiences or childrearing practices that create those personality traits. If we decide, on the other hand, that situational factors are more important, we would want to change the situations women are in, such as ending job discrimination. Finally, one other important theme is the importance of *values* in a scientific understanding of women. Values affect the scientific theories that are proposed and the way research is done. In particular, they affect the way research is interpreted, a point discussed earlier in the chapter. Readers need to become sensitive to the values expressed by a particular scientific position.

One further comment is in order to delineate the content of this volume. This is a book on the psychology of women, not a book on gender roles or gender differences. Some readers may find that we give too little attention to males. We would reply that the topic is women, not men. Certainly we will talk about male behavior, because part of the data on psychology of women comes from the data on gender differences, but we are most concerned with understanding women, and gender similarities must be included as part of that understanding. Thus if we say, for example, that women have certain adjustment problems in middle- and old-age, we are not implying that men do not have such problems. Rather we are saying that to understand women, we must recognize their problems, whether they are similar to or different from those of men. We are not suggesting that psychology of men is not important or worthy of study, but it is not the topic of this book. Our topic is the psychology of women. Sometimes it is different from the psychology of men, sometimes the same. In the following pages we shall explore what is known about the psychology of women and what remains to be understood.

Adam and Eve by Albrecht Dürer (Germany, 1471–1528).

2

IMAGES OF WOMEN IN MYTHOLOGY AND RELIGION

So the Lord God caused a deep sleep to fall upon the man, and while he slept took one of his ribs and closed up its place with flesh; and the rib which the Lord God had taken from the man he made into a woman and brought her to the man. Then the man said,

> *"This at last is bone of my bones*
> *and flesh of my flesh;*
> *she shall be called Woman,*
> *because she was taken out of Man."*

GENESIS 2:21–23

Eve, the first woman, responsible for the fall of humanity; Pandora, the first woman in Greek mythology, who released all the evils besetting humanity when she opened the forbidden box; Ishtar, the Babylonian earth mother and fertility goddess, but also goddess of war and destruction; Marilyn Monroe, a myth in her own time — how have women been represented in mythology, and what insight does this give us into the psychology of women? What does this tell us about attitudes toward women, how men view women, and how women view themselves?

JUNG'S THEORY

It may seem strange to begin a scientific book by looking at mythology, which is hardly amenable to study in the laboratory, to evaluation on the basis of numbers of bar presses or correct answers to true-false questions. Yet, according to some psychologists, myths do represent an important source of information about human psychology, and particularly about its unconscious aspects.

The psychologist Carl Jung and his followers have argued most strongly for analyzing mythology, together with dream contents, for a better understanding of the unconscious; the unconscious, according to Jung, has an important influence on the total personality. According to this theory, the personality of any given individual has its roots in history. (For a brief review of Jung's theory of personality, see Hall and Lindzey, 1970). The part of the psyche that contains these ancient memory traces is called the *collective unconscious*. It is a storehouse of memory traces inherited from all previous generations, and from animal ancestors as well — what Jung calls one's "racial" memory. Jung, of course, does not mean that these memories are inherited in the sense of being passed by genes and chromosomes, but rather that they represent universal inherited tendencies for people to think and to perceive in certain ways. The collective unconscious contains these universal symbols and interpretations that are shared by all people, ancient and modern. These symbols appear both in dreams and in myths.

The collective unconscious contains numerous *archetypes*, which are universal "inherited" ideas containing a large emotional component. For example, there is a mother archetype, which is the image of what a mother is, formed through all the centuries of human interaction with mothers. Thus, an infant interacts with its mother not only on the basis of what the mother does, but also on the basis of the baby's archetype of mother, possessed at birth and shared with all other people.

18

Therefore, following Jung's theory, one must look at history and mythology for a better understanding of modern attitudes toward women. These attitudes may result not only from interactions with women in the current social structure, but may also contain a component carried over from previous generations, according to Jung, in the collective unconscious. Thus, in looking at mythological views of women, we may actually be seeing our own unconscious views, free of the cover of rationalization.

Two important archetypes contained in the collective unconscious are particularly helpful in understanding the psychology of women. Like Freud, Jung recognized the inherent *androgyny* of all people — that any person, whether male or female, has both a masculine side and a feminine side. Jung used the term "anima" to refer to the feminine archetype in men, and "animus" to refer to the masculine archetype in women. Thus, the anima is a personification of the feminine psychological tendencies in a man, such as moods, hunches, receptiveness to the irrational, capacity for personal love, a feeling for nature, and a relation to the unconscious or spiritual (von Franz, 1964). The animus personifies the masculine psychological tendencies in a woman, including rationality, strong convictions, courage, and truthfulness. The anima, like the animus, may be either a positive or a negative force in the personality. For example, the negative part of a man's anima can be revealed in depressed moods, insecurity, unrealistic romanticism, or nasty, destructive remarks. The negative part of a woman's animus may be expressed as brutality, destructiveness, and a numbing of the emotions. But the anima and the animus, in their positive aspects, allow people to relate to and to understand members of the other gender. Thus, men understand women by virtue of their own feminine component, the anima, as women understand men through their animus.

A casual reading of Jungian views of psychology of women (for example, de Castillejo, 1973) may leave one with the feeling that his theory is very sexist in its orientation, with references to "feminine" tendencies, a woman with too strong a masculine component, or the need for women to get in touch with their own feminine natures. However, when referring to the "feminine principle," the Jungian analyst does not mean the feminine role as defined by a particular culture, but rather a principle or law that transcends any particular time, much like the law of gravity (Harding, 1971). The feminine principle represents the nonrational, the spiritual, and is the basis for human relationships. Further, the feminine principle is not possessed by women only, but is also part of men, although it is generally expressed more strongly in women. In addition, in the Jungian approach a differential valuing is not attached to the masculine as compared with the feminine — it is recognized that the masculine as well as the feminine can be either good or evil, and that both components must be in balance in a well-developed personality. Indeed, Jungian analysts contend that many of our contemporary problems, including the low status of women, may be attributed to the fact that ours is a masculine era, relying on science and rationality for solving problems, with a concomitant neglect of the feminine principle (Harding, 1971). Their suggestion is that we need to regain a sense of the feminine — of emotion, intuition, relatedness.

In summary, mythology can provide important information about psychology, in particular about the psychology of women. The importance of mythology is especially apparent from the theoretical perspectives of Jungian psychology, although scientific support for Jungian interpretations is lacking. Jung also provides some concepts useful in understanding the psychology of women, for example the anima and animus, which are the opposite-gender components in an individual's personality.

Let us proceed now to see how women have been portrayed in mythology.

FEMININE EVIL

One of the clearest images of women in mythology is their portrayal as the source of evil (Hays, 1964). In the Judeo-Christian tradition, Eve disobeyed God's orders and ate from the fruit of the tree of knowledge. As a result, Adam and Eve were forced to leave the Garden of Eden, and Eve, the woman, became the source of original sin, responsible for the fall of humanity. In a more ancient myth, the Greek god Zeus created the lovely maiden Pandora to bring misery to earth in revenge for the theft of fire by Prometheus. Pandora was given a box or jar containing all the evils of the world, which she was told not to open. But Pandora opened the box, and thus all the evils it contained spread over the world. In Chinese mythology the two forces Yin and Yang correspond to feminine and masculine, and Yin, the feminine, is seen as the dark, or evil, side of nature. In the story of Cleopatra, which is on the borderline between mythology and history, the Egyptian queen is seen as destroying Mark Antony through the powers of her sexuality.

Historically, perhaps the most frightening manifestation of the belief in feminine evil was the persecution of witches beginning in the Middle Ages and persisting into Puritan America. Guided by the Church in a Papal Bull of 1484, the *Malleus Maleficarum*, the Inquisition tortured or put to death unknown numbers of witches. The objective fact appears to be that the vast majority of those accused and tried were women (Hays, 1964). Thus, it is woman who is seen as being in collaboration with the devil, visiting evil upon humans.

In major myths from diverse cultures, then, as well as in historical occurrences, women are seen as being evil, and further as being morally weak, unable to resist temptation, false, and deceitful. How can such a negative view of woman be explained? One possibility is that these negative views are simply a result of male chauvinism. Men think women are inferior and express this in myth, or create such myths to "keep women down." However, there is also a psychological explanation: that socially organized attitudes toward women, such as those expressed in mythology, arise from basic tensions and anxieties experienced by men (Hays, 1964). That is, because men are in power in most societies, they will be the ones who shape the intellectual thought, including the myths. Men experience tension and anxiety that will be reflected in mythology. In particular, men experience tensions and anxiety about women, because women are unknown and mysterious — that is, they are different from men. The tendency to fear the strange or the unknown seems to be a strong human tendency (Hays, 1964; Beauvoir, 1952). Hence, men construct myths in which women are portrayed as the source of evil because men feel anxiety and fears about women.

In yet another interpretation, the Jungian analyst might view myths of feminine evil as resulting not from actual experience with women, but rather from the man's own anima, the feminine principle in his own personality. Thus, the myths of feminine evil result from man's inner, subjective conflicts with his own feminine nature (Harding, 1971).

In summary, a frequent image of women in mythology is that they are the source of evil. It seems likely that this view is an expression of the anxieties men feel about women. This dynamic may also help to explain the other mythical images of women, which will be explored in the following sections.

FERTILITY GODDESS/EARTH MOTHER

The procreative functions of women have been celebrated in myth with the worship of fertility goddesses and earth mothers. In Palestinian and Egyptian mythology, Astarte — like her Babylonian version, Ishtar — is the queen of heaven, the mother of all, who gives the power of reproduction and fertility in the fields to animals and to humans. By extension, she also becomes the goddess of sexual love and desire. In Egyptian mythology, Isis is the great mother and fertility goddess; in Greek mythology Aphrodite and Cybele are worshiped for their fertility. Even today we acknowledge the goddesses of creativity, the Muses.

Women in myth, then, have been worshiped for their creativity or fertility and thus valued and revered. But there is another side to the fertility goddess. Ishtar is the goddess of fertility, but she is also the goddess of bloodshed, war, and destruction. The Fates, three goddesses in Greek mythology, control the course of life, but also the time of death. The mother who has the power to give life also has the power to take it away (Lederer, 1968).

The earth mother/fertility goddess image of women in mythology, then, is at best an *ambivalent* image. ("Ambivalence" means having mixed feelings — positive and negative — about something.) Goddesses are worshiped for their powers of control: revered for their powers of fertility, yet feared for their ability to destroy life. This ambivalent attitude not only characterizes the images of women found in mythology but is also a continuing theme in psychology of women generally, as we shall see in later chapters.

WOMEN AS SEXUAL BEINGS

In addition to the fertility goddess image, the sexuality of women has been a prominent theme in myths and in history, an example being Aphrodite, the Greek goddess of love and sexuality, or the modern sex goddess, Marilyn Monroe.

But here, once again, the image of woman is an ambivalent one. Woman's sexuality is attractive and arousing, but also threatening, a source of fear (Lederer, 1968). The sex goddess can also be the castrating woman. The Pomo Indians of California have a myth in which the young girl has thorns about her vagina that the young man breaks off before marrying her. Twenty-two versions of the myth have been found in North America alone, and it also occurs in the mythology of Siberian tribes, as well as in that of India and New Guinea (Hays, 1964). Certainly the prevalence of this symbol of the castrating vagina attests to its importance in representing psychological functioning, as the notion of Jungian archetypes would suggest. In related myths, the female reproductive organs are seen as being a wound, a theme continued in Freudian theory (see Chapter 3).

At times in history, the ambivalence toward female sexuality has been exaggerated to the point of absurdity. An example is during the Victorian era, when women were categorized as one of two types, the virgin or the whore. The two aspects of female sexuality were transformed into two separate persons, the good woman and the bad woman.

How can this negative view of female sexuality be explained? Some authors argue that it arises from the concept of the woman as *chattel* (Millett, 1969). In many cultures, the woman has been viewed as a piece of property owned by her husband, or as chattel. (A good example of this attitude was the use of the chastity belt, which was popular in the Middle Ages and which still can, we are told, be purchased from mail-order houses. With this device, the man could lock away his property while he was gone.) Men fear the woman's sexuality because they fear her unfaithfulness; since the woman is viewed as chattel, or property, unfaithfulness means that a possession has been stolen, that there has been trespassing on the man's property. Fears of female sexuality, then, are related to the notion that women are property which can be stolen. Further, men's anxiety may result from the fact that maternity can be determined absolutely, but paternity cannot. Perhaps the fear of female unfaithfulness is also related to men's fears about their own sexual skills and inadequacies — will she find that other men are better lovers?

Expanding the explanation given for the myths of feminine evil, it seems quite possible that the taboos and myths surrounding female sexuality arise from male fear of female sexual processes because they are alien and mysterious (Hays, 1964). Menstruation and childbirth are processes never experienced by men, and they set women apart from men. Men fear these unknown, alien processes, and they create taboos to help control their fears. Mythology reflects the fantasies and anxieties men experience about female sexuality, as, for example, in the myth that female sexual organs are a result of castration.

Certainly attitudes toward sexuality and attitudes toward women are closely intertwined (Woudenberg, 1977). When sexuality is feared, women are feared. Those cultures which have positive sexual attitudes also tend to view women positively. Apparently the association arises at least in part because the one continuing source of interaction between men and women, and thus the way men "know" women, is through sex. Hence, it is not surprising that attitudes toward women and attitudes toward sexuality are related.

The question arises as to the direction of causation: do fears of sexuality cause negative attitudes toward women, or do negative attitudes toward women cause men to fear sex? Observations of the many sanctions against male homosexuality and masturbation suggest that sex is feared even when women are not involved. This, in turn, suggests that fears of sexuality are primary, and that these contribute to shaping attitudes toward women. With men's striving to be rational, sexuality remains elusive and poorly understood, a powerful source of pleasure, and yet a fearful challenge to their personal sense of adequacy. Does man project upon woman what he poorly understands in himself?

In summary, female sexuality is viewed ambivalently in mythology; it is seen as alluring, yet threatening. This ambivalence may arise from the anxieties men experience about female sexual processes, which are alien and mysterious to them.

THE MOON

From primitive times, the moon has been one of the symbols most closely associated with women (Harding, 1971; Briffault, 1927). All the Near Eastern fertility goddesses — Ishtar, Astarte, Cybele — are moon goddesses. The association between women and the moon probably arose in the minds of early peoples in several ways. First, from primitive times, the moon, like woman, was thought to be a source of fertility. Indeed, some tribes that had not yet discovered the sexual basis of reproduction believed that a woman could become pregnant if moonlight fell on her. In some communities the moon is called the Lord of Women. In such communities women have charge of matters concerned with the food supply, for they are believed to have the power of the moon to make things grow. Moon goddesses are mother goddesses and fertility goddesses.

A second source of the primitive association between woman and the moon was probably the common phenomenon of cyclicity. Early people probably noted that both the moon and women have a monthly cycle, and therefore must be associated. Indeed, the word "menstruation" means "moon change" (*mens-* refers to both "moon" and "month").

The waxing and waning phases of the moon symbolize the good/evil ambivalence that seems to be so characteristically a part of the view of woman. Thus, the moon symbolizes not only the fertility of its waxing phase, but also death, storms, and destruction in its waning. It is also thought to be the source of inner storms and conflict, and thus to influence lunacy. These two aspects of the moon — and of women — have sometimes even been represented by two separate goddesses. For example, in Greek mythology Aphrodite represents the Bright Moon and Hecate the Dark Moon (Harding, 1971).

Women were also thought to derive magical powers from their association with the moon. The moon was thought to control rain, and the functions of rainmaking and of controlling the weather were almost invariably in the hands of women (Harding, 1971). Closely related to the notion that women possess magical powers is the idea that women are filled with *mana* (Hays, 1964). Mana — a powerful force that infuses, particularly, the alien or mysterious — is an important concept among primitive peoples. Women are thought to be filled with this force because they also are unknown, mysterious to men. The mana notion is another expression of ambivalence toward women — the power of mana is at once attractive and frightening.

Interestingly, the moon goddess generally has a son who dies and is reborn, but she is regarded as being a virgin (Harding, 1971) — note the parallels with the Virgin Mary. The virginity is surprising in view of the goddess's chief function of being a mother, the source of fertility. Apparently the term "virgin" is best interpreted here as meaning "unmarried"; the moon goddess is the goddess of sexual love, but not of marriage. As such, she is a person unto herself. This is one of the few exceptions to the male as normative principle (to be discussed below) — the moon goddess is not defined in terms of her marriage or her relationship to a male god. She is depicted as the feminine principle itself, not a variation on the male.

In sum, woman is associated with the symbol of the moon, representing fertility but also the ambivalent forces of life and death.

THE MALE AS NORMATIVE

Throughout mythology the male is seen as normative, the female as a variant or deviation. That is, the male is the important one, the major representative of the species, the "normal" one, and the female is a variation on him. As Simone de Beauvoir expresses it, man is the Subject, woman is the Other (1952). Or, as another writer put it, woman is little more than a tail wagged by the male ego (Hays, 1964).

In the biblical creation myth (Genesis: 2), Adam, the man, is created first; Eve, the woman, is later fashioned out of his rib, almost as an afterthought. In this and many other creation myths, man is created first; he is the major, important part of the species. Woman comes second and is only a variant on the male, the normative. There are even myths in which a woman is created by castrating a man.

Perhaps the best example of the male-as-normative theme is in our language. We use the word "man" to refer not only to a male, but to people in general. When the gender of a person is unknown, we use the pronoun "he" to refer to "him." (Would we dare have said "to refer to her"?) The species as a whole is man; woman is merely a subset. This topic will be discussed in detail in Chapter 9.

To explain the concept of "normativeness," an analogy can be made to handedness. In our society, right handedness is normative, and left handedness is considered unusual or deviant. The world is basically set up for right-handed people, and lefties have difficulty adjusting in everything from finding scissors that fit them to finding a satisfactory place at the dinner table. Just as left-handed people live in a world made for the right-handed, so women live in a world made for men, in which the male is normative.

Throughout mythology and history, then, a dominant theme is that the male is normative. He is the chief member of the species and woman is a variation or deviation. It seems likely that psychological effects result from this view, particularly as it is expressed in language, although we are lacking empirical research to document such effects.

WOMEN IN THE JUDEO-CHRISTIAN TRADITION[1]

As people formed by Western culture, even in what is often termed the post-Christian age, our view of life and the world is profoundly shaped by the Judeo-Christian tradition. Therefore, it will help us to comprehend the

---

[1] The authors are indebted to the Rev. Clark Hyde for his assistance in preparing this section.

traditional Western understanding of women if we look at its religious basis, a basis that is so pervasive that it affects even those who claim no part of that religious tradition.

The basic source of "data" for this understanding is the Bible, which is the normative expression of the Judeo-Christian tradition. It is, whatever various theories of its inspiration might say, a very human book. It is the product of nearly 2000 years of human experience and reflection, and it contains a rich diversity of views on life and the human condition. It is therefore an extremely complex body of literature and cannot be oversimplified without doing violence to its integrity. Thus, while much of the biblical tradition is, in the strict sense, sexist, as we shall see, it also has great liberating insights into the relationship between women and men. The Judeo-Christian tradition runs the gamut, from the view of women expressed in the Eighteen Benedictions, in which the Rabbinic Jew thanked God that he was born neither a Gentile, nor a slave, nor a woman, to St. Paul's affirmation of the spiritual equality of women and men — "there is neither Jew nor Greek, there is neither slave nor free, there is neither male nor female, for you are all one in Christ Jesus" (Galatians 3:28).

Judaism   We begin by looking at the Old Testament and the religion of the people known collectively as Israel. This religious tradition must be understood in light of the attitudes of the people of the ancient Near East — Bablyon, Egypt, Assyria — attitudes that the Israelites at once shared and transcended. In the Old Testament there is a kind of tension between various understandings of women. Women are seen as subservient to men, with an assumption that this is an intrinsic part of the natural order. Yet at the same time, many aspects of femininity are valued highly in the religion of Israel, and it is safe to say that the status of women in the Jewish tradition was decidedly superior to that of women in all other civilizations of the Near Eastern or Mediterranean worlds.

Two experiences in the history of Israel were crucial to that people's formation of religious self-understanding and of their view of woman. These were: (1) the patriarchal and Exodus periods, a time of nomadic wanderings, and (2) the invasion and settlement of Canaan — now known as Palestine or the Holy Land — and the evolution of Israel into a settled agricultural and commercial nation. During both these times, extremely important religious revolutions took place for Israel that tied cultural views of women to the religious tradition.

During the period of the patriarchs and of the Exodus, roughly 2000 to 1200 B.C., Israel evolved from a disconnected group of nomadic tribes, to a united people with shared traditions and myths. The Israelites were constantly on the move seeking food for their herds, always ready to fight off marauding animals or other tribes competing for scarce grazing land. The tribes were closely knit bodies based on patriarchal kinship in which procreativity was highly valued and carefully regulated. The functions of hunter, herder, and warrior became exceptionally important, indeed necessary, to survival. In such societies, differences between women and men are emphasized (Barry, Bacon, and Child, 1957), masculine strength is highly valued, and males assume higher status than females. Procreativity, continuing the tribe, also becomes important, as does the need for order, in particular the need to regulate sexual relationships. Given these conditions, it is not surprising that we find Old Testament women viewed as the property or *chattel* of males, defined almost exclusively in procreative terms, their purpose being to produce children, preferably male children. Many institutions reflected this, such as the bride-price, in which a young man bought his wife from her father; the levirate marriage, in which a man was obliged to marry his brother's widow if she were childless so that his line would continue; and the nonreciprocal nature of divorce, possible at a man's whim, impossible for a woman. Thus, probably owing to cultural context, *male dominance* is a prominent theme in Judaism and the Old Testament.

The second important cultural period, the crossing of the Jordan and the settlement in Palestine, which occurred roughly between 1200 and 1000 B.C., brought Israel into contact with a settled agricultural people, the Canaanites. The Canaanites were concerned in their religious practices chiefly with fertility of the crops, a matter of urgent necessity for a struggling agricultural economy, and with human fertility. The Canaanites believed that they could promote fertility by imitative magic; that is, by performing the sexual act in religious ceremonies, they re-enacted the relationship between Asherah (Astarte), the earth mother, and Baal, the sky king, and thus, they believed, stimulated the crops to fertility. The most notable feature of this imitative magic was cultic prostitution in the temples, involving both male and female prostitutes as ministers of the religion. Women were highly involved, both as priestesses and as participants, since they symbolized the mother earth whose fertility was so valued.

The religious practices of the Canaanites had a great impact on the religion of Israel because of Israel's violent reaction against the perceived idolatry and immorality of the Canaanites. From roughly 1000 to 587 B.C., the champions of the orthodox Hebrew religion fought continually against both the abandonment of Hebrew religion for the none-too-subtle attractions of the fertility cult, and the attempt to introduce Canaanite practices and ideas into Yahwism.

One of the results of this conflict between the religion of Israel and that of the indigenous Canaanites was further negativism about the nature of women. Women were seen, in their sexuality, to be dangerous to pure Yahwism and, indeed, as agents of evil. The Old Testament expressions of the myth of feminine evil were fortified by the situation that Israel found upon settlement in Palestine. As Yahwism developed, it became more concerned with creation and the earth; but the creation myths that were added were attributed to Yahweh's male image, and not to any feminine deity, as in other Near Eastern religions. This served to reinforce the twin motifs of male dominance and feminine evil that are found throughout the Old Testament.

The prime example of the feminine evil theme is the figure of Eve. According to the myth of the Fall (Genesis 2, 3), Eve is the author of sin and the cause of man's expulsion from Paradise. Yet, Eve has her other side as well. Her name is said to mean "mother of all living," and her feminine creativity is given a great deal of prominence. Further, there is in both Old Testament creation myths (Genesis 2, the more ancient, and Genesis 1, the product of a later time), a recognition of the interdependence of women and men. According to Genesis 2, woman was created because God saw that "it is not good for man to be alone," and in Genesis 1, we find that "God created man . . . male and female he created them." Thus, even while woman is seen as the author of evil and the subject of man, she is yet seen as an indispensable part of God's creation.

This brings us to a third theme that runs through the Old Testament view of women: the high valuation placed on woman as mother and wife. Hebrew literature and mythology pay high tribute to the great mothers of the nation, such as Sarah, Rachel, and Miriam. The home is declared to be the woman's sphere. The domestic sphere was much more productive than it is in our post-industrial age, for it was the center of commercial and mercantile life. Thus, the woman's role was seen as vital to the health and strength of the nation.

In its public form, the religion of the Old Testament is a masculine prerogative; yet its central observances such as the Sabbath and the Passover take place in the home and include women as an integral part. There is no clearer expression of this understanding of woman as the mistress of the home than the thirty-first chapter of Proverbs:

> A good wife who can find?
> > She is far more precious than jewels.
> The heart of her husband trusts in her,
> > and he will have no lack of gain.
> She does him good, and not harm,
> > all the days of her life.
> She seeks wool and flax,
> > and works with willing hands.
> She is like the ships of the merchant,
> > she brings her food from afar.
> She rises while it is yet night and
> > provides food for her household and tasks for her maidens.
> She considers a field and buys it;
> > with the fruit of her hands she plants a vineyard.

· · ·

She opens her hand to the poor,
　　and reaches out her hands to the needy.

．　　．　　．

She opens her mouth with wisdom,
　　and the teaching of kindness is on her tongue.
She looks well to the ways of her household,
　　and does not eat the bread of idleness.
Her children rise up and call her blessed;
　　her husband also, and he praises her.
"Many women have done excellently,
　　but you surpass them all."
Charm is deceitful, and beauty is vain,
　　but a woman who fears the Lord is to be praised.
Give her of the fruit of her hands,
　　and let her works praise her in the city gates.

Throughout Jewish tradition, these three themes continue to exist in tension. The male is dominant, and woman is the subject of man according to the design of a masculine God. Women are the source of evil; through Eve, mankind fell from grace, and her sexuality is seen as a threat and a temptation. Yet, in the home the woman is highly regarded and, on occasion, called to perform acts of heroism on behalf of the nation.

Christianity   Christianity took over the traditional Jewish view of women, and that view was then magnified by the cultural context in which the Christian faith was formed. The Roman Empire of the first century A.D. was marked by decadence and sexual immorality that shocked the Jew and the ethical pagan alike (as the television series *I, Claudius* illustrated vividly). Further, during its first two centuries, the Christian Church believed that Christ would return at any moment, bringing the end of time, and so family life was considered to be of limited importance. Therefore, at the beginning, Christian theology heavily stressed the concepts of masculine dominance and feminine evil.

To the three themes discussed above, we must add a fourth, present in Jewish tradition but reaching its fruition in Christianity — that of the spiritual equality of women and men. Women were included in the ministry of Jesus in a way unknown in first-century society, Jewish and Gentile alike. Women were important actors in the most significant events of Jesus' life — from Mary who bore him, to the women who were the first to discover the empty tomb. Jesus, who taught by homely examples and cultural commonplaces, *never* used the concept of feminine frailty or evil to make a point (Sayers, 1946). Indeed, in his preaching, he made it quite clear that mutuality was to prevail in the relationship between men and women. For example, in his teaching on divorce (Mark 10:2–12), he applied to men criteria previously applied only to women and thus destroyed the double standard. There is no evidence that Jesus assigned women an inferior position, and every suggestion that he regarded women and men as spiritually equal.

Much of the Church's teaching downgrading women is attributed to St. Paul, the great apostle of early Christianity, and much of it deservedly so. Yet, at the same time, in Paul's churches women were accorded positions of trust and leadership. Paul also expanded on Jesus' teaching about divorce, and he said that marital relations must be based on absolute equality: "For the wife does not rule over her own body, but the husband does; likewise the husband does not rule over his own body, but the wife does" (I Corinthians 7:4). St. Paul is also responsible for the definitive statement of spiritual equality of women and men noted on page 26.

In the later Church the revolutionary impact of this teaching of the spiritual equality of women and men was blunted by the cultural context, but it remained a vital part of Christian tradition. In the early Church, ministers were expected to be married (I Timothy 2:1-5), and it was not until the fourth and fifth centuries that clerical celibacy became normative. In New Testament literature, pride and lack of faith are seen as the central sins. Only later, under the impact of conflict with Roman culture, did sexual sins (and the revived theme of feminine evil) take the prominence that characterizes much of Christian theology. In early Christian thought, Mary is seen primarily as the bearer of God, the mother of redeemed humanity, who by her "yes" to God reversed the effects of Eve's "yes" to the serpent. Only in later Christian theology is her virginity stressed, thus removing the threat of sexuality from the virtue of her motherhood.

In summary, three themes emerge from a study of the images of women in the Jewish tradition: male dominance, feminine evil, and the valued role of the female as mistress of the home. Christianity adds a fourth theme, the spiritual equality of women and men. These themes appear to have arisen through an interaction of the religions themselves with the cultures in which they developed (for example, the early Hebrew reaction to the Canaanite fertility cults). While patriarchal notions of male dominance prevailed, women were accorded a valued, if limited, status, finally brought to fruition in the Christian notion of spiritual equality of women and men, although a 2000 year history of Christian practice has substantially obscured this theme.

WHEN WOMEN WERE IN POWER . . .

The mythical images of women discussed up to this point have generally been negative, or at best ambivalent. We have attempted to explain these negative images in terms of anxieties experienced by men, who are in power and thus create the myths of the culture. Negative images of women occur in patriarchal societies — societies in which men have most of the political, legal, and economic power, and in which women have fewer privileges and rights, and lower status. The assumption is that images of women in mythology are so predominantly negative because virtually all societies, past and present, have been patriarchal.

In a provocative book, *Mothers and Amazons*, originally published in Germany in 1930, Helen Diner explored the nature of mythology and society in a time when women were in power — during matriarchal times. She relied on a theory developed by the Swiss anthropologist Bachofen in his *Das Mutterrecht* (Mother-right) in 1861. Bachofen argued that at the dawn of human history, human social organization passed through three successive stages. The first was one of general sexual promiscuity, with little social organization. In the second stage, social organization increased and a true matriarchy emerged. Apparently during this stage people had not discovered the nature of sexual reproduction, and instead believed in parthenogenesis, reproduction by the female alone through the development of an unfertilized egg. Women were thus viewed as extremely powerful, and they assumed control of the society. Not until the third stage, with the revolutionary discovery of paternity, did a patriarchy emerge. It should be noted that this theory is in disrepute among scholars (see, for example, Bamberger, 1974), who question whether matriarchies ever really existed. Nonetheless, conclusive proof for either side of the argument is lacking, and Diner's speculations are provocative enough to be worth considering.

If, at some early time, women were in power, if matriarchy did actually precede patriarchy, the myths emerging from such a period might be expected to present quite different views of women from those of a patriarchal society. According to Diner, in the earliest creation myths the female is the original life force, from which is then created the male. This would seem the logical mythical account to arise in a society that believed in parthenogenesis. For example, in Babylonian lore the original being, Thalat, gave birth to a divine couple from which the world was created. In the earliest Greek creation myth, the female earth emerges first from the primal vagina and then creates the earth, sky, and elements. Thus, in the earliest myths, the female is the original, the male the derivative. Creation myths in which the female is derived from the male, for example that of Adam and Eve, occurred later. This corresponds in time to a matriarchal society occurring first, followed by a patriarchal society. And in matriarchal society, the female is normative.

The Amazons, a legendary race of warrior women ruled by a queen, are perhaps the best known example of mythical matriarchy. Diner also argued that matriarchy was characteristic of the Spartans of Greece, of China through the Third Dynasty, among the common people of Japan, and in Tibet. The widespread belief that the female is the primal life force is attested to by myths of the virgin birth of Christ, Buddha, Quetzalcoatl, Montezuma, and Genghis Khan.

Thus, if early matriarchies did exist, they appear to have produced a much different view of women in mythology, for women were seen as the primary life force, the normative. Future research may yet discover matriarchal cultures, with a correspondingly more positive view of the female in myth.

NONCONSCIOUS IDEOLOGIES

Psychologists Sandra and Daryl Bem (1970) have argued that there is a nonconscious ideology influencing women's psychology. A nonconscious ideology is an ideology (set of ideas) to which we are exposed without being aware of it, either because (1) the ideas are so common and widely accepted that they are not noticed, much as a fish is not aware that it lives in a wet environment, or (2) the ideas are in a form that is subtle and not likely to be noticed or attacked. The myths and religious views discussed above are all good examples. A further example of a nonconscious ideology are the jokes in which women are portrayed as foolish, stupid, or incompetent (Zimbardo and Meadow, 1974). No one would argue against the content of a joke — that would be acting like a poor sport. And so such jokes became part of a nonconscious ideology that teaches that women are inferior, an ideology that is all the more dangerous because it is neither conscious nor overt, and therefore cannot effectively be attacked.

Here, we consider two more examples of nonconscious ideologies.

Example I: Jason and Medea revisited   Daniel Goleman (1976) analyzed the content of stories in adventure magazines for teen-age boys such as *Action for Men* and *Saga*, and romance magazines for teen-age girls such as *True Story* and *Real Romance*. He noticed that many of the plots in these magazines were simply modernized versions of the plots of ancient myths. As an example, here is a summary of the Greek myth of Jason and Medea:

> Jason had to retrieve the Golden Fleece to earn the right to the royal throne. The Fleece was the skin of a divine ram that was essential to his country's spiritual well-being; it was held by the king of a distant and hostile land. Jason set off with the Argonauts, an able-bodied band dedicated to helping him capture it. Each Argonaut had a special ability; Jason's was seduction, and he was unscrupulous in using women for his own ends.
>
> After many hardships, the Argonauts reached the country where the Fleece was held, only to find themselves hopelessly outnumbered. Medea, a young princess whose father had the Fleece under guard, saved the day. Bored with her home and boyfriends, she fell in love with Jason. Although her family warned her against this stranger, Medea betrayed her family ties, revealed her father's secrets for guarding the Fleece, and

fled with Jason. Totally devoted to Jason, Medea even slew her half-brother to help her lover escape with the Fleece.

Jason returned home triumphant and made Medea queen. But he cared more for ambition than for her. When she learned that Jason planned to divorce her and marry another princess to expand his kingdom, her love for him turned to hate. Enraged, Medea killed the would-be bride and her father, as well as her own sons by Jason.

Ashamed and repentant, Medea returned home to a forgiving family and a dull but safe marriage to the prince of a nearby kingdom. Jason died, heartbroken by the murder of his sons. (Goleman, 1976, p. 84)

Compare that plot with this one from a 1975 issue of *True Romance*.

Sixteen-year-old Becky hitch-hiked home to Portland after a year's absence, four months pregnant and unwed. Becky's odyssey began at a rock concert where she met Guy, a "gorgeous" school drop-out and wanderer, to whom she was immediately attracted. Her parents disapproved, and argued that there were "a lot of nice guys right in this neighborhood" she should date. In defiance, she met Guy in secret. When Guy decided to leave for a commune in Sacramento, Becky packed some clothes, left a note to her parents, and went with him.

With no one to tell her what to do, Becky found a new liberation in eating, sleeping, and making love as she pleased. But the bubble burst one day when Colette, a sexy redhead, moved into the commune. Guy was openly attracted to her and indifferent to Becky's hurt feelings. On top of this, Becky found she was pregnant and when she told Guy, he angrily blamed her for being careless. Becky, shaken, realized Guy had stopped loving her, if he ever had.

Becky returned home, where she learned that her rash departure had tragic effects on her family. Her mother, heartbroken and depressed, was in a mental hospital; her father was hardpressed to pay for her treatment. Even so, her father welcomed Becky back, and stood by her through the ordeal of giving her baby up for adoption. As her father assured her, "Families help one another when there's trouble." A chastened Becky wishes she could somehow undo all the damage she's caused, and resolves to build a better, more worthwhile life. (Goleman, 1976, p. 84)

What messages do such stories convey to the young people reading them? Girls reading the story are implicitly being told: (1) Beware of men — their seductiveness will lead to your downfall; (2) beware of sexuality — it, too, can be your downfall; (3) stay with your family, obey your parents, and don't be adventurous; (4) other women are the enemy (e.g., Colette); and (5) women are dangerous — they are capable of murdering their own children (Medea) or causing their mother's mental breakdown (Becky); in short, the myth of feminine evil is retold.

The more general point is that such stories are sources of nonconscious ideologies, and the ideologies of gender roles they present are quite similar to those found in age-old myths.

Example II: Genderisms in advertising   Anthropologist Erving Goffman (1977) analyzed the composition of photographs used in popular advertising. He noticed that the composition of the photographs often contained "genderisms," that is, subtle stereotyped themes. As an example, men were almost always shown with their heads higher in the photograph than women's, even when both the man and the woman were seated or in some other situation in which height should make little difference. According to Goffman's analysis, this positioning reflects a ritualized subordination of women. Typically one lowers one's head when in the presence of a person of superior authority and power, as when bowing to a king. Thus the lower position of women may reflect their subordinate status to men.

Once again we have a nonconscious ideology; the stereotyped idea is presented subtly. Nonetheless, it probably reflects widespread themes of male dominance and female subordination in our society, and indeed the composition of the photographs may help to perpetuate these themes.

In conclusion   We have suggested that mythology provides a way of increasing our understanding — although not the scientific way we will attempt in the remaining chapters — of the psychology of women, and particularly of the attitudes men hold toward women. Two persisting themes have been the ambivalence of attitudes toward women, and the view that the male is normative. Strikingly, these two themes are also found in scientific theory and research on women.

A final speculation is that mythology may be another source of a nonconscious ideology acting upon women. In earliest childhood, the little girl learns that she, Eve, was created from Adam's rib, and that God is male. Mythical creation stories, like jokes, are not subject to rational argument and debate. They are not, after all, supposed to represent actual historical fact. But will the little girl know that these stories represent the experience of a patriarchal society? Or will she simply believe that God is male, and that women are the source of evil in the world?

3

THEORIES OF FEMALE DEVELOPMENT

[Girls] notice the penis of a brother or playmate, strikingly visible and of large proportions, at once recognize it as the superior counterpart of their own small and inconspicuous organ, and from that time forward fall a victim to envy for the penis.

SIGMUND FREUD, Collected Papers

Understanding the nature of the differences between males and females has been a question that has fascinated people probably since the dawn of the human species. The nature of woman appears to have been particularly mysterious and intriguing, although too often her nature has been understood only from the male point of view. In the last chapter we saw how men have attempted to understand and explain women by constructing myths about them.

In the past century, science has come to dominate intellectual thought. And so it is not surprising that men (and sometimes also women) have more recently attempted scientific understandings of women. In the present chapter we will examine some major psychological theories, having their roots in science, that have been formulated to explain women and the differences between women and men. Each theory may offer some notions that account for part of the complexity. Each operates from one or several underlying premises, be they biological or cultural.

In later chapters we shall look at empirical data for a further understanding of women and gender roles. The reader can then contrast these theoretical views with what is known based on scientific data.

PSYCHOANALYTIC THEORY

The central author of this particular thesis was Sigmund Freud, an individual of remarkable insight. Despite the advent of new models of human psychological development and recent trends toward other forms of psychotherapy, few can doubt the influence of psychoanalytic theory in psychology, psychiatry, pediatrics, the understanding of literature, or even its revelance to theological matters, not to mention its penetration into the language of most lay people. Psychoanalytic theory not only describes human behavior, but it has also acted to shape human behavior. For example, Freud's theory of female sexuality (see Chapter 12) held that women could have two kinds of orgasm — vaginal or clitoral — and that the vaginal orgasm was the more "mature," that is, the better, of the two. Some women have spent hours trying to achieve the elusive vaginal orgasm, and have sought psychotherapy when they were unable to attain it, all as a result of Freud's theory. Certainly the theory has had an impact on human life, and in particular on women.

Basically, Freud viewed humans as being dominated by a reservoir of instincts and strivings. These instincts are focused in different regions of the body collectively referred to as the *erogenous zones*. Each zone is a part of the skin or mucous membrane highly endowed with blood supply and nerve endings that are very sensitive to stimulation. The lips and mouth constitute one such region, the anal region another, and the genitals a third. Thus Freud noted that sucking produces pleasure, as does elimination, and rubbing the genitals.

Stages of development   One of Freud's greatest contributions was to view human personality as being the result of *development*. That is, he saw the personality of an adult as the result of previous experiences, and he believed that early childhood experiences were most critical. He proposed a stage theory of psychosexual development, each stage being characterized by a focus on one of the erogenous zones. According to his view, all humans pass through the stages in a fixed, chronological sequence — first the oral, then the anal, and then the phallic stage — during the first five or six years of life. Thus during the first stage, the oral, the infant derives pleasure from sucking and eating and experiences the world mainly through the mouth. Following this is the anal stage, in which pleasure is focused on defecating.

In attempting to explain the development of gender identity and differences between males and females, Freud postulated that boys and girls pass through the first two stages of psychosexual development, the oral and the anal, in a similar manner. For both genders at this time, the mother is the chief object of love. It is during the *phallic stage*, around the ages of four to six, that the development of the genders diverges. As one might suspect from the name for this stage, females will be at somewhat of a disadvantage in passing through it.

During the phallic stage, the boy becomes narcissistically involved with his own penis. It is a rich source of pleasure and interest for him. A critical occurrence during the phallic stage is the formation of the *Oedipal complex*, named for the Greek myth of Oedipus, who killed his father and married his mother. In the Oedipal complex, the boy sexually desires his mother. His attachment to her is strong and intense. He also wishes to rid himself of the father, who is a rival for the mother's affection. But the father is too powerful an opponent, and the imagined consequences of attempting to do away with the father give rise to fears that the father will retaliate. He fears that the father will do him bodily harm, particularly to his beloved penis, so that the boy comes to feel *castration anxiety*. Through a complicated series of maneuvers the boy resolves the problem. He admits to an inability to possess the mother and do away with the father, the potential dangers being too great. He represses his libidinal impulses toward the mother, and makes the critical shift to identifying with the father. In the process of *identification* with the father, the boy introjects (takes into himself as his own) the values, the "thou-shalt-nots," of society as represented by the father and thus comes to have a conscience or superego. But more important for our purposes is that, in identifying with the father, he comes to acquire his gender identity, taking on the qualities the father supposedly possesses — strength, power, and so on.

The sequence of events in the phallic stage is considerably different for the girl. According to Freud, the first critical event is the girl's stark realization that she has no penis. Because children are so interested in their own and others' genitals during this stage, Freud believed that the girl will inevitably notice the boy's protrusion and her own cavity. Presumably she recognizes that the penis is superior to her own anatomy. She feels cheated and envious of males, and thus comes to feel *penis envy*. She also feels mutilated, believing that at one time she possessed a penis, but that it had been cut off — indeed Freud believed that the fires of the boy's castration anxiety are fed by the boy's observation of the girl's anatomy, which he sees as living proof of the reality of castration. Her desire for a penis, her penis envy, can never be satisfied directly, and instead becomes transformed into a desire to be impregnated by her father. Holding her mother responsible for her lack of a penis, she renounces her love for her mother and becomes intensely attached to her father, thus forming her own version of the Oedipal complex, sometimes called the Electra complex. Thus the sequence of events is reversed: for the boy, the Oedipal complex leads to castration anxiety, whereas for the girl, the parallel to castration anxiety — penis envy — occurs first and leads to the formation of the Oedipal complex. The desire to be impregnated by the father is a strong one, and persists in the more general form of maternal urges, according to Freud.

Passivity, masochism, and narcissism   Freud believed that there are three key female personality traits: passivity, masochism, and narcissism. Narcissism will be discussed in the section on Helene Deutsch's work, as she was particularly concerned with that quality. Here we shall focus on passivity and masochism.

In the outcomes of the Electra complex Freud saw the origins of the two well-known — at least to Victorians — feminine qualities, *passivity* and *masochism*. In choosing the strategy for obtaining the desired penis by being impregnated by the father, the girl adopts a passive approach — to be impregnated, to be done to, not to do — and this passive strategy persists throughout life. The desire to be impregnated is also masochistic, in that intercourse (in which, in Freudian terminology, the woman is "penetrated") and childbirth are painful. The female, therefore, in desiring to be impregnated, seeks to bring pain to herself.

Lest the foregoing strains the reader's credulity, perhaps some quotations from Marie Bonaparte, an early follower of Freud, will indicate the strength of these convictions.

> Throughout the whole range of living creatures, animal or vegetable, passivity is characteristic of the female cell, the ovum whose mission is to *await* the male cell, the active mobile spermatozoan to come and

penetrate it. Such penetration, however, implies infraction of its tissue, but infraction of a living creature's tissue may entail destruction: death as much as life. Thus, the fecundation of the female cell is initiated by a kind of wound; in its way, the female cell is primordially "masochistic." (1953, p. 79)

All forms of masochism are related, and in essence, more or less female, from the wish to be eaten by the father in the cannibalistic oral phase, through that of being whipped or beaten by him in the sadistic-anal stage, and of being castrated in the phallic stage, to the wish, in the adult feminine stage, to be pierced. (1953, p. 83)

Vaginal sensitivity in coitus for the adult female, in my opinion, is thus largely based on the existence, and more or less unconscious, acceptation of the child's immense masochistic beating fantasies. In coitus, the woman, in effect, is subjected to a sort of beating by the man's penis. She receives its blows and often, even, loves their violence. (1953, p. 87)

As we saw, the resolution of the Oedipal complex is critical for the boy's development, being necessary for the formation of his gender identity and superego. Unfortunately, for the girl the resolution of the Oedipal complex is neither as direct nor as complete. She was led to the Oedipal complex by her desire for a penis, a desire that can never truly be satisfied. More importantly, the prime motivation in the boy's resolving his Oedipal complex was his overpowering fear of castration. For the girl, castration is an already accomplished fact, and thus her motivation for resolution of the Oedipal complex is not so strong, being motivated only by the comparatively abstract realization that her desires for her father cannot be gratified.

Immature superego   For the female the Oedipal complex is never as fully resolved as it is for the male. It is not surprising, then, that related personality processes should differ for females and males. According to Freud, the girl's unsuccessful resolution of the Oedipal complex leads the female to lifelong feelings of inferiority, a predisposition to jealousy, and to intense maternal desires. Further, it leads females to be characterized by an *immature superego*. For the boy, one of the positive outcomes of resolving the Oedipal complex is the internalization, or introjection, of society's standards, thereby forming a superego. But the girl's attachment to the parents is never "smashed" as is the boy's, and she continues to be dependent on the parents for her values. She never internalizes her own values as completely as does the boy; continuing to rely on others, she thus is characterized by a less mature sense of morality, or an immature superego. In Freud's own words,

Their [girls'] superego is never so inexorable, so impersonal, so independent of its emotional origins as we require it to be in men . . . That they show less sense of justice than men, that they are less ready to submit to the great necessities of life, that they are more often influenced in their judgments by feelings of affection or hostility — all these would be amply accounted for by the modification in the formation of their superego which we have already inferred. (1948, pp. 196–197)

And again,

. . . Girls remain in it [the Oedipal conflict] for an indeterminate length of time; they demolish it last, and even so incompletely. In these circumstances the formation of the superego must suffer; it cannot attain the strength and independence which give it its cultural significance. (1933, p. 129)

In summary, Freud postulated a basic model for the acquisition of gender identity in the male, with a parallel model for the female. A basic assumption is the importance and superiority of the male phallus. It is so important to the boy that, in the throes of love for his mother, he fears that his father will harm the penis and he thus gives up his love for his mother and comes to identify with his father, thereby acquiring his own gender identity and introjecting the values of society. For the girl, on the other hand, penis envy, an instant recognition of the superiority of the penis and a sense of envy over not having one, is primary. She turns her love away from her mother and toward her father in an attempt to regain the penis, but is unsuccessful. Her Oedipal complex persists in modified form, is never completely resolved, and as a result her moral development is less adequate.

Criticisms of psychoanalytic theory   Numerous general and feminist criticisms of Freudian theory have been made.

From a scientific point of view, a major problem with psychoanalytic theory is that most of its concepts cannot be evaluated scientifically to see whether they are accurate. Freud believed that many of the most important forces in human behavior are unconscious, and thus they cannot be studied by any of the usual scientific techniques.

Another criticism that is often raised is that Freud derived his ideas almost exclusively from work with patients who sought therapy from him. Thus his theory may describe not so much human behavior as disturbed human behavior. In particular, his views on women may contain some truth about women who have problems of adjustment, but may have little to do with women who function well psychologically.

Many modern psychologists feel that Freud overemphasized biological determinants of human behavior and did not give sufficient attention to the influence of society and learning in shaping behavior. In particular, his views on the origin of differences between males and females, and on the nature of female personality, are heavily biological, relying mostly on anatomical differences — as the famous phrase has it, "Anatomy is destiny." In relying on anatomy as an explanation, Freud ignored the enormous forces of culture acting to create differences between females and males.

Feminists have raised numerous criticisms of Freudian theory, including those noted above (e.g., Weisstein, 1971; Sherman, 1971). They are particularly critical of Freud's assumption that the clitoris and vagina are inferior to the penis. Indeed, Freud's views have been termed "phallocentric." The superiority of the penis may have seemed a reasonable concept in the Victorian era in which Freud wrote, but it is difficult to believe today, and certainly has no scientific documentation backing it.

A related question is whether little girls would, in fact, instantly recognize the superiority of the penis. While case histories are available to document the existence of penis envy among women seeking therapy (see case history following), it remains to be demonstrated that penis envy is common among women, or that it has a large impact on their development. Indeed, empirical research indicates that in psychiatric studies the penis-envy theme is not nearly so common among women as is castration anxiety among men (Bosselman, 1960). This suggests that Freud, in writing from a male point of view, accurately observed the castration anxiety of the male, but was less accurate when constructing a parallel — penis envy — for the female.

A CASE HISTORY ILLUSTRATING PENIS ENVY

An unsuccessful artist who had always resented being a woman came to treatment very depressed and anxious at having allowed herself to become pregnant. Her husband had recently become extremely successful, and her envy of and competition with him were enormous, especially since she was blocked in her own professional development. She felt that the best way to "show up" her husband was to do the one thing he could not do — bear a child.

She expressed only hatred and contempt for her mother, who had been a dependent, ineffectual housebound woman. This resentment seemed to have started at the birth of her sister, three years younger, at which time the patient hid herself and refused to talk for days. The mother was hospitalized for depression when the patient was twelve. The father was an unsuccessful artist, an exciting, talented person whom the patient adored. She turned away from her mother and spent the next ten years of her life trying to be her father's son. He encouraged her painting and took her to exhibitions, partly to get away from the mother. However, he was very inconsistent and bitter, given to terrifying rages; he would alternate between leading her on and slapping her down. Her fantasy of being like a boy was brutally crushed at a time when she was preparing for a bas mitzvah; she thought she would be allowed to have one "as good as a boy's" but was suddenly humiliated publicly at puberty and sent home from the synagogue on the Sabbath because it was decided that she was now a woman and could no longer stay and compete with the men and boys. Menarche intensified her resentment of female functions, but she compensated with fantasies of having a son and traveling around the world with him — self-sufficient, no longer needing her family or her father. While in Europe on a scholarship, she fell in love and, while petting with the boy, had the only orgasm she has ever experienced. She feared his increasing power over her, experienced a resurgence of dependency needs and fled home. She felt she had spent her life trying to win her father's approval. But when she finally had a one-man show, he taunted her, "Why not give it up, go home, and make babies?"

After his death and her professional failure, she became increasingly depressed. At the age of thirty, she decided to get pregnant — after having been married four years. (She had previously been phobic about pregnancy and remained a virgin until her marriage.) She felt that her baby was conceived out of emptiness, not fullness, and then feared that the child would take her life from her, would deplete rather than fulfill her. Having a baby trapped her, she felt; she could no longer try to be like a man. It was as though she had had a fantasy penis which she finally had to relinquish.

There was plenty of evidence of typical penis envy in this case. As a girl, the patient even tried to compete with boys in urinary contests, and was furious because she always lost. She first associated her bedwetting with rage at not having a penis, but finally viewed it as a way to punish [her] mother for turning to [the] sister, and as an effort to recover the maternal solicitude she had lost. She envied, and was attracted to, men who had powerful drives for achievement and were free to pursue them. The penis was for her a symbol of such drives; to possess it would also save her from being like her mother. In one sense, she wanted a baby as a substitute for not having a penis; but she also had a burning wish to be a good mother — to prove her own validity as well as to "undo" her past. Her difficulty in achieving this wish forced her to work through her relationship with her mother, which she had contemptuously shelved, finding competition with men more exciting and less anxiety-provoking.

Source: Abridged from R. Moulton, "A Survey and Re-evaluation of the Concept of Penis Envy," Contemporary Psychoanalysis, 7 (1970):84–104. Used with permission of the author and publisher.

Feminists also note the similarities between psychoanalytic theory and some of the myths about women discussed in the previous chapter. In this context, Freud seems simply to be articulating age-old myths and images about women in "scientific" language. The mythical image of the female genitals as a wound is transformed into a theory in which females believe themselves to have been castrated. The image of women as sinful and the source of evil is translated into the scientific-sounding "immature superego." Certainly Freud's phallocentrism is a good example of a male-as-normative model. Basically, for Freud, a female is a castrated male. His model of development describes male development, female development being an inadequate variation on it.

Finally, feminists object to Freud's distinction between clitoral and vaginal orgasm and his belief that the vaginal orgasm is the more mature (better) one. This point will be discussed in detail in Chapter 12.

Nonetheless, it is important to recognize Freud's important contributions in his recognition of the importance of development in shaping human personality, and particularly in shaping gender identity.

VARIATIONS ON A FREUDIAN THEME

There were attempts within the psychoanalytic school to reform Freud's theory. Here we shall look briefly at some of the proposed variants that are relevant to women.

Alfred Adler   Adler is well known for his coining of the concepts of inferiority complex, compensation, and style of life. He theorized that women had a sense of inferiority not because they had no penis, but because of an unnatural male dominance in relations between women and men (Adler, 1927). Indeed, at one time he equated inferiority with unmanliness or femininity (Hall and Lindzey, 1970). Some women might respond to this sense of inferiority with a neurotic effort to obtain power and prestige — what he called the "masculine protest." Adler's contribution, then, to the psychology of women was his recognition that what is probably the very reasonable female envy of male political and economic power was mistaken by Freud to be envy of male anatomy.

Karen Horney   Several of the most prominent psychoanalytic theorists were women, and, not surprisingly, they made some modifications on Freud's theory. Horney's theoretical papers show an evolution over time in her own thinking. Originally she accepted Freud's ideas wholeheartedly; in a 1924 paper she eagerly documented the origins of penis envy and of the castration complex in women. However, she soon became critical of these notions, and in a 1926 paper she pointed out that Freudian notions really articulate the childish views boys have of girls (much as we have pointed out that they represent age-old myths), and that Freud's psychological theory of women had been phallocentric.

Her chief disagreement with Freud was over his notion that penis envy was the critical factor in female development. Horney used the master's tricks against him and postulated that the critical factor was male envy of the female, particularly of her reproductive potential ("womb envy"), and suggested that male achievement really represents an overcompensation for feelings of anatomical inferiority (a femininity complex). Bettelheim (1962) elaborated upon this notion with observations on puberty rites of primitive tribes, from which he concluded that womb envy is a very real force and that penis envy has been greatly exaggerated.

Helene Deutsch   In 1944, Helene Deutsch published a weighty two-volume work entitled *Psychology of Women*, the major attempt within the psychoanalytic school for a complete understanding of the psychological dynamics of women. In many ways, Deutsch is more of an observer and analyst than she is a theorist; her book contains numerous excerpts from case histories to illustrate major tenets of the psychoanalytic view of women.

Deutsch's major contribution was to extend Freud's analysis of female development, which essentially ended with the phallic stage and Oedipal complex, to later stages of development. She began in the prepuberty period because she saw the critical processes in woman's psychological development revolving around the transition from being a girl to being a woman. She then continued to describe female development and personality in adolescence and adulthood.

Deutsch largely retained a Freudian orthodoxy in her thinking. For example, she believed that to be a woman one must develop a "feminine core" in the personality, including the traits of narcissism, masochism, and passivity. She also held that instinct and intuition were very important to a feminine personality.

She elaborated on Freud's distinction between the function of the clitoris and the function of the vagina. She saw the switch from clitoral eroticism to a focus on the vagina as being an important task during prepuberty and adolescence. This switch represented a shift from activity to passivity, the clitoris representing the active, masculine component that the woman must give up to be truly feminine (Deutsch, 1924). Deutsch viewed this as the hardest task of libidinal development — a task further complicated by the beginning of menstruation, which revived feelings of castration.

Deutsch coined the term "masculinity complex" to refer to certain instances of women's failure to adjust. Such women are characterized by a predominance of masculine active and aggressive tendencies, which brings them into conflict with both their surrounding environment and their own feminine tendencies.

She proposed a typology of feminine women, what she called feminine-erotic types, eroticism being the heart of femininity. According to her, these types are derived from an interplay between narcissism and masochism; narcissism represents the self-protective functions — resisting the man — while masochism is equated with submission. The first feminine type is the woman who, when approached erotically, finds it difficult to refuse and yields easily. She apparently has a strong masochistic component and a weak narcissistic component. The second type of woman is more reserved, yielding only after she has established a secure relationship with the man. For this woman the narcissistic (self-preservative) and the masochistic functions are in balance. The third type is actually only a borderline feminine woman. She has the passive-erotic characteristics of the feminine woman, but also has a considerable admixture of masculinity that is evidenced particularly by a strong moral sense.

Deutsch viewed motherhood as the most critical feature in woman's psychological development. Indeed, the whole second volume of *Psychology of Women* was devoted exclusively to this topic, and she saw prepuberty and adolescence as mainly an anticipation of motherhood.

> Thus woman acquires a tendency to passivity that intensifies the passive nature inherent in her biology and anatomy. She passively awaits fecundation: her life is fully active and rooted in reality only when she becomes a mother. Until then everything that is feminine in the woman, physiology and psychology, is passive, receptive. (1944, Vol. I, p. 140)

Deutsch's view of the psychology of women is at once insightful and laden with the confusion of cultural and biological forces typical of psychoanalytic theory. For example, she believed that female passivity is a result of anatomy and biological functioning and failed to recognize that it is a culturally assigned part of the female role.

Erik Erikson   Erikson's reformulation and extension of psychoanalytic theory provides a more sophisticated view of social influences on development. Here we will concentrate on his major contribution to the psychology of women, his concept of inner space.

Erikson theorized that the key factor in female personality was not the reactive penis envy but rather a constructive, creative sense of a vital inner space. As he put it,

> But how, then, does a woman's identity formation differ by dint of the fact that her somatic design harbors an "inner space" destined to bear the offspring of chosen men and, with it, a biological, psychological, and ethical commitment to take care of human infancy? Is not the disposition for this commitment (whether to be realized in actual motherhood or not) the core problem of female *fidelity*? (1946, p. 5)

His major empirical evidence that this phenomenon exists comes from the play constructions of children. Children were asked to pretend to be motion picture directors, and to construct an exciting scene from a movie with a variety of miniature figures (people, animals, furniture, blocks). The girls generally produced an interior scene, with a configuration of furniture or an enclosure built with blocks. The people were inside, primarily in static positions, and the scene was generally peaceful. Occasionally there were portrayals of elaborate doorways. Boys, on the other hand, portrayed exterior scenes, sometimes with high walls with protrusions such as towers. The scenes depicted exciting action, often with downfall and ruin, such as automobile accidents. In sum, then, the girls portrayed inner, and the boys, outer space. Interestingly, the girls occasionally showed intrusions into their interior scenes by animals or dangerous men; their reaction was not fear or anger, but rather, pleasurable excitement and humor.

Certainly such observations could be criticized as the sole empirical basis for Erikson's assertions, although there is some independent supporting evidence (Franck and Rosen, 1949). His study has been criticized on the basis that it was poorly controlled and that the subjects were too old to rule out cultural factors as causes of the gender differences.

Erikson contrasted his understanding of women with the Freudian one as follows:

> . . . a shift of theoretical emphasis from the loss of an external organ to a sense of vital inner potential; from a hateful contempt of the mother to a solidarity with her and other women; from a "passive" renunciation of male activity to the purposeful and competent activity of one endowed with ovaries and a uterus; and from a masochistic pleasure in pain to an ability to stand (and to understand) pain as a meaningful aspect of human experience in general, and of the feminine role in particular. (1946, p. 13)

Another important contribution of Erikson was that he saw personal and gender identity as continuously subject to change and differentiation throughout the life of the individual, and that he did not concentrate exclusively on the infant/child period. As we shall see, this is particularly relevant in describing the developmental processes involved in identity acquisition in women.

SOCIAL LEARNING THEORY

A popular explanation for gender differences in behavior is "conditioning." That is, boys and girls act appropriately for their gender because they have been rewarded for doing some things and punished for doing others. The notion is that principles of operant conditioning explain the acquisition of gender roles. Thus, some behaviors are rewarded for girls while others are either not rewarded or they are even punished, so that the girl comes to perform the rewarded behaviors more frequently, the unrewarded ones less frequently or not at all. For example, little girls are rewarded for being quiet and obedient, while little boys are rewarded for athletics and achievement. Consequently, children acquire gender-typed behaviors because they are rewarded or approved. This is thought to be the essential process creating gender-typing.

Social learning theory is a major theoretical system in psychology, designed to describe the process involved in human development (see Bandura and Walters, 1963). In particular, it has been used to explain the development of gender differences (Mischel, 1966). In explaining the shaping of children's behavior, social learning theory uses the notion of *direct reinforcement* described above — that is, the idea that rewards and punishments are given differentially to boys and girls for gender-typed behaviors, and that children therefore come to perform the rewarded, gender-appropriate behaviors more frequently and the punished, gender-inappropriate behaviors less frequently. But social learning theory also emphasizes the importance of two additional processes: *imitation* and *observational learning*. Imitation means simply that children do what they observe others doing. Observational learning refers to situations in which children learn by observing the behavior of others, even though they may not actually perform the behavior at the time, perhaps not using the information until months or years later. These three mechanisms, then — direct reinforcement, imitation, and observational learning — are thought to underlie the process of gender-typing, that is, the acquisition of gender-typed behaviors, according to social learning theory.

Acquiring gender roles   Infants of both genders are biologically and psychologically dependent on the mother. According to the social learning approach, because the mother is the source of attention and care, the association of the mother's presence with comfort leads the child to value mother-presence and to experience anxiety or discomfort in her absence. Thus, as mother-presence comes to be equated with pleasure and mother-absence with discomfort, the mother takes on important meaning to the infant — she becomes an effective reinforcer of the child's behavior. In the course of development, the mother's demands and expectations for the child's behavior increase and the child learns to perform those acts that will bring about approval. The child's behavior comes to be keyed to the mother's approval or disapproval.

Applying the theory to the process of gender-role learning, the mother presumably reacts differentially to gender-typed behaviors in her child. For example, she may react positively when her daughter displays feminine behaviors, such as nurturance, and negatively when she displays masculine behaviors, such as aggressiveness. In effect, she rewards feminine behaviors and may punish masculine behaviors. Social learning theory asserts that these reinforcements will be effective in shaping the child's behavior.

Later, stimulus generalization occurs. That is, stimuli similar to the mother, for example, the father and other adults — also become effective reinforcers of behavior. These other adults also presumably react differentially to gender-appropriate behavior in the child, and apply reinforcements similar to those the mother has used. Thus male and female children are treated differently, the rewards being given in accordance with cultural prescriptions regarding appropriate behavior for males and females.

According to social learning theory, the next step of learning involves a new and important process, imitation. The child imitates the behavior of other people. The child's imitation is motivated partly by the power of authority figures, so that he or she is particularly likely to imitate parents or other adults. Behaving like a particular person gives the child the sense that she or he possesses that person's power. With regard to gender-role learning, the theory assumes that children tend to imitate the same-gender parent and other same-gender adults more than opposite-gender adults. That is, the little girl imitates her mother and other women more than she does men. The imitation of same-gender models furthers the gender-typing process. This mechanism of imitation helps to explain the acquisition of the complex and subtle aspects of gender roles that probably have not been the object of direct reinforcements. Further, imitation and direct reinforcement may interact. For example, the girl may imitate a behavior of her

FIGURE 3.1

Children learn gender roles in part by imitation of adults.

Source: Photo by Misha Erwitt / Magnum.

mother's and then be rewarded for it, once again furthering the process of gender-typing.

The child does not actually have to perform a behavior in order to learn it. A behavior may become part of the child's repertoire through observational learning. Such information may be stored up for use perhaps ten or fifteen years later, when a situation in adolescence or adulthood calls for a knowledge of gender-appropriate behaviors. For example, a young girl may observe her mother caring for an infant brother or sister. Although the little girl may not perform any infant-care behaviors at the time, much less be rewarded for them, she nonetheless may store up the information about infant care for use when she herself is a mother. Once again, gender-typing occurs through mechanisms other than direct reinforcement.

In more advanced learning, children also learn to anticipate the consequences of their actions. Here also, an action need not be performed for the child to understand the reinforcements or punishments that will result. The little girl knows in advance that her attempts to join Little League will be met with opposition, and perhaps even with direct punishments. Higher-order conditioning also occurs so that, for example, verbal cues may serve as strong reinforcements or punishments. The words "sissy" or "mannish" acquire a punishing quality all their own.

According to social learning theory, then, gender-typing results from differential rewards and punishments, as well as learning in the absence of direct reinforcement, by imitation of same-gender models and observational learning.

Evidence for social learning theory   Social learning theory has stimulated a great deal of research aimed at documenting the existence — or nonexistence — of the mechanisms it proposes. The research makes it possible to begin to assess the adequacy of the social learning model for the development of gender differences.

There have been numerous demonstrations of the effectiveness of imitation and reinforcements in shaping children's behavior, in particular gender-typed behaviors such as aggression. A good example is a study by the psychologist Albert Bandura (1965). In the first phase of this experiment, children were divided into three groups and shown one of three films. In all the films, an adult model was performing aggressive behavior, but in one film the model was rewarded; in another, punished; and in the third, left alone without consequences. The children's aggressive behavior was then observed. As the social learning approach would predict, children who had viewed the model being punished performed the least aggressive behavior. Further, and consistent with the findings of many other investigators (see Chapter 5), boys performed more aggressive behavior than girls. In the second phase of the experiment, the children were offered attractive reinforcements (pretty sticker pictures and juice treats) for performing as many of the model's aggressive responses as they could remember. Gender differences nearly disappeared in this phase, and girls performed nearly as many aggressive behaviors as boys.

This experiment illustrated several important points. The first phase demonstrated that children do imitate, and that they do so differentially depending on the perceived consequences of the behavior. Notice that in this phase the children themselves were not actually reinforced, but simply observed the model being reinforced. The second phase illustrated how gender differences in aggressive behavior can be influenced by reinforcements. When girls were given equal direct reinforcement for aggression, they were nearly as aggressive as boys. Certainly the experiment is evidence of the power of imitation and reinforcement in shaping children's behavior. However, even though these effects have been demonstrated in the laboratory, this does not necessarily imply that they are the mechanisms underlying the natural acquisition of gender differences (Baldwin, 1967).

Criticisms of social learning theory The mechanisms postulated by social learning theory — differential reinforcement, imitation, and observational learning — intuitively appear to be reasonable explanations for why gender differences develop. Nonetheless, it is important to remember that these ideas must be tested scientifically. The study by Bandura discussed above is one kind of test of social learning theory. But we still need to know some other things, namely (1) do parents and others actually reinforce the behavior of boys and girls differentially; and (2) do children really imitate parents and others of their own gender more than people of the other gender? The available evidence seems to support point (1), but not point (2).

There is evidence that parents treat boys and girls differently, and that they differentially reward some — though certainly not all — behaviors in boys and girls (Block, 1978; Sherman, 1978). In particular, parents emphasize different values for boys and girls (Block, 1973). Achievement and assertion are encouraged in boys, while girls are taught to control these characteristics; a sense of relatedness (concern for relationships with other people) is emphasized for girls.

The evidence does not support, however, the notion that children tend to imitate people of their own gender more than people of the opposite gender (Maccoby and Jacklin, 1974). When offered an opportunity to imitate either a male or a female model, young children do not tend to select the model whose gender is the same as their own; indeed, their choices appear to be fairly random with respect to the gender of the model. This raises the distinction between *learning* and *performance*. It is possible that children learn equally from models of both genders, but that they differentially perform what they have learned, depending on the perceived consequences of their behavior and the gender-appropriateness of the behavior. This point is illustrated in the study by Bandura mentioned above. Although the girls were less aggressive than the boys in the first phase of the experiment, they were almost equally aggressive in the second phase. The results from the second phase suggest that the girls had learned as much as the boys about the model's aggressive behavior, but that in the first phase they did not perform what they had learned, and did so only in the second phase when encouraged by reinforcements.

In summary, social learning theory postulates that three important mechanisms are involved in the development of gender differences: differential reinforcement, imitation, and observational learning. The power of reinforcements and imitation in influencing children's behavior has been demonstrated in numerous experiments. It also seems that parents do differentially reinforce some gender-typed behaviors. However, research calls into question whether children do imitate same-gender models more than opposite-gender ones. These latter results suggest that other, more complex processes must be involved, in addition to those postulated by social learning theory, in the development of gender differences.

THE COGNITIVE-DEVELOPMENTAL MODEL

In terms of impact, perhaps the closest equivalent in the second half of this century to Freud's work in the first half is the developmental theory founded by Jean Piaget. Kohlberg (1966) has extended Piaget's cognitive principles to the realm of gender roles.

Much of Piaget's thinking arose from his observations of the errors children made in answering questions such as those asked on intelligence tests. He concluded that these errors did not indicate that the children were stupid or ignorant, but rather that they had a different world view, or *cognitive organization* from that of adults. He discovered that the cognitive organizations of children change systematically over time, and he constructed a stage theory of cognitive (intellectual) development to describe the progression of these changes. Interestingly, concepts of gender and gender identity undergo developmental changes parallel to the development of other concepts.

Gender roles and gender constancy   If you ask a three-year-old girl whether she is a boy or a girl, she will answer correctly that she is a girl. But if you ask her whether she can grow up to be a daddy, she will incorrectly answer yes. A six- or seven-year-old girl will not make this error. The three-year-old understands the concept of gender, but does not yet have the concept of *gender constancy* — the knowledge that gender is a permanent part of the self or identity. The development of these concepts is amusingly illustrated by Kohlberg (1966, p. 95):

> (Jimmy has just turned four, his friend Johnny is four and a half)
> Johnny: I'm going to be an airplane builder when I grow up.
> Jimmy: When I grow up, I'll be a mommy.
> Johnny: No, you can't be a mommy. You have to be a daddy.
> Jimmy: No, I'm going to be a mommy.
> Johnny: No, you're not a girl, you can't be a mommy.
> Jimmy: Yes, I can.

Apparently Johnny has acquired the concept of gender constancy, while Jimmy hasn't.

According to Kohlberg, the acquisition of this basic concept of gender constancy and gender identity (around the ages of four to six) is the crucial basis for the acquisition of gender role. Once the little girl knows she is a girl and will always be a female, this gender identity becomes an important part of personal identity. Gender identity then determines basic valuations (whether a person or behavior is believed to be "good" or "bad"). Motivated to have a positive sense of self, the girl comes to see femaleness as good. She then associates this valuation with cultural stereotypes, so that the female role becomes attractive to her. And finally she identifies with her mother, who is a readily available example of the female role the girl wishes to acquire. Thus children are motivated to adopt gender roles as part of their attempt to understand reality and to develop a stable and positive self-concept.

Cognitive-developmental theory essentially views gender-role learning as one aspect of cognitive development. The child learns a set of rules regarding what males do and what females do, and behaves accordingly. Gender-role learnng is thus viewed not as externally imposed, but rather as largely self-motivated. The child essentially engages in self-socialization and self-selects the behaviors to be learned and performed on the basis of rules regarding the gender-appropriateness of the behavior.

Cognitive-developmental theory points up an important potential problem in female development. It asserts, quite reasonably, that normal, healthy children tend to value the self, and therefore their own gender. Therefore little girls grow up thinking "female is good." Unfortunately, this does not correspond to cultural valuations of gender roles, in which the male role is valued more highly. Thus the girl is placed in a conflict situation in which her human need is to value the female role, yet culture informs her that it is not a valued role. We shall discuss the implications of this situation further in the next chapters.

Criticisms of cognitive-developmental theory   Kohlberg's basic argument is that the acquisition of the concept of gender constancy and, with it, the concept of gender identity is the important first step in gender-typing. Once these concepts have been formed, say around five to seven years of age, the child essentially "self-socializes." What evidence is there supporting these ideas?

First, it is clear that there is a concept of gender constancy that develops in children around the ages of five to seven. Evidence comes from children's comments such as those quoted earlier in this chapter, and from their responses to direct questioning by psychologists (e.g., Marcus and Overton, 1978). There is also some evidence that kindergarteners who have acquired gender constancy prefer to observe same-gender models, as compared with opposite-gender models, whereas children who do not yet have a concept of gender constancy have no such preference (Slaby, 1974, cited in Maccoby and Jacklin, 1974, p. 365).

However, it is also clear that children's gender-typed interests appear when they are far too young to have acquired the concept of gender constancy (Maccoby and Jacklin, 1974). That is, gender-typed toy and game preferences appear when children are two or three, yet children do not develop gender constancy until they are between the ages of five and seven. This is inconsistent with Kohlberg's theory, which would say that gender-typed interests should not appear until after gender constancy develops.

It seems reasonable to conclude that Kohlberg's notion of gender constancy and "self-socialization" explains some aspects of gender-role development, but that other mechanisms — such as those in social learning theory — are also functioning.

We should also note that Kohlberg has presented his model of the development of gender identity for the male case only; thus, much of what we have said is based on our inferences of what the model would be for the female case. In fact, the model may break down in attempting to explain the acquisition of female gender identity. According to the theory, one of the child's main motives for adopting gender role is the power and value the child sees in that role; yet the female role has less power and value. Is the girl therefore less motivated to adopt her role than is the boy? Kohlberg (1966, pp. 121–122) attempts to avoid this problem by saying that girls are motivated by the competency and "niceness" they perceive the female role to represent. Certainly it would be desirable to have a more complete explication of the process of female gender-role development from the cognitive-developmental point of view.

IN CONCLUSION

We have considered the explanations provided by three of the major theories of psychology — psychoanalytic theory, social learning theory, and cognitive-developmental theory — for how females acquire a gender identity and gender-typed behaviors. Psychoanalytic theory stresses the importance of the girl's penis envy leading to the Oedipal complex, which is never fully resolved. Passivity, masochism, and an immature superego remain characteristic of women throughout life. According to social learning theory, male and female development run in parallel, both being motivated first by reinforcements from the mother and later from others; further gender-typed behaviors are acquired through imitation and observational learning. Cognitive-developmental theory views the acquisition of gender identity largely as an intellectual or cognitive process, part of the way a child comes to understand the world. The child first acquires a concept of gender identity, which then brings about modeling of gender-typed behaviors and attachments to the same-gender parent.

These various theoretical views operate from vastly different assumptions and provide very different understandings of the nature of gender identity and its acquisition. Cognitive-developmental theory sees the acquisition of gender identity as motivated by cognitive or intellectual factors — a rational process in comparison with the incest-sexual motivations of psychoanalytic theory or the pain-avoiding, reward-seeking motivations of social learning theory. Another distinction is the assertion of both cognitive-developmental theory and social learning theory that the child actively seeks to acquire gender role, as compared with the view of psychoanalytic theory, which sees the child as the passive recipient of anatomical determinants. Certainly it is an important observation that children do actively seek to acquire gender roles. On the nature-nurture continuum, while psychoanalytic theory represents the nature extreme (anatomy is destiny) and social learning theory the nurture extreme, cognitive-developmental theory emphasizes the interaction between the state of the organism (stage of cognitive development) and the information available from the culture. With regard to empirical verification of the theories, certainly there is much more experimental evidence supporting the notions of social learning theory and cognitive-developmental theory than there is for psychoanalytic theory.

Finally, the various theories postulate different sequences of processes in role acquisition (see Figure 3.2). In Freudian and social learning theory, parental attachment comes first and leads to identification, which leads to the acquisition of gender identity. But in cognitive-developmental theory, the process is reversed — gender identity is formed first, and it leads to modeling and attachment.

Since our basic purpose is to understand female development and gender-role development, what insights do these theories give us? No one theory by itself is adequate for understanding these developmental processes — there is no "right" theory. Yet no theory is completely wrong. Each contributes something to our understanding. Freudian theory was important historically in emphasizing the notion of psychosexual development, highlighting the notion that an individual's gender identity and behavior have their roots in previous experiences. To understand an in-

FIGURE 3.2

Theoretical sequences in the girl's gender identification.

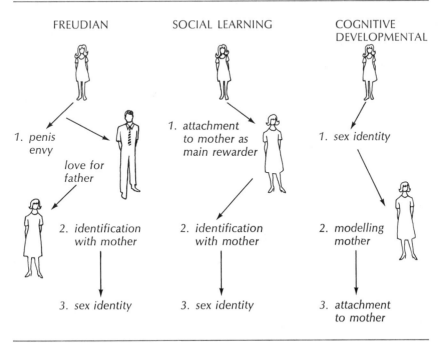

Source: After Kohlberg, 1966.

dividual's gender identity as an adult, or at any age, for that matter, one must look at the person's life history. A second important contribution from psychoanalytic theory is the concept of *identification*. Though one might dispute the factors Freud postulated as creating identification, the fact remains that children do identify strongly with the same-gender parent, and this identification is an important force in gender-role development.

Social learning theory is important in its emphasis on the social and cultural components of gender-role development — the importance of society in shaping gender-typed behaviors. It points out, quite correctly, that boys and girls are treated differently. Social learning investigators have also contributed some very impressive laboratory demonstrations of the power of reinforcements in shaping children's behavior, in particular gender-typed behaviors. Social learning theory also highlights the importance of imitation in the acquisition of gender role. Modern mothers who are concerned about freeing their children from gender-role restrictions might do well to keep these forces in mind. It is axiomatic that children do as you do (they imitate), not as you say. With respect to gender-role learning, girls tend to imitate their mothers. If a mother wants to avoid restrictive gender-role stereotypes for her daughter, it may help to encourage her to be a doctor or a lawyer; but in the end, the mother's own behavior may have a much greater impact than her verbal encouragements. If the mother devotes most of her time to cooking, cleaning, and sewing, and enjoys them, and further considers herself incapable of pounding a nail or fixing a leaky faucet, her daughter is likely to get interested in cooking, cleaning, and sewing, and to avoid pounding nails and fixing leaky faucets. If the mother portrays helplessness as part of the female role, the daughter is likely to start acting helpless. Mothers should consider carefully the kind of gender-role model they want to be to their daughters.

Finally, cognitive-developmental theory emphasizes that gender-role learning is a part of the rational learning processes of childhood (as contrasted with the libidinal motivations postulated by psychoanalytic theory). Further, the theory emphasizes that gender-role learning does not result solely from externally imposed forces of society, but arises at least in part from intrinsic motivation. Children actively seek to acquire gender roles, sometimes to the dismay of parents who want their children to be untouched by gender-role stereotypes. Gender roles seem to be helpful to children in structuring and understanding the reality of the world about them.

4

FEMININITY, MASCULINITY, AND ANDROGYNY

Everyone is partly man and partly woman.

The concepts of masculinity and femininity are intuitively appealing and meaningful to the average person. Most of us have a sense — perhaps not even well thought out — of what characteristics make a man "masculine" or a woman "feminine." Traditionally, of course, it was thought desirable for men to be masculine and women to be feminine. Such an assumption was made not only by lay people; it also underlies the theories in the previous chapter, and much of the traditional psychological research. In the last few years, however, a new ideal for both genders has been emerging — androgyny. In this chapter we shall see how psychologists have studied femininity, masculinity, and androgyny, and what the results of those studies have been.

THE CONCEPT OF
MASCULINITY-FEMININITY

There are several different ways of conceptualizing masculinity-femininity (M-F), and they vary in their complexity. These are illustrated in Figure 4.1.

The typology   The simplest view of M-F is that there are two types (hence the term "typology") of people, masculine ones and feminine ones. The notion is that we could categorize all human beings by placing each one into one or the other of these "boxes." It is then assumed that these two categories correspond very closely to a person's biological gender — that is, that virtually all females are in the feminine category and virtually all males are in the masculine category.

There are a number of problems with this conceptualization of M-F. Basically, it commits the *typological error*, which occurs any time we try to put people into simple categories or types (Rosenberg and Sutton-Smith, 1972). People are just not that simple, and a model that tries to put them into one of two categories — feminine or masculine — is guilty of oversimplification. It is a rather naive — not to mention conservative — model in its assumption that all or most women are feminine and all or most men are masculine. Its assumption that a female will consistently demonstrate nothing but feminine personality characteristics is certainly questionable. Finally, this model ignores all the variability from one woman to the next, not to mention the potentially great similarities between the genders. Nonetheless, this conceptualization is widespread and persisting.

FIGURE 4.1

Progressive conceptualization of masculinity-femininity.

1. The typological categorization

| masculinity | | femininity |

2. The unidimensional, bipolar continuum

masculinity ⟵————————————⟶ femininity

3. The two-dimensional scheme

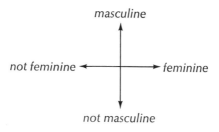

4. The multidimensional scheme

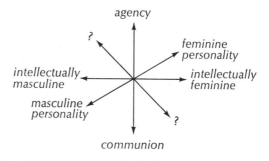

The continuum   A somewhat more sophisticated conceptualization is that masculinity-femininity can be represented by various gradations on a continuum (the second section of Figure 4.1). This, like the previous model, is intuitively appealing. The notion is that we can go beyond saying that a person is "masculine" and instead say that some people are very masculine, others moderately masculine, and others not very masculine, and similarly for femininity. Thus, for example, we might say that Burt Reynolds is more masculine than Jimmy Carter, who in turn is more masculine than Woody Allen. These people would presumably fall at varying points along a continuum or scale.

The continuum or scale is called a unidimensional, bipolar continuum. "Unidimensional" means simply one-dimensional, that is, that we can represent all the varieties of masculinity and femininity on a single scale. This is quite a different model from that used in discussing androgyny, whch requires two dimensions, as we shall discuss later in this chapter. The term "bipolar" simply means "two poles." The notion is that masculinity falls at one end or pole of this scale, femininity at the other end or pole. The idea, then, is that masculinity and femininity are opposites.

We shall postpone criticisms of this model until we have discussed the various psychological tests that have been constructed using it as a basis.

MEASURING MASCULINITY-FEMININITY

One of the first things that psychologists must do when they want to study a particular phenomenon of human behavior is devise a way to *measure* it. Often this takes the form of constructing a psychological test. Research on masculinity-femininity is no exception. Numerous psychological tests have been developed to measure it. Virtually all of them are based on the unidimensional, bipolar continuum model of M-F.

One example of a standard test of masculinity-femininity is the FE (for femininity) scale of the *California Psychological Inventory* (Gough, 1956). Some items from it are shown in Figure 4.2. It is a simple paper-and-pencil test, with a subject responding true or false to items, depending

FIGURE 4.2

Some sample items that differentiate males from females and are therefore used to measure masculinity-femininity.

Item	Response indicating femininity
Sometimes I have the same dream over and over.	True
I am somewhat afraid of the dark.	True
I think I could do better than most of the present politicians if I were in office.	False
I would like to be a soldier.	False
I think I would like the work of a librarian.	True
I want to be an important person in the community.	False

Source: Reproduced by special permission from California Psychological Inventory by Harrison G. Gough, Ph.D. Copyright 1956 by Consulting Psychologists Press, Inc.

on whether the items describe the subject or not. Then a score is computed that places the subject at some point along the bipolar continuum.

How are items chosen for such tests? They are chosen in a rather simple way — the criterion being that they must differentiate biological males from biological females. That is, an item is chosen if it shows marked gender differences, meaning that a much different proportion of males as compared with females will respond affirmatively to it. Therefore, an item such as "I prefer a tub bath to a shower" can appear on such tests, not because it reflects anything profound about the essence of masculinity or femininity, but simply because males tend to prefer showers and females tend to prefer tub baths. The implicit assumption, then, is that "femininity" is the quality of women that differentiates them from men.

What is the purpose of such tests? Many psychological tests are designed to differentiate one group from another. For example, a scale might be devised to measure the degree of a person's paranoia. Using this scale, a psychologist could tell whether a person was so disturbed as to need psychiatric care. By analogy, one might think that the purpose of M-F tests was to separate males from females. That is, of course, not the case, and there are certainly more efficient ways of telling who is male and who is female. Neither are M-F tests designed for use in applied settings such as deciding which of several candidates should be hired for a job. M-F tests have instead been designed to be used for research purposes. For example, they can be used in research designed to find out whether the degree of one's masculinity-femininity (or the extent of gender-typing) is related to certain other psychological characteristics. As an example of such research, it has been found that creativity and intelligence tend to be associated with cross-gender-typing (Maccoby, 1966). That is, boys who score more toward the feminine end of an M-F scale than the average for boys, and girls who score more toward the masculine end than the average for girls, tend to be more creative and intelligent than average. In other words, gender role nonconformity seems to have some benefits associated with it. This is an interesting result, and such research would not have been possible without some method of measuring M-F, such as an M-F test.

Criticisms of M-F tests   Perhaps the most important criticism of M-F tests is that they are based on the assumption that masculinity-femininity is unidimensional and bipolar (Constantinople, 1973). There is some question as to whether M-F is so simple that it can be scored on a single scale, or whether, instead, it might require several scales to capture its complexity. There is also a serious question as to whether M-F is bipolar. The bipolarity assumption means that masculinity and femininity are opposites of each other. Further, it means that the more masculine one is, the fewer feminine traits one exhibits. But is that necessarily true?

For example, if a man cultivates a "feminine" hobby such as cooking, that may increase his femininity, but does it necessarily decrease his masculinity — does it take away from the fact that he is a championship boxer? The more recent research on androgyny, to be discussed in the next section, provides an alternative model that is not subject to these criticisms.

Some other criticisms also deserve mention (Constantinople, 1973). One is that the psychologists who construct M-F tests never really get around to defining precisely what they mean by "femininity" or "masculinity." They typically settle for the meaning of gender differences when they choose items, with an implicit definition that femininity is whatever women are that men aren't. This may be very practical, but it does not give us much insight into what femininity or masculinity really is. Further, some tests emphasize gender-role preference (what I would like to be), while other measures emphasize gender-role adoption (what I actually do); it is not clear which of these tests measures true femininity or masculinity. For example, a girl might express rather masculine gender-role preferences, but might be very feminine in what she actually does, perhaps because she fears rejection from her peers if she does what she really wants to do. There is a contradiction between her gender-role preferences, which are masculine, and her gender-role adoption, which is feminine. Which is she, then, feminine or masculine? One M-F test might say feminine, and another might say masculine. Finally, there is a confusion between the masculinity-femininity of personality versus the masculinity-femininity of behavior (Spence and Helmreich, 1978). Should one be scored for femininity on the basis of one's personality traits (e.g., nurturance, sensitivity), or on the basis of behavior (e.g., cooking, child-rearing)? Generally, then, there is a problem in this area of research because of an ambiguity about exactly what is meant by "masculinity" and "femininity."

THE CONCEPT OF ANDROGYNY

The question that needs to be raised is, why can't a person be both feminine and masculine? In fact, most of us know people who are both. An example would be a woman who has strong achievement drives, is very successful at her career, plays tennis very well, and likes to wear jeans, and who at the same time likes to cook and sew, wear long dresses, and is very sensitive and caring. The problem is that traditional M-F tests can't handle her. The current work on androgyny was designed to study such people.

Androgyny means having both masculine and feminine psychological characteristics. It is derived from the Greek roots *andro*, meaning man (as in androgens) and *gyn*, meaning woman (as in gynecologist). An

FIGURE 4.3

The androgynous nature of humans is shown in this illustration from a seventeenth-century alchemy manuscript.

Source: Reprinted by permission of the Leyden University Library.

androgynous person, then, is a person who has both masculine and feminine psychological characteristics.

As shown in Figure 4.1, the concept of androgyny is based on a two-dimensional model of masculinity-femininity. The idea is that instead of masculinity and femininity being opposite ends of a single scale, they are two separate dimensions, one running from not feminine to very feminine, and the other from not masculine to very masculine. This would allow for androgynous people, that is, people who are high on both femininity and masculinity. It also would allow for feminine people, and for masculine people. In the third diagram of Figure 4.1, the androgynous people would be the ones falling in the upper right-hand quadrant. The two-dimensional model — unlike the unidimensional, bipolar model — allows for people who are both highly masculine and highly feminine, that is, androgynous.

MEASURING ANDROGYNY

Psychologist Sandra Bem (1974) has constructed a test to measure androgyny (see also Spence and Helmreich, 1978) that is shown in Table 4.1. It consists of 60 adjectives or descriptive phrases. Subjects are asked to indicate, for each, how well it describes them on a scale from 1 (never or almost never true) to 7 (always or almost always true). Of the 60 adjectives, 20 are stereotypically feminine,[1] 20 are stereotypically masculine, and 20 are neutral, that is, not gender-typed. Items 1, 4, 7, etc. in Table 4.1 are masculine; items 2, 5, 8, etc., are feminine; and 3, 6, 9, etc. are neutral. Therefore "self-reliant" is a masculine characteristic, "yielding" is feminine, and "helpful" is neutral.

Once the test has been taken, subjects are given two scores: a masculinity score and a femininity score. The masculinity score is the average of their self-ratings of the masculinity items, and their femininity score is the average of their self-ratings of the femininity items. This will give each person a score on each of the two scales shown in the two-dimensional diagram in Figure 4.1. The androgynous people should be in the upper right-hand part, which means they should be high on masculinity and high on femininity. Bem defines "high" as being above the median (the median is a kind of average). Therefore people are androgynous if they are above the median on masculinity and above the median on femininity (the median on each of these scales is generally about 4.9). A feminine person who scores high (above the median) on femininity but low

---

[1] Unlike the constructors of the M-F tests, Bem did not avoid defining M and F by simply relying on gender differences. Instead, femininity was defined as those characteristics that are considered socially desirable for women in our culture, and similarly for masculinity.

TABLE 4.1. Are you androgynous?

The following items are the Bem Sex Role Inventory. To find out whether you score as androgynous on it, first rate yourself on each item, on a scale from 1 (never or almost never true) to 7 (always or almost always true).

1. self-reliant	23. sympathetic	42. solemn
2. yielding	24. jealous	43. willing to take
3. helpful	25. has leadership	a stand
4. defends own beliefs	abilities	44. tender
5. cheerful	26. sensitive to the needs	45. friendly
6. moody	of others	46. aggressive
7. independent	27. truthful	47. gullible
8. shy	28. willing to take risks	48. inefficient
9. conscientious	29. understanding	49. acts as a leader
10. athletic	30. secretive	50. childlike
11. affectionate	31. makes decisions easily	51. adaptable
12. theatrical	32. compassionate	52. individualistic
13. assertive	33. sincere	53. does not use harsh
14. flatterable	34. self-sufficient	language
15. happy	35. eager to soothe hurt	54. unsystematic
16. strong personality	feelings	55. competitive
17. loyal	36. conceited	56. loves children
18. unpredictable	37. dominant	57. tactful
19. forceful	38. soft-spoken	58. ambitious
20. feminine	39. likable	59. gentle
21. reliable	40. masculine	60. conventional
22. analytical	41. warm	

SCORING:

(a) Add up your ratings for items 1, 4, 7, 10, 13, 16, 19, 22, 25, 28, 31, 34, 37, 40, 43, 46, 49, 52, 55, and 58. Divide the total by 20. That is your masculinity score.

(b) Add up your ratings for items 2, 5, 8, 11, 14, 17, 20, 23, 26, 29, 32, 35, 38, 41, 44, 47, 50, 53, 56, and 59. Divide the total by 20. That is your femininity score.

(c) If your masculinity score is above 4.9 (the approximate median for the masculinity scale) and your femininity score is above 4.9 (the approximate femininity median) then you would be classified as androgynous on Bem's scale.

Sources: Bem (1974), Bem (1977), Hyde and Phillis (1979).

(below the median) on masculinity would fall in the lower right-hand quadrant in Figure 4.1. Similarly, a masculine person who scores high on the masculinity scale but low on the femininity scale would fall in the upper left-hand quadrant. Finally, people who score low on both scales fall in the lower left-hand quadrant and are called "undifferentiated"

TABLE 4.2.   Percentages of college students classified as androgynous, masculine, feminine, or undifferentiated.

	Androgynous	Masculine	Feminine	Undifferentiated
Females	27	14	32	28
Males	32	34	8	25

Based on a sample of 715 students at the University of Texas.
Source: Spence and Helmreich, 1978.

because they don't rate themselves very highly on any of the adjectives, masculine or feminine. Therefore, having taken the Bem Sex Role Inventory, an individual can be placed in one of four categories: masculine, feminine, androgynous, or undifferentiated.

In her work with college students, Bem typically finds that about one-third of them are androgynous, according to her scale (see Table 4.2).

IS IT BETTER TO BE ANDROGYNOUS?

As an ideal, androgyny sounds good. It permits freedom from gender-role stereotypes and allows people to express their opposite-gender tendencies. But what are androgynous people like in reality? Do they function well psychologically, are they respected members of society? Or do they suffer from problems of confused gender identity? Does society view them suspiciously because of their gender-role nonconformity? There are a few studies available that give us some answers to these questions.

Pressure-to-conform study   Bem has done a number of studies to find out how androgynous people, as compared with stereotyped people, actually behave in various demanding situations (Bem, 1975; Bem and Lenney, 1976; Bem, Martyna, and Watson, 1976). Her general prediction in these studies is that androgynous people should do better in a wider variety of situations, because they are capable of being feminine or masculine when the situation calls for it. Stereotyped people, on the other hand, may do well when stereotyped behavior is required, but in situations demanding cross-gender behavior, they will do poorly.

The "pressure-to-conform study" was one such experiment (Bem, 1975). Subjects were brought to the laboratory in groups of 4 males and 4 females. They were then placed in individual booths equipped with microphones and earphones. Their task was to judge how funny some cartoons were; they thought that they were participating in an experiment on humor. The cartoons had previously been rated by an independent set of judges and half of them had been judged very funny, half of them not at all funny.

Subjects were asked to rate how funny each cartoon was. Before giving their rating, however, they heard what they thought were the others in their group giving their ratings. In fact what they were hearing was a tape recording, with voices saying that a particular cartoon was funny when it wasn't and vice versa.

The idea was that subjects who stuck to their guns and gave their opinions of the cartoons honestly, refusing to be influenced by the others would be displaying the "masculine" trait of independence. Those whose opinions were swayed by the others and gave ratings similar to them, rather than really telling how funny the cartoons were, would be showing the "feminine" characteristic of compliance or conformity. Bem feels that independence in this situation is a good characteristic.

Her prediction for the outcome of the study was that those subjects who had been classified as masculine by the Bem Sex Role Inventory would be independent or nonconforming. Feminine subjects, on the other hand would be more likely to conform. Androgynous subjects should be able to be masculine or feminine. In this situation, Bem believes that independence is the most desirable behavior, and therefore she predicted that androgynous subjects would be independent. The results turned out exactly as predicted — masculine and androgynous subjects did not differ significantly from each other, and both groups were significantly more independent than the feminine subjects.[1]

Good-listener study   In another study, the subject listened as a lonely transfer student poured out a list of troubles in adjusting to college life (Bem, 1976). The interaction was watched from behind a one-way mirror and subjects were scored for their responsiveness and sympathy for the talker, as a measure of their nurturance.

The idea is that the "feminine" quality of nurturance is what is called for in this situation. Bem predicted that feminine subjects would be more nurturant than masculine subjects. Androgynous people, able to be either masculine or feminine, should do what is appropriate, namely, be nurturant. The results turned out as predicted: feminine subjects and androgynous subjects of both genders did not differ from each other, and both groups were significantly more nurturant than masculine subjects.

In sum, these two studies, when taken together, indicate that an-

---

[1] If you are a psychology student, you might want to notice that this and the next study are means by which Bem can begin establishing the *validity* of the Bem Sex Role Inventory. That is, to be valid, the scale should be able to differentiate various groups of people, based on theoretical predictions. That is precisely what this study does.

drogynous people probably function better in a wider variety of situations than do gender-typed people. Because they have both masculine and feminine characteristics in their repertoire, they are capable of being masculine when that is appropriate (as in the pressure-to-conform study when independence is appropriate) and they are capable of being feminine when that is appropriate (as in the good-listener study, where nurturance is most appropriate).

Self-esteem   The traditional assumption in psychology was that gender-typing was a good thing in terms of personal adjustment. That is, it was thought that the well-adjusted person would be appropriately gender-typed (feminine if a female, masculine if a male), and that people who were not so gender-typed would be poorly adjusted. But even some of the traditional research, based on the unidimensional, bipolar model of M-F, contradicted these assumptions. For example, high femininity in females has been shown to be correlated with high anxiety and low self-esteem (e.g., Cosentino and Heilbrun, 1964: Gall, 1969; Gray, 1957; Sears, 1970; Webb, 1963). High masculinity in adult men has been correlated with high anxiety, high neuroticism, and low self-acceptance (Harford et al., 1967; Mussen, 1962).

With a test to measure androgyny now available, we are in a position to see how well-adjusted androgynous people are, and how their adjustment compares with that of gender-typed people. Research indicates that androgynous people and masculine people tend to be high in self-esteem, in comparison with feminine people and undifferentiated people who tend to be lower in self-esteem (Bem, 1977; Spence et al., 1975). The ordering of groups, from highest to lowest in self-esteem, has been found consistently to be: androgynous, masculine, feminine, undifferentiated (Spence and Helmreich, 1978). These results, then, give no evidence that androgynous people are poorly adjusted, suffering from confusions of gender-role identity. Instead they indicate that androgynous people have high self-esteem, an important psychological characteristic. The point that masculine people tend to have higher self-esteem than feminine people is certainly worth noting. The implications of this finding will be discussed further in Chapter 7.

These findings have important implications in the area of mental health and psychotherapy. This will also be discussed in Chapter 7. Briefly, it is being suggested now that the old model of gender-typing as part of mental health be replaced with a new ideal of androgyny as a model of mental health (Kaplan, 1976).

Androgyny as an ideal   *Psychology Today* magazine recently asked its readers for their ideas about masculinity (Tavris, 1977). When the women respondents described their notion of the ideal man, they basically described someone who was androgynous. Ideally, they wanted someone who was self-confident, successful, and willing to fight for his family and his beliefs ("masculine" characteristics), but who was also warm, gentle, and willing to lose ("feminine" characteristics). This suggests the possibility that androgyny is emerging as an ideal in our society.

Of course, *Psychology Today* readers are scarcely a random sample of the American population; they tend to be more educated and more liberal than the average American. It would be a mistake to conclude that blue-collar workers yearn for androgyny. Also, the survey did not ask men about their ideal woman, so we cannot tell whether androgyny has emerged as an ideal for women. This study does suggest an important area needing research — namely, how do people react to androgynous people in comparison with gender-typed people?

Problems?   Androgyny sounds so wonderful, but are there any problems with it? Basically, the concept has become popular so recently, and the research is so new and relatively small in quantity, that it is probably too early to tell. But at least two possible problems can be raised.

First, androgyny is advantageous in freeing people from the restrictions of rigid gender-role stereotypes. In so doing, however, it may be setting up an extraordinarily demanding, perhaps impossible, ideal. For example, in the good old days, a woman could be considered reasonably competent ("successful") if she could bake bread well. To meet new standards and be androgynous, she not only has to bake bread well, but also has to repair cars. That is, androgyny demands that people be good at more diverse things, and that may be difficult. Indeed, the characteristics required to be androgynous sometimes seem almost mutually contradictory. For example, on the Bem Sex Role Inventory, in order to be androgynous, one needs to be forceful and dominant ("masculine" items) and also shy and soft-spoken ("feminine" items). It is hard to see how a person could be all of those at once. Of course, the ideal androgyn would be expected to display different characteristics in different situations, depending on what was most appropriate; but knowing what is most appropriate is also rather difficult.

Some feminist scholars have also raised a second criticism of androgyny (Orloff, 1978). They regard it as essentially a "sell-out" to men. That is, to become androgynous, women need to add masculine traits to their personalities, or become more like men. The argument has been made that what we should do, rather than to encourage women to become more like men, is to concentrate on valuing those things that women do and are. To these scholars, rediscovering and cherishing womanhood would be preferable to encouraging androgyny. This, of course, is a matter of personal values.

STAGES OF GENDER-ROLE DEVELOPMENT

A friend of ours recently recounted the following story. Both she and her husband hold Ph.D.'s and are professors of political science. Both are feminists, and they try to have an egalitarian marriage and run an egalitarian household. Yet one day their little son came home from kindergarten, glibly telling them how women could be nurses and not doctors, and men could be doctors and not nurses. To say the least, our friend was quite dismayed by this. She had certainly never told her son such things, and in fact had told him quite the opposite. Probably some of you have had similar experiences, or know of people who have, and can appreciate the frustration parents feel when, after all of their efforts to teach their children about gender-role equality and freedom, the children still keep coming up with the same tired, old stereotypes that people have traditionally held. However, some recent research and theory in psychology provide an explanation for this phenomenon, not to mention a ray of hope for parents.

Psychologist Joseph Pleck (1975) has proposed that children go through stages in their understanding of gender roles. Basically, he has applied cognitive-developmental theory to children's understanding of gender roles, much as Kohlberg did (as discussed in Chapter 3). Kohlberg, however, stopped his theoretical descriptions when children were five or six; Pleck has extended the theory to describe older children and adults (for other, similar theorizing, see Block, 1973; Rebecca et al., 1976).

According to Pleck's theory, there are three stages of gender-role development, and these stages parallel the stages of moral development in children (the stages of moral development having already been well documented by psychologists). In the first stage of moral development in children, the premoral phase, children are dominated by their desire to gratify their own impulses, and seek to be good only to avoid punishment. In the corresponding *first stage of gender-role development*, the child's gender-role concepts are disorganized. The child may not even know her or his own gender yet, and has not yet learned that only men are supposed to do certain things, only women others. (In Kohlberg's terms, such children have not yet acquired the concepts of gender identity or gender constancy.) In the second stage of moral development, conventional role conformity, children conform to rules mostly to get approval from others, particularly authorities. In the corresponding *second stage of gender-role development*, children know the rules of gender roles and are highly motivated to conform to them themselves, and also to make others conform to them. This stage begins in childhood and probably reaches its peak in adolescence when gender-role conformity is strongest. In the third stage of moral development, the postconventional phase, moral judgments are made on the basis of internalized, self-accepted principles rather than on the basis of external forces. In the corresponding *third stage of gender-role development,* people manage to go beyond (transcend) the limitations of gender roles imposed by society; such individuals develop psychological androgyny in response to their own inner needs and values.

Of course, some adults never make it out of the second stage of moral development to move on to the third stage. An example would be the man who donates a lot of money to a charity because it will get him respect and approval from important people, rather than because of an internalized belief that the charity is a good cause and he should support it. So, too, some people never go beyond the second stage of gender-role development and move on to androgyny; they remain for their entire lives restricted by rather tight limitations of gender roles.

Pleck's theory is informative in answering the question originally posed, namely, why do children who should have very flexible ideas about gender roles instead have rigid — sometimes absurdly rigid — ideas? This theory suggests that children, as part of their cognitive development and their attempts to understand how the world works, must go through a stage of gender-role restrictiveness. Essentially, they must first learn that only men can be doctors and only women can be nurses before they can learn that there are exceptions to that rule and that girls can become doctors. Feminist parents probably cannot realistically expect that their children will skip stage two of gender-role development. What they can hope for, and provide the stimulus for, is their children eventually reaching stage three and androgyny.

No one has collected systematic data to test this theory as yet, although there is some fragmentary supporting evidence (Block, 1973). As Pleck noted, the theory helps to make sense out of some apparently conflicting studies. For example, some studies show that daughters of working mothers have quite traditional gender-role concepts when they are young (Hartley, 1959, 1960); but another study showed that maternal employment is associated with daughters' high achievement and androgyny later in life (Siegel et al., 1963). Perhaps the kind of roles parents model make little difference in childhood, when all children are in a conforming stage, but by late adolescence or adulthood these people are able to benefit from the liberated models their parents provided.

5

GENDER DIFFERENCES IN PERSONALITY AND BEHAVIOR

Certainly woman's aptitude for facile tears comes largely from the fact that her life is built upon a foundation of impotent revolt; it is also doubtless true that physiologically she has less nervous control than man and that her education has taught her to let herself go more readily. This effect of education, or custom, is indeed evident, since in the past men like Benjamin Constant and Diderot, for instance, used to pour out floods of tears, and then men ceased weeping when it became unfashionable for them.

SIMONE DE BEAUVOIR, The Second Sex

All of you have probably heard dialogues such as the following:

MCP*: "Of course she did that, because she's so emotional. Women are just more emotional than men."

AF**: "Women *are not* more emotional than men. How can you say that?"

MCP: "Yes they are."

AF: "No they're not."

et cetera, et cetera.

Debates such as these are often not productive because they essentially end up setting one person's opinion against another's. The more productive approach is to realize that MCP's statement, "Women are just more emotional than men," is scientifically testable. That is, one can collect actual data on men and women to see if it is true. In this chapter we shall consider research that has done just that — looked at gender differences in various personality characteristics and behaviors — to see how different the personalities of women and men are. Research on gender differences in abilities will be discussed in Chapter 8.

STEREOTYPES, REAL DIFFERENCES, AND THE NATURE–NURTURE ISSUE

Before we look at the various personality characteristics and behaviors that have been investigated, it is important to make a distinction among the following: gender-role stereotypes, psychological gender differences that have been empirically determined to exist ("real" differences), and the causes of gender differences, whether biological or environmental.

Gender-role stereotypes are simply the things (behaviors, personality traits) that people expect from males and females. Research shows that, even in modern American society, and even among college students, there is a consensus that males and females do differ psychologically in many ways (Rosenkrantz et al., 1968). A list of these stereotyped traits is given in Table 5.1.

---

* MCP = male chauvinist pig
** AF = ardent feminist

TABLE 5.1. Stereotyped personality characteristics

There is a consensus among Americans that the following are characteristics of men and women.

Masculine Characteristics Considered Socially Desirable

Very aggressive
Very independent
Not at all emotional
Almost always hides emotions
Very objective
Not at all easily influenced
Very dominant
Likes math and science very much
Not at all excitable in a minor crisis
Very active
Very competitive
Very logical
Very worldly
Very skilled in business
Very direct
Knows the ways of the world
Feelings not easily hurt
Very adventurous
Can make decisions easily
Never cries
Almost always acts as a leader
Very self-confident
Not at all uncomfortable about being aggressive
Very ambitious
Easily able to separate feelings from ideas
Not at all dependent
Never conceited about appearance

Feminine Characteristics Considered Socially Desirable

Very talkative
Very tactful
Very gentle
Very aware of feelings of others
Very religious
Very interested in own appearance
Very neat in habits
Very quiet
Very strong need for security
Enjoys art and literature very much
Easily expresses tender feelings

Source: Rosenkrantz et al., 1968.

When actual data are collected on the behavior and personality of females and males, the stereotypes turn out to be true in some cases ("real" differences), but not in others. For example, there is a stereotype that males are more aggressive than females; this turns out to be a real difference, as we will see later in this chapter. On the other hand, there is a stereotype that women are less intelligent than men, although actual research shows this not to be true; there are no gender differences in IQ. In this case, the stereotype is false. A *real difference*, then, is a gender difference that has been found to exist based on data collected on the personality or behavior of males and females.

Finally, if a gender difference (a real difference) is found, it requires one more step of analysis — and a very difficult one — to determine whether the difference is biologically or environmentally caused. For example, because there is a well-documented gender difference in aggression, we cannot automatically infer that it is biologically caused (e.g., by sex hormones), nor can we automatically decide that it is produced by environmental factors (e.g., socialization). Gender differences may be caused by environmental factors, biological factors, or both.

GENDER DIFFERENCES VERSUS INDIVIDUAL DIFFERENCES

Suppose we say that a particular study of kindergarten children showed boys to be more aggressive than girls. Just what exactly does that mean?

Such a statement generally means that there were average differences between males and females, and that these differences were statistically significant. It most certainly does not mean, however, that all the males were more aggressive than all of the females. With data on gender differences, the distributions, while showing average differences, generally overlap to a great extent (see Figure 5.1). Typically there is a great deal of variability among members of one gender (individual differences). Therefore one should not be surprised to find an aggressive little girl in the kindergarten in our imaginary study. There may be some very aggressive little girls, but the boys, on the average are more aggressive. And, particularly if the number of subjects is large, a statistically significant gender difference may be found even though the average scores of males and females are fairly close.

The point is that even when there are average gender differences in a particular trait, there are almost always still large individual differences — differences from one female to the next and from one male to the next. Often these individual differences are more important than the average gender differences. A finding that females are less aggressive than males should certainly not lead one to expect that all females are unaggressive.

FIGURE 5.1

Examples of distribution of scores for males and females that might lead to statistically significant gender differences in the trait.

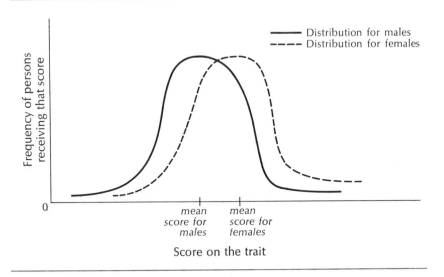

Often in this book we will make a statement such as "males are more aggressive than females" as a kind of shorthand for the more precise — but awkward — "males, on the average, are more aggressive than females." Individual differences and the great overlap of distributions should always be kept in mind, however.

MACCOBY AND JACKLIN: THE PSYCHOLOGY OF SEX DIFFERENCES

At this point, there are literally thousands of studies investigating psychological gender differences. These studies have attempted to document the "real differences," using the terminology introduced above. This should mean that we have a thorough understanding of which behaviors show gender differences and which do not. Unfortunately, things are a bit more complicated than that. Often the results of different studies contradict each other. For example, some studies of gender differences in infants' activity levels find that boys are more active, while others find no differences. In such cases, what should we conclude? Are boys more active than girls?

Another problem is that sometimes a single study that finds a gender difference will be widely cited and included in textbooks, and the five other studies of the same behavior that found no gender difference will be ignored. It seems likely that this occurs particularly when a finding of gender differences confirms the stereotypes held by authors and the general public. As an example, many child psychology texts cite the finding that boys are more active than girls, and further argue that this may be a source of later gender differences and of the active assertiveness of the adult male role. However, in the actual studies of infants' activity levels, two of the reports found gender differences that were not statistically significant (Knop, 1946; Lewis et al., 1963). According to the rules of science, a gender difference should be statistically significant before it is worth talking about. A third study that is cited as evidence, in fact, used male infants only as subjects (Bell, 1960). It is difficult to see how such a study could be evidence for gender differences.

To bring some order out of this chaos, Stanford psychologists Eleanor Maccoby and Carol Jacklin attempted to review systematically the huge number of studies of psychological gender differences, publishing their findings in a book entitled *The Psychology of Sex Differences* (1974). In all, they reviewed over 2000 articles and books, most of them published after 1966. They made particular efforts to find studies that had tested for gender differences in psychological characteristics but had found none. They concluded that some widely held beliefs about gender differences have little or no scientific evidence backing them. They also found that there are some gender differences that are very solidly documented. Maccoby and Jacklin's conclusions will be mentioned frequently in this chapter in our discussion of gender differences in personality, and also in Chapter 8 in our discussion of gender differences in abilities.

Maccoby and Jacklin's book instantly became a classic in the field, in part because the authors are highly respected psychologists, and in part because there was a great need for such a book. Later, however, the book was criticized — perhaps the most serious criticisms coming from Berkeley psychologist Jeanne Block (1976a, 1976b). She argued that Maccoby and Jacklin had a bias toward finding no gender differences. She found some clerical errors in their tallying of studies and felt that their categorizing of studies was sometimes arbitrary. Finally, young subjects were overrepresented in the studies surveyed by Maccoby and Jacklin; 75 percent were based on subjects 12 years old or younger, and nearly 40 percent were based on preschoolers. This, of course, is not Maccoby and Jacklin's fault; it simply reflects the way psychologists have chosen to do their research. Nonetheless, it means that we know very little about gender differences in adults, and most of that is based on data from college students — still scarcely a broad age range. Block pointed out that many gender differences do not appear until adolescence, and so findings of no gender differences with young children may be misleading.

In the sections that follow, we will cite Maccoby and Jacklin's conclusions when they seem to be accurate and will refer to other sources if they have provided convincing evidence that Maccoby and Jacklin's conclusions are not accurate.

We shouldn't leave this discussion, however, without noting a moral that emerges. Often a very interesting gender difference will be found in a study, and the study will be given a great deal of publicity, including being included in textbooks and professors' lectures. Students need to develop a critical attitude in such cases. The first question one should ask when hearing such a report is, has this finding been replicated? *Replicated* means that the study has been repeated independently by other scientists and the same results obtained. A single study that finds a gender difference is not very convincing. Are there other studies of the same behavior that find no difference? Or have many different scientists all found this difference consistently? One study doth not a gender difference make.

Now let us proceed to see whether there is evidence for gender differences in a variety of personality characteristics and behaviors. We have put them in roughly the following order: those for which there is good evidence of a gender difference come first, those where the evidence is somewhat mixed come next, and, finally, those in which there appears to be no gender difference.

AGGRESSIVENESS

Gender differences   Perhaps the most consistently documented psychological gender difference is in aggressiveness, with males being more aggressive than females (Maccoby and Jacklin, 1974). This difference holds up for every one of the many different kinds of aggression that have been studied, including physical aggression, verbal aggression, and fantasy aggression. Further, this gender difference has been found in all cultures in which the appropriate data have been collected.

Developmentally, this difference appears about as early as children begin playing with each other, around the age of two or two and a half. The difference continues consistently throughout the school years. Of course, as people get older, they become less aggressive, at least in the physical sense. For example, it is rare to see adults rolling around on the floor as they punch each other, compared with the frequency with which that occurs on an elementary school playground. We have less information available on gender differences in adult aggression, but we do know that the vast majority of crimes of violence are committed by men (although female crime is on the increase). According to the results of social psychologists' research on aggression (most of it done in the laboratory with college students), there are some situations in which there are no gender differences; but it is rare for women to be more aggressive than men (Frodi et al., 1977). In particular, women are likely to be as aggressive as men when it appears that it would be justified or even prosocial to be aggressive.

It also seems that men and women react differently to provocation: what angers a man (and leads him to be aggressive) tends to make a woman anxious, not angry or aggressive.

What causes the gender difference?   The causes of the gender difference in aggressiveness have been hotly debated, with the nature and nurture teams battling against each other. The nurture team attributes gender differences in aggressiveness to the greater size and musculature of males and/or differences in the levels of the sex hormone testosterone. These factors will be discussed in detail in Chapter 10.

On the nurture side, a number of culture forces might produce the observed gender difference: (1) Aggressiveness is a key part of the male role in our society, and unaggressiveness or passivity a key part of the female role. Following the logic of cognitive-developmental theory, as soon as children become aware of gender roles, girls realize that they are not supposed to be aggressive and boys know that they should be. As we noted in Chapter 3, this logic does not work very well in explaining how gender differences develop so early, but it may be helpful in explaining gender differences among older children. (2) Children imitate same-gender adults more than opposite-gender adults, and they see far more aggression in men than in women, particularly on TV and in movies. Hence boys imitate men, who are aggressive, and girls imitate women, who are unaggressive. (3) Boys receive more rewards for aggression and less punishment for it than girls do. These reinforcements might be in a physical form, such as spanking, or in a verbal form such as comments from adults like "Boys will be boys" in response to a boy's aggression, and "Nice young ladies don't do that" to a girl's aggression. Boys also may be rewarded in the form of status or respect from their peers for being aggressive, while girls receive no such reward. Actual studies, however, indicate that boys are punished more for aggression than girls are by both parents and teachers (Maccoby and Jacklin, 1974; Serbin et al., 1973; Hyde and Schuck, 1977). This poses a problem for this explanation. However, psychologists believe that some kinds of punishments for aggression may actually increase a child's aggression rather than decrease it. Therefore the punishments that boys receive may actually make them more aggressive. (4) A somewhat more complex cultural argument takes into account the fact that, simply because of the way our culture organizes child care, the major disciplinarians of small children are women — mothers and teachers. Research indicates that children's identification with a punishing adult is important in what kind of effects the punishment will have. If the child is highly identified with the adult, punishment will decrease aggression, whereas if the child is not identified with the adult, punishment increases aggression (Eron et al., 1974). Little girls are more highly identified with their mothers and female teachers than boys are. Hence punishment by mothers and female teachers would decrease the aggression of girls and increase the aggression of boys. There are some empirical data to support this explanation (Hyde and Schuck, 1977). One implication of this line of reasoning is that if we want to reduce the aggressiveness of boys, or increase the aggressiveness of girls, or minimize gender differences, we will need to get fathers more involved in caring for their children and get more men to be nursery school and elementary school teachers.

FIGURE 5.2

Gender differences in aggressiveness appear early.

Source: Photo by Cary Wolinsky / Stock Boston.

The question of what causes gender differences in aggressiveness is a complex one that has not been completely resolved by scientific data. Perhaps the best conclusion to make at this point, and the one that seems to agree best with the existing data, is that there are probably rather small biologically-based gender differences in aggressiveness, and that cultural forces act to magnify these differences considerably (Hyde and Schuck, 1977).

Dominance   The majority of studies show that males are more dominant than females (Block, 1976b). Dominance behaviors may involve things like getting one's own way, or having a reputation for toughness in a kind of human pecking order. Such behaviors may be a bit more subtle to get at than the kinds of physical aggression discussed in previous sections. Nonetheless, they are important for two reasons: First, they are more important in adult interactions than are behaviors such as punching and kicking. Thus they may be important in how women function in the world of work or in other adult interactions. Second, dominance is an important reflection of a person's *status*. Dominant individuals have higher status than subordinate individuals. Feminist theorists have noted that gender is an important status variable, with men having higher status than women (e.g., Henley, 1973). Thus gender differences in dominance behaviors may reflect the differential status of women and men, or may even contribute to that differential status.

To illustrate the way psychologists measure dominance and find gender differences, let us consider in detail a study by Kathrynn Adams and Audrey Landers (1978). Copies of paintings were shown to pairs of college student subjects; however, one member of each pair was really a confederate of the experimenters. The subjects saw pairs of paintings, and their initial task was to write down which one of each of the twenty pairs they thought was more attractive. The pairs had previously been rated as being equal in attractiveness by other subjects. After subjects had made their individual decisions, the experimenter told them that they must come to a joint decision on which of each pair was more attractive. On six of the pairs, the confederate voiced his or her opinion second and disagreed with the subject. If the subject stuck to her or his guns, the confederate would offer a challenge, and the process continued up to a possible twenty challenges. The number of challenges that the subject withstood was a measure of the subject's dominance.

In this study, there was a significant gender difference. Males withstood an average of about nine challenges, whereas females withstood an average of about six. Based on this finding, Adams and Landers concluded that males were more dominant than females.

Dominance was essentially defined by Adams and Landers as resistance to another's attempts at influence. Some people would dispute this definition. They might say that this study does not demonstrate gender differences in dominance, but rather demonstrates gender differences in influenceability or conformity. Maccoby and Jacklin included in their category of behaviors classified as dominance such things as attempts to influence another child's behavior, attempts to influence an adult's behavior, reputation (ranked by peers) for "toughness" among children, and leadership. The point is that there is no standard definition of a term like "dominance." It is defined by different researchers in different ways, and at best it is a complex concept. Thus it is not surprising that it is a complex matter to determine whether there are gender differences in dominance.

SELF-CONFIDENCE

Suppose a group of students take their first exam in Introductory Psychology. Immediately after they complete the exam and before they receive their grades, we ask them to estimate how many points (out of a possible 100 points) they think they got on the exam. Most studies indicate that we will find a gender difference, with females estimating that they will get fewer points than males estimate (Block, 1976b; Berg and Hyde, 1976). Psychologists interpret this as indicating that females have lower self-confidence than males do.

This difference between males and females has been found consistently in many studies. Even in a study involving a group of preschoolers, with an average age of four-and-a-half years, girls had lower expectancies for their performance on various tasks than boys did (Crandall, 1978). This was also found to be true of elementary school children (Crandall, 1969).

The gender difference in self-confidence is an important one. There is evidence that people with low expectations for success avoid engaging in challenging tasks. Thus this gender difference may have important effects on women's careers and accomplishments, a point to be discussed further in Chapter 8.

Although there is a fairly consistent gender difference in self-confidence, we need to place some qualifications on the general result (Lenney, 1977). First, whether females give lower estimates of their expectancies depends on the kind of tasks involved. For example, females do not give lower estimates if they are made to think a task is gender-appropriate for them. Second, the gender difference depends on the kind of feedback given to people about their performance. If females are given clear and unambiguous feedback about how well they are doing, or how good their abilities are, then their estimates are not lower than males. Finally, the gender difference depends on the presence or absence of social comparisons or social evaluations. If social comparisons are present, then women give low estimates; but if they work alone or in situations where they do not expect their performance to be compared with others, then their estimates are not lower. Therefore it seems that women have lower self-confidence than men in some situations, but not in others.

Before leaving the topic of self-confidence, we need to note one further complication, namely in interpretation of the results. The objective, statistical result in the studies we have been discussing is that males estimate they will get more points on the exam or some other task. To use the terminology of Chapter 1, the *interpretation* of this result is that males have more self-confidence than females, or that *females are lacking in self-confidence*. This interpretation carries with it the implication that females have a kind of psychological deficit. Would it be possible to make a different interpretation that would still be consistent with the data? An alternative interpretation is that males' estimates are too high (rather than females' being too low) and that males are unrealistically confident. This alternative is just as reasonable an interpretation of the gender difference, but this interpretation implies a problem for males. As it turns out, with tasks such as these it is possible to decide which interpretation is more accurate, because we can find out how students actually did on the exam. As it turns out, males tend to overestimate their performance by about as much as females underestimate theirs, although some studies find girls' estimates to be accurate and boys to be inflated (Crandall, 1969; Berg and Hyde, 1976). Therefore, there is some truth in each interpretation — men are probably a bit overconfident and women a bit underconfident.

ACTIVITY

There has been quite a bit of debate among psychologists as to whether there are gender differences in activity level. Certainly if you ask the average parent or teacher, they will tell you that boys are more active. Most child psychology texts have maintained that this is true. Maccoby and Jacklin (1974), however, concluded that the data were ambiguous — some studies showed no differences and a few showed that females were more active. Then Block (1976b), in her critique of Maccoby and Jacklin, concluded that the evidence does show that boys are more active than girls; of the 59 relevant studies, 24 found boys significantly higher, three found girls significantly higher, and the rest found no difference.

Where does that leave us? It seems reasonable to conclude that boys are more active than girls, although the difference is probably not quite so marked as the difference in aggressiveness. It is also well-established that the great majority — about 80 to 85 percent — of hyperactive children are boys (Stewart et al., 1966; Chess, 1960).

What causes this gender difference? The arguments are similar to those made about aggressiveness, and the issue has not been resolved in either case. What we do not know is how much the developmental precocity of girls contributes to this difference. Stated briefly, girls are ahead of boys in development. As children grow older, they learn to control their activity more. It might be, then, that the lower activity of girls represents simply a greater ability to control activity because of their being somewhat more mature than boys.

ANXIETY

Most studies show that girls are more fearful, timid, and anxious than boys (Block, 1976b). Once again, though, the difference is not simple. Most of the studies that find differences are based on self-reports, but studies based on direct observations often find no gender difference (Maccoby and Jacklin, 1974). To illustrate the difference between self-reports and direct observations, suppose a psychologist is trying to determine whether girls are more fearful of dogs than boys are. If the psychologist is using the self-report method, he or she would interview children and ask them if they are afraid of dogs. Using the method of direct observation, the psychologist would bring a dog into the room and see whether the children behave fearfully.

What we know, then, is that girls and women are more willing to admit that they have anxieties and fears. It is possible that these self-reports reflect the fact that females actually are more fearful and anxious than males. But it is also possible that males and females experience the same levels of fear and anxiety and that females are only more willing to admit them. This might be a result of gender-role stereotypes, which portray women as fearful and timid and men as fearless and brave. This would encourage women to admit their feelings and men to pretend not to have them. At this point, however, studies have not been able to resolve this issue.

EMPATHY

Empathy means feeling the emotion another person is feeling. It essentially involves putting yourself in another's place emotionally. According to stereotypes, females are more empathic than males, as part of the general stereotype of emotional expressivity in females and emotional inexpressivity in males. Is this stereotype a real difference?

Psychologist Martin Hoffman (1977) reviewed studies of empathy and concluded that the majority do show females to be more empathic. Even in studies of newborn infants, girls are more likely to cry in response to a tape recording of another infant crying. The gender difference in empathy is found consistently at all ages through college, the oldest group to be studied. The difference is often a small one, but girls consistently have the higher empathy scores. Hoffman concluded that the greater empathy of females is probably related to their tendency to experience guilt over harming others, and to their greater tendency to imagine themselves in the other's place.

What does this difference mean? Hoffman made an interesting concluding comment:

> Since empathy and guilt are the major prosocial affects known at this time, the findings suggest that females may have a more highly developed affective base for prosocial behavior than do males. (1977, p. 720)

That is, we need not take the finding of greater empathy in females as just one more piece of evidence that women are overemotional, crying at the slightest provocation. Instead, it is important to recognize that empathy is one of the nobler of human emotions, enabling one to act for the benefit of others. And females appear to have more of it.

INFLUENCEABILITY

Most social psychology texts state that women are more influenceable than men. Women are said to be more easily persuaded, more suggestible, and more conforming. As one text puts it:

> The most consistent and strongest factor that differentiates people in the amount they conform is their sex. Women conform more than men. . . . (Freedman et al., 1970, p. 239)

However, psychologist Alice Eagly (1978) reviewed the available studies on influenceability and concluded that the evidence did not support such claims. In fact, most studies in the area of persuasion and conformity show that there is no gender difference. The one exception is in studies of group pressure to conform, in which females do show more conforming responses; however, that may simply reflect the tendency of females to try to preserve harmony in a group.

Conformity is probably a good example of a gender difference that gets into textbooks despite an absence of evidence for it. Probably this has occurred in part because the finding of a gender difference would agree with stereotypes that women are influenceable and conforming, and men are independent and nonconforming. Indeed, one study that is sometimes cited as evidence for the gender difference in fact used male subjects only (Asch, 1956).

SOCIABILITY

It is also part of conventional wisdom that females are more "social" than males. Maccoby and Jacklin (1974), however, have concluded that this belief is unfounded and that there are actually no gender differences in sociability.

To measure sociability in infants, psychologists showed them various pictures, some of human faces, some of geometric forms. The idea was that if the female infants spent more time gazing at human faces, this would indicate that they were more interested in social stimuli. There were a few scattered reports that this was the case, but when Maccoby and Jacklin reviewed all the evidence, they concluded that there was no evidence of a gender difference.

In childhood, it seems that boys and girls are equally responsive to social reinforcement. There does not seem to be a gender difference in the amount of time spent interacting with playmates. In fact, at some ages it appears that boys actually spend more time with friends. The pattern of social interaction, however, does tend to be somewhat different — boys tend to congregate in large groups or gangs, while girls are more likely to interact in pairs or small groups.

The evidence, then, does not support the notion that females are more social or dependent on social reinforcements.

IN CONCLUSION

In this chapter we have tried to assess the evidence for gender differences in some important personality characteristics and behaviors. For some of these — particularly for aggression and self-confidence — there was good evidence of a difference. For others — activity, anxiety, and empathy — there seemed to be a gender difference, but a smaller one. Finally, for some — influenceability and sociability — there was no good evidence of a gender difference.

The danger in focusing so much on gender differences is that we will start to think that males and females have entirely different personalities. While there are some differences, as we have seen, what is perhaps more impressive are the similarities. Even for stereotyped traits such as influenceability and sociability, there appear to be no gender differences. And we have not even begun to discuss a long list of characteristics that have probably never shown a gender difference in anyone's research and have, therefore, been omitted from mention — for example, honesty, conscientiousness, sincerity. It is important to remember that *gender similarities* are probably more the rule than gender differences.

6

FROM INFANCY TO OLD AGE: DEVELOPMENT ACROSS THE LIFESPAN

At age twelve I was among the first of my friends to begin to menstruate and to wear a bra. I felt a mixture of pride and embarrassment. For all of my life I had been a chubby, introspective child, but a growth spurt of a few inches, along with my developing breasts, transformed me one summer into a surprisingly slim and shapely child-woman. The funny thing was that on one level I had always known this would happen. Yet it was as if a fairy godmother had visited me. I felt turned on, but I was mostly turned on to myself and the narcissistic pleasure of finding I was attractive to boys.

FROM Our Bodies, Ourselves

The chubby little baby girl playing with her toes; the young woman with a newly-completed degree in business, applying for her first job and being asked if she can type; the woman at 68 whose husband died a week ago, who must figure out how to reorganize her life after 40 years of marriage: What do these people have in common? They are all the same person, at different stages of her life.

Traditional developmental psychology has been biased in the age range it has studied and considered important. In part, as a legacy of psychoanalytic theory, early childhood was thought to be extremely important, and many felt that a person's personality was permanently determined by the age of five or six. Developmental psychology was equated with child psychology. The current trend in developmental psychology, though, is to study human development across the entire lifespan, from infancy through old age. The idea is that our personalities continue to develop or change, not only in childhood, but also in adulthood. In this chapter we shall consider the development of female personality and roles across the lifespan.

INFANCY

As noted above, psychologists have spent an extraordinary amount of time studying children, particularly preschoolers and infants. The study of gender differences has been no exception. Investigations of infant gender differences have had two primary motives. First, it has been thought that if gender differences were found in newborns—say when they are only one day old — they must surely be due to biological factors, since gender-role socialization can scarcely have had time to have an effect. The idea, then, was to try to discover the biological causes of gender differences by studying newborns. Second, many investigators think it is important to study the way parents and other adults treat infants, in order to discover the subtle (and perhaps not so subtle) differences in the way adults treat boy babies and girl babies, beginning the process of socialization at a tender age. We shall review research in these two areas below.

Infant gender differences   Establishing what behaviors in infants show gender differences has the same complications as does establishing any gender difference (as discussed in Chapter 5). To this is added the further complication of trying to establish whether these differences really mean anything in terms of later behavior, in childhood or adulthood. As in

Chapter 5, many of our conclusions will be based on the reviews by Maccoby and Jacklin (1974) and Block (1976).

First, it should be noted that most infant behaviors do not show gender differences. That is, *gender similarities* are the rule for most behaviors. For example, in a study of infants at three weeks of age and again at three months, twelve behaviors were measured (Moss, 1967). At three weeks, only six of the twelve showed significant gender differences, and at three months, only four of the six still showed gender differences (males fussed more, were more irritable [cried and fussed], and were more often awake and passive, while females slept more). Only four of twelve variables, then, showed stable gender differences at three weeks and three months. The majority of behaviors showed gender similarities.

Nonetheless, there are some behaviors for which there is evidence of gender differences. Newborn girls seem to have greater *tactile sensitivity* (sensitivity to touch) than newborn boys (Block, 1976). This may be measured, for example, by blowing air on the baby's cheek or stomach and seeing whether she or he responds.

There are probably differences in *activity level*, with boys having the higher activity (Block, 1976). In small infants, this may be measured by counting the amount of swinging arms or kicking legs. In older babies, it might be measured by counting the number of squares the baby crawls across on a playroom floor. The differences here, however, are small and rather inconsistent; Maccoby and Jacklin concluded there were no differences, but Block, in re-reviewing the evidence, concluded that there were.

One widely cited study found evidence of greater separation distress in female infants (Goldberg and Lewis, 1969; Messer and Lewis, 1972). This refers to the distress an infant feels when separated from the mother, in this case by placing a barrier between the two. This might indicate greater attachment or dependency in girls. However, more recent research has shown that minor manipulations of the experimental procedure could eliminate or even reverse the gender difference (Jacklin et al., 1973; Maccoby and Jacklin, 1974). Thus there is not good evidence to support the notion of greater separation distress or dependency of female infants.

Some evidence does exist, then, for very early gender differences in at least two behaviors, tactile sensitivity and activity level. The next question is, what does this mean? The results by themselves are of little interest, except perhaps to a trivia expert. They become important if they predict later behavior, in childhood or adulthood. For example, if people high in tactile sensitivity in infancy turn out to be high in empathy in adulthood, then the greater tactile sensitivity of girl infants may explain the greater empathy of girls and women (discussed in Chapter 5). To get evidence for this supposition, however, requires *longitudinal developmental research*. This means starting out with a group of infants and following them through their lives until they are adults. The research for a project of this type is very time-consuming and costly, so not much of it has been done. There are some suggestions of the kind of results that may occur. For example, tactile sensitivity in infancy has been related to vigor, assertiveness, and persistence in the late preschool years (Bell et al., 1971). Ironically, this would predict that girls should be more vigorous and assertive than boys. Further research in this area should be extremely informative.

Adults' treatment of infants   The other area of interest in infant research concerns whether, even at this early age, parents and other adults treat males and females differently.

Once again, *gender similarities* seem to be the rule; for the most part parents treat male and female babies similarly (Maccoby and Jacklin, 1974). Nonetheless, there do seem to be some differences. Boys are handled more roughly (Maccoby and Jacklin, 1974), and boys generally receive more responses from adults, such as being held by the mother (Lewis, 1972).

Some of these studies are based on direct observations of parent-child interactions, while others are based on parents' self-reports of their behavior toward their babies. The problem with this is that not only do parents influence infants, but infants also influence parents. Therefore, if there are differences in the behavior of boys and girls, these may cause the differences in parental treatment rather than the reverse. For example, if boys cry more, that may explain why they are held more.

A well-designed experiment, the *Baby X Study*, controlled these factors (Seavey et al., 1975). The adult subjects (all nonparents) were told they were participating in a study on infants' responses to strangers. They were brought into an observation room and a three-month-old infant (actually a female) in a yellow jumpsuit was put on the floor in the room with them. One third of the subjects were told the baby was a boy, one third were told she was a girl, and the other third were given no gender information. Three toys were near the baby — a small rubber football (a "masculine" toy), a Raggedy Ann doll (a "feminine" toy), and a plastic ring (a "neutral" toy). The interactions between the subject and the baby were observed from behind a one-way mirror for three minutes. The frequency of using each of the toys was recorded, and ratings were made of the behavior of the adults toward the infant. Afterward, the subjects also rated their own impressions of the infant.

A number of interesting results emerged. With regard to choice of toy, there was an interaction between gender of the subject and gender-label of the baby. The results are shown in Table 6.1. The football was not really very popular in any condition, probably because it does not seem to be a very appropriate toy for such a small baby. This suggests the interesting speculation that the age of the child is more important than the gender in determining toy choice, although this would have to be investigated in a separate experiment. As expected, the doll was used most frequently

TABLE 6.1. Mean frequency of toy choices for babies by the adults in the
Baby X Study

Gender of Subject	Baby Labelled	Toy		
		Football	Doll	Teething Ring
Male	Boy	.33	.72	.61
	Girl	.50	1.61	.94
	No label	.85	.71	1.42
Female	Boy	.57	.71	1.00
	Girl	.50	1.27	1.05
	No label	.40	1.23	.70

Source: Seavey et al., 1975.

when the baby was introduced as a girl. On the ratings of the interactions, and on the subjects' ratings of the babies, however, there were no significant differences depending on the label given to the baby. Some of the most interesting results came from the neutral label group. Many of them inquired what the baby's gender was. Most of them had formed an opinion of what the baby's gender was by the end of the session (57 percent of male subjects and 70 percent of female subjects thought that it was a boy) and had stereotyped rationales for their beliefs. Those who thought it was a boy noted the strength of the grasp or lack of hair, while those who thought it was a female remarked on the baby's roundness, softness, and fragility.

What can we conclude from this study? It would seem that gender is important in adults' interactions with children, something that is particularly evident when the adults are not told a child's gender. However, the effects are not simple, and they may not be large. None of the ratings of the interactions showed gender-label effects. Neither did the adults automatically give a football to the "boy." Further, the effects depended not only on the gender-label given the baby, but also on the gender of the adult subject. Future research will have to untangle the complexities of adults' treatment of boy babies compared with girl babies.

CHILDHOOD

Gender differences   Already by the early preschool years, several reliable gender differences have appeared. One is in *toy and game preference*. By two or three years of age, girls sew, string beads, and play at housekeeping, while boys play with guns, toy trucks, tractors, and fire engines, and do carpentry (Maccoby and Jacklin, 1974). What we don't know is what causes this early gender-typing of activities or interests. It may be that it has some biological basis, since it appears so early. But it is also true that there has been a chance for several years of socialization to take place.

Another difference that appears early is in *aggressiveness*. About as soon as aggressive behavior appears in children, around the age of two, there are gender differences; boys are more aggressive than girls. This difference persists throughout the school years (see Chapter 5).

Socialization   The forces of gender-role socialization become more prominent in childhood. The child's own immediate family may begin to have different expectations for her or him. For example, girls may be expected to help with the dinner dishes, boys to take out the garbage. The culture at large also has a tremendous impact. The schools, whether purposely or unwittingly, often transmit the information of gender-role stereotypes (Chafetz, 1974, p. 88ff.). We recently heard the story of a second-grade teacher urging on a little girl balking at doing a mathematics problem by saying "you must learn to do your arithmetic so you'll be able to do the marketing for your husband when you grow up." Children's readers still depict girls and women in restrictive, boring, passive, supportive, or downright stupid roles (Weitzman et al., 1972). Television is also a major transmitter of stereotyped information to the growing girl, depicting women as chiefly preoccupied with the shininess of their floors and the whiteness of their wash (McArthur and Resko, 1976). Indeed, much of the absurdity of gender-role stereotypes may arise not from the actual roles of men and women, but rather from the caricatures of these roles portrayed on television, which the young girl may see as an important source of information about the nature of the adult world.

It is also true that there is considerable variation from one family to the next in the way children are socialized to gender roles. Very "liberated" parents may take great pains to give trucks to their daughters and dolls to their sons and to make sure that the mother and father share equally in child-care duties. A more traditional family will probably encourage more traditional roles.

One factor that creates variation both between and within families in socialization forces is the size of the family and the child's ordinal position among siblings (Sutton-Smith and Rosenberg, 1970). For example, girls with sisters, as compared with girls with brothers, are significantly more interested in "feminine" activities.

School   It seems that girls make the adjustment to school with much greater ease than boys do. Boys are referred for psychological evaluation and are found in remedial classes considerably more frequently than girls are (Andrews and Cappon, 1957; Dreger et al., 1964; Spivack and Spotts, 1965; Werry and Quay, 1971). (Note how this contrasts with adjustment problems in adulthood, see Chapter 7.). Girls' interactions with teachers seem to be more pleasant and less full of conflict. In one study, kindergarten girls related to adults twice as frequently as boys did (Lott, 1978).

Tomboys   Despite the results on gender differences and socialization, not every girl conforms. One study found that 63 percent of a group of junior high girls said they were tomboys, and 51 percent of a sample of adult women recalled having been tomboys in childhood (Hyde et al., 1977). Not every girl, then, is staying at home playing with dolls. In fact, probably the majority are engaging in the active games that have traditionally been called "masculine." Perhaps tomboyism is simply childhood's version of androgyny.

Although many social critics emphasize the restrictiveness of girls' socialization, it is probably true that opposite-gender behavior is far less tolerated for boys than it is for girls. Many parents tolerate their daughters climbing trees and playing baseball, but get very upset at a son playing with dolls. It is, after all, far worse to be a sissy than to be a tomboy. As one investigator commented,

> . . . demands that boys conform to social notions of what is manly come much earlier and are enforced with much more vigor than similar attitudes with respect to girls. (Hartley, 1959, p. 458)

It seems, then, that particular areas exist in which there are gender differences in childhood, and that socialization does occur to some extent. It is also true, however, that gender similarities are the rule, and that many girls are allowed a great deal of freedom and are encouraged to achieve in school. Severe gender-role pressures probably do not come until later in adolescence. But in a sense, this may be even more difficult for the girl than would be consistent gender-role restrictions. Throughout most of her childhood she is free to pursue achievements, and only later is she told that these achievements are not appropriate.

ADOLESCENCE

If the behavior and development of males and females are so similar for about the first ten years of life, how do the gender differences in adult personality and roles arise? In the early years, females do better in school and have fewer adjustment problems than boys. Yet in adulthood females have low-status jobs and contribute less than men in the professions (Chapter 8) as well as having a higher incidence of mental illness (Chapter 7). Although the groundwork for these differences is prepared in childhood, the real precipitating factors most likely occur in adolescence. These will be discussed below.

The femininity-achievement incompatibility   In adolescence, a cultural rule starts to be enforced on the girl: achievement and femininity are incompatible — that is, to achieve is gender-inappropriate. If the girl continues to achieve she will be unfeminine, and to be feminine is not to achieve. The girl is caught in a situation in which two equally important systems of values are in conflict. One is the desire for a positive sense of self, the sense that one is a worthwhile, productive person. Achieving, getting good grades, and excelling have been encouraged and rewarded so far, providing a major avenue for establishing the self as having worth and value. But the reward system changes abruptly at adolescence. The competing system is the desire to be a good female, to conform to gender-role expectations, and to be feminine, with whatever rewards that carries. The desire to be a competent, worthwhile person is now incompatible with the desire to be good in the female role; society at large does not value the female role (Broverman et al., 1972).

The reward system may change in adolescence for either or both of two reasons. One is that heterosexual relationships, popularity, and dating rise to importance; thus the peer group may begin enforcing the rules of the femininity-achievement incompatibility. Parents, too, may change their teachings as they begin to see popularity and marriageability as important for their daughter. The timing of the change in the parents' emphasis, of course, varies greatly from one family to the next. In one, the girl may be urged to stop studying and to start having boyfriends when she is in sixth grade, while in another, achieving a college education will be viewed as far more important than dating, and the parents do not begin asking about marriage prospects until the young woman announces that she is going to go to graduate school and get a Ph.D.

Data on the changing social emphases at adolescence and their impact on the girl are rather slim. One recent study compared preadolescent (fifth grade) girls and adolescent (tenth grade) girls on a measure of gender-role stereotyping. The tenth grade girls had significantly higher stereotyping scores, indicating that the tenth grade girls rated women significantly lower than men on socially-valued traits related to competence (Baruch, 1975). Another study found that 26 percent of the college women studied experienced conflict over the contradictory role expectations ("masculine" and achievement-oriented versus "feminine" and family-oriented) that their families had for them (Komarovsky, 1946).

Perhaps most relevant is a study of the self-concept of students in the third through twelfth grades (Rosenberg and Simmons, 1975). The results indicated that gender differences were small among the younger children and that striking gender differences emerged during adolescence. At that time, girls became more self-conscious than boys; the adolescent girls were increasingly people-oriented, while adolescent boys stressed achievement and competence. In another study, high school juniors and seniors were asked whether they would most like to be independent,

FIGURE 6.1

In early adolescence, the girl learns that her status will be determined by her attractiveness, not her achievements.

Source: Photo by Eve Arnold / Magnum.

successful, or well-liked (Rosenberg, 1965). Adolescent girls emphasized being well-liked (60 percent compared with 35 percent of the boys), while boys were much more likely to stress success (46 percent compared with 29 percent).

Certainly the origin of the double-bind for females, probably the single most important influence on female personality, lies in the conflict between achievement and femininity (Horner, 1970a, 1972). The adolescent girl is caught in a classic double-bind situation in which she wants both of two alternatives, but the two alternatives are incompatible. She wants both to be feminine and to achieve, but the two are perceived as being incompatible. Certainly here would appear to be the origins of much of the ambivalence and conflict in female personality — the adolescent girl finding it difficult to combine, because of imposed cultural contingencies, being a worthwhile individual and a proper female (Broverman et al., 1972). In this we see one source of the adjustment problems some adult women have.

Dating and friendship   The rituals of dating are also an important force influencing adolescent female personality development. Competition against other girls for the attention of boys becomes essential to success; other females become the enemy. The competition is in itself somewhat frustrating since the competitor must remain passive in such an important battle; the girl cannot directly choose the boy and call him for a date. On the other hand, the passive aspects of this social interaction for the female should not be overemphasized. The antics displayed by many teenage girls in their attempts to attract male attention are about as passive as a three-ring circus complete with wild animals and neon lights.

A fairly common phenomenon of adolescent female dating is the date with an "older man," which is not only common, but encouraged. This phenomenon is probably related to the differences in developmental levels of females and males. Puberty and the accompanying growth spurt occur about two years earlier in girls than boys (Hyde, 1979). The teenage girl with a discerning eye can tell that many of the males of her own age are less mature than she is, and that to relate to someone of her own maturity, she must date an older male. The unfortunate result is that the female is in the position of being naive and inexperienced, the male wise, worldly, and knowing. This might be seen as a force pushing the female into the subordinate role in adulthood.

One rule that becomes quickly apparent in the dating game is that females are valued for their appearance, males for their achievements. This phenomenon has been documented in a number of social psychology studies. For example, in one study snapshots were taken of college women and men (Berscheid et al., 1971). A dating history of each subject was also obtained. Judges then rated the attractiveness of the women and men in the photographs. For the women there was a fairly strong relationship between attractiveness and popularity; the women judged more attractive had had more dates in the last year than the less attractive women. There was some relationship between appearance and popularity for men, but it was not so marked as it was for women. In another longterm study, begun in the 1930s, fifth and sixth grade girls were rated as to the attractiveness of their appearance (Elder, 1969). Years later they were tracked down. As it turned out, the more attractive the preadolescent, the more "successful" she had been in getting a husband. The most beautiful girls had married well-to-do, sucecssful men. It seems that a woman's status is determined by her appearance, a man's by his achievements.

Another noticeable phenomenon among adolescent females is the formation of girl-groups or cliques, tight-knit groups of girls engaging in mutual sharing and often more than a little plotting. The student of behavior wishing to identify such phenomena can generally spot these cliques by the immense amount of giggling that emanates from them. These groups may serve important functions for the developing girl by helping her to discover the nature and meaning of both femininity and sexual impulses (Douvan and Adelson, 1966). Unfortunately, the latter function at least is not as well served for girls who are less likely than boys to exchange sexual information (Kinsey et al., 1953).

A potentially much more useful function of girl-groups is the formation of real friendships with other females. Unfortunately, female friendships tend to be devalued since many teenage girls will instantly break plans with girl friends if a male asks for a date. Indeed, the girl-group phenomenon of adolescence, which has great potential for helping the female build her developing self-concept, may have a negative impact. Because of the low value placed on these friendships (spending time with males is far more desirable) and because of the competitiveness for male attention, many girls develop a bitter feeling toward their relationships with other females. This is probably planting the seed of the negative attitudes women hold toward other women and, therefore, of their own low self-esteem. College women often write in autobiographies that in high school they much preferred the company of boys to that of other girls — who are, they say, mean, jealous, spiteful, and untrustworthy. One cannot help but see a paradox (and unhealthiness) in so many females ascribing these negative characteristics to all females other than themselves. Of course, this problem does not result from any innate characteristics of females. Most likely it is a result of the low status of women and a belief that a girl's status is determined by her popularity and, later, whom she marries. At any rate, the girl-group may have a negative impact on the adolescent girl's developing sense of self and what it means to be female.

The search for identity   According to Erik Erikson (1950) adolescence is the stage in which the primary developmental crisis is a quest for identity. For the male, adult identity will be defined largely in occupational terms (Angrist, 1969) — "I am a doctor." Adolescence and the growing identity then become a preparation for this adult identity — "I must start to take science courses and become a responsible student in order to become a doctor."

For the adolescent girl, however, this process seems to be considerably different (Psathas, 1968). She does not anticipate that work outside the home will be a major source of identity for her (Douvan, 1970). College women often say they are preparing themselves to be teachers or social workers, not because they want to educate the minds of youth or do good works for humanity, but rather so that they "will have something to fall back on" (in case of unexpected widowhood or divorce). Job or occupation is simply not seen as a major source of identity. Instead, the major source of identity is the husband and later the children — that is the wife-mother role. The man sees himself as a doctor; the woman sees herself as a doctor's wife. On the most glorious day of her life, her wedding day, a portrait is taken that soon appears in the newspaper. The caption says "Mrs. Robert Jones," not Susan Jones or Susan Smith-Jones, leaving not a trace of her former name (identity) and giving all-too-clear evidence that from that time on, her identity is defined in terms of her husband.

Therefore, in the late adolescent period, when the male is actively striving to develop an adult identity, we see the female postponing identity formation in an attempt to maintain a flexible identity that can adapt itself to the as-yet-unknown husband (Angrist, 1969). Forming a distinctive identity might make the girl unmarriageable. For example, a girl may decide to become the best nuclear physicist in the world. But if she later meets the man of her dreams, with the one exception that he has no plans to be married to the world's best nuclear physicist, she may have eliminated a good marriage prospect for herself. Shirley Angrist (1969) uses the term "contingency training" to describe this phenomenon. Flexibility is built into women's personality in the socialization process by contingency training. Woman lives by adjusting to and preparing for anticipated and unanticipated contingencies: the unknown qualities of the future husband, lack of guarantee of marriage, possible economic necessity of work, possible childlessness, children leaving home, and divorce or widowhood. For the adolescent female, the marriage/unknown-husband contingency is certainly the most salient (Psathas, 1968). While a flexible personality may be a detriment to professional achievement (Chapter 8), in other areas it may be very valuable. If contingencies are truly beyond one's control, the ability to adapt is very functional.

Another way of looking at female identity formation is to recognize the distinction between *personal identity* and *vested identity*.[1] Personal identity refers to the person's identity as a unique individual, and in particular to those behaviors and activities that are intrinsically rewarding to the individual. Vested identity, on the other hand, refers to those behaviors and activities for which the person receives extrinsic rewards (for example, a paycheck), those behaviors that are expected by society, perhaps because of the gender of the individual. For example, a twelve-year-old girl may very much enjoy (derive intrinsic gratification from) active sports and the thrill of scientific discovery. These are important components of her personal identity. In contrast, her vested identity, par-

---

[1] The authors thank Lois Ventura and Sherry Ziegler for suggesting the distinction between these concepts, although in somewhat different terms.

ticularly in the future, will consist of being a housewife and mother and conforming in other ways to the expected female role. She will receive extrinsic rewards for performing these behaviors, and will be viewed negatively if she does not carry these out — for example, if she chooses not to have children or chooses not to marry. A critical process of adolescence and early adulthood is to match personal identity with vested identity as an adult. This is accomplished particularly through the process of occupational choice. For example, a boy who experiences the intrinsic gratification of the thrill of scientific discovery may begin studying hard and preparing himself for a career as a physicist or an experimental psychologist. Or, if he enjoys working on cars, he may prepare himself to be a mechanic. For him, vested adult identity, the things that are extrinsically rewarding, are likely to be congruent with personal identity, those things that are intrinsically rewarding. For females, however, the adult vested identity of housewife/mother is normative, it is expected. Hence the wide variations that exist in the personal identities of growing girls often cannot be reflected through occupational choice in their adult vested identities. The girl who would enjoy being an athlete or a scientist has her role aspirations channeled into being a housewife and mother. She is often not encouraged to choose a vested identity that will be congruent with her personal identity.

Of course, today not every young woman makes marriage her major goal. Particularly among college women, a career may be the foremost concern, with marriage and children seeming at most a remote occurrence in the future. Today, then, it seems that three alternative female identity patterns have emerged (Dellas and Gaier, 1975):

1. Traditional role and stereotype: Awaiting marriage
2. Achievement and role success: Achievement in valued areas of our androcentric society
3. Bimodal identity: Commitment to family and career

Unfortunately, none of these three alternatives escapes the double-bind (Denmark and Goodfield, 1978) that will remain as long as there is an incompatibility between femininity and achievement. The adolescent girl who chooses the traditional role today may find herself and others wondering why she didn't accomplish more in the world of work (Luria, 1974). The girl who chooses the achievement-oriented identity will be questioned for her lack of husband and children. And the girl who chooses the bimodal identity will later suffer the pulls between the conflicting areas of her life.

A study of women graduating from college in the years 1967 to 1970 provides some information on the life expectations of women in late adolescence (Luria, 1974). Similar studies of women a generation ago indicated that their typical expectation was not to hold a paying job, but rather to devote their lives to being housewives, mothers, and volunteer workers. In contrast, the majority of college women in this recent study expected to hold paying jobs at least during some periods in their lives. However, the transformation is not radical — most of them still did not anticipate holding jobs while their children were preschoolers, but did plan to work once their children entered school. As the investigator concluded,

> Thus, while motivation to work is not low on the average . . . the conditions under which these women say they will work are still highly constrained by their prospective view of their job as mothers of preschoolers and infants. (Luria, 1974, p. 316)

In sum, while we have suggested that personality development may be quite similar in females and males during infancy and childhood, adolescence represents a major divergence. The expectations for the girl suddenly change and become conflicting: achievement is not rewarded as it was formerly, femininity is demanded, and achievement and femininity are seen as being incompatible, creating a double-bind, or ambivalence, in female personality. Later in adolescence, identity formation becomes a key process, but the contingencies are such that it may not occur at this stage and may instead be postponed.

EARLY ADULTHOOD

Wife, housewife, mother   Most adult women define their identity almost completely in terms of their wife-mother role. Therefore it is important to consider the merits and disadvantages of this traditional course of action.

Young wives typically enjoy the intimacy and sharing of their marital relationship, and generally find the early years of marriage to be rewarding (Campbell et al., 1975). Achievement urges are often suppressed at this time, in favor of "accomplishing" the wife-mother role. Some authors have suggested that wives experience "vicarious achievement" through their husband's job, making the husband's job a "two-person career" (Lipman-Blumen, 1972; Papanek, 1973).

Overall, however, marriage seems to favor men rather than women. Married women report more depression than married men do; married men are less depressed than never-married men, but married women do not have a similar advantage over never-married women (Radloff, 1975). Single men report less life satisfaction than married men, but for women the difference is reversed — single women report more satisfaction than married women (Gurin et al., 1960; Bradburn and Caplovitz, 1965).

The housewife role is a rather mixed one in terms of satisfactions and frustrations. According to interviews with London housewives, 70 percent were dissatisfied with the housework aspects of their roles. The common reasons for dissatisfaction were monotony, loneliness, long hours (on the average, they worked 77 hours per week), and a lack of structure. The most frequently mentioned advantage was autonomy, or being one's own boss (Oakley, 1974).

The mother role is probably the most satisfying part of the traditional complex of female roles. Even here, however, there may be problems. The feeding demands of small infants leave many mothers constantly exhausted, and it is not until infants are several months old that they can respond with one of their heartwarming smiles. Interactions with young children are stimulating in their own way, but many women feel a need for some interactions with other adults during the day. Certainly the pressures on married couples to have children are high. Interestingly, however, married couples without children report greater happiness than married couples with children (Campbell et al., 1975).

Women and work   The fact that the majority of American women hold jobs outside the home is one of the best kept secrets in our country. Among women between the ages of 18 and 64, 57 percent hold jobs (U. S.

FIGURE 6.2

The fact that the majority of American women (57 percent) hold jobs outside of the home, is one of the best kept secrets in our country.

Source: Photo by Steven Lewis / The Picture Cube.

Department of Labor, 1978). The working woman, then, is not a variation from the norm, she *is* the norm. Below we shall consider some stereotypes about women and work, and what the actual data say.

Stereotype 1: Women are working only for pin money. The idea behind this stereotype is that most women are only providing a second income, that the husband supports the family, and the wife is working only to provide a few frills. In fact, however, most women work because of stark economic necessity. In 1977 nearly two-thirds of all women in the labor force were single, widowed, divorced, separated, or had husbands whose earnings were less than $10,000 (U. S. Department of Labor, 1978). The majority of women workers were the sole supporters of their families, or were married to men whose incomes would have put them below the poverty line.

Stereotype 2: Women shouldn't be hired for jobs requiring training, because they will just quit when they get married or pregnant. The assumption here is that women are more likely to quit their jobs than men are. Overall, that is true. However, when occupational level and income are controlled, males and females do not differ significantly in turnover rates (Mead and Kaplan, 1965, p. 52). This simply means that women are found disproportionately in dull, dead-end jobs, and there is a high turnover rate in those jobs, whether men or women are in them. Given the same job and the same pay, females and males have about the same turnover rate. Today, most women are in the labor force for more than just a few years. In 1970, the average woman could expect to spend 22.9 years of her life in the labor force (U. S. Department of Labor, 1978).

Stereotype 3: Women are often sick, and thus miss too many days of work. In fact, in 1974 women averaged 5.1 sick days per year and males averaged 4.8, scarcely a difference worth talking about (U. S. Bureau of the Census, 1976, p. 88).

Stereotype 4: A woman who is really ambitious and qualified can get ahead anyway. It is true that some women get ahead, but they are relatively few in number. All other factors aside, what the woman worker must often face is simple job discrimination. For example, the average woman worker is as well-educated as the average man worker — both have a median of 12.6 years of schooling — but she makes only three-fifths as much as he does, when both work full-time year around (U. S. Department of Labor, 1978). In 1977 women were 79 percent of clerical workers, but only 22 percent of managers and administrators (U. S. Department of Labor, 1978). Most investigators agree that women are discriminated against in employment. Given the same education, job, experience, and so on, they are given less pay and are promoted more slowly (see review by Almquist, 1977).

Aside from these statistical analyses, there are several interesting studies that have documented the psychological aspects of job discrimination against women. A classic study demonstrated that, even when the work of a female is identical to that of a male, it is judged as inferior (Goldberg, 1968; replicated by Pheterson et al., 1971). Female college students were given scholarly essays in a number of academic fields to evaluate. All of the subjects rated the same essays, but half of them rated essays bearing the names of male authors (for example John T. McKay), while the other half rated the same essays with the names of female authors (Joan T. McKay). The essays were identical except for the names of the authors. The results were that the essays were rated higher when the author was male, even when the essay was in a traditionally feminine field such as dietetics. It appears that the work of males is valued more

FIGURE 6.3

Women aspiring to nontraditional careers must often face various forms of psychological discrimination; for example, many people do not want to work for a woman boss and have difficulty recognizing a woman in a leadership role.

Source: Photo by Abigail Heyman / Magnum.

even if it is identical to that of females. It is interesting to note that the raters in this study, those who gave lower value to female work, were themselves females.

Surveys show that many people do not want to work for a woman boss (Kanter, 1977). Social psychology studies have documented that it is difficult for a woman to assume and be recognized in a leadership role. For example, one study investigated this by using the phenomenon that the person seated at the head of a table is usually recognized as being the leader of a group (Porter et al., 1978). Subjects were shown photographs of groups seated around a table and were asked to rate the leadership attributes of each member of the group. A man seated at the head of the table in a mixed-gender group was clearly seen as the group's leader, but a woman occuping that position was ignored. Women at the head of the table were recognized as leaders only when the group was all-female.

In sum, even though job discrimination is legally prohibited, women must still deal with various psychological forms of discrimination in their attempts to achieve in the world of work.

Working mothers   Of all mothers with children under 18 years of age, 51 percent were in the labor force in 1977 (U. S. Department of Labor, 1978). Even among mothers with children under six years of age, 39 percent work outside the home (U. S. Department of Labor, 1976). Thus there are a lot of working mothers — 15.5 million, to be exact (U. S. Department of Labor, 1978). What do we know about how being a mother and holding a job interact psychologically?

In adulthood, it seems that the femininity-achievement incompatibility of adolescence is rerun under a new format, the work-mother incompatibility (Epstein, 1970; Hoffman, 1974b; Chafetz, 1974). That is, many people believe that women with children should stay at home and take care of them and should not hold jobs. The belief is that a working mother cannot be a good mother.

Psychologist Lois Hoffman (1974b) has done a detailed review of research on the effects of maternal employment on children. She concluded that there was no evidence that school-age children suffer either emotional or intellectual deprivation as a result of their mothers being employed. Indeed, working mothers seem to encourage more independence in their children, something that would generally be considered a good idea. Some evidence also exists that working mothers provide different role models for their children and that, at least for daughters, this may be beneficial. It also appears that the effects of the mother's employment depend on her psychological state — for example, her attitude toward working.

The conflicts experienced by working mothers have been extensively documented (Paloma and Garland, 1971; Bailyn, 1970; Holmstrom, 1972;

Fogarty, Rapoport and Rapoport, 1971; Hartley, 1960). The woman may be caught working two full-time jobs, and feeling that she is doing neither adequately. She may experience feelings of guilt that she is neglecting her children in order to work. Because of the complex demands on her time, there may also be conflicts with her wife role, with less time remaining for her husband. Children must still be fed and taken to the doctor, even with an eight-hour workday. If the working mother has an understanding husband, he may help out with the cooking, cleaning, or babysitting, but the clear understanding remains that these are all her responsibilities, and he is being a "nice guy" to help her. Even highly-liberated professional women are not free from the restrictions and conflicts of roles. Such women tend to demand that their husbands be even brighter than they, and speak of their husbands as being exceptionally talented (Birnbaum, 1975). This represents a subtle kind of role conformity, in which the exceptionally talented woman still ensures that her husband is brighter than she. As one feminist put it, "We won't be really liberated until we are free to marry men who are dumber and shorter than we are."

Divorce   The Census Bureau has estimated that, if present trends continue, one-fourth of women born between 1935 and 1939 will have seen their first marriages end in divorce by the time they reach age 50 in the 1980s (Census Bureau, 1972). Divorce rates are high, but remarriage rates are also high. However, remarriage rates for women are lower than those for men. In 1969, 221 out of every 1000 men remarried, whereas 135 out of every 1000 divorced women remarried (Scanzoni and Scanzoni, 1976). Accordingly, of the 6.5 million Americans who are currently divorced, 4 million are women (O'Leary, 1977).

The psychological processes involved in divorce and the period following it have been studied extensively (e.g., Bohannon, 1970; Brown et al., 1976; Weiss, 1976). Divorce is a period of transition and grief, and many have likened it to the process of bereavement following the death of a spouse. Divorce counselor Mel Krantzler speaks of divorce as "the death of a relationship" and believes that a time of grieving is essential to emotional healing. The change in status and roles may be stressful. A woman has to shift from the role of wife to that of divorcée, which may be particularly difficult for the woman who has defined much of her identity by the wife role.

In interviews, divorced and separated mothers note a number of added stresses in their lives (Brown et al., 1976). Their financial burdens are increased, as are their responsibilities. The divorced mother generally not only has to rear her children, but support them as well. Then, on top of that, she has to see to it that the car is repaired, in addition to many other tasks that her husband might have done formerly. Conflicts between work and children, which we have noted earlier, seem to intensify. None-theless, many women noted some advantages to their single parent status, such as an increased sense of autonomy and independence.

The single woman   It is difficult to remember how radical the concept of the Mary Tyler Moore Show — now in reruns — was when it began in the late 1960s. It was about an attractive, bright woman in her thirties who was *happily single,* and who never, in the course of the series, got married. The concept of a woman being purposely single and being happy was a new one.

The number of high school and college women who do not intend to marry is about 5 to 6 percent (Douvan and Adelson, 1966); even in data collected in 1973 and 1975, the percentage has not increased (Donelson, 1977).

Nonetheless, being a single woman is increasingly being viewed as a valid alternative lifestyle for women. In 1974, nearly one-quarter (23.4 percent) of women aged 24 were in the "never married" category; the comparable figure in 1960 was 16 percent (*Current Population Reports,* 1974). Census experts are not entirely sure whether these statistics indicate a trend toward not marrying, or a trend toward marrying later.

Two advantages are typically mentioned in discussions of being a single woman (Donelson, 1977). One is freedom. There is no necessity to agree with someone else on what to have for dinner, what TV program to watch, or how to spend money. There is the freedom to move when it is advantageous to one's career — or to stay put and not to move to follow a husband's career. The other advantage is a sense of self-sufficiency and competence. The single woman has to deal with the irritation of fixing the leaky faucet herself, but having done so, she gains a sense that she is competent to do such things. As noted earlier, single women have higher reported life-satisfaction than married women.

In a society as marriage-oriented as ours, it is not surprising that there are disadvantages to being a single woman. Most of the social structures for adults involve couples' activities, and the single person is often excluded. Loneliness is another disadvantage that is mentioned frequently.

Sociological studies indicate that higher levels of intelligence, education, and occupation are associated with singleness among women (Spreitzer and Riley, 1974). One sociologist concluded from these data that high-achieving women may consider marriage too confining and therefore choose not to marry (Havens, 1973). Note that this is a much different matter from saying that such women are not likely to be chosen. The decision is apparently theirs. For most women, however, being single is not a result of an early, explicit decision, but rather is a result of many small choices, many not made deliberately (McGinnis, 1974). These women may essentially drift into singleness and, once there, discover that they like it

MIDDLE AGE

Most women move through adulthood and into middle age with their identity defined chiefly in terms of others — husband and children. In this context, it is clear why middle age can be a difficult time for some women. Below we shall discuss the "empty nest" syndrome, one of the problems that may arise during this period.

The empty nest   During middle age the children leave home — to go to work, to go away to college, to get married. For the middle-aged woman, a major source of identity — motherhood — has been taken away. The term *empty nest syndrome* has been used to describe the cases of depression in women at this time. Sociologist Pauline Bart (1971) has investigated the empty nest syndrome. Interestingly, her research indicates that it is the "supermothers," not those who chose nontraditional careers, who are most susceptible to this depression. The supermothers have invested so much of themselves in the mother role that they have the most to lose when it has ended. Confirming these results, a study of graduates of an Eastern women's college who had been out of college 35 years and were in their late fifties indicated that women employed full-time had significantly lower symptom scores than women not employed outside the home (Powell, 1977).

Sociologist Lillian B. Rubin (1979) has recently challenged many ideas about the empty nest syndrome. Her results are based on a study of 160 women, a cross section of white mothers aged 35 to 54, from the working, middle, and professional classes. To be included in the sample, they had to have given up work or careers after a minimum of three years and to have assumed the traditional role of housewife and mother for at least ten years after the birth of their first child. Therefore this group should be the most prone to the empty nest syndrome. Typically these women said, "My career was my child." Contrary to the empty nest, Rubin found that, although some women were momentarily sad, lonely, or frightened, they were not depressed in response to the departure or impending departure of their children. The predominant feeling of every woman except one was a feeling of relief. For mothers who have sacrificed so much for their children, such a reaction is probably not too surprising. Rather than experiencing an immobilizing depression, most of the women found new jobs and reorganized their daily lives. Rubin felt that the women's movement had helped many of the women by raising their sights to other careers and opportunities.

What should we conclude, then? Probably some women do experience empty nest depressions, but not every woman does. Among those who do experience such depression, the experience may be brief. What is probably most important is the ability of the majority of women to adjust to the radical changes that occur in their lives and roles at this time.

Work   In an earlier section we noted the strains on women who work and have families in young adulthood. Then we noted fewer problems with depression among women who hold jobs outside the home. In the long run, is a woman better off psychologically to work or to have a career, or not?

Research on highly educated women now in their forties indicates that employed wives have higher self-esteem than women who are housewives exclusively (Birnbaum, 1975). These results contradict those found in women in their twenties: The family-oriented women possessed higher self-esteem, presumably because they were gaining satisfaction from having small children, while the career women experienced greater self-doubt during their struggle to establish a career. It appears that the career role, while adding some conflicts particularly in early adulthood, may provide a rewarding payoff — a more positive sense of self-esteem in middle age.

THE ELDERLY WOMAN

Some have suggested that there is a "double standard of aging." That is, as a man reaches middle age and beyond, he may appear more distinguished, but a woman of the same age does not seem to become more beautiful. As we saw in a previous section, a woman's value in her youth is often judged by her appearance, which may decline with age. Here we shall examine some of the research on women in old age.

Widowhood   There are far more widows than widowers. In the United States the ratio of widows to widowers is estimated at about four to one (Berardo, 1968). This is the result of two trends: the longer life expectancy of women, and the tendency of women to marry men older than themselves. Opportunities for remarriage are limited because there are so few men compared with women in this age group. Among all elderly persons (over age 65) in 1970, there were 722 men for every 1000 women. The Census Bureau predicts that by 1990 the ratio will be 675 men for every 1000 women (Census Bureau, 1973). Therefore it is fairly frequent for women to face the last 15 years or so of their lives alone. The average age of widowhood is 56 and more than half of all the women over 65 are widows (Berardo, 1968; U.S. Department of Commerce, 1973) with all the accompanying problems of adjustment.

A number of psychological processes occur in the bereavement of women during the year following the death of a husband (Parkes, 1970). These occur in approximately the following order:

1. Shock or numbness — In the first few days after the death of a husband the usual reaction is not intense emotion, but rather a sense of numbness.

2. Yearning and intense mourning — There is intense preoccupation with thoughts of the dead husband, grieving is intense, and there is a great deal of crying.
3. Anger and protest — There may be anger or bitterness directed toward relatives, a doctor, clergy, or to the dead husband for leaving her alone.
4. Disorganization — Even by the end of the first year of bereavement, most widows expressed little interest in planning for the future.
5. Mitigation (reduction of the pain) — There are periods of time when grief is reduced, and the woman may discover ways to protect or defend herself from the pain she is experiencing.
6. Identification — The woman expresses identification with the dead spouse, perhaps behaving or thinking like him, perhaps expressing opinions he would have had.

Of course, there is variation from one woman to the next in how widowhood is experienced. Two factors that appear to be relevant are the woman's age, and whether the husband's death was quick and unexpected, or the result of a long illness and therefore expected. The very elderly woman seems psychologically better prepared for her husband's death.

It seems that the death of a spouse is harder on men than it is on women (Spreitzer et al., 1975) as evidenced by low morale, mental disorders, and high death and suicide rates (Bock and Webber, 1972). Put another way, women seem to cope better with widowhood. One reason for this appears to be that women are more likely to have deep friendships that they have developed over the years from which they can draw emotional support (Blau, 1973). Nevertheless, social isolation and loneliness are problems for widows (Lopata, 1973).

Role exiting   Sociologist Zena Blau (1973) uses the term *role exiting* to describe the chief social process of aging. By this she means that the elderly must face the process of leaving behind roles that they formerly had, and many of these roles may have been critical to their own sense of identity. For example, in widowhood, there is an exit from the wife role and this may be difficult. Mandatory retirement from one's job creates another kind of role exiting. Traditionally this has been more of a problem for men than for women because men had more of their identity defined by their jobs. But as we see more women developing commitments to careers, retirement and the accompanying loss of a role may become a problem for women as well.

Gender roles and androgyny   Some scholars have suggested that gender roles become more relaxed or even reversed among the elderly. With the

TABLE 6.2.   Percentages of males and females who are classified as androgynous in four age groups

| | Age | | | |
Gender	13–20	21–40	41–60	61 and over
Females	26	31	11	7
Males	9	4	31	40

Source: Hyde and Phillis, 1979.

children grown, the woman is less restricted to the mother role. In some marriages, because the husband is older than the wife, he may have retired while she continues to hold a job. Thus he may do many of the household chores while she is the breadwinner.

This shifting of gender roles might suggest that the elderly become increasingly androgynous. To see whether this is true, subjects from age 13 to 85 were asked to complete the Bem Sex Role Inventory, discussed in Chapter 4 (Hyde and Phillis, 1979). Based on their scores, subjects were categorized as androgynous, feminine, masculine, or undifferentiated. The results, shown in Table 6.2, indicate that men become more androgynous with age, but that women become less androgynous with age.[1] In fact, the percentage of feminine women increased in the oldest age categories. Perhaps this means that both men and women become more feminine with age, resulting in more androgynous men and more feminine women.

IN CONCLUSION

We have traced female development across the lifespan. Gender similarities seem to be the rule in infancy and childhood, with many gender differences not emerging until adolescence. The femininity-achievement incompatibility exerts an important force on female development. The postponement of identity formation, and forming an identity in terms of the wife-mother role are also important.

---

[1] These data were cross-sectional (collected on many different people at different ages) and not longitudinal (collected on the same group of people repeatedly as they grew older). Therefore it is important to be cautious in concluding from them too much about actual developmental changes.

7

PROBLEMS OF ADJUSTMENT AND PSYCHOTHERAPY

I was eighteen when I started therapy for the second time. I went to a woman for two years, twice a week. She was constantly trying to get me to admit that what I really wanted was to get married and have babies and lead a "secure" life; she was very preoccupied with how I dressed, and just like my mother, would scold me if my clothes were not clean, or if I wore my hair down; told me that it would be a really good sign if I started to wear makeup and get my hair done in a beauty parlor (like her, dyed blond and sprayed); when I told her that I like to wear pants she told me that I had a confusion of sex roles . . . I originally went to her when my friends started to experiment with sex, and I felt that I couldn't make it, and that my woman friends with whom I had been close had rejected me for a good lay. . . .

FROM Women and Madness

Stories such as the one told by this woman are all too common among women who have been patients in psychotherapy. What is known about the experiences of such women? In this chapter we shall explore some of the adjustment problems women have, the evidence on whether there is sexism in traditional psychotherapy, and newly emerging therapies for women.

GENDER RATIOS AND MENTAL ILLNESS

Studies consistently show that more women than men are patients in psychotherapy (Gove and Tudor, 1973; Chesler, 1972). One British study found the lopsided ratio of 35 women for every one man in psychotherapy (cited by Chesler, 1972). This is probably an overestimate of the differential. Based on a survey of many studies, it seems likely that there are about two women in psychotherapy for every one man (Gove and Tudor, 1973).

How should this differential be interpreted? One possibility is that it simply means that more women than men are mentally ill. This may be a result of the stresses or unhealthiness of the female role (Gove and Tudor, 1973). Another possibility is that women in fact have no more adjustment problems than men do, but women are just more willing to admit their problems and seek psychotherapy (Phillips and Segal, 1969). It is not possible at this time to say which of these interpretations is correct. Possibly they are both correct to some extent.

It is also true that the diagnoses given to women differ substantially from those applied to men. Women are more frequently diagnosed as depressed, hysterical,[1] neurotically anxious, and phobic. Men, on the other hand, are termed alcoholic, organic (referring to psychological disorders caused by organic or physical problems such as brain damage), and anti-social (Gove and Tudor, 1973; Howard and Howard, 1974).

Space does not permit a discussion of all possible problems of adjustment in women. Below we shall consider two that are of special interest: depression, and alcoholism and drug abuse.

---

[1] For many centuries, hysteria was thought to be a problem caused by a wandering uterus! Now the term is used to refer to someone who overreacts to situations, responding in a hystrionic or melodramatic way (adjectives like "coquettish" or "seductive" may be used). In extreme cases, the person converts the high levels of anxiety into a physical symptom, such as blindness.

PROBLEMS OF ADJUSTMENT
FOR WOMEN

Depression   The symptoms of depression include (1) emotional aspects — a dejected mood, apathy; (2) cognitive aspects — a low self-evaluation and negative expectations about the future; (3) motivational aspects — motivation is low and there is an inability to mobilize oneself to action; and (4) behavioral aspects — appetite loss, sleep disturbance, loss of interest in sex, and tiredness (Beck and Greenberg, 1974).

Among persons with serious depression requiring hospitalization, the ratio of women to men is about two to one (Gove and Tudor, 1973). It has been estimated that the incidence of depression may be as high as 8 percent among women, compared with 4 percent among men (Roth, 1959). Even in large-scale surveys of the general American population, women have reported more symptoms of depression than men do (Radloff, 1975). It seems reasonable to conclude that there is more depression among women than among men.

Why do women have more problems with depression? There are a variety of factors associated with depression in women, including the empty nest syndrome, postpartum factors, and organic (physical) factors, such as involutional depressions (depression related to aging and specifically to menopause). There is even some evidence that sex-linked genetic factors are related to manic-depressions (Winokur et al., 1969).

Freud believed that overly dependent people are prone to depression. When they experience a loss, such as the death of a loved one, or a symbolic loss, such as perceived rejection by someone close to them, they become depressed. Further, Freud viewed women as naturally more dependent than men. Therefore, his theory would account for the greater occurrence of depression in women based on their greater dependency.

Behaviorist psychologists believe that depression occurs when the reinforcements one is accustomed to — for example, a satisfying job or a congenial spouse — are suddenly withdrawn. The person responds by reducing activities. If there is not some reinforcement for the person's remaining efforts, he or she sinks further into depression. The pattern of inactivity itself may be rewarded if the person gets special attention for being "sick." Following these notions, a behaviorist might explain the greater occurrence of depression in women as being a result of women not receiving sufficient reinforcements for their actions (an assumption that is not too difficult to make); or as a result of women being especially likely to find themselves in situations in which their customary reinforcements are withdrawn (for example, having to leave one's friends and job and move to follow a husband's career, or having the children leave home when they grow up).

Two other factors are relevant in discussing the causes of depression in women: women's roles and learned helplessness.

A large-scale survey of 2,829 women in the general population investigated the relationship between *women's roles* and reported symptoms of depression (Radloff, 1975). There was some evidence that the marital role for women contributes to depression. Married women have higher depression scores than married men and never-married women. The housewife role has also been proposed as a source of women's depression. Many of the tasks of a housewife are unchallenging, repetitive, and lacking in a sense of accomplishment, as, for example, making beds that will just be unmade that evening and made again the next day. In this study, full-time housewives were more depressed than married men, but so were working wives. Therefore, it doesn't seem that getting a job, by itself, is the cure for women's depression. It is also possible that part of the problem is that women continue all of their (depressing) housewife responsibilities even though they take jobs outside the home.

Following in the behaviorist tradition, psychologist Martin Seligman's (1975) theory of *learned helplessness* as a cause of depression may be helpful in explaining depression in women (Radloff, 1975; Radloff and Monroe, 1978). Seligman believes that depressives have a history of learning that they are incapable of successful mastery and control over their lives. In short, they have learned to regard themselves as helpless. When confronted with a difficult situation, they feel that they cannot deal with it successfully, and depression results. The sense of helplessness and lack of control Seligman talks about sound very much like the powerlessness that feminists say is characteristic of women. If women in our society do indeed lack power — in everything from interpersonal relationships to national politics — this may contribute to a sense of helplessness and thus to depression. Further, traits that women are socialized for, such as passivity, may contribute to helplessness. One study showed that girls receive more task-irrelevant praise, while boys get the task-relevant praise (Dweck and Reppucci, 1973). Perhaps even at a very early age, girls learn that they will not be rewarded for what they do.

How can one deal with this situation? First, it is probably possible to apply some "preventive medicine" based on the learned helplessness theory. Child-rearing practices and other factors should be examined to see whether they encourage helplessness in females, and if they do, they should be changed. As two authorities commented,

> . . . young women will do well to concentrate on preventing future depressions by cultivating habits of self-respect and self-reliance and by leading a balanced life, participating in a variety of activities rather than depending on family ties alone for emotional and intellectual sustenance. (Beck and Greenberg, 1974, p. 130)

But psychological changes in women alone will probably not be enough. As long as the society around them is unresponsive to their actions, problems will still result. As the same authors commented,

A woman can learn to be aware of what she wants, to take direct action to get it, and to take credit for her successes. But to avoid helplessness, her environment must cooperate. (1974, p. 130)

Alcoholism and drug abuse   Just as depression has been a "feminine" problem, alcoholism has been a "masculine" problem. In the Victorian era, drinking was viewed as a male-only activity, and the prohibition movement was led by women. However, the percentage of women who drink has risen steadily, and current figures indicate that about 77 percent of men and 60 percent of women drink at least occasionally (Calahan et al., 1969). However, while there is now tolerance of social drinking for women, there is little tolerance for drunken women, and the drunk woman is viewed with more scorn and disgust than the drunk man (Gomberg, 1974).

In Europe and America, the ratio of male alcoholics to female alcoholics is about four to one (Willis, 1973). However, such statistics are based on patients seen in therapy. It may be that there are actually as many women alcoholics as men alcoholics (Block, 1962), but that the women are just less likely to be noticed. For example, no one notices the drunken housewife, but the drunk man who must show up at work on Monday morning and fails to do so is much more conspicuous.

What is known psychologically about alcoholic women? Traumatic events — in particular, loss of a parent during childhood, psychiatric illness in the family, or alcoholism in the family — are all more likely among women alcoholics than among women in the general population (Gomberg, 1974). There is actually one longitudinal study available, although the sample is small (Jones, 1971). The Oakland Growth study was a longitudinal study begun in the 1920s, with continuing followups. When the women in the study were in their late forties, they were categorized as to whether they were abstainers, light, moderate or heavy drinkers, or problem drinkers. It was then possible to examine the data collected on them when they were younger to see what characterized the problem drinker as compared with others. For the future problem drinker, adolescence was a severe crisis. According to the researcher, the following is characteristic of the future problem drinker (pp. 67–68):

At fifteen, life is full of adolescent self-doubt and confusion. She fears and rejects life, is distrustful of people, follows a religion which accentuates judgment and punishment. She escapes into ultrafemininity.

The composite picture, then, is a history of emotional deprivation, with a submissive, passively resentful girl undergoing a stressful adolescence, fearful of dependency relationships and trying to solve her problems with superfemininity (Gomberg, 1974).

There appears to be a strong relationship between depression and drinking problems in women (Schuckit et al., 1969; Schuckit, 1972). There is also a rather high rate of alcoholism among husbands of alcoholic women. The evidence suggests that alcoholism may begin with the husband and be transmitted to the wife, although the reverse rarely occurs (Gomberg, 1974).

While the alcoholic woman is superfeminine on the surface, the evidence also suggests that she is ambivalent and in conflict about her femininity, with her aggressive and assertive tendencies barely pushed beneath the surface (Gomberg, 1974).

The data on drug addiction also indicate a male:female ratio of about five to one (Willis, 1973). These statistics are for addiction to illicit drugs such as morphine and heroin, however. Data also show that large numbers of women are hooked on legal prescription drugs such as tranquilizers and diet pills. Physicians simply seem to be more willing to suggest drugs as cures for women's problems. For example, female depressives receive more drugs, and stronger ones, than males with the same symptoms (Stein et al., 1976). In another study, women accounted for 58 percent of the frequent users of major tranquilizers, 70 percent of the minor tranquilizer users, and 66 percent of the sedative users (Cooperstock, 1971). In a study of repeat prescriptions of drugs, more women (5 percent) than men (3.3 percent) received ten or more prescriptions within a year (Cooperstock, 1976). Thus dependence on or addiction to legal prescription drugs is a serious problem for some women and, once again, gender roles seem to play a part.

SEXISM AND PSYCHOTHERAPY

With the rise of the women's movement in the late 1960s, psychotherapists and the institution of psychotherapy became the object of sharp attacks for sexism (e.g., Chesler, 1972). What evidence is there that sexism in psychotherapy is a problem?

The Broverman study   By far the most frequently cited study used as evidence of sexism in psychotherapy is one done by psychologist Inge Broverman and her colleagues (1970). They investigated the judgments of clinicians (psychiatrists, clinical psychologists, and social workers) on criteria of mental health for males and females. The clinicians in the sample were given a personality questionnaire with a series of bipolar rating scales of gender-typed personality characteristics, for example:

very	*not at all*
aggressive	*aggressive*

└──┘

One third of the clinicians were instructed to indicate on each item the pole to which a mature, healthy, socially competent *male* would be closer. Another third were told to do this for a *female*, and the remaining third were told to do so for an *adult*. Three interesting results emerged. First, while there were no significant differences between the standards for males and for adults, there were differences between the standards for females and for adults. This is a good example of the "male as normative" principle in psychology. The standards for human mental health are for males, and females are a deviation from them — or, as one feminist put it, "a normal, average, healthy woman is a crazy human being." A second result was that socially desirable personality characteristics tended to be assigned to males, undesirable ones to females. For example, a mature, healthy, socially competent woman is supposed to be more submissive, more excitable in minor crises, have her feelings more easily hurt, and be more conceited about her appearance than a mature, healthy, socially competent man. A third result was that there was no difference in the results depending on whether the clinician-rater was a man or a woman (more than one-third of the clinicians were females). Apparently female clinicians are no more exempt than males from these views of "healthy" womanhood.

On the basis of this study, it appears that the same double-bind situations that bring women to therapy may be present in the therapy situation. Basically the woman has two alternatives: she can adjust to female norms, in which case she will have a number of undesirable personality characteristics (for example, excitable in minor crises); or she can develop certain desirable human traits such as independence and assertiveness, in which case she may be accused of rejecting her femininity, and therefore of being abnormal. Of course, not every clinician is guilty of such situations, and there has been some dispute over the Broverman results (Fabrikant, 1974), but the general trends discovered in this study are disturbing.

As evidence of sexism in psychotherapy, there are some problems with the Broverman study. The basic problem is that it does not provide a direct measure of what we are concerned with: whether therapists, in their treatment of patients, act in a sexist manner. This study does not measure what therapists actually do in therapy, but rather what their attitudes are, based on their responses to a paper-and-pencil questionnaire. What we need are data on therapists' actual treatment of patients (Stricker, 1977), but these are in short supply. We shall review those that are available in a later section. Another problem with the Broverman study is that it is now about ten years old. It is possible that therapists have changed their attitudes substantially in the last ten years, in response to changing attitudes about gender roles in our culture.

APA: Defining sexism in psychotherapy   In 1974, the American Psychological Association appointed a task force to investigate sex bias and sex-role stereotyping in psychotherapeutic practice. In an initial report, they attempted to catalogue the kinds of practices that can reasonably be considered to indicate sex bias in psychotherapy (APA, 1975). These ideas were based on a preliminary survey of women psychotherapist members of APA.

The report identified four general areas in which sex bias and sex-role stereotyping occur. These are listed below.

1. Fostering of traditional gender roles.

Example:
The therapist assumes that the woman's problems will be solved by marriage or being a better wife.

> My therapist suggested that my identity problems would be solved by my marrying and having children; I was 19 at the time and in no way ready for marriage.

2. Bias in expectations and devaluation of women:

Example:
The therapist denies self-actualization or assertiveness for female clients and instead fosters concepts of women as passive and dependent.

> Whenever a female becomes active, assertive, and aggressive in group situations the label "castrating bitch" is applied to her.

3. Sexist use of psychoanalytic concepts.

Examples:
a. The therapist maintains that vaginal orgasm is a prerequisite for emotional maturity and thus a goal of therapy.
b. The therapist labels assertiveness and ambition with the Freudian concept of "penis envy."

4. Responding to women as sex objects including seduction of female clients.

Regarding the point about seducing clients, the 1978 revision of the American Psychological Association's ethical code states: "Sexual intimacies between therapist and client are unethical." A recent survey investigated the sexual activities of a sample of licensed Ph.D. psychologists with their patients (Holroyd and Brodsky, 1977); 5.5 percent of the male and 0.6 percent of the female psychologists returning the questionnaire admitted having engaged in sexual intercourse with a patient during the time the patient was in therapy, and an additional 2.6 percent of male and 0.3 percent of female therapists had intercourse with patients within three months of termination of therapy. These are probably best regarded as minimum figures, because they are based on the self-reports of the therapists and some might not be willing to admit such activity, even though the questionnaire was anonymous. Of those therapists who had intercourse with patients, 80 percent repeated the activity with other patients.

The Task Force report is helpful in providing a cataloguing of the kinds of practices in therapy that may be sexist or sex-biased. Nonetheless, the information is based on self-reports. We are still lacking data, based on direct observations of therapy sessions, that would tell us more accurately the nature and extent of sex bias. In addition, it could be that there are some very subtle sexist practices that neither patient nor therapist is aware of, which could be discovered only by analysis of direct observations of therapy sessions. For example, it could be that therapists give more verbal reinforcements (e.g., *mm hmm*) when female clients are talking about being mothers than when they are talking about their careers.

Other evidence   As noted above, the Broverman study provides some evidence of stereotyped attitudes on the part of therapists, but by itself it does not provide very direct evidence of sex bias in therapy. A number of other studies have been done to try to provide better evidence. These are called *analog studies* because they investigate a situation that is analogous to the therapy situation rather than the therapy situation itself. Space does not allow us to review all of them here, so instead we shall consider in detail one analog study that is fairly typical.

Beverly Gomes and Stephen I. Abramowitz (1976) mailed a case history to a sample of psychotherapists. The therapists were asked to rate the patient whose history they read on a number of scales such as emotional maturity (very inadequate to very adequate) and mental disorder (extremely disturbed to mildly disturbed). The case history a particular therapist received was actually one of four case histories prepared by the investigators. All four were identical, except that half said the person was male, and half said she was female; they also differed in the concluding pargaraph. In half the cases, it described the person with a number of "feminine" adjectives such as warm and dependent. In the other half, the person was described as having "masculine" characteristics such as ambitious and cold. Therefore the case history a therapist received might be about a feminine woman, a masculine woman, a feminine man, or a masculine man. In all other respects, however, all the case histories were identical.

On the ratings of mental disorder, there were no significant differences in the ratings given to male compared with female patients, nor to masculine versus feminine patients. Neither was there any difference between the ratings of male and female therapists. The absence of difference between ratings of males and of females suggests that there may not be as much sex bias among therapists as one would think from the Broverman study. As the authors concluded,

The overall failure to detect prejudice against women or sex-role non-conformists among any therapist subgroup would tentatively appear to exonerate clinicians of the charges of unwitting antifemale sentiment and norm-enforcement. (Gomes and Abramowitz, 1976, pp. 10–11)

This study is interesting, then, because of its failure to find sex bias.

Other studies using a similar technique have found that liberal female clients receive lower adjustment ratings from politically conservative therapists (Abramowitz, Jackson, and Gomes, 1973) and that female clients receive a *better* prognosis — prediction for successful cure — than male clients (Abramowitz et al., 1976).

The problem with analog studies such as the one by Gomes and Abramowitz is that they still do not look at the actual therapy session. Further, the subjects (therapists) may have guessed the purpose of the study and tailored their responses to look respectable — that is, unbiased. Other investigators have used a confederate posing as a client who told the therapist a standard story, and the therapist's responses were measured (e.g., Shapiro, 1977).

A few investigators have studied actual therapist-client behaviors, such as length of time the patient is kept, or remains, in therapy or in the hospital (e.g., Chesler, 1972). The problem with these "real life" measures is that it is possible that female patients are harder to cure than male patients, something that can't be controlled in real life studies, but can be controlled in studies like the one by Gomes and Abramowitz.

Conclusion   Where does all of this leave us? Is sexism a problem in psychotherapy? Probably three conclusions are reasonable at this point. First, the scientific evidence is not very good for the existence or non-existence of sexism in psychotherapy. Many of the studies have problems or contradicting results. However, it seems unlikely that there would be so many tales of sexism around — such as those found by the APA Task Force — if there were no sexism. It probably does exist, and one hopes that future research will document exactly where and what it is. Second, it is probably true that some therapists are sexists, but that not every therapist is a sexist. This may account for the failure of most studies to find overall evidence of sex bias. But if only one therapist in ten is a sexist and you get that therapist, you may have a very unpleasant experience. It is probably wise, therefore, to become sensitized to problems of sex bias so that you can spot them. Whether a therapist is a sexist probably depends on a number of factors, such as his or her political beliefs, personality, and individual reactions to a particular client. Third, from the research it would appear to be inaccurate to say that male therapists are biased and female therapists are not. Many studies find no differences between male and female therapists in their bias. Probably more important than the therapist's gender is her or his attitudes about gender roles.

HOW TRADITIONAL THERAPIES WORK FOR WOMEN

One of the most important factors influencing a woman's experience in therapy is the theoretical orientation of the therapist and the corresponding type of therapy she or he uses. Below we shall consider three kinds of therapy to see how they relate to women and whether they are likely to be biased.

Psychoanalysis   Psychoanalysis is a system of therapy based on Freud's theory (see Chapter 3). Both Freudian theory and psychoanalysis have received sharp criticisms from feminists. Some feminists feel that psychoanalysis is inherently, or at least very likely to be, sex-biased (e.g., American Psychological Association, 1975). Others, however, feel that it can be applied in an unbiased way, and even speak of feminist psychoanalysis (e.g., Shainess, 1977).

The problem with psychoanalysis is that some of its central concepts *are* sex-biased. For example, women's achievement strivings may be interpreted as penis envy. Women who enjoy orgasm from masturbation may be regarded as immature and thus be urged to strive for the more mature, vaginal orgasm. The evidence indicates that women in psychoanalysis have sometimes been convinced that they are inferior, masochistic, and so on (American Psychological Association, 1975).

Therefore, although feminist or nonsexist psychoanalysis may be a possibility, clients should be sensitized to the potential sexism of psychoanalysis.

Behavior therapy   Behavioral therapy (behavior mod) is a set of therapies based on principles of classical conditioning (usually associated with Pavlov) and operant conditioning (usually associated with Skinner). In contrast to psychoanalysis, behavior therapy attempts no in-depth analysis of the patient's personality or unconscious motives. Instead, the focus is on problematic behavior and how it can be modified by learning principles, such as rewarding desired behaviors or punishing undesired ones. A number of specific therapy techniques may be used. One is *systematic desensitization*. The patient and therapist make a list of events that arouse the patient's anxiety, and these are listed in a "hierarchy" from least anxiety-provoking to most anxiety-provoking (see Table 7.1). The patient is then trained in deep muscle relaxation. Next, the patient relaxes and, while relaxed, is asked to imagine the least anxiety-provoking item on the hierarchy; if there is any tension, the patient goes back to concentrating on relaxation. Once the patient is relaxed while imagining that situation, the therapist moves on to the next situation on the hierarchy, and so on, until the patient is relaxed while imagining the most anxiety-provoking situation.

TABLE 7.1.   A client's hierarchy for systematic desensitization

most anxiety-
arousing
	1. An argument she raises in a discussion is ignored by the group.
	    2. She is not recognized by a person she has briefly met three times.
	        3. Her mother says she is selfish because she is not helping in the house (studying instead).
	            4. She is not recognized by a person she has briefly met twice.
	                5. Her mother calls her lazy.

least anxiety- arousing	6. She is not recognized by a person she has briefly met once.

Source: After Wolpe and Lazarus, 1966.

Once patients feel relaxed imagining these events, they are often able to feel relaxed and confident when actually confronting them.

Another therapy technique that is practiced is *positive reinforcement,* in which desired behaviors are rewarded. *Observation* and *imitation* can also be used, such as assertiveness training for women, which we will discuss later in this chapter. Finally, *aversive learning procedures* — in which some unpleasant stimulus functions to eliminate an undesired behavior — may be another technique applied. For example, the drug antabuse may be given to alcoholics; if they drink, the drug causes unpleasant body reactions such as nausea and vomiting. Such therapy is called *aversive counterconditioning.*

There is no inherent sexism in the concepts of behavior therapy (Lazarus, 1974). It does not assume that there should be gender differences, or that only women should engage in certain behaviors. Certainly behavior therapy does contain value judgments, but these should be applied equally to females and males. For example, assertiveness is valued by behavior therapists, but it should be valued both for males and for females. Of course, it would be possible for an individual behavior therapist to be sex-biased, but there is nothing in the theoretical system itself that is biased.

As an example of the treatment of a particularly common problem for women, the behavior therapist would attack depression by trying to increase the level of positive reinforcement the woman receives in her environment (Beck and Greenberg, 1974). For example, it might be that her husband is unresponsive, or even that he responds negatively, to her attempts at conversation or her work around the house, or to discussion of her own job. Her husband might be trained to be more responsive to her, thus providing more positive reinforcement. Or she may receive little positive reinforcement in her job, in which case she might be encouraged to alter her work or find a different job that would provide more positive reinforcement.

Gestalt therapy   Gestalt therapy is a system of psychotherapy formulated by Fritz and Laura Perls in the 1940s. It is one of a group of therapies known as humanistic therapy because of their emphasis on treating the whole person (Perls, 1969; for reviews of Gestalt applied to women, see Brien and Sheldon, 1977; Polster, 1974). The basic aim of Gestalt therapy is to help people develop more intelligent behavior. This is done by helping them realize that alternatives or choices are open to them, which they often did not realize. With an awareness of choices, there is a greater range of action available. With the realization of these alternatives, though, comes responsibility. That is, the patient is encouraged to take responsibility for his or her life. It is no longer sufficient to blame one's unhappiness on forces around oneself (husband, job, etc.). With the realization of alternatives comes the responsibility for molding one's own life in an exciting way. This philosophy is helpful to women who often have the unpleasant feeling of being "stuck" in a lifestyle they don't seem to want. Gestalt therapy should help them to realize they have other alternatives open to them, and should give them the energy to move into those alternatives.

The following case illustrates the way Gestalt therapy worked for one woman's problems.

> One depressed woman named Polly felt she was "sick." Home alone with the children all day, she was very lonely and isolated. Her husband wanted to be her only adult contact. As her depression continued, her ex-therapist and her husband felt she should be hospitalized. Gradually, she saw that she had been accepting her husband's idea of a suitable lifestyle for her. She realized two things she wanted: adult companionship and self-understanding. At this point, depressed, frightened, yet resolute, she came into Gestalt therapy.
>
> Directing Polly away from focusing on what was *wrong* with her led her to open many new avenues. In addition to meeting new friends, she took a trip to India with an anthropology class and rekindled an old interest in flying planes. More important than these specific changes, however, was her realization that her depression was the result of turning her energies inward. Laura Perls recently said in a workshop in San Francisco that "depression is the opposite of expression." This was certainly the case with Polly. (Brien and Sheldon, 1977, p. 123)

Like behavior therapy, there is nothing inherent in the theory of Gestalt therapy that makes it sex-biased, although of course it would still be possible for an individual therapist to be biased.

NEW THERAPIES
FOR WOMEN

With the critiques of traditional therapies, particularly psychoanalysis, has come the suggestion that there is a need for feminist therapy or nonsexist therapy, or therapies especially tailored to the needs of women. In this section we shall discuss some of these alternatives.

Feminist therapy and nonsexist therapy   Feminist and nonsexist therapies may be characterized as allowing

> clients to determine their own destinies without the construction of culturally prescribed sex-role stereotypes based upon assumed biological differences. Both approaches attempt to facilitate equality (in personal power) between females and males. (Rawlings and Carter, 1977, p. 50)

Clinical psychologists Edna Rawlings and Dianne Carter (1977) distinguish between nonsexist therapy and feminist therapy. Feminist therapy, in particular, includes an advocacy of positions of the women's movement. They state that *nonsexist therapy* has the following particular values and assumptions:

1. The therapist should be aware of her or his own values.
2. There are no prescribed gender-role behaviors.
3. Gender-role reversals (e.g., female breadwinner, male at home) are not labeled pathological.
4. Marriage is not regarded as any better an outcome of therapy for a female than for a male.
5. Females are expected to be as autonomous and assertive as males; males are expected to be as expressive and tender as females.
6. Theories of behavior based on anatomical differences (e.g., Freud, Erikson) are rejected.

The assumptions of *feminist therapy*, according to Rawlings and Carter, are:

1. The inferior status of women is due to their having less political and economic power than men. Power analysis is central to feminist thought (see, for example, Chapter 9) and to feminist therapy.
2. The primary source of women's pathology is social, not personal; external, not internal.
3. The focus on environmental stress as a major source of pathology is not used as an avenue of escape from individual responsibility.
4. Feminist therapy is opposed to personal adjustment to social conditions; the goal is social and political change.
5. Other women are not the enemy.
6. Men are not the enemy either.

7. Women must be economically and psychologically autonomous.
8. Relationships of friendship, love, and marriage should be equal in personal power.
9. Major differences between "appropriate" gender-role behaviors must disappear.

Terminology in this area is not standardized, however, so some therapists might refer to themselves as feminist therapists when in fact their assumptions correspond to what we have here called nonsexist therapy.

Perhaps the two points that are most central to feminist therapy, and that most distinguish it from traditional psychotherapy, are points 2 and 5 above. Regarding point 2, traditional therapies have viewed people's problems as being internal (within the individual) and have correspondingly prescribed personal changes to achieve better adjustment. Feminist therapists, in contrast, view women's problems as being external in origin, caused by oppression in the society around them. From this follows point 5: if the problems are external in origin, then the goal should be to change society, not oneself.

Assertiveness training   Assertiveness training — a technique of behavior therapy — has become popular among women, and it can take place either as a part of formal psychotherapy, in informal self-help groups, or in classes. (For more detailed discussions, see Jakubowski-Spector, 1973; Jakubowski, 1977). First, some terms need to be defined.

Assertion or assertiveness involves standing up for one's basic interpersonal rights in such a way that the rights of another person are not violated. Assertion should be a direct, honest, and appropriate expression of one's feelings. *Aggression,* in this context, involves standing up for one's rights in such a way that the rights of the other person are violated. It involves dominating, humiliating, or putting down the other person. *Nonassertion* is failing to stand up for one's rights and, consequently, permitting one's rights to be violated by others (Jakubowski-Spector, 1973).

Women tend to have more problems with being assertive than men do. In part it is because assertiveness is confused with aggressiveness, and aggressiveness is definitely not part of the feminine role — but then neither is assertiveness. Passivity and many of the other traits females are socialized for are contrary to assertiveness. Women are often concerned with maintaining harmonious relationships with others, and they may fear that being assertive will cause friction. The problem is that there is a cost in always swallowing one's feelings—a sense of frustration, ineffectiveness, or hurt. Some would even argue that depression can result from lack of assertion (Jakubowski, 1977). Because assertiveness is a valuable human quality, many women are taking assertiveness training.

Assertiveness training often consists of role playing, in which students respond to people who are being aggressive or infringing on their rights, the idea being that assertiveness is learned through practice and through seeing models of assertive behavior. The following is an example of how high-quality assertion can be used to resolve a conflict.

> A graduate professor often continued evening class ten minutes or more beyond the normal class period. Although many students were irked by this behavior, one student was assertive and approached the professor after class one evening.
>
> *Student*:   I recognize that sometimes we get so involved in the discussion that you may not realize that the class is running overtime. I'd appreciate your ending the class on time because I have several commitments which I need to keep immediately after this class.
>
> *Professor*:   I don't really think that I've been late so often.
>
> *Student*:   I guess that you haven't noticed but the last three classes have been ten or fifteen minutes late. Is there any way I could help you end it on time?
>
> *Professor*:   As a matter of fact there is. I'm often so interested in the class that I don't look at my watch. It'd help me if you'd raise your hand five minutes before the end of the class period. If I don't stop in five minutes, signal me again.
>
> *Student*:   I'd be happy to do that. (Jakubowski, 1977, pp. 157–158)

Notice that the student was assertive, expressing her feelings directly, but in a way that showed regard for the professor. She did not show aggression (for example, "You're so damned inconsiderate of us, making us stay late all the time.") Neither was she nonassertive (in this case, doing nothing and continuing to suffer). The situation proceeded to a satisfactory resolution.

Consciousness-raising groups as therapy for women   With the rise of the feminist movement and consciousness-raising groups, and corresponding criticism of traditional psychotherapy, has come the suggestion that consciousness-raising groups may serve as a form of therapy for women (for reviews, see Brodsky, 1977; Kirsh, 1974).

A consciousness-raising group is usually a group of eight or so women. Consistent with beliefs of the women's movement, there is no leader; rather, all members are considered equal. The groups usually meet on a regular basis, such as for two hours one evening every week, lasting anywhere from a few weeks to a year or more. The participants talk about themselves, about their feelings, their experiences, and problems they are having. Beyond this, there is an analysis of how society's gender-role stereotypes create many of these problems. Many positive results may come from this. The women often realize that they have many problems in common, which can relieve the feeling of abnormality resulting from the sense of being the "only one" with a problem. The sense of competition with other women may decrease and real bonds between women may develop. Other women become role models of effectiveness. The major

FIGURE 7.1

Some have argued that consciousness-raising groups are better for women than psychotherapy.

Source: Photo by Owen Franken / Stock Boston.

goal, however, is a heightened awareness of themselves as women.

Therapy is not the goal of consciousness-raising groups, although the groups may be therapeutic. Feminists are careful to point out the difference in ideology between C-R groups and psychotherapy:

> The basic difference in the structures is that the patient-therapist relationship is unequal and hierarchical, contrasted with the peer equality among women in consciousness-raising groups. The basic difference in the ideologies is that traditional psychotherapy stresses adjusting the inner workings of individuals to fit society; consciousness-raising groups emphasize the need to change society by showing individuals that their "person" problems are rooted in socio-cultural phenomena. (Kirsh, 1974, pp. 336–337.)

Note that this is quite similar to the principles of feminist therapy discussed earlier. Because consciousness-raising groups are not specifically designed to be therapy, women with serious problems are generally referred to a feminist therapist.

There has been some research into the psychological effects of participating in a C-R group, although the research has been rather unsystematic, in part because some C-R groups are suspicious of the motives of professional researchers. Some of the changes that have been reported include:

increased autonomy, activity, and self-esteem; expanded jobs and career orientation; desire for more egalitarian relationships with men; a new understanding of the concept of "mother"; "finding one's anger"; and more positive feelings about other women (Kirsh, 1974; Kincaid, 1977). These, of course, would all be considered positive outcomes, whether from a C-R group or from psychotherapy. More research in this area is needed.

ANDROGYNY AS A MODEL OF MENTAL HEALTH

To this point we have discussed studies that are critical of setting traditional standards of masculinity and femininity as criteria of mental health (e.g., Broverman et al., 1970). These studies argue that it makes little sense to call traits such as passivity and submissiveness healthy for women. Now that we know what women shouldn't be like, what should they be? Is it possible to state in some positive way what characteristics a healthy, well-adjusted woman should have?

One suggestion that has been raised is that androgyny should be the new model of mental health for women, and for men as well (Kaplan, 1976). The idea is that assertiveness and self-confidence ("masculine" traits) and interpersonal sensitivity and emotional expressiveness ("feminine" traits) are all desirable, so why not put them all together in one individual? The result would be the androgyn. The research reviewed in Chapter 4 indicates that the androgynous person tends to be more healthy than the gender-typed individual, since androgynous people have higher self-esteem and seem to function more effectively in a wider variety of situations. Thus there is also some scientific evidence to support androgyny as a model of mental health. Perhaps if the young women of today become more androgynous than the women of previous generations, women will have fewer problems of adjustment such as depression. It will be interesting to see if this actually occurs.

However, one should not expect that androgyny will be the perfect medicine for all of women's psychological problems. Some psychologists have pointed out problems with androgyny as a model of mental health (e.g., Kaplan, 1979). One of the basic problems seems to be that a person may have an androgynous combination of personality characteristics, but may apply them in the wrong situations. For example, a woman might be assertive and demanding to her husband when he needs her nurturance, and then become soft and nurturant when it would be better for her to be firm and assertive. Thus, having androgynous personality characteristics does not ensure that they will be used in the most adaptive way.

Androgyny holds a great deal of promise as a vision of mental health free from gender-role stereotypes, but it will require a great deal of societal change and more sophisticated scientific understanding before that vision is realized.

8

ABILITIES, ACHIEVEMENT, AND MOTIVATION

When Samuel Johnson was asked which is more intelligent, man or woman, he replied, "Which man, which woman?"

Part of the lore of the culture is that women are less intelligent than men. Put bluntly, they are dumb — witness the expression "dumb broad." An additional truism is that women's thought processes are less rational, more illogical than men's, more influenced by emotion. A familiar scene in movies and comics is the male shaking his head over his inability to understand the mind of his wife or girl friend. (This might in fact be evidence of inferior male intelligence or perceptiveness, but it never seems to be interpreted that way.)

Is there any scientific evidence to support the notion that women are less intellectually competent than men? In this chapter we shall explore empirical evidence regarding the intellectual and achievement characteristics of women, and whether these characteristics seem to differ from those of men.[1] It is important to remember that the finding of a gender difference does not say anything about what causes it, i.e., whether biological or environmental factors are responsible. We shall then examine motivational differences between females and males with the goal of better understanding the relationship between women's abilities and their achievements.

ABILITIES

General intelligence   There is no evidence to support the hypothesis that females are less intelligent than males. In fact, research has consistently shown that there are no gender differences in general intelligence. One of the most thorough studies of this sort was done in Scotland. All the children in the country who were born on February 1, May 1, August 1, and November 1 in 1926 were given the Stanford-Binet intelligence test. The average IQ for boys was 100.51, and for girls 99.7. This difference was not statistically significant, despite the large size of the sample (Scottish Council for Research in Education, 1939). Another extensive Scottish study showed boys four points higher on an individual IQ test, girls two points higher on a group IQ test (Scottish Council for Research in Education, 1949). While these differences were statistically significant, the fact that they were so small and in opposite directions once again indicates that neither gender is superior to the other in general intellectual performance.

---

[1] The reader who wishes to explore this subject in more detail may consult one of the excellent reviews available (Sherman, 1978; Maccoby and Jacklin, 1974; Maccoby, 1966; Tyler, 1965).

These results need to be interpreted with some caution, because of the nature of IQ-test construction. It became clear to the early test constructors that, because of both biological and cultural factors, boys would do better on some kinds of tests, while girls would do better on others. They decided to balance these subtests so that there would be no gender differences in overall measured intelligence. Therefore, saying that there are no gender differences in overall tested intelligence essentially means that the test constructors succeeded in their goal of eliminating gender differences.

There is some evidence of gender differences in the development of intelligence, however. Girls tend to test somewhat higher than boys during the early school years, while boys surpass girls in high school. This might be due in part to higher drop-out rates among low-testing boys (Maccoby, 1966).

In conclusion, a multitude of studies in the past five decades (of which we have cited only a few) fail to indicate any gender differences in general intelligence. Rather than looking at global assessments, it is more revealing to analyze patterns of specific abilities in male and in females.

Verbal ability   Females are superior to males in verbal ability (Sherman, 1978; Maccoby and Jacklin, 1974). Developmentally, girls appear to have a slight advantage at the beginning of language development, around the ages of two or three; but for the most part there are few gender differences during childhood. Gender differences in verbal ability increase in prominence beginning at about age eleven, and the superiority of females increases through high school and possibly beyond. Girls do better not only at relatively simple verbal tasks such as spelling, but also at more complex tasks such as analogies and creative writing (Maccoby and Jacklin, 1974). In high school a smaller proportion of girls than of boys need remedial reading training. Further, Margaret Mead found girls to be more verbally precocious than boys in all the diverse cultures she has observed (Mead, 1958).

Motor skills   The traditional results from differential psychology indicate that boys surpass girls not only in muscular strength, but in speed and coordination of gross body movements. On the other hand, in finger dexterity and fine movements, females are generally superior (Maccoby and Jacklin, 1974; Anastasi, 1958).

Research in physical education indicates that, in general, large gender differences in motor performance do not appear until adolescence; there are correspondingly few physical differences between males and females until puberty with its onset of hormonal differences leading to larger height and musculature in the male (Singer, 1968). For example, Bayley's Scale of Motor Development (1936) does not differentiate the genders prior to five years of age. In general, developmental curves for physical performance (for example, speed in the 100-yard dash, grip strength) in males increase during childhood and show sharp increases during adolescence. The curves for girls are parallel to those for boys during childhood (girls being at only slightly lower levels), but during adolescence girls' performance levels off or even declines. Once again we see that in childhood, gender similarities are more the rule than gender differences; gender differences do not become prominent until adolescence. In physical performance, adolescent gender differences probably result from both actual physical differences and cultural factors (lack of training for girls, gender inappropriateness of athletic competition for girls). As evidence of the importance of environmental factors such as nutrition and training, it has been noted that in the Olympic games, the first four places in the women's 100 meter dash in 1952 showed faster times than the winner in the 1896 men's event (Jokl, 1964).

The extent and importance of early gender differences in motor skills, and in particular their relevance to gender differences in adult abilities and occupations, might well be debated. Some authors argue that gender differences in childhood activities (with boys using large muscles in sports, girls using fine muscles in embroidery) are natural determiners of gender differences in adult roles, with men hunting and farming, women sewing and cooking. This is at least in part related to the issues of gender differences in motor activity (Chapter 5). Our view is that prepuberal physical differences are not large, do not result in very great differentials in children's activity, and are probably not a good rationalization for differences in adult roles (D'Andrade, 1966).

Spatial ability   Females show poorer spatial ability than males do. Tests of spatial ability generally involve testing the ability to visualize three-dimensional objects on the basis of a two-dimensional picture and to do mental rotations and other manipulations on them (see Figure 8.1).

Some researchers have speculated that gender differences in this ability might be due to different childhood experiences, boys playing with erector sets, girls with dolls (Sherman, 1967). However, the exact causes of the gender difference in spatial ability are not yet known. It is interesting to note, however, that gender differences in spatial ability do not appear until adolescence (Maccoby and Jacklin, 1974).

While many occupations do not rely heavily on spatial ability, there are some in which it is very important — for example engineering, technical drawing, and mechanics (Smith, 1964). It might therefore be tempting to attribute the small number of women in these fields to women's relatively low spatial ability. However, the gender difference in spatial ability is not nearly large enough to account for the fact that only 1 percent of the engineers in the United States are women (Bird, 1968; Hyde and Rosenberg, 1976).

FIGURE 8.1

Sample item and solution from a test of spatial ability.

The test below is made up of pictures of blocks turned different ways. The block at the left is the reference block and the five blocks to the right are the answer blocks. One of these five blocks is the same as the reference block except that it has been turned and is seen from a different point of view. The other four blocks could not be obtained by turning the reference block. For example:

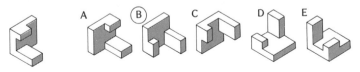

The illustration below shows that "B" is the correct answer.

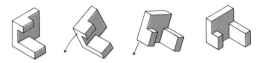

Source: From R. E. Stafford, *Identical Blocks*, form AA, 1962. Used with the permission of R. E. Stafford and Harold Gulliksen.

Mathematical ability   On numerical tests, boys do better, although here again the results are not simple. The differences do not appear consistently in school until age 12–13 (Maccoby and Jacklin, 1974). In early childhood, there seem to be no gender differences (Gesell, 1940). In fact, girls learn to count earlier (that wonderful resource, verbal ability?). Once the differences do appear in school-age children, they seem to most favor boys in tests of numerical *reasoning*, while girls are equal or even superior in numerical *computation* (Anastasi, 1958). This pattern of abilities persists through high school and into adulthood.

Reasoning ability   Once again, there seems to be an absence of gender differences in reasoning ability until adolescence (Maccoby and Jacklin, 1974). Then, the observed gender differences depend on the content of the material. As we have already seen, boys excel in numerical reasoning. However, girls usually excel in tests of verbal reasoning such as analogies (Anastasi, 1958). There is therefore no support for the notion that women are less logical or less rational than men.

Perceptual speed   The ability known as perceptual speed involves being able to perceive details quickly and accurately and to shift attention from one item to the next rapidly. Tests of perceptual speed are generally timed, and involve comparison of two strings of letters or numbers to see whether they are identical (see Figure 8.2). This seems to be the basic aptitude necessary for most forms of clerical work (Andrew and Patterson, 1959).

FIGURE 8.2. Sample items from a test of perceptual speed

Instructions: Compare each line of the COPY at the bottom of the page with the corresponding line of the ORIGINAL at the top. Each *word* or *abbreviation* or *digit* in the copy that is not exactly the same as in the original is one error. In each line, mark every word or abbreviation or figure that is wrong. Then count the errors you have marked in the line and enter the total number in the column at the right. The first line has been done correctly to show you just how to mark and where to enter the total number of errors in the line. Work quickly and accurately.

ORIGINAL

Name	Address	Amount
Dr. Jane Frazier	Madison, Ind.	$7385.96
Mr. Michael Crane	Atlanta, Ga.	1435.64
Dr. Frank Thompson	Troy, N. Y.	2537.96
Miss Mary James	Washington, Conn.	4994.73

COPY

Name	Address	Amount	Number of Errors
~~Miss~~ Jane Fraşier	Madison, ~~Wis.~~	$73$$.96	5
Dr. Michael Crane	Atalanta, Ga.	1434.54	——
Dr. Frank Thomson	Troy, N. J.	2538.96	——
Mrs. Marie Jones	Washington, Conn.	4884.73	——

Source: From *General Clerical Test*. Reproduced by permission. Copyright 1944, renewed 1971, © 1969 by The Psychological Corporation, New York. All rights reserved.

Women are consistently better than men on these tests. In one study, only about 18 percent of men scored equal to or above the median score for women. Even when only clerical workers were tested, only 21 percent of male clerical workers reached or exceeded the median for women clerical workers (Andrew and Patterson, 1959).

This gender difference appears very early — the youngest age group tested has been five-year-olds, and even here girls are superior to boys (Miele, 1958; Gainer, 1962); and the gender difference is consistent at intervening age levels (Schneidler and Patterson, 1942). It therefore seems improbable that gender differences are due to differential practice, since it is hard to believe that five-year-old girls have had more clerical experience than five-year-old boys. Training on perceptual speed problems does not erase gender differences unless only the males are given training (Longstaff, 1954) — that is, through training, males can be brought to the level of untrained females, but if males and females are given equal training, females remain superior in performance.

Artistic and musical abilities   In early childhood, girls draw more detailed figures than boys do. In later years, artistic ability becomes difficult to evaluate because of differences in training. Tests of art appreciation tend to favor women (Anastasi, 1958).

In simple tests of auditory discrimination and memory, there appear to be no gender differences. Women show more aesthetic appreciation of music but differential experience probably plays a major role here. When only subjects with no formal music training are studied, there are no gender differences (Anastasi, 1958).

Whether due to experience or to innate factors, the artistic and musical aptitudes of women have equipped them to have some impact as professionals in the arts, as we shall see in the section on achievement. There are many excellent female authors and musicians. Fortunately, society demands sopranos and altos as well as tenors and basses. In prehistoric times, women may well have invented several art forms, including decorated pottery and patterns in weaving. Interestingly, these woven patterns suggest rather advanced spatial and numerical concepts in the women who created them (Hays, 1964).

Structure of abilities   We have seen evidence of gender differences in the profile of abilities, with women being better in some areas — such as verbal ability and perceptual speed — and men in others — such as spatial and mathematical abilities. The pattern of abilities may affect an individual's organization or structure of abilities. For instance, a female with high overall verbal ability may have more differentiated or specialized verbal abilities (Anastasi, 1970).

These different profiles of abilities may also lead to differences in problem-solving strategies. For instance, an arithmetic story problem might be solved by any one of three strategies — a verbal solution, a numerical solution, or a spatial solution. People generally choose to solve problems in the mode in which their ability is best — that is, they have a preferred strategy. Traditionally, psychologists have concerned themselves only with whether the answer to a particular problem is right or wrong. Recently, they have become more concerned with the ways in which people get the answer. We may find in the future that a male and a female both got the correct answer to a problem, but that the female used a verbal strategy, while the male used a spatial one. Such discoveries will greatly increase our understanding of the cognitive processes of women.

How large are the differences?   We have concluded that there are reliable gender differences in some — though certainly not all — abilities. Of the reliable differences, in verbal, mathematical, and spatial abilities and perceptual speed, how large are the differences between females and males? The answer seems to be, not very large (Sherman, 1978). In fact, they are not large enough to appear reliably in every study. Even in those studies in which they do appear, the difference between the means for males and females is generally small.[2] One implication is that the gender differences are so small as to be irrelevant in practical situations such as job counseling. It would be a great mistake, for example, to urge a high school girl against an engineering career because females on the average are lower than males in spatial ability. The gender difference is far too small to predict that an individual female will not have adequate spatial ability for such a career. A far better indicator would be her own score on a spatial ability test.

COGNITIVE STYLE

Field dependence   Psychologist Herman Witkin and his colleagues (1954, 1964) have carried out a series of experiments from which they conclude that women have a field-dependent style, whereas men are field independent. This contrast has also been termed analytical *versus* global functioning — men are analytical, whereas women are global in their perceptions. Typical of the tests used in these studies is the rod-and-frame test (Figure 8.3). The subject is seated in a dark room facing a luminous rod inside a luminous frame. Both the rod and frame are tilted at an angle, and the subject's task is to adjust the rod to the true vertical. The tilt of the frame serves as a distraction in the task, so that people make errors from the true vertical in adjusting the rod. People who are very accurate in judging the true vertical are called field independent because they have been able to make their judgments independent of the misleading frame or field, while people who make errors are said to be field dependent. Because women make larger errors on the average than men on this test, Witkin infers that women are field dependent, men field independent, in their cognitive styles. It should be noted that this may hold only in visual tests. In other tasks, performed with their eyes closed, women did as well as men.

The interpretation Witkin places on his research is an interesting instance of the large leap of faith that is often made between results and interpretations, particularly when research confirms stereotyped expectations (Chapter 1). Some psychologists are beginning to think that what is essentially a gender difference in susceptibility to an illusion has unjustifiably been interpreted to conform to gender-role stereotypes, namely that women are dependent and men independent.

---

[2] In statistical language, the difference between the means is probably no more than 0.25 SD (standard deviations) (Maccoby and Jacklin, 1974). The gender difference seems to account for only about 1 percent of the variance in verbal ability and 4 percent of the variance in spatial ability (Sherman, 1978).

FIGURE 8.3

The Rod-and-Frame apparatus is used to measure field-dependence and field-independence.

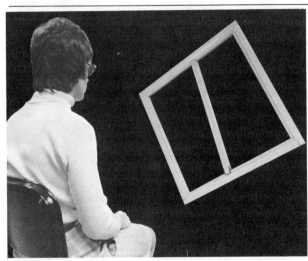

Error in judgment of the true vertical indicates field-dependence.

Accuracy in judgment of the true vertical indicates field-independence.

Source: After Witkin et al., 1954.

On the basis of these criticisms, it is difficult to know what these results on cognitive style mean, except that women and men have different styles of perceiving and processing information, in this instance, when the field or context is misleading.

The Sherman hypothesis   Psychologist Julia Sherman (1967) hypothesized that many of the observed gender differences in abilities and cognitive style are simply due to gender differences in spatial ability. She believed that these spatial-ability differences were in turn due to different early experiences for boys and for girls — that boys' play experiences, for example, gave them a better education in spatial relations.

Where we observe many gender differences in abilities and cognitive style, there may be only one fundamental one. It is particularly likely that this is the case for field dependence-independence, because the content of the embedded-figures test (another test that, like the rod-and-frame test, is used to measure field dependence-independence) is so similar to that of many tests of spatial ability.

There is some evidence backing Sherman's hypothesis. Results indicate that, indeed, when differences in spatial ability are removed, no significant gender differences remain on the rod-and-frame test (Hyde, et al., 1975). Also, gender differences in a test of arithmetic reasoning are eliminated by removing differences in spatial ability.

To summarize, we have seen that there are no gender differences in general intelligence, but there are some differences in special abilities. Girls are superior on tests of verbal ability and perceptual speed, while boys are superior in spatial visualizing ability and mathematical ability. Males tend to be more accurate on the rod-and-frame test, a measure of cognitive style; this result has been used as evidence that males are more analytical than females, but the results are probably due simply to differences in spatial ability.

ACHIEVEMENT

School achievement   At all grade levels, girls consistently get better grades than boys, even in those areas in which boys score higher in ability tests. Gender differences on standardized school achievement tests such as the Stanford Achievement Test closely parallel differences in tested abilities. Boys score higher in science, social studies, and arithmetic reasoning, while girls do better in spelling, language usage, and, less consistently, in arithmetic computation (Anastasi, 1958). The school progress of girls is also superior to that of boys. Girls less frequently have to repeat a grade, and are more frequently accelerated and promoted.

Vocational achievement   Stop for a moment and think of the name of a famous woman scientist. Write it down. Probably at least 90 percent of you wrote "Marie Curie," and the rest of you wrote nothing because you couldn't think of her name. Who else is there?

This illustrates how few women have achieved real eminence in science and how little recognition we give to those who have. (Other examples would have been Anna Freud, Jane Lawick-Goodall, and Margaret Mead.) Standard biographical dictionaries generally show that less than 10 percent of the people who have achieved eminence have been women, and generally more than half of these are listed because they were sovereigns by birthright (Anastasi, 1958) or the wives or mistresses of famous men!

THE STORY OF A GIFTED WOMAN:
BEATRIX POTTER

> Beatrix Potter is best known as the author and illustrator of *The Tale of Peter Rabbit*. But her biography reveals a great deal about the struggles of a gifted woman trying to express her creativity and interest in the field of biology.

She was born in 1866, and by the age of eight, was already carefully drawing and labeling caterpillars. She became particularly interested in fungi, and through her teens and twenties, she devoted as many hours as possible of every day to a search for new species she had not previously observed. She then painted each one that she saw.

By 1894, her studies of fungi and lichens were sufficiently advanced for her to take an interest in research from abroad suggesting that lichens result from symbiosis, a relationship between two organisms in which each is necessary for the other's survival. To test this hypothesis, she enlisted the help of her uncle, a distinguished chemist. On the basis of her research, Potter discovered the intimate interdependency between the fungus and alga which together formed the lichen.

It was through her uncle that she gained her first audience with the scientific establishment. He took her to the Royal Botanic Gardens to present her work. The assistant director was found sorting gums. "I know nothing about fungi," he told them brusquely. "I am exclusively tropical." One after another of the scientists greeted her with apathy. The director dismissed her paintings of fungi as being too artistic to meet scientific criteria.

Although continually rebuffed by the scientific community, she continued her work on lichens, began work on spores, and started drafts of a paper describing her findings. As such, she was the first Britisher to explain the symbiotic relationship involved in a lichen and to begin to understand the germination of spores.

Her uncle became increasingly furious over her rejections by the scientific establishment and determined that her views would be heard. In 1897 a paper entitled "On the Germination of the Spores of Agaricineae" by Helen B. Potter was read to the Linnean Society of London. It was read by a friend; Beatrix Potter was not present because only men were allowed to attend the meetings.

But the prospects for her work to be appreciated remained nonexistent. Two years later she gave up her study of spores, finding the response of children to the books she wrote and illustrated to be much more satisfying. Her first book, complete with illustrations, was about a rabbit. Unable to get a publisher, she paid to have it printed. *The Tale of Peter Rabbit* has been on the list of children's bestsellers ever since its publication 70 years ago. Many of the psychological themes of Potter's own life are reflected in the characters, most notably frustration, a sense of being kept from a desired goal. For example, Peter Rabbit can't roam the garden at will because of the upraised rake of the pursuing gardener, MacGregor. Gifted in both science and art, Beatrix Potter finally found a socially acceptable, gender-appropriate way to express her creativity, by writing and illustrating children's books.

At the age of 47 she married, for the first time, a lawyer and spent her last 30 years living happily in the country. One wonders what great contributions she might have made to science had she not been so thwarted in her efforts.

Source: Naomi Gilpatrick. "The Secret Life of Beatrix Potter." *Natural History*, 81(8) (1972), p. 38.

An early statistical study of eminent women, collecting a total of 868 names representing 42 nations and extending from the seventh century B.C. to 1913, showed that the largest number (38 percent) had achieved eminence in literature. Women's high verbal ability has apparently been put to some use. However, the highest degree of eminence (as measured by the number of lines allotted in the biographical dictionaries) was obtained by sovereigns, political leaders, and mothers and mistresses of eminent men. Women achieved eminence in a number of other non-intellectual ways, such as tragic fate, beauty, and being immortalized in literature (Castle, 1913).

Even in fields traditionally assigned to women, the top-ranking, most prestigious positions are held by men. We have already seen that women express more aesthetic appreciation for art, yet most of the eminent artists are men. Professional interior decorating and clothing design are dominated by men. The world's great chefs are men.

In more recent years, there still remains a gap between the accomplishments of women and of men. In 1968, 3 percent of American lawyers were women, as were 7 percent of American doctors (Bird, 1968). In a 1965 sample from *Who's Who in America*, women comprised only 4.5 percent of the listings, down from 8.5 percent in 1925 (Chafetz, 1974, p. 132.) Women more frequently distinguished themselves in the arts, while men did so in business. Certainly a contemporary study like Castle's would have a host of interesting characters to add to the list — Indira Gandhi, Golda Meir, Eleanor Roosevelt, Jane Lawick-Goodall, Margaret Mead, Isadora Duncan, and Coco Chanel, to name a few.

Studying the adult achievements of women labeled as gifted during the school years provides some insight into the "gap at the top" syndrome. The Stanford Gifted Child Study (Terman and Oden, 1947) is perhaps the most extensive research of its kind. More than 600 children with IQ's above 135 (which represents the upper 1 percent of the population) were identified in the California schools. Their progress was then followed into adulthood. The adult occupations of the women, whose childhood IQ's were in the same range as the men's, were on the whole undistinguished. Few became professionals. While IQ showed a fairly close relationship to accomplishment among men, it showed essentially no relationship among women. In fact, two thirds of the women with IQ's 170 or above (certainly at the genius level) were housewives or office workers. One cannot help but be struck by the enormous waste of resources this represents.

In summary, in terms of achievement, girls surpass boys in school achievement in all areas, but in terms of professional achievement, females lag behind males. This deficit in achievement is particularly surprising in view of the high verbal abilities of females and their school successes; it is probably a result of a variety of forces including discrimination and gender-role socialization. In later sections of this chapter we shall explore various motivational factors that may also help to account for the lesser professional achievements of women.

GIFTED WOMEN

The professional woman   How many women Ph.D.'s are there? What is the female Ph.D. like? Is she less productive than her male colleagues in terms of papers and books published, scholarly research, and professional participation? What are some of the psychological characteristics of these women? Are children a hindrance to them? A survey by Simon et al. (1967) provides considerable information on these points.

The percentage of Ph.D.'s who are women varies a great deal from one field to another. Slightly more than 20 percent of the Ph.D.'s in psychology are earned by women.

A common finding of the classic literature in differential psychology is that women Ph.D.'s are less productive than their male counterparts. However, according to the Simon survey, the notion that many of these women are employed part time or not at all, and that they are less productive than their male colleagues is a myth without support. The survey found that 96 percent of the unmarried women and 87 percent of the married women with no children worked full time. Even among the married women with children, 60 percent worked full time, and 25 percent part time.

Professional productivity was measured by the number of articles and books published. Using this index, there appears to be no difference in productivity between men and women Ph.D.'s. While there are differences in the patterns in different fields, combining the data across all fields indicates that 58 percent of all the men surveyed had published at least one article, 58 percent of the unmarried women had done this, as had 66 percent of the married women. Approximately 23 percent of the men had published at least one book, as had 21 percent of the unmarried and 20 percent of the married women. The mean number of articles published was 5.2 for men, 4.1 for unmarried women, and 5.3 for married women.

One of the most striking facts about these professional women was that only 50 percent of them were married, as opposed to a marriage rate of about 90 percent among their male colleagues. On the other hand, it did not appear that marriage or children were serious hindrances to the professional lives of those women who were employed full time (those employed only part time or not at all were not included in the productivity figures). In fact, there was a slight tendency for the married women to produce *more* than their male colleagues, whereas the unmarried women produced slightly less.

This survey provided less evidence of pay or promotion discrimination than have others (such as Astin and Bayer, 1972). The authors estimated that the men earned on the average about $700 per year more than the women — a difference, but a smaller one than many other studies report. Simon et al. suggest that the crucial areas in which these women, largely in colleges and universities, experience discrimination are more subtle than pay and promotion, and involve factors like prestige and acceptance among their colleagues. The female Ph.D. may be left with a feeling that she is a member of a minority group that has not yet gained acceptance.

The creative personality in females   What is the successful, achieving, creative woman like? Is she a mannish distortion of femininity? Is she unhappy and lonely? Is she filled with frustrations and conflicts?

In recent years, there have been two theoretical approaches to the creative personality in women. Many of the popular writers on women, such as Margaret Mead and Simone de Beauvoir, have suggested that women become creative and productive by becoming masculine. They say that the inhibition of aggression found in most women is a handicap. In order to be successful and creative, women must throw off the shackles of femininity and start acting more like men. An opposing view is the MacKinnon repression theory which says that masculine women repress their femininity, and that this repression will lead to a lack of creative spontaneity (Helson, 1966). In response to the philosophy that femininity *per se* damages creativity and productivity, it is surprising that we find that more feminine men are more creative on the average. It may be instructive to look at some of the empirical data that have been gathered on the personalities of creative women.

Psychologist Ravenna Helson (1966) has studied the personalities of college women with artistic and imaginative interests, and has identified what she calls the imaginative-artistic (IA) syndrome associated with creativity. Women who conform to this syndrome seem to mistrust personal relationships. They are impulsive, rebellious, have a strong investment in their own inner lives, and are independent in making judgments. They are not masculine, nor have they taken an overall masculine identification. They are not dominant individuals. Instead, they show a goal-directed pattern of effort that is conducted in a feminine way. That is, they express their creativity in a way that is a compromise with existing social norms. In seeking to encourage creativity in women, Helson suggests not that their masculine tendencies be encouraged, but rather that working conditions be made more congenial to them and that better incentives to their productivity be offered.

In another study, Helson (1971) looked at the personalities of creative women mathematicians. The traits most characteristic of these women, as compared with their less creative counterparts, were rebellious independence, narcissism, introversion, and a rejection of outside influence; strong symbolic interests and a marked ability to find self-expression and self-gratification in directed research activity; and flexibility both in general attitudes and in mathematical work. Lest these women seem unduly bizarre, it should be noted that these traits have all been ascribed to the creative person, whether male or female. While they seem to appear more clearly in women mathematicians than in men mathematicians, it could well be argued that the women manifested the essential characteristics of the creative person. It is interesting that these characteristics seem more abnormal or less admirable in women than in men.

The Queen Bee syndrome   A very interesting phenomenon characteristic of some highly sucecssful professional women has recently been documented: the "Queen Bee syndrome" (Staines et al., 1974). Some female antifeminists have the characteristics typical of people who resist social change: they are politically conservative, religious, less educated, and older. However there is another group of female antifeminists with quite different characteristics: they are successful professionals in a man's world. They are the Uncle Toms of the women's movement, women who try to keep other women down, even though they are in a position to advance women's cause.

The Queen Bee rejects the feminist notion that many of women's problems are external in origin, the result of political and economic discrimination. Instead, she believes that the system is open and fair and that an individual succeeds on his or her own merits. If *she* can make it, then so can other women. Women who don't make it have no one but themselves to blame. Because of her belief in individual determinants of success, she also rejects the collective strategies of the women's movement for effecting social change.

The Queen Bee also generally is a "supermother," achieving not only in her career but also in the traditional feminine role of wife and mother. Her dedication to these traditional virtues is so strong as to appear almost defensive. Queen Bees are more likely, as compared with a control group of traditional women and another control group of feminists, to say that their husband's job has priority over theirs and to agree that children of working mothers tend to be maladjusted.

There are several possible explanations for this striking phenomenon. First, Queen Bees have been co-opted by the establishment. The first few members of minorities who are admitted to organizations are often co-opted. The system tolerates countermilitants most easily, and these few "tokens" are rewarded for not rocking the boat. Indeed, their success may almost be conditional on their countermilitancy. The Queen Bee's status and acceptance may be somewhat precarious, being dependent on her not adopting a militant stance. Second, the Queen Bee's antifeminism is a means of excluding the competition. Being the only successful woman around can be a lot of fun. Newer, younger women entering the ranks may take away her special, unique status. In addition, the Queen Bee may have had to overcome many obstacles to achieve her position, and therefore hates to see other women attain rank without the initiation rites. Hence, she has little interest in promoting the entry of women into her profession and indeed may make some efforts to keep them out. Finally, the Queen Bee is getting a lot of rewards from the system as it is. She is praised for being so feminine, yet thinking like a man. The status quo is comfortable for her, and she can be expected to have little animosity toward a system that rewards her so well.

In the context of the psychology of women, the Queen Bee syndrome is distressing yet not too surprising. Certainly it can at least in part be traced to the femininity-achievement double-bind. The Queen Bee has found one means for resolving this bind — or perhaps her solution represents no resolution at all. Staines et al. conclude on a hopeful note that the incidence of this syndrome may be decreasing and it is probably not very common to begin with. Certainly one hopes that as women begin to understand their own psychology better, such syndromes will be avoided.

ACHIEVEMENT MOTIVATION

A striking paradox has emerged in this chapter. Women start out life with good abilities, yet they end up in adulthood with lower status and less achievement than men. Little girls have better verbal ability than little boys, and in this age of rhetoric we should certainly appreciate the importance of verbal ability. Girls also have better fine motor coordination, and in a technological age, this is certainly more useful than brute strength. Girls also do much better in school. Yet in adulthood we find them in unpaid occupations such as being housewives, or in unrewarding ones such as being clerks. Why?

There is currently a high consciousness about discrimination against women, and certainly discrimination is an important source of women's low achievement. (See Chapter 6 for a more complete discussion.)

However, we believe that discrimination on the basis of gender is not the entire answer to "why women fail." Society has subtler ways of achieving its goals, in which women may internalize low drives to achieve, and may perpetuate this pattern in other women. Some of the personality factors that may act on women's achievements are achievement motivation, the motive to avoid success, and expectations about success. We shall examine these processes in women in the following sections.

The *achievement motive* is the desire to accomplish something of value or importance through one's own efforts, to meet standards of excellence in what one does. There are several methods for measuring this.

The most commonly used is a projective technique in which subjects' stories in response to an ambiguous cue are scored for achievement imagery (McClelland et al., 1953). Subjects are shown a series of pictures and are asked to write a story about each picture after being told that this is a test of creative imagination. They are told to cover such questions as: What is happening? What has led up to this situation? What will happen? What is being thought? One of the pictures shows a young man standing on a sidewalk with a broom in his hand, looking off into the distance. Below are two stories written by different subjects about this picture:

> The boy works in the grocery store. He has just graduated from high school and hasn't enough money to go to college. He is standing there thinking about how long it will take him to save enough to get his education. He doesn't want to remain a store clerk all his life, and wants to make something of himself.

> It seems that this young man has been told by his father to clean up the sidewalk. This has prevented him from going off to the beach for the day with his pals. He is watching them go off in their car and is feeling left out and sore at his father.

The first story would be scored as indicating a high achievement motive, while the second indicates a low achievement motive.

Most of the classic literature on gender differences asserts that females have a lower level of achievement motivation than males (Tyler, 1965; Hoffman, 1972). These gender differences are of considerable interest because achievement motivation is related to achievement behaviors such as test performance and occupational choice. Thus, the lower achievement motivation of females might help to explain their lesser occupational achievement, and might therefore represent a kind of "internalized barrier to achievement." Theories were constructed to explain the developmental forces, such as socialization, that might lead females to have low achievement motivation (Hoffman, 1972). It was also believed that, while females were not motivated for achievement, they were motivated by social concerns, or by a *need for affiliation*. That is, females were thought to be motivated not by internalized standards of excellence (achievement motivation), but rather by a desire for approval from other people (Hoffman, 1972). Indeed, some authors even suggested that girls' achievement behavior (for example school achievement) was not motivated by achievement motivation as it was for boys, but rather by a need for affiliation (the teacher's approval).

There is a need to reassess these results, however. From a review of available research, there actually appears to be little evidence for lower achievement motivation in females (Maccoby and Jacklin, 1974). The results are complex because achievement motivation may be tested under any of several conditions. In the simplest case (the "neutral" or "relaxed" condition), subjects are simply given the test. Under such conditions, females actually show higher achievement motivation than males. The test may also be given under "achievement arousal" conditions. For example, before taking the test, subjects might be given an anagrams test that they are told measures not only intelligence, but also capacity to organize and to evaluate situations quickly and accurately, and to be a leader. Under these conditions, males' achievement motivation increases sharply, while females' does not. These results indicate that females generally have a high level of achievement motivation, but that certain situations — for example, competitive ones — do not arouse their achievement motivation as they do males'. We shall return to this idea when we discuss the motive to avoid success in the next section. Gender differences in achievement motivation appear to depend on the situation in which the motive is measured.

Gender differences in achievement motivation also probably depend on age and stage of development. While females may generally have a high level of achievement motivation, at various periods of a woman's life achievement may become anxiety provoking, so that she temporarily suppresses her achievement motivation (Bardwick, 1971). For instance, a girl who, because of a strong desire to go to medical school and become a doctor, has earned straight A's through her junior year in college, suddenly meets the man of her dreams. He has no plans for being married to a doctor, but rather wants a competent wife, housewife, and mother for his children. So she abandons all medical school plans. However, after her children are all in school, she may revive her educational goals and become a successful professional. Achievement may have been very anxiety-provoking to the young woman when she was of marriageable age, but having "accomplished" the female role, she may again express achievement motivation, and achievement can then become a source of satisfaction. Probably this relationship of achievement motivation to stage of development, as well as the failure of females to increase their achievement motivation under competitive situations, are results of the perceived incompatibility of femininity and achievement (see Chapter 6).

The belief in women's need for affiliation also needs reassessment (Maccoby and Jacklin, 1974; Stein and Bailey, 1973). This belief was based on the notion that females are more sensitive to interpersonal reinforcement; yet available research does not indicate that this is true. Much of what appears to be affiliative needs in females may actually be achievement needs expressed in a gender-appropriate fashion. Thus the traditional housewife may be highly motivated to be an outstanding cook and to throw fantastic dinner parties not because of her needs for social approval, but because this is a socially acceptable, gender-appropriate means of expressing her very real achievement strivings. She is displaying achievement that is gender-appropriate for women.

In summary, females appear to have high levels of achievement motivation on the average. This motivation, however, is not aroused by achievement-arousal conditions, as is the case with males. Gender differences in achievement motivation appear to depend on the situation in which they are tested, as well as on the stage of development.

MOTIVE TO AVOID SUCCESS

In 1969 Matina Horner reported on the results of research on an anxiety about success called *motive to avoid success* or *fear of success*, among bright, high-achieving women.

In attempting to understand the basis of gender differences in achievement motivation, Horner first observed that achievement situations, such as test taking, are more anxiety-provoking for females than for males. In order to measure this phenomenon, Horner devised a projective test in which subjects were asked to complete a story that begins: "After first-term finals, Anne (John) finds herself (himself) at the top of her (his) medical-school class." Females wrote about Anne, males about John.

Males' stories generally indicated happiness and feelings of satisfaction over achievement. For example:

> John is a conscientious young man who worked hard. He is pleased with himself. John has always wanted to go into medicine and is very dedicated. . . . John continues working hard and eventually graduates at the top of his class.

Females' responses, on the other hand, were often bizarre:

> Anne starts proclaiming her surprise and joy. Her fellow classmates are so disgusted with her behavior that they jump on her in a body and beat her. She is maimed for life.

The negative imagery expressed by females generally fell into one of three categories — fear of social rejection, worries about maintaining womanhood, and denial of the reality of success. For example:

Social rejection fears:

> Anne is an acne-faced bookworm. She runs to the bulletin board and finds she's at the top. As usual she smarts off. A chorus of groans is the rest of the class's reply . . .

Worries about womanhood:

> Unfortunately Anne no longer feels so certain that she really wants to be a doctor. She is worried about herself and wonders if perhaps she isn't normal . . . Anne decides not to continue with her medical work but to take courses that have a deeper personal meaning for her.

Denial of reality:

> Anne is a code name of a nonexistent person created by a group of medical students. They take turns writing exams for Anne.

In her sample of undergraduates at the University of Michigan, Horner found that 65 percent of the females, as compared with less than 10 percent of the males, told stories that fell into one of these three categories.

This motivational variable also seems to be related to performance (Horner, 1972; Karabenick and Marshall, 1974). When put in a competitive situation, females who did not show fear of success improved their scores over those they achieved when working individually, while females high in fear of success did worse in competition. The motive to avoid success, then, seems to be aroused in achieving, competitive situations. Attitudes of male peers are also important in evoking it (Horner, 1972). While all the females in the sample were intellectually talented, most of those high in fear of success were majoring in humanities and planned traditional careers such as housewife or teacher; those who were low in fear of success aspired to graduate degrees and careers in scientific areas like math and physics.

Presumably the motive to avoid success is related to the perceived conflict between achievement and femininity and the perceived connection between achievement and aggressiveness, which is also gender-inappropriate for females. Thus, for women, the rewards of achievement are contaminated by the accompanying anxiety.

Horner collected her original data in 1965 for her doctoral dissertation. The results were published in a 1969 *Psychology Today* article. They attracted quite a bit of attention, to put it mildly. The New York *Times* and other newspapers featured stories about the research. The article was reprinted a number of times and was required reading for many students. The research was — and is — appealing for a number of reasons. It appeared just at the time of rising interest in women and the women's movement. In particular, it seemed to offer a sensible explanation for why more women had not succeeded in high-status occupations — they simply feared success.

In the cold light of day some 10 or 15 years later, the research doesn't seem to provide the surefire answers it originally did. Horner's research has been criticized on a number of grounds (Tresemer, 1974; Shaver, 1976; Zuckerman and Wheeler, 1975): (1) Other studies using Horner's techniques often find men having as much or more fear-of-success imagery than women. Therefore there is no reason to believe that the motive to avoid success is found only in women, or even that it is more frequent in women. If that is the case, then it cannot be used to explain the lesser occupational achievements of women.[3] (2) Anne's success was in a gender-

---

[3] The failure to find gender differences in motive to avoid success in other studies cannot be explained by the fact that they occurred later, when gender-role standards became liberated. There appears to be no trend over time as to which studies show women having more fear of success and which don't (Zuckerman and Wheeler, 1975).

inappropriate field, namely medical school. Therefore the research may not indicate a generalized fear of success, but rather a fear of being successful at something that is gender-inappropriate. Perhaps if Anne had been doing well in nursing school, she would not evoke much anxiety. One study has shown just that (Cherry and Deaux, 1978). (3) Women are responding to another woman, Anne, not themselves, in writing the stories. Perhaps they feel anxious about Anne's success, but would not feel anxious about their own success. (4) In technical language, Horner's technique confounds gender of subjects with the gender of the stimulus cue. That is, women write about Anne, men about John. From this, we cannot tell whether women are higher in fear of success than men, or whether successful women (cues) arouse more anxiety than successful men. Perhaps if men wrote about Anne, they too would indicate bizarre reactions to her. In fact, one study has shown that to be exactly what happens (Monahan et al., 1974). This suggests that Horner's techniques may simply be measuring cultural stereotypes about women rather than murky unconscious conflicts.

Where does this leave us? Is there a motive to avoid success that keeps some women from achieving, or that at least makes them miserable if they do? Our intuitive feeling is that there probably is such a phenomenon, but we also must say that there is not much scientific evidence for it. In Chapter 1, we noted that one of the critical steps in psychological research is *measurement*. That is, when a researcher has some phenomenon to study, she or he must first devise a way to measure it. In Horner's case, she chose to measure the motive to avoid success by using a *projective test*. The idea is that subjects are given an ambiguous cue. Their stories about that cue presumably reflect a projection of their own unconscious motives. Most psychologists now consider projective tests to be poor methods of measurement, and might prefer some more direct method, perhaps a paper-and-pencil checklist (such as Bem used in measuring androgyny, as discussed in Chapter 4). Our feeling is that the motive to avoid success probably exists, but no one has been able to measure it adequately as yet (Macdonald and Hyde, 1979).

WHEN A WOMAN SUCCEEDS
IT IS JUST LUCK

Suppose a college woman gets an A on a calculus exam. When she thinks about her success, or when others think about it, what will they believe caused it? To what will they attribute her success? This is called the *attribution process*, and it has been studied in detail by social psychologists. Typically four kinds of causes have been studied: ability, effort, luck, and task ease. Applied to the example given here, people might think that the woman got an A because of her own high mathematical ability, because she studied hard (effort), simply because she was lucky, or because the exam was easy. These four kinds of causes can be further categorized into two groups, those attributing the event to *internal* sources (factors within the individual, that is, ability and effort) and those attributing the event to *external* sources (forces outside the individual, that is, luck and task ease).

There do appear to be important gender differences in attributions. Women are more likely than men to attribute their success to external sources, in particular luck; men, in contrast, attribute success to their own abilities (Deaux and Farris, 1974, cited in Deaux, 1976; Feather, 1969; McMahan, 1972; Simon and Feather, 1973). This is also true if people explain the performance of another person; they generally think that a woman succeeds because of luck, and that a man succeeds because of his skill or ability (Deaux and Emswiller, 1974). In short, when a woman succeeds, everyone thinks it was just luck.

What about the other side of the story, failure? Here the results are not so consistent as they are for success, but there seems to be some tendency for women to be more likely than men to attribute failure to internal sources, namely to their own lack of abilities (McMahan, 1971, 1972; but see Feather, 1969). The general pattern appears to be, then, that when women fail, it reaffirms their belief in their own lack of abilities; and when they succeed, they can't believe it was due to their own abilities, and instead attribute it to luck.

Recall a related result discussed in Chapter 5. It has been found that women have lower expectations for success than men do, for a wide variety of tasks and age groups (Crandall, 1969). Indeed, this gender difference has been discovered as early as the preschool years. Further, people with high expectations of success tend to do better. For example, when people are randomly assigned to high-expectancy and low-expectancy groups, the high-expectancy group tends to perform better (Tyler, 1958). Therefore, women may achieve less because they expect to achieve less.

There appears to be a rather insidious, self-fulfilling prophecy or multiplier effect operating here. Females expect not to do well, which promotes not doing well. When females fail, it reinforces their belief in their own lack of abilities, further lowering their expectation of success and making success less likely. When females succeed, they attribute it to luck, and thus expectations of their own success are not increased. Indeed, this may help to explain why the consistent school successes of girls as compared with boys do not create high expectations of further success among girls — success is interpreted as being due to luck. It should be noted, of course, that we are talking about average differences between females and males. Certainly there are women who take pleasure in successes and attribute them to their own abilities. But women, on the average, are more likely to attribute success to luck and to have low expectations for future success. Certainly these are further internalized sources — as the motive to avoid success may also be — contributing to women's lack of achievement.

It is important to recognize the situational and social factors influencing these phenomena. As noted above, in competitive situations women have lower expectations for success than men do; however, in noncompetitive situations, women state expectancies similar to men's (House, 1974). These results parallel those for achievement motivation noted earlier in this chapter. Women's achievement motivation is as high or higher than men's in neutral situations, but men's becomes higher when competition is involved. Apparently women's gender-role concerns are more prominent when the situation involves competition.

Conclusion   In this chapter we reviewed evidence on gender differences in abilities, noting that females are superior in some areas (verbal ability, perceptual speed) and males are better in others (mathematical ability, spatial ability). Girls do better in school, yet men's adult achievements in the world of work exceed those of women's. There is a disparity, then, between the abilities and school achievement of females, on one hand, and their adult work achievements on the other.

Two general classes of factors help to explain this discrepancy: external[4] barriers to achievement, and internal (or intrapsychic) barriers to achievement. External barriers are factors such as job discrimination and, as noted in Chapter 6, there is ample evidence that this exists, both in obvious and subtle forms. Internal barriers or intrapsychic factors — such as low achievement motivation in competitive situations, motive to avoid success, low expectations for success, and particular patterns of causal attributions — also seem to exist. Of course, the internal barriers may be caused by external forces; for example, a woman may have low expectations for success on her job because she has experienced job discrimination. Thus, a combination of external and internal factors is important in explaining the lesser achievements of women. It is also important to recognize both sets of factors when trying to bring about the social change necessary to allow women to achieve more.

---

[4] The use of *external* and *internal* here should not be confused with the language of external and internal used in discussing causal attributions earlier in this chapter.

9

WOMEN AND LANGUAGE

Women are the decorative sex. They never have anything to say, but they say it charmingly.

OSCAR WILDE

Suppose that you found the following caption, torn from a cartoon: "That sunset is such a lovely shade of lavender, isn't it?" If you had to guess the gender of the speaker, what would you say? Most people would guess that the speaker was a woman. Most of us have ideas about what is "appropriate" speech for males and females, and "lovely" and "lavender" just don't sound like things that a man would (or should) say. In this chapter we shall explore the evidence on the difference between how women and men speak and communicate nonverbally, and on how women are treated in the English language.

GENDER DIFFERENCES IN LANGUAGE USE

Stereotypes   The example given above illustrates certain stereotypes about men's and women's speech — namely, that women use adjectives like "lovely" and "lavender" and men don't. Exactly what *are* the stereotypes concerning women's and men's speech?

Cheris Kramer (1974, 1976) investigated this question by analyzing 156 cartoons containing adult human speech from 13 consecutive issues of *The New Yorker*. In addition, she had 25 female and 25 male students indicate, for each caption, whether they thought a man or a woman had said it. Kramer later expanded her study to include cartoons from *Ladies Home Journal*, *Playboy*, and *Cosmopolitan*. She found that male characters were more likely to swear, while female characters were more apt to use adjectives such as "nice" and "pretty." Generally men's speech was stronger than women's, with more exclamations and harsh words. Male speakers were more likely to be putting down someone, while when a woman spoke, it was likely that her words were themselves the joke. Students had no trouble identifying which lines had been spoken by males and which by females. Stereotyped identifications could be made in about 75 percent of the cases. Students of both genders stereotyped women's speech as stupid, vague, emotional, confused, and wordy. Men's speech was characterized as logical, concise, businesslike, and controlled.

With these stereotypes in mind, do they indicate "real" differences between men's and women's speech? What evidence exists on the actual speech patterns of women and men?

Correctness   There is some indication that women's speech tends to be more "correct" than men's (Thorne and Henley, 1975, p. 17). For example, in one study of the pronunciation of words ending in "-ing," males pronounced it "in'" 62 percent of the time, compared with only 29 percent for females (Shuy, 1969). Generally, it seems that females' speech is closer to the normative speech of their culture, while males' is more likely to contain errors or subcultural forms (Kramer, 1974).

Tag questions   Linguist Robin Lakoff (1973) originally hypothesized that women use more tag questions than men. A tag question is a short phrase at the end of a declarative sentence that turns it into a question. An example would be "This is a great game, isn't it?"

More recently, data have been collected to see whether Lakoff's ideas are correct (McMillan et al., 1977). College students participated in a group problem-solving task in either same-gender or mixed-gender groups of five to seven people. The discussions, which involved solving a mystery and lasted thirty minutes, were tape recorded, and later were coded and analyzed by the experimenters. They found that the women used about twice as many tag questions as the men, a difference that was statistically significant.

Using the terminology of Chapter 1, we have a statistical result that women use significantly more tag questions than men do. How should that finding be interpreted? The standard interpretation has been that men's lesser tendency to use tag questions indicates the self-confidence and forcefulness of their speech. Women's greater tendency to use them is interpreted as indicating uncertainty or weak patterns of speech. As Lakoff put it,

> These sentence types provide a means whereby a speaker can avoid committing himself, and thereby avoid coming into conflict with the addressee. The problem is that, by so doing, a speaker may also give the impression of not being really sure of himself, of looking to the addressee for confirmation, even of having no views of his own. (1975, pp. 16–17)

This interpretation implies that women's speech is somehow deficient, reflecting undesirable traits such as uncertainty. Are other interpretations possible? To interpret this difference in a way that would be more favorable to women, we might say that the tag question is intended to encourage communication, rather than to shut things off with a simple declarative statement. The tag question encourages the other person to express an opinion. Rather than reflecting uncertainty, women's greater use of tag questions may reflect greater interpersonal sensitivity and warmth (McMillan et al., 1977).

The researchers in the experiment discussed above attempted to determine which of these interpretations was more accurate (McMillan et al., 1977). They did this by comparing the use of tag questions in same-gender versus mixed-gender groups. They reasoned that, if tag questions reflect uncertainty, then women should use more tag questions when men are present (mixed-gender groups) than when only women are present (all-female groups). This hypothesis was confirmed by the data, thus supporting the "greater female uncertainty" interpretation. However, men also used more tag questions in mixed-gender groups than they did in all-male groups. The researchers had not hypothesized this, as it did not seem that men should be more uncertain when women were present. Thus the interpretation of this gender difference is still unclear, and more sophisticated experiments will be necessary before a definitive statement can be made. The more important point to keep in mind, however, is that often alternative interpretations, one favoring men, the other favoring women, can be made of the same statistical results.

Intonation   Say the phrase "Are you coming?" in a number of different ways. By varying the way you say it, you can convey a variety of feelings, from cheerful politeness to stern irritation. This is done by varying the intonation pattern, that is, the combination of high pitches plus low pitches.

Studies indicate that females and males tend to use somewhat different intonation patterns (Brend, 1971; McConnell-Ginet, 1978). Women are more likely to use intonation patterns of surprise, unexpectedness, cheerfulness, and politeness. Further, men have only three contrasting levels of pitch in their intonation, whereas women have four; the additional level that women have is the highest one. The distinctive intonation patterns used by women are probably advantageous in allowing them to express a wider range of emotions. However, they may also contribute to women's speech appearing overly emotional and high-pitched.

Interruptions   Researchers have repeatedly found that men interrupt women considerably more often than women interrupt men (McMillan et al., 1977; Zimmerman and West, 1975). To give an idea of the magnitude of the difference, some data from one study are shown in Table 9.1. Notice that women interrupt women about as often as men interrupt men. However, women very seldom interrupt men, while men quite frequently interrupt women.

Once again, we have a statistical result that men interrupt women considerably more than women interrupt men. How should this gender difference be interpreted? The typical interpretation made by feminist social scientists involves the assumption that interruptions are an expression of *power* or *dominance*. That is, the interrupter gains control of a conversation, and that is a kind of interpersonal power. The gender difference, then, is interpreted as indicating that men are expressing power and dominance over women. This pattern may reflect the subtle persistence of traditional gender roles; it may also help to perpetuate traditional roles.

This power interpretation will also be discussed in the section on nonverbal communication later in this chapter. Such interpretations have become central to feminist research and theory.

Total talking time   The stereotype is that women talk a lot more than men. Women are reputedly always gabbing on the telephone or over the back fence. In the study of cartoon captions discussed at the beginning of this chapter, women's speech was characterized by students as being "wordy" (Kramer, 1974, 1976).

What about the empirical data? Is this stereotype a real difference? In fact, there does seem to be a real difference, but it is just the opposite of the stereotype. In terms of total talking time, men talk more than women (Swacker, 1975; Argyle et al., 1968; Strodtbeck et al., 1957).

Other differences   Some other gender differences in speech have been documented. For example, males use more hostile verbs than females do (Gilley and Collier, 1970). Women say more supportive words, such as *mm hmm* (Hirschmann, 1974, cited in Thorne and Henley, 1975, p. 231; Fishman, 1978). Generally, the differences fall along the lines one would expect from gender-role stereotypes.

The gender differences in language use that we have discussed seem to be found rather consistently. Indeed, male-female differences in language are found in all cultures around the world (Bodine, 1975). Nonetheless, it is important not to overestimate the extent of the differences. In many ways, females and males use essentially the same vocabulary and grammar. Thus, while certain features of male and female language differ, it would be unwise to say that there are separate female and male languages. Gender similarities are the rule in language just as they are in other behaviors (Kramer et al., 1978).

TABLE 9.1.   Mean number of interruptions per half hour, according to gender of interrupter and gender of interruptee in mixed-gender groups

Gender of Interruptee	Gender of Interrupter	
	Female	Male
Female	2.50	5.24
Male	0.93	2.36

Source: McMillan et al., 1977.

BODY LANGUAGE:
NONVERBAL COMMUNICATION

The popularizers of the "body language" concept have pointed out the fact that we often communicate far more with our body than with the words we speak. For example, suppose you say the sentence "How nice to see you" while standing only six inches from another person or while actually brushing up against them. Then imagine, in contrast, that you say the sentence while standing three feet from the person. The sentence conveys a much different meaning in the two instances. In the first, it will probably convey warmth and possibly sexiness. In the second case, the meaning will seem much more formal and cold. As another example, a sentence coming from a smiling face conveys a much different meaning than the same sentence coming from a stern or frowning face.

Here we shall see what evidence there is on whether there are differences between women and men in nonverbal styles of communication, and what those differences mean.

The politics of touch   Studies consistently show that men touch women considerably more frequently than women touch men (Henley, 1973; Jourard, 1966). Having demonstrated the existence of a gender difference, we must now proceed to an interpretation of its significance.

Feminist scientists have interpreted this particular gender difference as a reflection of dominance relations between men and women, with men expressing dominance by touching women, which in turn reinforces women's subordinate role (Henley, 1973, 1975). Below we shall outline some of the theorizing and data that lead to and support that interpretation.

In his essay "The Nature of Deference and Demeanor," Erving Goffman (1956) argued that, between a superior and a subordinate, relations will be asymmetrical. That is, the superior will have the right to certain familiarities with the subordinate that the subordinate is not allowed to reciprocate. Goffman further argued that touch by one person to another operates in this way. As an example, he considered the status system in a hospital, where doctors (the superiors) touch patients (the subordinates), but the reverse would seem unreasonable and presumptuous. Certainly there are many other examples. The boss puts his hand on the secretary's shoulder while giving her instructions, but she scarcely puts her hand on his shoulder when she returns the typed letters. Age, too, is a status dimension, with adults having status over children. We see adults walk up to a baby and stroke its cheek or tickle its sides, liberties they would scarcely take with another adult.

Psychologist Nancy Henley (1973) did the original research and theorizing suggesting that these principles apply to relations between women and men — namely, that touch is a means by which men express dominance over women. In her original study, an observer spent 60 hours recording instances of touching in places such as a shopping center, a bank, and a college campus. For each instance, the gender, age, and approximate socioeconomic status of the two persons involved were recorded. Of the 28 instances of touch between people of approximately equal age and socioeconomic status, 23 involved a man touching a woman, while only five involved a woman touching a man. Thus men do touch women considerably more than women touch men. To verify the dominance interpretation of this result, Henley examined the touch relationships along the other dimensions — both of which are status indicators — namely, socioeconomic status (SES) and age. Regarding SES, there were fourteen cases in which the toucher was of higher status than the person being touched, while there were only five cases in which the toucher was judged to be of lower status. The results were similar for age. In 36 cases the

FIGURE 9.1

Men touch women more than the reverse, which may be an expression of power and dominance.

Source: Photo by Antonio Mendoza / The Picture Cube.

toucher was judged to be at least ten years older than the person being touched, while there were only seven cases in which the toucher was at least ten years younger than the person being touched. From Henley's study it would be reasonable to conclude that (1) there is a gender difference in touching, with men touching women more than the reverse, and (2) higher-status, dominant individuals tend to touch lower-status, subordinate individuals more than the reverse.

A recent study provides further confirmation and elaboration of Henley's conclusions (Summerhayes and Suchner, 1978). Subjects were shown photographs of female-male interactions and were asked to rate the extent to which each person dominated the interaction. The photographs varied along two dimensions: the status differences between the two people as indicated by their age and dress (female higher, versus equal, versus male higher), and who was touching whom (female toucher, versus no touching, versus male toucher). They found that when either a man or a woman touches another person, the effect is to reduce the perceived dominance of the person being touched. They even found that lower-status women could reduce the status of higher-status men by touching them. In some of the interactions, however, the effects of touch did not work quite this systematically, suggesting that the effects of touch are not simple.

Of course, a touch does not always convey the meaning of dominance. A touch can also convey feelings of sexuality or of solidarity and friendship. Which of these meanings is conveyed depends on the situation. Friendship tends to be conveyed if the touch is between persons of approximately the same status and the touch is reciprocal, such as a handshake or a mutual hug (our prior discussion has been concerned with nonreciprocal touch, that is, one person touches another but the touch is not returned). While it is fairly easy for a man to convey dominance by a touch, it is probably more difficult for a woman to do so, and she is likely to have the touch interpreted as having a sexual meaning.

What are the practical implications of this research and theorizing? First, men who are concerned about establishing egalitarian relationships with women need to become aware of their use of touch. It can signal dominance and unequal roles even though one is not aware of doing so and does not intend to do so. Second, women who are concerned with trying to be more assertive and dominant in their interpersonal relations may want to consider increasing their use of touch. The risk in this approach is that the touch will be mistaken for a sexual message. One is therefore advised to aim for sexually neutral areas of the body, such as the shoulder or forearm.

Interpersonal distance   Generally it seems that in the United States, men prefer a greater distance between themselves and another person, while there tends to be a smaller distance between women and others. For example, women stand closer to other women in public exhibits than men do to men (Baxter, 1970). In a study of the initial speaking distance set by an approaching person, it was found that women were approached more closely than men (Willis, 1966). In another study, subjects seated themselves an average of 4.6 feet from a female stimulus person and an average of 8.5 feet from a male — i.e., they sat about twice as far from the male as from the female (Wittig and Skolnick, 1978). Thus it seems that interpersonal distance works much like touch — women are more likely to be touched and they are more likely to be approached closely.

These results can be interpreted in a manner similar to the interpretation of the results on touching. That is, it might be said that women essentially have their personal space or "territory" violated, and that this expresses dominance over them. On the other hand, an alternative interpretation would be that women have a small interpersonal distance as a result of, or in order to express, warmth or friendliness. More sophisticated research will be necessary to sort out these possibilities (see, for example, Wittig and Skolnick, 1978).

Smiling   Women tend to smile more than men although, once again, it is not clear how this difference should be interpreted (Mehrabian, 1971). Smiling has been called the female version of the "Uncle Tom shuffle" — that is, rather than indicating happiness or friendliness, it may serve as an appeasement gesture, communicating, in effect, "please don't hit me or be nasty." Smiling seems to be a part of the female role. Most women can remember having their faces feel stiff and sore from smiling at a party or some other public gathering at which they were expected to smile. The smile, of course, did not reflect happiness, but rather a belief that smiling was the appropriate thing to do. Women's smiles, then, do not necessarily reflect positive feelings, and may even be associated with negative feelings.

There is really very little research on smiling and its implications for women and gender roles. There is one interesting study, however, of smiling in interactions between parents and children (Bugental et al., 1971). When fathers were smiling they tended to make more positive statements to their children, compared with when they were not smiling. Mothers' statements, on the other hand, were no more positive when they were smiling than when they were not. Parents, and particularly mothers, smiled more when they thought they were being observed than when they thought they were not being observed. This suggests that smiling is indeed part of a role people play. Finally, it seemed that children had learned to sort out the contradictory messages (smile accompanied by a negative statement) they got from their mothers; they ignored the smile and responded to the negative statement.

HOW WOMEN ARE
TREATED IN LANGUAGE

To this point we have discussed women's communication styles, both verbal and nonverbal. The other aspect that needs to be covered in our discussion of women and language is how women and the concept of gender are treated in our language. Feminists have sensitized the public to the peculiar properties of terms like "chairman" and "man" used to refer to the entire species.[1] Here we shall discuss patterns that emerge in the way the English language treats women and concepts of gender.

Male-as-normative   One of the clearest patterns in our language is the normativeness of the male, a concept discussed in Chapter 2. The male is regarded as the normative (standard) member of the species, and this is expressed in many ways in language. These ways include the use of "man" to refer to all human beings, and the use of "he" for a neutral pronoun (as in the sentence "The infant typically begins to sit up around six months of age; he may begin crawling at about the same time"). The male-as-normative principle in language can lead to some absolutely absurd statements. For example, there is a state law that reads "No person may require another person to perform, participate in, or undergo an abortion of pregnancy against his will" (Key, 1975).

Sometimes students in their essays mistakenly use the phrase "the male species" (the expression they really mean to use is "the male of the species"). But in a way they are expressing the principle well — the male is the species.

At the very least, the male-as-normative usage introduces ambiguity into our language (Beard, 1946). When someone uses the word "men," does *he* mean males, or does he mean people in general? When Dr. Karl Menninger writes a book entitled *Man Against Himself*, is it a book about people generally, or is it a book about the tensions experienced by males?

Some people excuse such usage by saying that terms like "man" are generic. Such an explanation, however, is not adequate. To illustrate how weak the "generic" logic is, consider the objections raised by some men who have recently joined the League of Women Voters. They have complained that the name of the organization should be changed, for it no longer adequately describes its members, some of whom are now men. Suppose in response to their objection they were told that by "woman," we mean "generic woman," which of course includes men. Do you think they would feel satisfied?

The male-as-normative principle is also reflected in the *female as the exception* phenomenon. Recently a newspaper reported the results of the

---

[1] Someone once commented cutely that feminists have a bad case of "pronoun envy." (Key, 1975)

Bowling Green women's swimming team and the Bowling Green men's swimming team in two articles close to each other. The headline reporting the men's results was "BG swimmers defeated." The one for the women was "BG women swimmers win." As another example, suppose a male doctor discovers a vaccine for cancer. The headline might read "Doctor discovers cancer vaccine." But if the doctor happens to be female, the headline would likely be "Woman doctor discovers cancer vaccine." The point is that we consider athletes and prestigious professionals to be normatively male. In cases where they are female it seems important to note this as an exception.

Parallel words   Another interesting phenomenon in our language is how parallel words for males and females often have quite different connotations (Lakoff, 1973; Key, 1975; Schulz, 1975). For example, consider the following list of parallel male and female words:

Male	*Female*
bachelor	spinster
dog	bitch
master	mistress

Note that the female forms of the words generally have negative connotations; a bachelor is viewed as a carefree, happy person, while a spinster is the object of pity. Also note that the negative connotation to the female words is often sexual in nature. For example, a man who is a master is good at what he does or is powerful, but a woman who is a mistress is someone who is financially supported in return for her sexual services. Another example would be the sentences "He's a professional" and "She's a professional." The former implies that the man is a doctor or lawyer or very good at what he does, while the latter implies that the woman is a prostitute.

Of course, many of these parallel words originally had equivalent meanings for male and female. An example is *master* and *mistress*, terms originally used to refer to the male and female heads of the household. Over time, however, the female term took on negative connotations, a process known as *pejoration*. Linguist Muriel Schulz (1975) has argued that this process is caused simply by prejudice. That is, terms applied to women take on negative meanings because of prejudice against women (see also Allport, 1954).

Euphemisms   Generally when there are many euphemisms for a word, it is a reflection of the fact that people find the word and what it stands for to be distasteful or stressful (Schulz, 1975). For example, consider all the various terms we use instead of "bathroom" or "toilet." And then there is the great variety of terms such as "pass away" that we substitute for "die."

Feminist linguists have argued that we similarly have a strong tendency to use euphemisms for the word "woman" (Lakoff, 1973; Schulz, 1975). That is, people have a tendency to avoid using the word "woman," and instead substitute a variety of terms that seem more "polite" or less threatening, the most common euphemisms being "lady" and "girl." In contrast to the word "man," which is used quite frequently and comfortably, "woman" is used less frequently and apparently causes some discomfort or we wouldn't use euphemisms for it.

Infantilizing   A 25-year-old man wrote to an advice columnist, depressed because he wanted to get married but had never had a date. Part of the columnist's response was

> Just scan the society pages and look at the people who are getting married every day. Are the men all handsome? Are the girls all beautiful?

This is an illustration of the way in which people, rather than using "woman" as the parallel to "man," substitute "girl" instead. As we noted in the previous section, this in part reflects the use of a euphemism. But it is also true that "boy" refers to young males, "man" to adult males. Somehow "girl," which in a strict sense should refer only to young females, is used for adult women as well. Women are called by a term that seems to make them less mature than they are; women are thus infantilized in language. Just as the term "boy" became very offensive to black activists, so "girl" has become offensive to feminists.

There are many other illustrations of this infantilizing theme. When a ship sinks, it's "Women and children first," putting women and children in the same category. Other examples in language are expressions for women such as "baby," "babe," and "chick." The problem with these terms is that they carry a meaning of immaturity and perhaps irresponsibility.

How important is all of this?   Although many of the tenets of the women's movement — such as equal pay for equal work — have gained widespread acceptance, the importance of changing our language to eliminate sexism has not. Many people tend to regard these issues as silly or trivial. Just how important is the issue of sexism in language? (For a review, see Blaubergs, 1978.)

It is true that language reflects thought processes. This being the case, sexism in language may be the symptom, not the disease (Lakoff, 1973). That is, things like the generic use of "man" and "he" may simply reflect the fact that we do think of the male as the norm for the species. The practical conclusion from this is that what needs to be changed is our thought processes, and once they change, language will change with them.

On the other hand, one of the classic theories of psycholinguistics, the Whorfian hypothesis (Whorf, 1956), states that the specific language we learn influences our mental processes. If that is true, then things like the generic use of "man" make us think that the male is normative. This process might start with very young children when they are just beginning to learn the language. If such processes do occur, then social reformers need to pay careful attention to eliminate sexism in language because of its effect on our thought processes.

An important study demonstrated that, even when "he" and "his" are used in explicitly gender-neutral contexts, people tend to think of males (Moulton et al., 1978). College students were asked to make up stories creating a fictional character who would fit the theme of a stimulus sentence. The students were divided into six groups; for three of the groups, the stimulus sentence was

> In a large coeducational institution the average student will feel isolated in —— introductory courses.

One of the groups received *his* in the blank space, another received *their*, and the third received *his or her*. Another three groups received one of the alternative pronouns in the stimulus sentence:

> Most people are concerned with appearance. Each person knows when —— appearance is unattractive.

Averaging the responses of all groups, when the pronoun was "his," only 35 percent of the stories were about females; for "their," 46 percent were about females, and for "his or her" 56 percent were about females. Females were chosen as characters more often for the second stimulus sentence (concerned about appearance) than for the first. But the important point is that, even though a sentence referred to "the average student," when "his" was used most people thought of males. Though a linguist may say that "he" and "his" are gender-neutral, they are certainly not gender-neutral in a psychological sense. It seems likely that both processes — thought influencing language and language influencing thought — occur to some extent. Insofar as language does have the potential for influencing our thinking, sexism in language becomes a critical issue (e.g., Martyna, 1979; Moulton et al., 1978).

SOME PRACTICAL SUGGESTIONS

Some people believe in theory that it would be a good idea to eliminate sexism from language, but in practice they find themselves having difficulty doing this in their speaking or writing. Here we shall discuss some practical suggestions for avoiding sexist language (for reviews, see Blaubergs, 1978; Miller and Swift, 1977) and for dealing with some other relevant situations.

Toward nonsexist language   The use of generic masculine forms is probably the most widespread and difficult problem of sexist language. The following are some ways to eliminate or avoid these usages.

One possibility is to switch from the singular to the plural, because plural pronouns do not signify gender. Therefore, the generic masculine in (1) can be modified as in (2):

1. When a doctor prescribes birth control pills, he should first inquire whether the patient has a history of blood clotting problems.
2. When doctors prescribe birth control pills, they should first inquire whether the patient has a history of blood clotting problems.

Another possibility is to reword the sentence so that there is no necessity for a pronoun, as in

3. A doctor prescribing birth control pills should first inquire whether the patient has a history of blood clotting problems.

One of the simplest solutions is to use "he or she" instead of the generic "he," "him or her" instead of "him," and so on. Therefore, the generic masculine in (1) can be modified to

4. When a doctor prescribes birth control pills, he or she should first inquire whether the patient has a history of blood clotting problems.

Many feminist scholars, however, believe that the order should be varied, so that "he or she" and "she or he" appear with equal frequency. If "he or she" is the only form that is used, women still end up second!

One final possibility is the singular use of "they" and "their." For years people have been saying sentences like "Will everyone pick up their pencil?" and English teachers have been correcting them, saying that the correct form is "Will everyone pick up his pencil?" Since it is so natural to use the plural in this situation, and to do so eliminates the sexism, why not go ahead and do it?

With a little practice, these strategies can be used to eliminate the generic masculine.

Space does not permit a complete discussion of all possible practical problems that may arise in trying to avoid sexist language. Usually a little thought and imagination can solve most problems. For example, the salutation in a letter, "Dear Sir," can easily be changed to "Dear Madam or Sir," or "Dear Sir or Madam," or simply "To Whom It May Concern." The tendency to use euphemisms for "woman" can be changed by becoming sensitive to this tendency and making efforts to use the word "woman."

One other solution to the problem of generic masculine pronouns should also be mentioned — namely, the creation of some new singular pronouns that are gender-neutral. Unfortunately, at least ten alternatives

for these new pronouns have been proposed, confusing the situation somewhat (Blaubergs, 1978). One set that has been proposed is "tey" for he
or she, "tem" for him or her, and "ter" for his or her. Thus one might say:
The scientist pursues ter work; tey reads avidly and strives to overcome
obstacles that beset tem. Entire books have been written with this usage
(e.g., Sherman, 1978). Although in an ideal sense these new pronouns
have a great deal of merit, they do not seem to be catching on. Probably
they would need to be adopted by a number of respected, widely-circulated
sources in order to find their way into the ordinary person's language. If
the *New York Times*, the *Washington Post, Time, Newsweek*, Walter
Cronkite, and the President all started using "ter," "tey," and "tem," they
would probably have a chance. Such widespread adoption does not seem
to be a very immediate possibility, however.

This brings us to the topic of institutional change in language use.

Institutional change   It is encouraging to note that a number of institutions have committed themselves to using and encouraging nonsexist language. For example, several textbook publishers have issued guidelines for
nonsexist language and refuse to publish books that include sexisms (e.g.,
McGraw-Hill Book Company in 1974; Scott, Foresman and Company in
1972). The American Psychological Association has guidelines for the use
of nonsexist language in articles in the journals it publishes (APA, 1975).
These are all good sources for the reader wanting more detail on how to
eliminate sexist language.

Many occupational titles, particularly in government agencies, have
also changed. For those who worry about the linguistic properties of nonsexist language, it is worth noting that some of the changes introduce
definite improvements. For example, "firemen" has been changed to "fire
fighters." In addition to being nonsexist, the newer term makes more
sense, since what the people do is fight fires, not start them, as one might
infer from the older term.

Language, women, and careers   The discussion of gender differences in
language use in the first part of the chapter raises an important practical
question for women aspiring to careers in male-dominated occupations
such as business. From the data presented in that part of the chapter, it
seems reasonable to conclude, at least tentatively, that the average woman
has some language characteristics that suggest that she is uncertain of herself or lacking in confidence. These are certainly not qualities that help
one get ahead in the business world. Should women attempt to modify
their language on the job, much as blacks speak standard English when
the situation calls for it? And how should women modify their language?

One possibility is for women to become conscious of their "feminine"
speech patterns, to eliminate them and substitute "masculine" ones.
Women could stop using tag questions and high tones and start interrupt-

ing more. Although we have no data on the point, it is our opinion that this approach would probably not work very well, simply because many people feel threatened by "masculine" women. This approach also adopts male values and assumes that the male should be the norm.

As an alternative, we would suggest that women try to achieve androgynous speech, that is, speech that has both the desirable qualities of "feminine" speech and the desirable qualities of "masculine" speech. Such speech would convey confidence and forcefulness together with a concern for the feelings of others. Such a combination of qualities should contribute to success in many careers.

10

BIOLOGICAL INFLUENCES ON WOMEN'S BEHAVIOR

. . . an extraordinarily important part of the brain necessary for spiritual life, the frontal convolutions and the temporal lobes are less well developed in women and this difference is inborn. . . . If we wish a woman to fulfill her task of motherhood fully, she cannot possess a masculine brain. If the feminine abilities were developed to the same degree as those of the male, her maternal organs would suffer, and we should have before us a repulsive and useless hybrid.

MOEBIUS, Concerning the Physiological
Intellectual Feebleness of Women, 1907

Traditionally it was believed that biological differences between females and males created psychological differences. It was also popularly thought that biological influences were particularly potent forces on women's behavior. The turn-of-the-century psychologist quoted above believed that male and female brains differed and that the female brain was defective. Women are also thought to be the victims of their "raging hormones." In this chapter we shall examine the evidence on whether biological gender differences create psychological gender differences, and on whether women's behavior is controlled by biological forces.

The biological factors that may influence women and gender differences fall into three major categories: genetic factors, sex hormones, and brain differences.

GENES

Normal humans possess a set of 46 chromosomes. Since chromosomes occur in pairs, there are 23 pairs, classified as 22 pairs of autosomes (non-sex chromosomes) and one pair of sex chromosomes. The female has a sex chromosome pair denoted XX, while the male sex chromosome pair is XY. Therefore, there are no genetic differences between males and females except for the sex chromosomes.

Traits that are controlled by genes on the sex chromosomes are called *sex-linked traits*. For such traits, the female will have a pair of genes controlling a particular sex-linked trait, but a male will have only one gene for that trait, because he has only one X chromosome. (The function of the Y chromosome and the functions of any genes on it are not yet well understood by geneticists; for our purposes, we will consider the Y chromosome genetically inert.) Sex linkage is a source of gender differences when one form of a gene (*allele*) is dominant or recessive to the other possible allele, as in the example of blue eyes (b) recessive to brown eyes (B). Normally, to manifest a recessive trait, both alleles must be recessive, while the dominant trait is manifested if both members of the pair are dominant, or one dominant and one recessive. However, for genes on the X chromosome, a male will have only one allele, and will therefore manifest the recessive if the one allele present is recessive. The female, of course, with two X's, needs two recessives to manifest the recessive trait. Thus if a trait is sex-linked recessive, it will be manifested more frequently by males than by females. A good example is color blindness.

This basic genetic gender difference is thought to be a source of the biological resiliency of the female compared with the male (for a popularized discussion, see Montagu, 1952). Women are known to be generally less susceptible to disease than men. Some sources of this difference are sex-linked recessive genetic diseases, such as hemophilia. Most diseases or other harmful genetic effects are recessive, while beneficial effects are generally dominant (the biological utility of this system is apparent). We have just seen that it is easier for a man to manifest a sex-linked recessive trait, since he needs only one recessive gene, while a woman needs two recessives. Therefore, men are more likely than women to be affected by sex-linked recessive defects such as hemophilia and color blindness.

Except for color vision, there is no behavior for which there is good evidence of sex-linked genetic influence. There was some early evidence that spatial visualizing ability was influenced by an X-linked gene (Stafford, 1961; Hartlage, 1970; Bock and Kolakowski, 1973; Yen, 1975). However, more recent studies using larger samples fail to find evidence for this (Bouchard, 1977; DeFries et al., 1976).

One other important function of the sex chromosomes is to direct the course of prenatal gender differentiation. In doing this, they interact with hormones. This brings us to a second biological factor that may influence gender differences.

SEX HORMONES

Hormones are powerful chemical substances manufactured by the various endocrine glands of the body. Endocrine glands secrete hormones into the blood stream so that they can have effects throughout the body, including target organs far from the endocrine gland that secreted them. Among the endocrine glands are the gonads (ovaries and testes), pancreatic islets, pituitary, thyroid, and adrenal glands.

The "male" sex hormone is called *testosterone*. It is one of a group of "male" hormones called androgens, which are manufactured by the testes. The "female" sex hormones are *estrogen* and *progesterone*, which are manufactured by the ovaries. If these hormones influence behavior, then they may create gender differences.

Actually, it is a mistake to call testosterone the "male" sex hormone and estrogen and progesterone "female" hormones. Testosterone, for example, is found in females as well as males. The difference is in amount, not presence or absence. In women, testosterone is manufactured by the adrenal glands, and the level in women's blood is about one-sixth that in men's (Salhanick and Margulis, 1968).

The differences in levels of sex hormones may affect behavior at two major stages of development: prenatally (the time between conception and birth), and during and after puberty (adulthood). Endocrinologists refer to the effects that occur prenatally as *organizing effects* because they cause a relatively permanent effect in the organization of some structure, whether in the nervous system or the reproductive system. Hormone effects in adulthood are called *activating effects* because they activate or deactivate certain behaviors. In order to understand the prenatal effects, we must first discuss the process of prenatal gender differentiation.

Prenatal gender differentiation At the moment of conception, there are gender differences. If the fertilized egg contains two X chromosomes, then the genetic gender of the individual is female; if it contains one X and one Y chromosome, the genetic gender is male. The single cell then divides repeatedly, becoming an embryo, then a fetus. Interestingly, during the first two months of human prenatal development, it appears that the only differences between females and males are in genetic gender. That is, anatomically and physiologically males and females develop identically during this period. Beginning approximately during the third month of pregnancy, and continuing through about the sixth month, the process of prenatal gender differentiation occurs (for an extended discussion, see Money and Ehrhardt, 1972). First, the sex chromosomes direct the differentiation of the primary sex characteristics, or gonads (see Figure 10.1). An XX chromosome complement directs the differentiation of ovaries; an XY complement produces testes. The gonads then have the important function of secreting sex hormones. Thus the fetal internal environment

FIGURE 10.1

The sequences of prenatal differentiation of females and males.

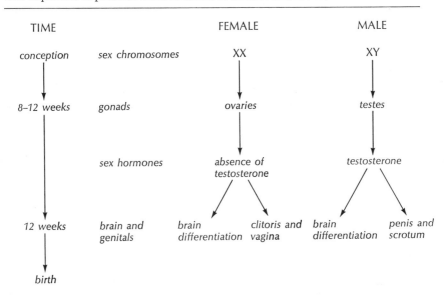

or physiology becomes different for females and males because of endocrine differences.

The sex hormones further affect the course of fetal differentiation. In particular, the male testes produce testosterone. The presence or absence of testosterone seems to be the critical factor determining the direction of further differentiation. If testosterone is present, the male penis forms. If testosterone is not present (or present only in small amounts), a clitoris and vagina differentiate. In addition to influencing the process of anatomical gender differentiation, the sex hormones also influence the developing brain. The structure most affected seems to be the hypothalamus. The importance of this differentiation will be discussed later in the chapter.

Prenatal sex hormone effects   Male fetuses and female fetuses, then, live in different hormonal environments. Does this have any effect on their later behaviors?

Most of the evidence we have in this area is based on experiments done with animals. It may be that the effects on humans would not be the same. But let us consider the animal experiments, and then see what is known about similar processes in humans.

Prenatal sex hormone exposure seems to affect mainly two behaviors: sexual behavior and aggressive behavior. The organizing effects of sex hormones on sexual behavior have been well documented. In a classic experiment, testosterone was administered to pregnant female guinea pigs (Phoenix et al., 1959). The female offspring that had been exposed to testosterone prenatally were, in adulthood, incapable of displaying female sexual behavior (in particular, lordosis, which is a sexual posturing involving arching of the back and raising the hindquarters so that the male can insert the penis). It is thought that this occurred because the testosterone "organized" the brain tissue (particularly the hypothalamus) in a male fashion. These female offspring were also born with masculinized genitals, and thus their reproductive systems had also been organized in the male direction. But the important point here is that the prenatal doses of testosterone had masculinized their sexual behavior. Similar results have been obtained in experiments with many other species as well.

In adulthood, these hormonally masculinized females displayed mounting behavior, a male sexual behavior. When they were given testosterone in adulthood, they showed about as much mounting behavior as males did. Thus the testosterone administered in adulthood *activated* male patterns of sexual behavior.

The analogous experiment on males would be castration at birth followed by administration of female sex hormones in adulthood. When this was done with rats, female sexual behavior resulted. These male rats responded to mating attempts from normal males the way females usually do (Harris and Levine, 1965). Apparently the brain tissue had been organized in a female direction during an early critical period when testosterone was absent, and the female behavior patterns were activated in adulthood by administration of ovarian hormones.

Similar effects have also been demonstrated for aggressive behavior. Early exposure to testosterone increases the fighting behavior of female mice (Edwards, 1969). Female rhesus monkeys given early exposure to testosterone show a higher incidence of rough-and-tumble play (Young et al., 1964). Thus it appears that early exposure to testosterone also organizes aggressive behavior in a "masculine" direction.

What relevance do these studies have for humans? Generally, the trend is for hormones to have stronger effects on lower species, and less effect on humans (Beach, 1947). It would be unethical, of course, to do experiments like the ones mentioned above on human subjects. Nonetheless, a number of "accidental" experiments of this sort have occurred when pregnant women were given drugs containing hormones. The offspring of these women have been studied in detail by psychologist John Money and his colleagues. Money has concentrated particularly on the gender identity these individuals develop.

Biology and gender identity   Gender identity — the knowledge that one is a male or a female, and the integration of this fact into one's personal identity — is a very basic psychological characteristic. Is gender identity biologically determined (by chromosomes, by hormones, or by anatomical sex characteristics), or is it modifiable by environment?

On the basis of a long program of research, Money Hampson, and Hampson conclude that the acquisition of gender role and of basic gender identity is contingent upon the environment (Money, 1961, 1970, 1972; Hampson, 1965). Many of their data come from individuals with morphological incongruities leading to contradictions among their various sexual characteristics.

In order to discuss gender identity, it is important first to understand the distinctions among the six variables of gender: (1) chromosomal gender (XX in the female versus XY in the male); (2) gonadal gender (ovaries versus testes); (3) hormonal gender (estrogen and progesterone versus testosterone); (4) internal accessory organs (uterus and vagina versus prostate and seminal vesicles); (5) external genital appearance (clitoris and vaginal opening versus penis and scrotum); and (6) assigned gender (It's a girl! or It's a boy!) and gender role. Normally, of course, all of these variables are in agreement, apparently indicating that chromosomal gender determines gender identity. That is, normally the female's XX chromosome complement causes differentiation of the ovaries during fetal development (actually, it is not the presence of XX, but the absence of a Y chromosome that causes this), and the ovaries produce the appropriate female hormones, which cause further feminine differentiation of the internal accessory organs and external genitalia. The appearance of

the external genitalia determines the gender assignment — the announce-
ment "It's a girl!" — which then leads to rearing as a female.

However, a number of "accidents" during the course of development
may result in the gender indicated by one or more of these variables
disagreeing with the gender indicated by the others. In these cases, the
gender of assignment and rearing may or may not correspond to the
genetic gender, but the child seems to accept the assigned gender and to
develop successfully in it. Hence, Money, Hampson, and Hampson (1955)
conclude that gender identity is learned as a result of environmental
factors.

One sort of individual they have studied is the pseudohermaphrodite,
in whom there is a contradiction between external genital appearance and
one of the other biological gender variables (genetic gender, gonads, hormones, or internal reproductive structures). In genetic females, this often
results from a condition known as the "adrenogenital syndrome." These
females as fetuses develop ovaries normally, but during the course of
prenatal development, the adrenal gland begins to function abnormally
(as the result of a recessive genetic condition) and an excess amount of
androgens is produced. Prenatal sexual differentiation does not follow the
normal course. As a result, the external genitalia are partly or completely
male in appearance — the labia are partly or totally fused, and the clitoris
is enlarged to the size of a small penis. Hence, at birth, these genetic
females are identified as being males.

Money (1972) cited one case of a matched pair of these individuals.
Both were diagnosed as males at birth. One was from that time on reared
as a male. He developed normally as a male, functioned normally in
groups of boys, had outdoor, athletic, and sporting interests, and easily
accepted the stereotype of the male role in marriage. The other child,
because of further medical problems, returned for treatment and was at
that time correctly rediagnosed as a female. Her external genitals were
feminized surgically, and the internal reproductive structures were already
feminine. She was reared as a female, and managed fairly successfully to
adopt the female role, although she did have tendencies toward what
Money calls "tomboyism." Despite identical genetic gender and genitals,
these individuals could become either males or females, depending on the
gender of the assignment and rearing.

Hampson says:

> Psychologic sex or gender role appears to be learned, that is to say, it is
> differentiated through learning during the course of the many experiences
> of growing up. In place of a theory of innate constitutional psychologic
> bisexuality we can substitute a concept of psychosexual neutrality in hu-
> mans at birth. Such neutrality permits the development and perpetuation
> of many patterns of psychosexual orientation and functioning in accord-
> ance with the life experiences each individual may encounter and trans-
> act. (1965, p. 125)

The position of "psychosexual neutrality" argues that, from the time of gender assignment (in accordance with external genitalia), maleness or femaleness is continually reinforced. Gender identity may result solely from environmental contingencies, although certainly biological factors make some outcomes more likely.

An important related finding is that there appears to be a critical period for gender assignment and for the formation of gender identity. Up until the age of about 18 months, the child's gender may be almost arbitrarily reassigned, as in the case of the pseudohermaphrodite, and the child will accept the new gender and develop normally in it. Reassignment after that age can lead to serious conflicts in the child, and normal development in the new gender is unlikely. Note that this is in agreement with the view of cognitive-developmental theory (Chapter 3), which asserts that the formation of gender identity occurs at about the age of three years, and that this becomes a permanent, life-long concept.

The position espoused by Money and the Hampsons of psychosexual neutrality at birth and the immense importance of the environment in the formation of gender identity has not been accepted without challenge. First, it should be noted that in almost all the cases given as evidence, sex reassignment was supplemented by appropriate surgical or hormonal therapy. That is, the individual's biological characteristics were modified to correspond to the assigned gender. Hence, it is not reasonable to say that gender could be assigned independent of biological gender characteristics. In fact, the very success of the reassignment often depends on the proper anatomical and hormonal modifications. Second, there are often traces of behaviors that are opposite to the behavior of gender of rearing. For example, born and raised as males, five patients showed interest during childhood only in activities typically characteristic of girls. A sixth patient, born and raised as a female, always showed masculine tendencies. All possessed genitalia normal to the assigned gender, and had no apparent physical defects, until adolescence, when they developed secondary sex characteristics normal for the opposite gender (Baker and Stoller, 1967). It appears that the pubertal cross-gender body change in effect agreed with their earlier gender wishes. One can therefore cite cases that contradict the rule that postnatal environmental forces determine gender identity. Finally, it is difficult to know how relevant the abnormal cases studied by Money are to understanding the normal process of acquiring a gender identity.

Nonetheless, Money's data do provide impressive evidence of the extent to which gender identity is a product of environmental forces.

Hormone effects in adulthood   The effects of sex hormones in adulthood that are of interest to us fall into two categories. First, sex hormone levels in women fluctuate over the menstrual cycle. This raises the question of whether these hormone fluctuations would cause fluctuations in mood or other psychological characteristics. This topic will be discussed in detail in Chapter 11. Second, levels of sex hormones differ in men and women. For example, as noted earlier, women have only about one-sixth the level of testosterone in the blood that men do. Could it be that these different levels of hormones "activate" different behaviors in men and women?

As noted above, studies done with animals indicate that sex hormones administered in adulthood may have effects on both aggressive behavior and sexual behavior. Once again, however, we have little information on whether there are similar effects on humans. Several studies have shown increased sex drive in women as a result of the administration of testosterone (reviewed by Kane et al., 1969). A study of eighteen young men indicated that there was a significant correlation between testosterone production rate and a measure of hostility and aggression (Persky et al., 1971). Another recent study looked at testosterone levels existing in husbands and wives in relation to their sexual behavior (Persky et al., 1978). Intercourse frequency was not related to either partner's average testosterone levels, but it was related to wives' testosterone levels at their ovulatory peaks. The wives' self-rated sexual gratification also correlated significantly with their own plasma testosterone levels.

Probably sex hormone levels do have some effects on adult human behaviors, particularly aggressive and sexual behaviors. It is also likely that these effects are not so strong as they are in animals, and that they are more complex and interact more with environmental factors.

THE BRAIN

Although the quote at the beginning of this chapter may seem quaintly sexist, there are some differences between human male and female brains (Money and Ehrhardt, 1972). These differences are in two major areas: the hypothalamus, and the organization of the left and right hemispheres.

The hypothalamus   Gender differences in the hypothalamus seem to be the result of differentiation of brain tissue in the course of fetal development, much as is the case for the reproductive organs (see Figure 10.1). Recall that the sequence of normal development consists of the sex chromosomes directing the differentiation of gonadal tissue into ovaries or testes. The gonads then secrete appropriate-gender hormones, which cause further reproductive-system differentiation. The fetal gonadal hormones also cause appropriate-gender differentiation of the hypothalamus.

Basically, then, brain differentiation in the fetus is a process much like reproductive-system differentiation. Earlier researchers believed that the embryo began with no differentiation on the basis of gender and therefore humans were inherently bisexual. It now appears to be more accurate to say that nature's primary impulse is to create a female. That is, if no additional forces intervene, female development occurs. The critical variable is the presence or absence of testosterone. If it is present, male characteristics develop; if absent, female characteristics. Thus it seems that, biologically, the female is normative! The male is a variant created by the addition of testosterone.

It appears that one of the most important organizing effects of prenatal sex hormones is the determination of the estrogen-sensitivity of certain cells in the hypothalamus (for a review, see Taleisnik et al., 1971). Once again, it is the presence or absence of testosterone that is critical. If testosterone is present during fetal development, certain specialized receptor cells in the hypothalamus become insensitive to estrogen; if no testosterone is present, these cells are highly sensitive to levels of estrogen in the bloodstream. This is important because of the hypothalamic-pituitary-gonadal regulating feedback loop (see Chapter 11). In this process, gonadal hormone output is regulated by the pituitary, which is in turn regulated by the hypothalamus. The hypothalamus responds to the level of gonadal hormones in the bloodstream. Male hypothalamic cells are relatively insensitive to estrogen levels, whereas female hypothalamic cells are highly sensitive to them. We also know that estrogen (and progesterone as well) lowers the threshold of central nervous system (CNS) excitability in adults. Hence, the estrogen-sensitivity effect in the female amounts to a much greater increase in CNS excitability in response to estrogen than in the male. The estrogen-sensitivity effect is a result of the organizing effect of hormones. Hormones administered in adulthood activate male and female nervous systems differentially depending on prenatal determination (organizing effects) of estrogen sensitivity.

What are the observable consequences of these gender differences in the hypothalamus? One consequence is the determination of a cyclic or acyclic pattern of pituitary release of hormones (e.g., Barraclough and Gorski, 1961). The hypothalamus directs pituitary hormone secretion. It appears that a hypothalamus that has undergone female differentiation will direct the pituitary to release hormones cyclically, creating a menstrual cycle, whereas a male hypothalamus directs a relatively steady production of pituitary hormones.

The gender differences in the hypothalamus may have some consequences for behavior, too, although these have not been well documented in humans (for a review, see Reinisch, 1974). As discussed earlier, the organization of the hypothalamus in a male or female direction may have some influence on both sexual and aggressive behavior.

Right hemisphere, left hemisphere   The brain is divided into two halves, a right hemisphere and a left hemisphere. It is thought that these two hemispheres carry out somewhat different functions. In particular, in right-handed, normal persons, the left hemisphere seems specialized for verbal tasks, and the right hemisphere for spatial tasks. The term *laterali-*

zation usually refers to the extent to which a particular function, say verbal processing, is handled by one hemisphere rather than both. Thus, for example, if verbal processing in one person is handled entirely in the left hemisphere, we would say that that person is highly lateralized or completely lateralized. If another person processes verbal material using both hemispheres, we would say that that person is bilateral for verbal functioning.

Brain lateralization research is a very active, exciting area in psychological research at the moment. Because there are gender differences in both verbal ability and spatial ability (see Chapter 8), it is not surprising that various theories have been proposed using gender differences in brain lateralization to account for the observed differences in abilities. We shall review these theories and the evidence for them below (for a detailed review, see Sherman, 1978).

The *Buffery and Gray hypothesis* (1972) is that the left hemisphere becomes dominant for verbal functions earlier in girls, leading to less bilateral processing of spatial information. Buffery and Gray believe that bilateral representation of spatial information causes better spatial performance, and so they argue that the lesser bilaterality of females for spatial processing explains their poorer spatial performance.

The *Levy hypothesis* (Levy, 1972; Levy-Agresti and Sperry, 1968) is that females are like left-handed males in that they are more likely to be bilateral for verbal functions. She further hypothesized that the best spatial and verbal performance occurs with the most lateralization of these functions. The bilaterality of verbal functioning in females would impair spatial functioning, so that females, like left-handed males, would have poorer spatial ability.

Interestingly, the Buffery and Gray hypothesis and the Levy hypothesis contradict each other — one assumes that more bilaterality means better performance, while the other assumes that less bilaterality causes better performance.

The *Harshman and Remington hypothesis* (1976, cited in Sherman, 1978) is that, because females mature earlier than males, at young ages females are more lateralized than males; but when males are fully mature, they are more lateralized than females, both for verbal and spatial functions. Harshman and Remington believe that this greater lateralization of spatial function leads to better spatial performance in males.

One kind of experiment that psychologists use to test hypotheses such as these is the *tachistoscope* study. A tachistoscope is an instrument that contains a viewer through which the subject looks at slides as the experimenter presents them. If the subject keeps her or his eyes fixated on a center focus point, stimuli can be presented to the right half of the visual field or to the left half. Stimuli presented to the right half of the visual field are transmitted to the left hemisphere. Thus if a subject is better at recognizing verbal stimuli presented in the right visual field than in the left, that person would be said to be left-hemisphere dominant for verbal functions.

On the basis of studies of this kind and others, the Buffery and Gray hypothesis can be rejected (Sherman, 1978). There is little evidence to support it, and other evidence that contradicts it. The Levy theory can be rejected for the same reasons. The Harshman and Remington hypothesis also has little evidence backing it, but because the evidence is more ambiguous, judgment on it should probably not be made as yet (Sherman, 1978).

You may be somewhat dismayed by such an inconclusive statement after discussing these theories. Brain lateralization is a very active area of research, and there are often flashy newspaper or magazine articles on a scientist who has discovered *the* cause of gender differences in abilities based on right-hemisphere/left-hemisphere differences. It is worthwhile for you to know the kinds of theories that have been proposed and the fact that there is contradicting evidence. When the next theory comes along, you should know that it needs to be evaluated carefully, and how one could go about testing it, for example by using tachistoscope studies. Such theories are also sometimes evaluated using clinical studies of brain-damaged people.

From a feminist point of view, it is interesting to note that all of these theories were constructed to explain the female *deficit* in spatial ability. None of them tries to account for female *superiority* in verbal ability. Perhaps the theories will become more adequate when they do so.

One other hypothesis that has been advanced is the *bent-twig hypothesis* (Sherman, 1971, 1978). It states that because of earlier maturation of verbal abilities, females come to rely more on verbal processing and left-hemisphere processing than males do. Because of this differential experience, when faced with spatial problems, girls do not do as well as boys do. Thus a slight biological difference in maturation rates is magnified by later experiences. More data will be needed to test this hypothesis.

In sum, there do seem to be some gender differences in the use of the hemispheres of the brain. In particular, there is evidence that females use the left hemisphere for spatial functions more than males do (Sherman, 1978). However, the exact differences and the effect these have on gender differences in abilities have yet to be untangled by research.

IN CONCLUSION

We have considered three major classes of biological influences on gender differences and women's behavior: genes, hormones, and brain factors. Genes are not likely to be sources of gender differences, except when the genes are on the X chromosome, as for traits such as color blindness.

Hormones have effects prenatally as well as in adulthood, particularly on sexual and aggressive behaviors, and possibly on behaviors related to the menstrual cycle. Regarding brain factors, gender differentiation of the hypothalamus in a female direction controls the cyclic functioning of the menstrual cycle, and may be related to both aggressive and sexual behavior. Finally, there may be some gender differences in the functioning of the hemispheres of the brain, but the exact nature of these differences is not yet well known.

11

PSYCHOLOGY AND WOMEN'S HEALTH ISSUES

(There is) an imperative need for women every-where to learn about our bodies in order to have control over them and over our lives. We seek to communicate our excitement about the power of shared information; to assert that in an age of pro-fessionals, we are the best experts on ourselves and our feelings; to continue the collective struggle for adequate health care.

FROM Our Bodies, Ourselves

One of the most important parts of the feminist movement of the last decade has been the women's health movement. It is based on the belief that women need to know more about their bodies in order to have more control over them. One of the best books to come out of that movement is *Our Bodies, Ourselves*, written by the Boston Women's Health Book Collective (1976).

In this chapter we shall consider some of the topics that are important in the women's health movement — menstruation, menopause, pregnancy and childbirth, abortion, and mastectomy. We will give brief information on the physical and medical aspects of each of these topics, and concentrate on the psychological research that has been done on them.

MENSTRUATION

Biology of the menstrual cycle   It is estimated that the human female is born with approximately 500,000 primary follicles in both ovaries, each follicle containing an egg or ovum. ("Follicle" here refers to a group of cells in the ovary that encapsulates an egg and has nothing to do with the term "hair follicle.") A single menstrual cycle involves the release of one egg from a follicle, allowing it to move down the oviduct (fallopian tube) for possible fertilization and implantation in the uterus. Hence not more than 400 eggs are ovulated from puberty through menopause. The remaining follicles degenerate.

It is important to note that the menstrual cycle occurs only among primates (monkeys, apes, and humans), and not in lower species. Many people mistakenly compare the estrous cycle of the dog and other mammals, in which sexual receptivity and fertility occur at the time of slight bleeding during estrus or "heat," to the menstrual cycle. There are two major differences between the two types of cycles. First, the estrual female is sexually receptive only during the estrous phase of the estrous cycle, while menstrual females are continually capable of sexual behavior during the menstrual cycle. Second, menstruation occurs only for menstrual females, and not for estrual females (Turner and Bagnara, 1971). Thus the human female is continually sexually receptive and ovulates or is fertile about midway between periods of bleeding or menstruation.

A menstrual cycle can be separated into four phases, each describing the state of the follicles and ova within that phase (see Figure 11.2). It would be most convenient to call the period of menstruation the first phase, since it is easily identifiable, but physiologically it represents the

FIGURE 11.1

Schematic cross section of the female pelvis, showing sexual and reproductive organs.

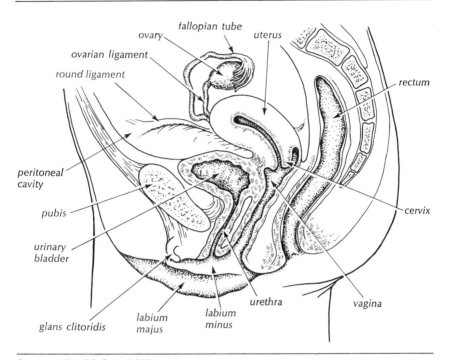

fallopian tube

ovary

uterus

ovarian ligament

round ligament

rectum

peritoneal cavity

pubis

cervix

urinary bladder

urethra

vagina

glans clitoridis

labium majus

labium minus

Source: After McCary, 1973.

last. The first phase, called the *follicular phase*, extends approximately from day 4 to day 14 after menstruation begins. (In counting days of the cycle, day 1 is the first day of menstruation.) During this phase, a follicle matures and swells. The termination of this phase is marked by the rupturing of the follicle and the release of the egg (*ovulatory phase*). During the next phase, the *luteal phase*, a group of reddish-yellow cells, called the corpus luteum, forms in the ruptured follicle. The final phase, marked by *menstruation*, represents a sloughing off of the inner lining (endometrium) of the uterus, which had built up in preparation for nourishing a fertilized egg.

These cyclic phases are regulated by hormones that act in a negative feedback loop with each other (Figure 11.3), so that the production of a hormone increases to a high level, producing a desired physiological change. The level is then automatically reduced through the negative feedback loop. Here we are concerned with two basic groups of hormones — those produced by the ovaries, most importantly estrogen and progesterone,

FIGURE 11.2

Changes in hormone levels over the phase of the menstrual cycle.

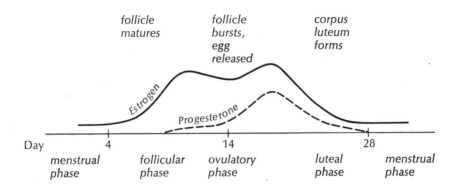

and those produced by the pituitary gland, most importantly follicle-stimulating hormone (FSH) and luteinizing hormone (LH). We also need to consider control of the activity of the pituitary by the hypothalamus, an important region of the brain on its lower side (Figure 11.3), by LH-releasing factor and FSH-releasing factor. The overall pattern of the negative feedback loop is that the activity of the ovary, including its production of estrogen and progesterone, is regulated by the pituitary, which in turn is regulated by the hypothalamus, which is sensitive to the levels of estrogen produced by the ovaries.

The regulation of the menstrual cycle involves interactions among the levels of these hormones. The follicular phase of the cycle is initiated by the pituitary gland sending out follicle-stimulating hormone (FSH), which signals the ovaries to increase production of estrogen and to bring several follicles to maturity. The resulting high level of estrogen, through the feedback loop, signals the pituitary to decrease production of FSH and to begin production of luteinizing hormone (LH), whose chief function is to induce ovulation. Temporarily, FSH and LH induce even more estrogen production, which further lowers the amount of FSH. At this point the LH becomes dominant, causing the follicle to rupture and release the egg. The corpus luteum then forms in the ruptured follicle. The corpus luteum is a major source of progesterone. When progesterone levels are sufficiently high, they will, through the negative feedback loop, inhibit production of LH, and simultaneously stimulate the production of FSH, beginning the cycle over again.

FIGURE 11.3

Schematic diagram illustrating the negative feedback loops controlling hormone levels during the menstrual cycle. FSH and LH are produced by the pituitary gland and influence production of estrogen and progesterone in the ovaries. The hypothalamus is sensitive to levels of these hormones and, in turn, regulates levels of FSH and LH. (See text for further explanation.)

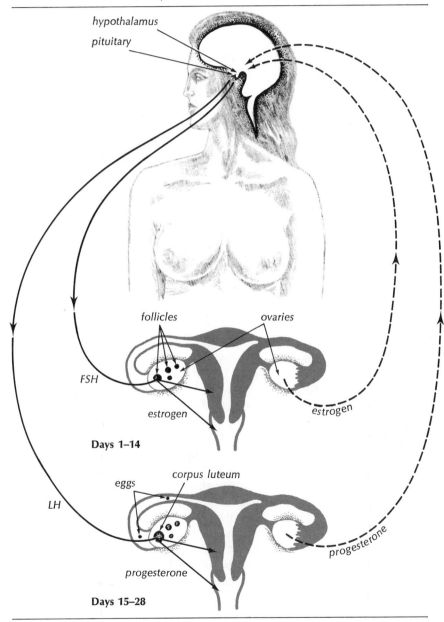

Source: After Appel, 1972.

Estrogen has a number of functions and effects in the body. It maintains the lining of the vagina and uterus and provides the initial stimulation for breast growth. Its nonreproductive functions include increasing water content and thickness of skin and retarding growth rate. At the beginning and the end of the mentrual cycle, estrogen is at a low level. In between these two times, it reaches two peaks, one immediately prior to and during ovulation, the other in the middle of the luteal phase (Figure 11.2). It appears that mature ovarian follicles are the major producers of estrogen.

Progesterone is especially important in preparing the uterus for implantation of the fertilized ovum, maintaining pregnancy, and regulating the accessory organs during the reproductive cycle. The corpus luteum is a major source of progesterone. Hence progesterone level peaks during the luteal phase, and is otherwise low.

Psychological correlates of the menstrual cycle   The notion that women experience changes in personality or mood depending on the phase of the menstrual cycle is well known to the lay person (for example the Sally-is-blue advertisements) and scientist alike. In this section we shall examine the evidence on the nature and extent of these moods and behavior shifts, and their relationship to the hormone cycles occurring during the menstrual cycle.

In 1931, R. T. Frank gave the name "premenstrual tension" to the mood changes that occur during the three or four days immediately preceding menstruation (approximately days 23 to 26 or 28 of the cycle). This phase is characterized by negative feelings, including depression, anxiety, irritability, and low self-esteem. There is by now an extensive literature on this phenomenon, and the more general one of fluctuations in mood and behavior corresponding to the menstrual cycle (see Parlee, 1973, for a critical review).

Four types of studies have been used to document the existence of a premenstrual syndrome. First, attempts have been made to correlate observable behaviors with cycle phase. For example, it has been found that a large proportion of the criminal acts of violence and suicides committed by women occur during the four premenstrual and four menstrual days of the cycle (Dalton, 1964). Forty-five percent of the female industrial workers who call in sick, 46 percent of the women admitted to psychiatric care, and 52 percent of female accident-emergency admissions are in the eight premenstrual or menstrual days. In addition, 54 percent of the children brought to a clinic with minor colds were brought during their mothers' eight premenstrual and menstrual days, perhaps indicating an increase in mothers' anxiety at this time (Dalton, 1966). The premenstrual syndrome, then, may have rather important and far-reaching consequences. On the other hand, it is important to notice that the eight premenstrual and menstrual days do constitute 36 percent of the total days in a cycle. Hence a statistic like "49 percent of criminal acts committed by women are during this period," which appears impressive considered by itself, may not represent a substantial or meaningful increase over the 36 percent expected randomly. And even with these presumed hormone effects, it is important to note that women commit far fewer crimes than men do. Other studies attempting to demonstrate behavioral changes over the menstrual cycle have failed to find such fluctuations for intellectual performance (Sommer, 1972; Golub, 1976) and reaction time (Zimmerman and Parlee, 1973).

A second type of study used to document the premenstrual syndrome is based on questionnaires requesting that women report retrospectively their symptoms and moods at various phases of the cycle. Such studies are largely useless since the questionnaires have not been adequately developed. In addition, retrospective accounts, particularly of such evanescent phenomena as moods in relation to menstrual cycle, are notoriously unreliable and have not been demonstrated to correlate with other indicators of premenstrual symptoms, that is, their validity is not established (Parlee, 1973).

A third type of study uses daily self-reports made by women throughout the cycle. Such studies generally find positive moods around the time of ovulation, and various symptoms, such as anxiety, irritability, depression, fatigue, and headaches, premenstrually (see summary by Parlee, 1973).

A fourth approach avoids direct questioning of subjects about symptoms, and instead uses a kind of projective technique, in which subjects tell stories at regular intervals throughout the cycle. These stories are then subjected to a standardized scoring for themes manifested in them. An example is a study by Ivey and Bardwick (1968), who recorded the spontaneous stories of twenty-six college women at ovulation and premenstruation over two menstrual cycles and then scored them using Gottschalk and Gleser's Verbal Anxiety Scale. Their findings for these normal subjects (the results are much like those in the classic work of Benedek and Rubenstein, 1942, using psychiatric patients) were that anxiety about death, mutilation, and separation were highest premenstrually, while self-confidence and self-esteem were higher at ovulation. Ivey and Bardwick provide the following examples:

From one woman at ovulation:

We took our skis and packed them on top of the car and then we took off for up north. We used to go for long walks in the snow, and it was just really great, really quiet and peaceful.

Mutilation anxiety from the same woman premenstrually:

. . . came around a curve and did a double flip and landed upside down. I remember this car coming down on my hand and slicing it right open and all this blood was all over the place. Later they thought it was broken because every time I touched the finger, it felt like a nail was going through my hand.

From another woman at ovulation:

Talk about my trip to Europe. It was just the greatest summer of my life. We met all kinds of terrific people everywhere we went, and just the most terrific things happened.

Hostility from this same woman premenstrually:

. . . talk about my brother and his wife. I hated her. I just couldn't stand her . . . I used to do terrible things to separate them.

In summary, the results of the research using all of these approaches do seem to indicate that there are fluctuations in mood corresponding to the phases of the menstrual cycle.

It is tempting to speculate that these mood-behavior changes are related to, or perhaps even caused by, changes in hormone levels occurring during the cycle (Bardwick, 1971). In particular, it seems that high levels of estrogen (at ovulation) are associated with positive moods, while low levels of estrogen premenstrually are associated with negative moods.

However, such a conclusion has been severely criticized on a number of counts (Parlee, 1973). First, virtually all of the data (with some exceptions discussed below) presented to support this contention are correlational in nature; causal inferences are then made from these data, an unwise procedure at best. That is, the data simply demonstrate a correlation between cycle phase or hormone levels and mood. From this it is unwarranted to infer that hormones actually cause or influence mood. From these data an equally tenable conclusion would be that the direction of causality is the reverse — that psychological factors affect hormone levels and menstrual-cycle phase. For example, gynecology texts state that stress may delay menstruation or precipitate its onset; many women in concentration camps during World War II ceased menstruating. Social factors may also have an influence; for example, females living together in a college dormitory came to have menstrual cycles more closely synchronized as the academic year progressed (McClintock, 1971). In sum, the inference that hormone level influences mood is not completely justifiable on the basis of the available data, although further data may yet substantiate this conclusion.

One study (Paige, 1971) that partially answers the objection about correlational data involved scoring the spoken stories of 102 married women four times during a single menstrual cycle: on days 4, 10, 16, and two days before the onset of menstruation. Other data were also collected to try to disguise the purpose of the study. The subjects fell into three groups: (1) those who were not taking oral contraceptives and never had; (2) those who were taking a combination pill (combination pills provide a steady high dose of both estrogen and progestin, a synthetic progesterone, for twenty or twenty-one days); and (3) those who were taking sequential-type pills (which provide fifteen days of estrogen, followed by five days of estrogen-progestin, similar to the natural cycle, but at higher levels). Nonpill women experienced statistically significant variation in their anxiety and hostility levels over the menstrual cycle as previous studies had shown. Women taking the sequential pill showed the same mood changes that nonpill women did, which agrees with the predicted outcome, since their artificial hormone cycle parallels the natural one. Combination-pill women showed *no* mood shifts corresponding to the menstrual cycle: their hostility and anxiety levels remained constant. Therefore it appears that the steady high level of both hormones leads to a steady level of affect. This study serves as a pseudo-experiment with respect to hormone levels, thereby answering, in part, the objections with regard to causal inferences on hormone-behavior relations.

A second criticism of this area of research is that the term "premenstrual syndrome" or "premenstrual tension syndrome" is only vaguely defined. For instance, some authors have defined it so broadly as to include "any combination of emotional or physical features which occur cyclically in a female before menstruation" (Sutherland and Stewart, 1965, p. 1182). While it would be worthwhile to know what percentage of the female population is afflicted with premenstrual symptoms, estimates of this percentage vary considerably from one study to another. In one study, premenstrual irritability was found in 69 percent of the sample, depression in 63 percent, and both symptoms together in 45 percent (Sutherland and Stewart, 1965). In another study, the responses of approximately 30 to 50 percent of 839 young married women to a questionnaire indicated mood cycles in irritability, tension, and depression (Moos, 1968). On the other hand, another investigator noted that 56 percent of the women in his sample did not report any significant premenstrual tension symptoms (Rees, 1953). In view of the vagueness of definition, it is not surprising that these estimates are not consistent, and until the "syndrome" is more clearly defined, we can have no really accurate estimate of its incidence. At least from these data it seems fair to conclude that the premenstrual syndrome is far from universal among women. It is possible that 50 percent of women have no premenstrual symptoms.

A third, and very real, problem with this area of research is the problem of subject expectations. Subjects may report more negative feelings premenstrually because such feelings are culturally prescribed — brainwashing through menstrual drug ads — or because they feel the experimenter expects them, since they must certainly be aware of the investigator's interest in their menstrual cycle.

Psychologist Diane Ruble (1977) did a clever experiment to determine whether subjects' expectations influence their reporting of premenstrual symptoms. College student subjects were tested on the sixth or seventh day before the onset of their next menstrual period. They were told that they would participate in a study on a new technique for predicting the expected date of menstruation using an electroencephalogram (EEG), a method that had already been successfully tested with older women. After the electroencephalogram had been run, the subject was informed of when her next period was to occur, depending on which of three experimental groups she had been assigned to: (1) the subject was told she was "premenstrual" and her period was due in 1 or 2 days; (2) the subject was told she was "intermenstrual" or "midcycle" and her period was not expected for at least a week to 10 days; or (3) she was given no information at all about the expected date of menstruation (control group). The women then completed a self-report menstrual distress questionnaire. The results indicated that subjects who had been led to believe they were in the premenstrual phase reported significantly more water retention, pain, and changes in eating habits, than did subjects who had been led to believe they were around midcycle. (In fact, subjects in these groups did not differ significantly in when their periods actually arrived.) There were no significant differences between the groups in ratings of negative moods, however. This study indicates that, probably because of learned beliefs, women overstate the change in body states that occur over the menstrual cycle. When they think they are in the premenstrual phase, they report more problems than when they think they are at midcycle.

A subtle problem of interpretation also exists in menstrual cycle research. A typical conclusion is that symptoms increase or that mood is negative premenstrually. Perhaps, however, the premenstrual state is the "usual" one, and what occurs is really a decrease in symptoms, or a positive mood shift, at ovulation. This is essentially a problem of establishing a baseline of behavior — and what should that be? Should it be the average for males? Or are males irrelevent to this research? This is a complex question needing further resolution.

We should also note the tremendous cultural influences on menstrual-cycle mood shifts. In many primitive societies and religions, the menstruating woman is seen as unclean, and many taboos arise to prevent her uncleanness from spreading to others (Stephens, 1961). For example, she may not be permitted to cook while menstruating, or she may even be isolated from the rest of the community in a separate hut outside the village. Such superstitions become subtler in modern America, but they still persist. For example, many couples abstain from sexual intercourse during the woman's period. A recent survey of 960 California families showed that half the men and women had *never* had sex during menstruation (Paige, 1973). There is also considerable evidence of cultural influences on menstrual distress. For example, groups of married women were compared, according to their religious preference, on attitudes toward menstruation and variations in anxiety during the cycle (Paige, 1973). Most of the Jews and Catholics said they would never have sex during menstruation, as compared with less than half the Protestants. Protestants did not experience much fluctuation in anxiety level between the ovulation and premenstrual phase, while Catholics showed extreme fluctuations. These cultural variations in menstrual attitudes and symptoms may be related to religious teaching regarding menstruation (Paige, 1973). In any case, Protestant, Catholic, and Jewish women all have the same hormone cycles, but the correlated psychological cycles are different, so that the psychological cycles must surely be influenced by culture.

Finally, this area of research has seen too little attention devoted to coping mechanisms (Maccoby, 1972). Most women are simply not dissolved in tears, reduced to a state of incompetency, for three to six days each month. Certainly women must develop mechanisms for coping with these mood shifts, particularly if they are so regular and predictable. In fact, it might be reasonable to expect that the women who experience the largest mood shifts would develop the best strategies for coping with them. Unfortunately, we have little empirical evidence on these points. Our own interviews with undergraduates suggest that increased activity, "keeping busy," is the most common coping strategy. Another common coping mechanism is sleeping more than usual — a kind of escapism, but also a very practical means of dealing with feelings of fatigue. In addition, because the premenstrual syndrome is so well known, it is easy to deal with accompanying symptoms such as depression — most women quickly spot that the depression is associated with the onset of menstruation and proceed about their business, unconcerned that they are displaying serious psychological symptoms as they know that the symptoms will disappear in a few days.

In assessing the practical implications of this research, some important considerations should be kept in mind. First, the *magnitude* of the mood shift depends very much on the individual woman. It is a function of her psychological adjustment, as well as her current experiences. Certainly in practical situations, the magnitude and content of the mood shift are most important. For instance, it is much more important to know that a particular woman experiences mood shifts so small as to be unnoticeable in her work and interpersonal relations, than to know that she experiences slight mood shifts detectable only by sensitive psychological tests. Hence the most important characteristics are individual ones, just as they are for men.

Second, in making practical decisions about hiring people, certainly performance is more important than mood. Most of the available research documents mood cycles. Few attempts have been made to demonstrate cycles in performance, such as intellectual or athletic performance, and most of these have demonstrated an absence of such cycles in females (Golub, 1976; Sommer, 1973). Thus there is no substantial evidence that the behaviors required in a work situation are influenced by menstrual-cycle phase.

In addition, it is possible that monthly hormonal cycles exist in men also (Parlee, 1978; Delaney et al., 1976; Ramey, 1972, Hersey, 1931), but until quite recently they have not been the subject of scientific investigation — probably because they produce no obvious symptoms like menstruation.

In summary, research suggests that menstrual-cycle changes in hormone levels may be related to corresponding changes in mood. Mood is generally positive at ovulation or mid-cycle, when estrogen levels are high, while it is negative, with feelings of depression, anxiety, and irritability, at the time of low estrogen levels premenstrually. The existing research has many problems: most of it is correlational in nature, and subject expectations complicate interpretations. Cultural factors may also contribute to mood shifts. In addition, probably a substantial proportion of women either do not experience such mood cycles, or their cyclic fluctuations are so small as to be undetectable.

MENOPAUSE

Physical and psychological changes   A number of physical as well as psychological changes occur during the climacteric. *Climacteric* refers to the gradual aging of the ovaries over the years, leading to a decline in their efficiency. Most importantly, estrogen production declines, leading to the most obvious symptom of the climacteric, menopause, which occurs on the average at age 47. Another effect is the atrophy of genital tissue and shrinking of the breasts.

A number of symptoms occur at this time: physical symptoms such as "hot flashes"; psychological symptoms such as depression, irritability, crying spells, and inability to concentrate; and what may be psychosomatic symptoms such as dizziness, headaches, and heart pounding.

Do all women experience these menopausal symptoms? In a survey of 638 women aged 45 to 55, conducted in London in 1964–1965, 30 to 50 percent of the women reported experiencing dizziness, palpitations, insomnia, depression, headache, or weight gain, and most of these women reported experiencing several of these symptoms rather than just one. About 50 percent of the women experienced hot flashes, and half of the 50 percent said the flashes were acutely uncomfortable (McKinlay and Jeffreys, 1974). It is generally estimated that only about 10 percent of all women suffer severe distress at menopause. Thus it might be concluded that at least as many as 50 percent (perhaps 80 to 90 percent) of all women suffer some of these uncomfortable menopausal symptoms, only about 10 percent are severely affected, and a sizable proportion — at least 10 percent and perhaps as many as 50 percent — display none of these symptoms.

Psychological problems of menopause include depression, irritability, anxiety, nervousness, crying spells, inability to concentrate, and feelings of suffocation. In rare cases, the depression may be extremely severe (involutional melancholia) in a woman who has no previous history of mental problems. It is estimated that about 10 percent of women suffer from serious depression during menopause. Less severe depression during menopause is more common.

These psychological symptoms, however, involve a subtle problem of interpretation similar to the one mentioned in conjunction with the premenstrual-tension syndrome. Women are said to have "more" problems during menopause. More than what? More than men? More than at other times in their own lives? Investigating the latter question, psychologists Bernice Neugarten and Ruth Kraines (1965) studied symptoms among women of different age groups. They found that adolescents and menopausal women reported the largest number of problematic symptoms. Postmenopausal women reported the smallest number of problematic symptoms. Apparently, menopause does not permanently "wreck" a woman. Among the adolescents, psychological symptoms were the most common (for example, tension), while among the menopausal women, physical symptoms such as hot flashes were most common. Menopausal women showed an increase in only five categories of psychological symptoms: headache, irritability, nervousness, feeling blue, and feelings of suffocation (the latter being associated with hot flashes). Thus menopause does not seem to be the worst time of a woman's life psychologically; probably it is not as bad as adolescence.

Biology or culture?   The difficulties associated with menopause are attributed to biology (in particular, to hormones) by some, and to culture and its expectations by others.

From the biological perspective, the symptoms of menopause appear to be due to the woman's hormonal state. In particular, the symptoms appear to be related either to low estrogen levels or to hormonal imbalance. The former hypothesis, called the *estrogen-deficiency theory*, has been the subject of the most research. Proponents of this theory argue that the physical symptoms, such as hot flashes, and the psychological symptoms, such as depression, are caused by declining amounts of estrogen in the body. It is also worth noting that, hormonally, this period is similar to the premenstrual period, with its declining estrogen levels, and that the psychological symptoms are also similar: depression and irritability.

The best evidence for the estrogen-deficiency theory comes from the success of estrogen-replacement therapy. Physicians may prescribe estrogen either in its natural form, Premarin, or in a synthetic form such as Stilbestrol, Progynon, or Meprane. Estrogen-replacement therapy is very successful in relieving low-estrogen menopausal symptoms like hot flashes, sweating, cold hands and feet, osteoporosis, and vaginal discharges. It may also relieve psychological symptoms such as irritability and depression (see Bardwick, 1971, for a review). The success of this therapy suggests that low estrogen levels cause menopausal symptoms and that increasing estrogen levels relieves the symptoms.[1]

On the other hand, advocates of the environmental point of view note the cultural forces that may act to produce psychological stress in women around the time of menopause. The aging process itself may be psychologically stressful in our youth-oriented culture. The menopausal years remind a woman forcefully that she is aging. Menopause also means that the woman can no longer bear children. For women who have a great psychological investment in motherhood, this can be a difficult realization. In Chapter 6 we reviewed research on the empty nest syndrome and found that some investigators question whether this is a time of depression among women. Further, we noted that menopausal symptoms do not occur in women in cultures in which women's status rises at this time (Bart, 1971).

We have a strong cultural bias toward expecting menopausal symptoms. Thus any quirk in a middle-aged woman's behavior is attributed to the "change." It simultaneously becomes the cause of, and explanation for, all the problems and complaints of the middle-aged woman. Given such expectations, it is not surprising that the average person perceives widespread evidence of the pervasiveness of menopausal symptoms. Ironically, idiosyncrasies in women of childbearing age are blamed on menstruation, while problems experienced by women who are past that age are blamed on the *lack* of it.

As a way of resolving this biology-culture controversy, it seems reasonable to conclude that the physical symptoms of menopause, such as hot flashes, are probably due to declining estrogen levels, and that the psychological symptoms, such as depression, may be due to low estrogen levels or culturally imposed stresses, or a combination of both.

PREGNANCY AND CHILDBIRTH

Pregnancy is marked by radical hormone changes, in which both estrogen and progesterone levels are high. Early in pregnancy, the corpus luteum is responsible for this production, while later in pregnancy, the placenta is the major source of the two hormones.

Research on the exact emotional states of women during pregnancy has produced conflicting results and opinions (reviewed by Sherman,

---

[1] Any possible benefits of estrogen-replacement therapy should be weighed against the dangers, because there is increasing evidence linking it to cancer of the uterus (Mack et al., 1976; Marx, 1976; Weiss et al., 1976).

1971), and the radiant contentment of the pregnant woman is far from a well-established fact. Benedek's view (1959) that pregnancy is a time of "vegetative calm" is countered by the view that pregnancy is a time of crisis (Bibring et al., 1961; Taylor, 1962). Some support for the former view comes from one study in which it was concluded that pregnancy was a time of unusual well-being (Hooke and Marks, 1962). In another study, pregnant women were found to be introverted, passive, dependent, and in need of love and affection (Caplan, 1960). But feelings of dependency may produce anxiety in women who pride themselves on self-sufficiency (Hamilton, 1955). Supporting the "crisis" view, pregnant Jewish women showed more depression as measured by the Rorschach inkblot test (though not by another personality test, the MMPI) than a nonpregnant control group (Riffaterre, 1965). Negative attitudes and moods would not be surprising in view of the fact that some children are unwanted (Sherman, 1971, p. 170). For example, in a sample of Scottish women, 41 percent did not want the pregnancy, 18 percent did not mind, and 41 percent desired it (Scott et al., 1956). In another study, 80 percent of the women were happy about their first one or two children, but only 31 percent were happy about the fourth or more (Gordon, 1967). Further evidence of negative attitudes regarding pregnancy comes from data on the substantial number of induced abortions. In the sample of females in the Kinsey study, about 20 to 25 percent had had an induced abortion sometime in their lives (Gebhard et al., 1958).

Emotional state seems to be related to stage of pregnancy (Sherman, 1971, p. 177). During the first three months, depression and fatigue are not at all uncommon. Women's emotions are generally most positive during the second trimester (months 4 to 6). The last trimester may be more stressful and anxious, as the woman begins to worry about how the delivery will go, whether the baby will be healthy, and so on. As Sherman concludes,

> So far as emotional state in pregnancy is concerned, the weight of the evidence suggests that it is not generally a period of unusual well-being. However, such feelings occur in some women during middle pregnancy, and there may be a decrease in psychotic reactions during pregnancy. Milder emotional disturbances, however, apparently increase, especially during the last six weeks (1971, p. 179).

Parturition, or childbirth, represents a major shock to the body. Estrogen and progesterone levels drop sharply, and it may take as long as several months for the levels to return to normal and for menstruation to resume. Psychologically, there is the well-known syndrome of *postpartum depression*, in which the woman, immediately after childbirth and perhaps for a week or more, feels depression. Suicide attempts are more frequent than usual. Estimates of the proportion of women experiencing some postpartum emotional disturbance or depression range from 25 to 67 percent

(Sherman, 1971). Severe disturbance is rare; postpartum psychosis occurs in about one woman in every 400 (Gordon and Gordon, 1967).

Psychological and social influences on the symptoms of the pregnancy and postpartum periods should be noted. Our culture is full of lore on the psychological characteristics of pregnant women — the glow of radiant contentment, the desire for dill pickles and ice cream. Perhaps pregnant women display these symptoms simply as a result of learning rather than because of hormones. The proper behavior for pregnancy is learned through the process of gender-role socialization, and the behaviors are displayed when the time comes. Positive moods might be further related to a strong desire for a child. Negative moods might be related to not wanting the child, fear of the dangers of childbirth, or fear of responsibility for the child. Postpartum depression might be related to the sudden change that has occurred in one's life, not wanting the baby, fearing responsibility for it, or even such a simple factor as being in a hospital and being separated from one's husband and family. Separation from the baby, which is often enforced for the first twelve to twenty-four hours in the hospital, may also contribute to depression (Klaus et al., 1972). It has been demonstrated that postpartum emotional reactions are influenced by both past and present stresses (Gordon et al., 1965). Thus depression symptoms could be as easily explained by psychological and social factors as by hormonal ones. Probably, in reality, postpartum depression is a result of a combination of biological factors (shock to the body, radically diminished hormone levels), and social-psychological factors.

ABORTION

A number of methods of abortion are available (see Hyde, 1979, for a more complete discussion). The most commonly used method is vacuum curettage (also called dilation and evacuation (D and E), vacuum suction, and vacuum aspiration). It is done on an outpatient basis with a local anesthetic. The procedure itself takes only about ten minutes and the woman stays in the doctor's office, clinic, or hospital for a few hours. The woman is prepared as she would be for a pelvic exam, and an instrument is inserted into the vagina. The instrument dilates (stretches open) the opening in the cervix. A nonflexible tube is then inserted through the opening until one end is in the uterus. The other end is attached to a suction-producing machine, and the contents of the uterus, including the fetal tissue, are sucked out. Recent statistics indicate that D and E is the safest method of abortion, not only during the first trimester, but through the twentieth week of pregnancy (U. S. Public Health Service, 1976).

It is a common belief that making the decision to have an abortion and having one are times of extreme psychological stress, and that psychological problems may result. In fact, however, according to research that has been done on women who have had legal abortions, the experience is not traumatic (see review by Osofsky and Osofsky, 1972). Most women report feeling relieved and happy after the abortion. Fewer than 10 percent of women experience psychological problems afterward, and most of them had problems before the pregnancy and abortion.

Women generally appear to be well adjusted after having an abortion, but well adjusted compared with what? That is, what is the appropriate control or comparison group? One comparison group that has been studied is women who requested an abortion but were denied it. Women in this group have a much higher rate of disturbance than women who have had abortions. Another group that has been studied is children who were born because an abortion request was denied. They, too, show a high incidence of psychiatric disturbance (Forssman and Thuwe, 1966).

The highly publicized "Akron ordinance," passed by the voters of Akron, Ohio, requires that women requesting an abortion be told

> that abortion may leave essentially unaffected or may worsen any existing psychological problems she may have, and can result in severe emotional disturbances.

According to the research discussed above, the psychological "information" being given is not really true, at least as far as the scientific evidence shows at this time. It seems unfortunate that people can vote to have incorrect information conveyed, particularly on such an important issue.

MASTECTOMY

Breast cancer is the most common form of cancer in women. It is rare in women under 25, and a woman's chances of developing it increase every year after that age. About 1 out of every 15 American women (7 percent) develops breast cancer at some time in her life (Lanson, 1975).

Because breast cancer is relatively common, every woman should do a breast self-exam monthly, around midcycle (*not* during one's period, when there may be natural lumps). Unfortunately, psychological factors such as fear prevent some women from doing the self-exam or, if they discover a lump, from seeing a doctor immediately. This is unfortunate because the more quickly breast cancer is discovered and treated, the better the chances of recovery.

In fact, not all breast lumps are cancerous. There are three kinds of breast lumps: cysts (fluid-filled sacs, also called fibrocystic disease or cystic mastitis), fibroadenomas, and malignant tumors. The important thing to realize is that 80 percent of breast lumps are cysts or fibroadenomas and are therefore benign, that is, not dangerous. Techniques for diagnosis of breast cancer are controversial. Most physicians feel that the most definitive method is the excisional biopsy, in which a small slit is made in the breast, the lump is removed, and a pathologist determines whether it is cancerous. Other diagnostic techniques include needle aspiration, thermography, mammography, and xeroradiography.

If a malignancy is confirmed, what is the best treatment? This is also controversial. The treatment usually is some form of mastectomy, that is, surgical removal of the breast. In radical mastectomy, the most serious form of surgery, the entire breast, as well as the lymph nodes and underlying muscles are removed. Advocates of this procedure argue that it is best to be as thorough as possible, and that the muscle and lymph nodes should be removed in case the cancer has spread to them. In modified radical mastectomy, the entire breast and lymph nodes, but not the muscles, are moved. In simple mastectomy, only the breast, and possibly a few lymph nodes are removed. In partial mastectomy or lumpectomy, only the lump and some surrounding tissue are removed. Unfortunately, the data do not provide definite evidence of whether the more radical procedures lead to a higher survival rate (Lanson, 1975).

Breast cancer and mastectomy are topics with important psychological consequences. The psychological impact of a mastectomy can be enormous (Asken, 1975). Severe depression as well as suicides following mastectomy have been reported (Ervin, 1973). Our culture is very breast-oriented. For a woman whose identity has been defined in terms of her beauty and her voluptuous figure, mastectomy may be perceived as a destruction of her womanhood and a blow to her sense of identity. There may be effects on her sexual expression, and she may feel that no man would want her in such a disfigured condition.

A recent systematic study of 41 women who had mastectomies indicated that 60 percent judged their postmastectomy emotional adjustment to be excellent or very good, but 10 percent judged it not very good, poor, or very poor (Jamison et al., 1978). About one-fourth of the women reported having suicidal thoughts following the mastectomy. About 15 percent sought professional help for their emotional problems related to the mastectomy. Interestingly, however, it was not the postmastectomy period that was rated as most difficult psychologically; rather, the period immediately following discovery of the lump was reported as being the worst. About three-quarters of the women reported that their sexual satisfaction in marriage had not changed or was better, but one-quarter reported a change for the worse. In sum, this study provides evidence of successful coping by the majority of mastectomy patients, but it also indicates that a substantial minority of women suffer considerable psychological stress. It is extremely important for mastectomy patients and their husbands to have counseling available. The American Cancer Society has organized support groups for mastectomy patients in many towns.

IN CONCLUSION

In this chapter we have discussed the psychological aspects of some topics considered important by the women's health movement. We considered the evidence on whether women experience menstrual-cycle fluctuations in mood and whether these shifts are caused by fluctuating hormone levels. Although there is a great deal of research in this area, there are fundamental problems with the research itself which makes it difficult to draw firm conclusions. Our conclusion is that some, though not all, women experience menstrual-cycle fluctuations in mood. There is evidence of both hormonal and cultural influences on the fluctuations; it seems likely that cultural forces act to increase the woman's perception of relatively small body changes.

Our conclusions about menopause were similar. Some, though not all, women experience psychological symptoms such as depression and irritability. Once again, the perception of a body change is magnified by cultural factors — expectations that there should be menopausal depression, loss of role and the empty nest, and so on.

Research on the psychological aspects of pregnancy indicates that a woman's psychological state depends on the stage of pregnancy she is in; negative moods are more common in the first and third trimesters, and positive moods are more common in the second. Once again, environmental factors probably influence the woman's perception of her body changes.

Research on the psychological consequences of having an abortion indicate that it is generally not a traumatic experience.

Finally, we emphasized the psychological aspects of mastectomy, something physicians often fail to recognize.

In all these cases, we feel that as women inform themselves more about the functioning of their bodies, they should also inform themselves about the *psychological* aspects of these processes.

12

FEMALE
SEXUALITY

Clitoral stimulation is more intensive and produces a more violent reaction. . . . Vaginal stimulation is much more relaxing and much less intense. I like it. I love clitoral stimulation . . . vaginal stimulation is soothing and produces a rhythmical rocking and rotating of the pelvis. . . . It is never intense as clitoral stimulation, yet feels extremely good in its own way. The best analogy I can contrive is the difference between someone lightly and caressingly stroking your bare back or arm or face and being violently, exhaustingly tickled. The former resembles vaginal, the latter clitoral stimulation. Vaginal stimulation soothes me and produces an involuntary contented hum deep in my throat. The vaginal stimulation of intercourse produces a closeness, a coordination, a sense of oneness unmatched by any other sexual activity.

S. FISHER, Understanding the
Female Orgasm

It is not coincidental that the liberation of women and the sexual revolution are taking place simultaneously. Historically, sex for women has always meant pregnancy, which has meant babies, and which, in turn, has meant a life devoted to motherhood. For the first time in the history of any species, we are now able to separate sex from reproduction, both in theory and in practice.

As a result, women are now free to be sexy without making a twenty-year commitment to motherhood. And so, perhaps, we may begin to consider the real nature of female sexuality, uncomplicated by reproductive functions (and fears).

PHYSIOLOGY

Only recently has female sexual physiology been the subject of scientific investigation. Most of our contemporary knowledge in this area is due to the important work of William Masters and Virginia Johnson (1966). Here we will give only a summary of their results, concentrating on the female response. Readers who wish more detail should consult the original technical reports (Masters and Johnson, 1966, 1970), or one of the analyses of their results intended for the lay person (Brecher and Brecher, 1966; Belliveau and Richter, 1970).

Masters and Johnson distinguish four phases in sexual response, although it should be noted that these stages flow together. The first phase is *excitement*. In the female, the primary response is *vasocongestion* or engorgement of the tissues surrounding the vagina. This simply means that a great deal of blood accumulates in the blood vessels of the pelvic region. A secondary response is the contraction of various muscle fibers, which results, among other things, in erection of the nipples.

Perhaps the most noticeable response in this period is the moistening of the vagina with a lubricating fluid. This seems quite different from the most noticeable response in males, erection of the penis. In fact, Masters and Johnson have discovered that the underlying physiological mechanisms are the same, namely vasocongestion or engorgement. It is fairly common knowledge that engorgement causes erection in the male. Masters and Johnson believe that the droplets of moisture that appear on the walls of the vagina during sexual excitation are fluids that have seeped out of congested blood vessels in the surrounding region. Hence the physiological underpinnings are the same in males and in females, although the observable response seems different.

FIGURE 12.1

Female sexual and reproductive anatomy.

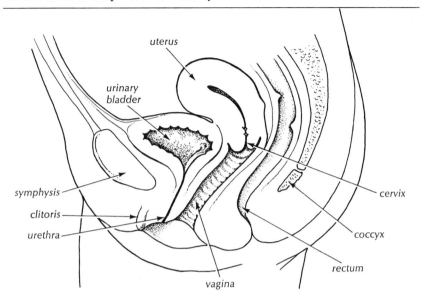

Source: After Belliveau and Richter, 1970.

Lubrication marks only the beginning of female sexual response, however. In the excitement phase, a number of other changes take place, most notably in the clitoris. The clitoris, located just in front of the vagina (see Figure 12.2), is, like the penis, a shaft with a bulb or "glans" at the tip. The glans is densely packed with highly sensitive nerve endings. Hence clitoral stimulation contributes greatly to female sexual response. In sexual intercourse, the clitoris is stimulated both by direct clitoral-area friction, and by movement of the penis through the labia minor (inner lips), which causes the "hood" or prepuce of the clitoris to move back and forth across the glans of the clitoris, resulting in stimulation of this organ. Hence the clitoris is always stimulated in intercourse.

In response to further arousal, the clitoral glans swells, and the shaft increases in diameter probably also due to engorgement. This may be in response to the stimulation described above, to stimulation in another area of the body, such as the breasts, or to purely psychological stimulation, such as an erotic train of thought.

The vagina also responds in this phase. Think of the vagina as a barrel in the resting state, divided into an outer third (or lower third, in a woman standing upright) and an inner two thirds (or upper two thirds). During the successive stages of sexual response, the inner and outer por-

FIGURE 12.2

The external genitals of the human female.

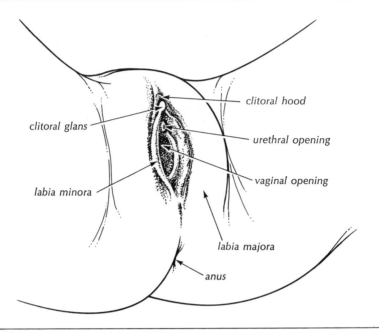

clitoral hood

clitoral glans

urethral opening

vaginal opening

labia minora

labia majora

anus

Source: After Belliveau and Richter, 1970.

tions react in very different ways. In the latter part of the excitement phase, the inner two-thirds of the vagina undergoes a dramatic expansion or ballooning. This produces a tenting or pulling apart of the vaginal walls surrounding the cervix (see Figure 12.3).

In the second phase of the woman's sexual response, the *plateau phase*, the major change is the appearance of the "orgasmic platform" (Masters and Johnson, 1966). This refers to the outer third of the vagina when it swells and is engorged with blood, with its diameter reduced by as much as 50 percent (see Figure 12.3). Hence while the upper portion of the vagina expands during excitement, the lower or outer portion narrows during the plateau phase. The orgasmic platform therefore grips the penis (if there happens to be a penis in the vagina at that point), resulting in a noticeable increase in the erotic stimulation experienced by the male.

The other major change occurring during the plateau phase is the elevation of the clitoris. The clitoris retracts and draws away from the vaginal entrance, but continues to respond to stimulation. A number of autonomic responses also occur, including an increase in pulse rate, and a rise in blood pressure and in rate of breathing.

FIGURE 12.3

Female sexual and reproductive organs during the plateau phase of sexual response. Notice the ballooning of the upper part of the vagina, the elevation of the uterus, and the formation of the orgasmic platform.

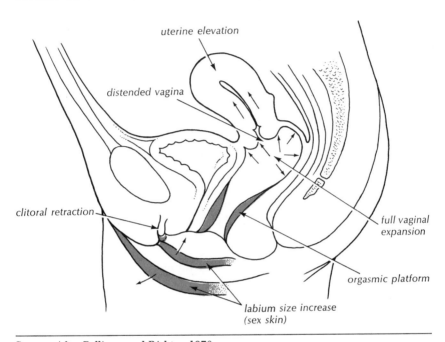

Source: After Belliveau and Richter, 1970.

Once again, these complex changes seem to be the result of two basic physiological processes, vasocongestion (the blood vessels becoming engorged with blood) and increased muscular tension, which occur similarly in both men and women. Readiness for orgasm occurs when these two processes have reached adequate levels. As Masters and Johnson describe it, in the plateau phase "the female gathers psychological and physiological strength from the stockpile of mounting sexual tension, until she can direct all her physical and mental forces toward a leap into the third or orgasmic phase of sexual tension expression."

The female *orgasm*, the third phase of sexual response, consists of a series of rhythmic muscular contractions of the orgasmic platform. Generally there is a series of three to twelve contractions, at intervals of slightly less than a second. The onset of the subjective experience of orgasm is an initial spasm of the orgasmic platform preceding the rhythmic contractions.

The sensations of orgasm in the female have been described as follows:

In the female, orgasm starts with a feeling of momentary suspension followed by a peak of intense sensation in the clitoris, which then spreads through the pelvis. This stage varies in intensity and may also involve sensations of "falling," "opening up," or even emitting fluid. Some women compare this stage of orgasm to mild labor pains. It is followed by a suffusion of warmth spreading from the pelvis through the rest of the body. The experience culminates in characteristic throbbing sensations in the pelvis. (Katchadourian and Lunde, 1972, p. 58).

Contrary to popular belief, orgasm does not signal the end of sexual response. In the fourth or *resolution phase* of sexual response, the major physiological changes are a release of muscular tensions throughout the body and a release of blood from the engorged blood vessels. In the female, the breasts, which were formerly enlarged with nipples erect, return to the normal state. The clitoris returns to its normal, unretracted position and shrinks to normal size. The orgasmic platform relaxes, and the ballooned upper portion of the vagina shrinks. The return of the female to the unstimulated state may require as long as a half hour following orgasm. If the woman reaches the plateau phase without having an orgasm, the restoration process takes longer, often as much as an hour. Indeed, prostitutes who habitually experience arousal without orgasm may experience cumulative physiological effects, resulting in chronic engorgement of the vaginal tissues (Masters and Johnson, 1966).

COMMON FALLACIES

Because sexuality has been so often the subject of superstition and so seldom the subject of scientific research, even modern American culture is filled with distorted ideas about it. A discussion of several misconceptions about female sexuality and the results of relevant scientific research follow.

Clitoral and vaginal orgasm   Freud believed that women can experience two different kinds of orgasm — clitoral and vaginal. According to his view, little girls learn to achieve masturbatory orgasm through stimulation of the clitoris. However in adulthood, they have to learn to transfer the focus of their sexual response from the clitoris to the vagina, and to orgasm from intercourse. Since some women fail to make this transfer, they can only experience clitoral orgasm, and are therefore "vaginally frigid." Freud thought that the only mature female orgasm was vaginal.

Masters and Johnson have dispelled this myth by showing convincingly that, physiologically, there is only one kind of orgasm. The major response is the contraction of the orgasmic platform. That is, physiologically an orgasm is the same, whether it results from clitoral stimulation or from vaginal stimulation. Indeed some women are even able to have orgasms through breast stimulation — and the physiological response is identical to that occurring from vaginal intercourse (Masters and Johnson, 1966). Moreover, even in ordinary vaginal intercourse, the clitoris is stimulated as described above. Hence the clitoris participates fully even in vaginal intercourse.

While it is well established that orgasms resulting primarily from vaginal and clitoral stimulation are physiologically the same, psychologically they may be experienced differently. The sensations arising from heterosexual intercourse and clitoral masturbation, for example, may be quite different. Physiologically, the orgasm is the same, but attending conditions (presence of the male and contact with his body) may lead to quite different perceptions of the sensation.

Recent research indicates that women who prefer vaginal stimulation to clitoral stimulation have high levels of anxiety as compared with women who prefer clitoral stimulation or both. This provides further evidence against Freud's belief that vaginal orgasm represents more maturity or better adjustment than clitoral orgasm (Fisher, 1973).

The single, satiating orgasm   It has long been thought that women, like men, experienced only one orgasm, followed by a "refractory period" of minutes or even hours when they are not capable of arousal and orgasm. Recent research shows that this is not true and that, in fact, women can have multiple orgasms. Kinsey (1953) discovered this, reporting that 14 percent of the women he interviewed experienced multiple orgasms. The scientific establishment dismissed these reports as unreliable, however.

Observations from the Masters and Johnson laboratory have provided convincing evidence that women do indeed experience multiple orgasms within a short time period. Moreover, these multiple orgasms do not differ from single ones in any significant way except that there are several. They are not minor experiences. In fact, the second and third orgasms are usually experienced subjectively as more satisfying than the first.

Physiologically, after an orgasm, the vaginal region loses its engorgement of blood. However, in the female, but not in the male, this process is immediately reversible. That is, under continued or renewed erotic stimulation the region again becomes engorged, the orgasmic platform appears, and another orgasm is initiated. This is the physiological mechanism that makes multiple orgasms possible in females. In some women, this process may continue to the point of exhaustion.

Most frequently, multiple orgasms are attained through masturbation rather than intravaginal intercourse, since it is difficult for the male to postpone his orgasm for such long periods, and his stimulation would be necessary for the orgasms to continue.

Sex during pregnancy   Until recently, most physicians as well as the general public have believed that having intercourse during the last stages of pregnancy or too soon after giving birth was dangerous because of possible infection or discomfort to the woman. Women were often forbidden by their doctors from having intercourse from the sixth month of pregnancy through three months postpartum, a total of six months, probably creating some marital strains. This long prohibition appears not to be necessary except in unusual cases. In fact, during the second trimester of pregnancy, there is an increased sexual responsiveness in women (Masters and Johnson, 1966).

Ordinarily, intercourse may continue safely until four weeks before the baby is due, although this is clearly an individual matter. Usually by the third week postpartum, the woman is physically sufficiently recovered for coitus, and her sexual responsiveness also generally returns at this time. Hence it appears that the prohibition need be only slightly less than two months. As we shall see, breastfeeding can be sexually arousing, tied in physiologically to the sexual-response system of the female. The sexual responsiveness of women who breastfeed returns sooner after giving birth than it does for those who don't.

Sexuality and the elderly   It is a popular belief that a woman's sexual responsiveness is virtually gone by the time she is 60 or so, and perhaps even ceases at menopause. Some people believe that sexual activity is a drain on their health and physical resources, and deliberately stop all sexual activity in middle age in order to prevent or postpone aging. Once again, Masters and Johnson have exploded these myths.

As they conclude, "There is no time limit drawn by the advancing years to female sexuality." For the male, also, under conditions of good health and emotional adjustment, there is "a capacity for sexual performance that frequently may extend beyond the eighty-year age level." One important factor in maintaining sexual responsiveness is a regularity of sexual expression. Inactivity cannot prolong one's sex life.

It is true that certain physiological changes occur in the woman in her later years that influence her sexual activity. The ovaries sharply reduce their production of estrogen at menopause and the vagina loses much of its resiliency, the amount of lubrication becoming substantially reduced. However, it is common for women to be given hormone-replacement therapy after menopause, which minimizes these changes. Application of lubricants is also helpful. Sexual performance seems to depend much more on the opportunity for regular active sexual expression and physical and mental health than it does on hormone imbalance (Masters and Johnson, 1966).

PSYCHOLOGICAL ASPECTS

Gender differences in sexuality   It is a stereotype in our culture that female sexuality and male sexuality are quite different. Women are reputed to be uninterested in sex and slow to arouse. Men, in contrast, are supposed to be constantly aroused. What is the scientific evidence on gender differences in sexuality?[1] There is evidence of differences in two areas: orgasm consistency and masturbation. Evidence is more mixed in two other areas: desire for sex and motives for having intercourse, and arousal to erotic materials. These will all be discussed below.

There is some evidence that males and females differ in the consistency with which they have orgasms during heterosexual intercourse. Women, on the average, seem to be less consistent at having orgasms — at least during coitus — than men are. Investigators have repeatedly found that about 30 percent of married women never have orgasms, or do so only occasionally, during intercourse with their husbands (for example, Kinsey et al., 1953; Terman, 1951). Kinsey estimated that the average married female in his sample had orgasms about 75 percent of the time during intercourse with her husband (Kinsey et al., 1953, p. 375). Kinsey believed that males have orgasms 100 percent of the time, or so close to it that he did not bother to tabulate comparable statistics for them. He also found that about 36 percent of the women in his sample had never had an orgasm before marrying. These data generally reflect the phenomenon that it is harder for females to have orgasms. In fact, one book on female sexuality contains a chapter entitled "The Struggle for Orgasm" (Kronhausen and Kronhausen, 1964), and it expresses how some women feel — as if they have to struggle to have an orgasm.

More recent surveys seem to indicate a trend toward women having orgasms with greater consistency during marital sex. In the Hunt survey (1974), only about 10 to 15 percent of the women reported having orgasms seldom or never. This increased consistency of orgasm might be related to a number of factors, including the increased variety of techniques — such as cunnilingus — that are used in marital sex at the present time. The trend generally seems to be in the direction of diminishing what formerly was a large gender difference in orgasm consistency.

One striking gender difference that emerged in the Kinsey studies was in masturbation. In that sample, 92 percent of the males had masturbated to orgasm at least once in their lives, as compared with 58 percent

---

[1] Much of the evidence to be cited comes from the Kinsey report, which was based on interviews with over 11,000 subjects (Kinsey et al., 1948, 1953). There are two main criticisms of it: (1) the sample is not a random or representative sample of the United States population, and this might lead to mistaken statistics; and (2) it is based on people's self-reports of their sexual behavior, which may not be accurate (Hyde, 1979). The recent survey by Hunt (1974) is more up-to-date, but subject to the same two criticisms.

of the females (Kinsey et al., 1953). Not only did fewer women mastur-bate, but also, in general, those who did masturbate had begun at a later age than the males. Virtually all males said they had masturbated before age 20 (most began between ages 13 and 15), but substantial numbers of women reported masturbating for the first time at age 25, 30, or 35.

Unlike some other gender differences in sexuality — which were pres-ent in the older Kinsey study but which seem to have evaporated by the time of the more recent Hunt study — gender differences in masturbation still seem to be a very real phenomenon. Hunt (1974) found that 94 percent of the males and 63 percent of the females in his sample had masturbated to orgasm at least once, percentages that are very close to those found by Kinsey a generation before. Hunt found that both boys and girls in his sample appeared to have begun masturbating earlier than those in Kinsey's study, but girls still began later than boys.

One question we must ask, however, is whether this is a real gender difference or just an inaccuracy induced by using self-reports. In our cul-ture, particularly in previous decades, more restrictions have been placed on female sexuality than on male sexuality. It might be that these re-strictions have discouraged females from ever masturbating. On the other hand, they might simply lead females to not report masturbating. That is, perhaps women do masturbate but are simply more reticent to report it than men are.

There are, of course, no data to answer that question directly. How-ever, a comparison of the Kinsey data and the Hunt data can provide a clue. In the time intervening between these two studies, presumably restrictions against female sexuality lessened to some extent. A likely consequence of this change is that women began to feel freer to admit that they engaged in various forms of sexual behavior; for example, many more women report that they engage in premarital sex and in oral-genital sex now than at the time of the Kinsey study. Yet the percentage of women who say they masturbate has remained relatively constant (58 percent in the Kinsey study, 63 percent in the Hunt study). This suggests that the women in Hunt's study would have felt free to say that they masturbated if they really did; after all, they were willing to say that they engaged in premarital sex and oral-genital sex. Thus we can conclude that those who said they did not masturbate were being honest. In the absence of direct evidence, however, this reasoning is purely speculative.

The data suggest, then, that there is a substantial gender difference in the incidence of masturbation — virtually all males masturbate to or-gasm, while about one-third of all women never do.

Another area in which there is some evidence of a gender difference is desire for sex and motives for having intercourse. In a 1920 survey, two-thirds of the wives reported that they desired intercourse less fre-quently than their husbands did (cited by R. R. Bell, 1966, p. 137). Though Kinsey provided no direct data on this point, he noted that early in marriage, many husbands desired intercourse more frequently than their wives did, although the pattern was often reversed in middle age (Kinsey et al., 1953, p. 353). Traditionally then, there appeared to be a gender difference in desire for intercourse, with men wanting it more frequently than women did.

In the recent Hunt survey, however, fewer than 5 percent of the wives said they wished marital intercourse was less frequent (Hunt, 1974). Thus it seems that the "I have a headache" syndrome in women is mostly a thing of the past. In fact, in the recent *Redbook* survey, one-third of the wives said that they wished they had intercourse *more* frequently than they did (Levin and Levin, 1975).

There is a stereotype that men and women differ in their motives for having sex. Men — at least according to the stereotype — are more interested in the physical aspects of sex and have a "love 'em and leave 'em" attitude. Women, on the other hand, are thought to be most interested in love and romance and to be concerned with the interpersonal more than the physical aspects of the relationship. Unfortunately, there are no direct studies that assess whether these stereotypes are actually true. Psychologist Judith Bardwick reported the following answers from women responding to the question, "Why do you make love?":

> Because it's a means of getting closer to him.
> I guess because I love him.
> A very social thing to do — a way of reaching people.
> Mostly to see my boyfriend's enjoyment.
> Since we're getting married, it's not wrong. (1971, pp. 55, 56)

Bardwick sees such responses as indicative of the importance that women attach to love and close relationships. What we do not know, unfortunately, is how men would respond to this same question. One study provides some evidence, however. When college males were asked to give the reason for engaging in their first act of intercourse, the most common response was curiosity, followed by "just wanting to"; love for the girl was the reason in only 14 percent of the cases (Shope, 1975, pp. 196–197).

Another stereotype is the existence of a gender difference in arousal to erotic materials, men being much more responsive to them than women are. Is there any scientific evidence that this is true?

The females in the Kinsey sample were considerably less likely to report responses to erotic materials than the males. For example, about half of the males reported having been aroused at some time by erotic stories; although almost all the women had heard such stories, only 14 percent had been aroused by them. These data are often cited as evidence that women are not as easily aroused as men.[2]

---

[2] Actually, however, the Kinsey data were not that simple. Kinsey noted wide variability in women's responses and speculated that perhaps one-third of all women are as erotically responsive as the average male. Further, there were no gender differences in certain behaviors; for example, about the same number of females as males reported having been aroused by erotic literary materials.

Studies done in the last decade, however, have provided little evidence that males and females differ in their arousal to erotic materials. For example, in one study the responses of 128 male and 128 female university students to erotic slides and movies were studied (Schmidt and Sigusch, 1970). The slides and movies showed petting and coitus. In several tests for gender differences, either there were no differences, or the differences were small, with about 40 percent of the females reporting a stronger arousal response than the average male. All the females and almost all the males reported genital responses to the slides and movies. And women, not men, showed an increase in petting and coitus in the 24 hours after seeing the erotic stimuli. Therefore, there seems to be little basis for saying that women are not erotically responsive to such materials.

An interesting study by psychologist Julia Heiman (1975) provides a good deal of insight into the responses of males and females to erotic materials. Her subjects were sexually experienced university students, and she studied their responses as they listened to tape recordings of erotic stories. Not only did Heiman obtain subjects' self-ratings of their arousal, as other investigators had done, but she also got objective measures of their physiological levels of arousal. To do this, she used two instruments: a penile strain gauge and a photoplethysmograph. The penile strain gauge is used to get a physiological measure of arousal in the male; it is a flexible loop that fits around the base of the penis. The photoplethysmograph measures physiological arousal in the female; it is an acrylic cylinder that is placed just inside the entrance to the vagina. Both instruments measure vasocongestion in the genitals, which is the major physiological response during sexual arousal. These physiological measures are a great advance since they are not subject to the errors or distortions that may occur when subjects simply rate their own arousal.

Subjects heard one of four kinds of tapes. There is a stereotype that women are more turned on by romance, while men are more aroused by "raw sex." The tapes varied according to which of these kinds of content they contained. The first group of tapes was *erotic*; they included excerpts from pornographic material and popular novels giving explicit descriptions of heterosexual sex. The second group of tapes was *romantic*; a couple were heard expressing affection for each other, but they did not actually engage in sex. The third group of tapes was *erotic-romantic*; they included erotic elements of explicit sex and also romantic elements. Finally, the fourth group of tapes served as a *control*; a couple were heard engaging in conversation but nothing else. The plots of the tapes also varied according to whether the male or the female initiated the activity and whether the description centered on the female's physical and psychological responses or on the male's. Thus the tapes were male-initiated or female-initiated and female-centered or male-centered. Three important results emerged from the study:

1. Explicit sex (the erotic and erotic-romantic tapes) was most arousing, both for women and for men. The great majority of both males and females responded most, both physiologically and in self-ratings, to the erotic and erotic-romantic tapes. Women, in fact, rated the erotic tapes as more arousing than men did. Neither men nor women responded — either physiologically or in self-reports — to the romantic tapes or to the control tapes.
2. Both males and females found the female-initiated, female-centered tape to be the most arousing.
3. Women were sometimes not aware of their own physiological arousal. Generally there was a high correlation between self-ratings of arousal and objective physiological measures of arousal, both for men and for women. When men were physically aroused, they never made an error in reporting this in their self-ratings — it's pretty hard to miss an erection. But when the women were physically aroused, about half of them failed to report it in their self-ratings. (One might assume that women who were sophisticated enough to volunteer for an experiment of this sort and who were willing to insert a photoplethysmograph into their vagina would not suddenly become bashful about reporting their arousal; that is, it seems likely that these women honestly did not know when they were aroused.)

In sum, then, Heiman's study indicates that females and males are quite similar in their responses to erotic materials, but that women can sometimes be unaware of their own physical arousal. This study, however, dealt only with the preliminary stages of arousal; perhaps women vary in the point at which they recognize their arousal.

Development of ideas about sexuality   The earliest sexual experiences many people have are in masturbation. But as we have seen, the data indicate that substantial numbers of females never masturbate, and many of those who do, do so later in life than males do. This may have important consequences in other areas of sexuality as well.

Childhood and adolescent experiences with masturbation are important early sources of learning about sexuality. Through these experiences we learn how our bodies respond to sexual stimulation and what the most effective techniques for stimulating our own bodies are. This learning is important to our experience of adult, two-person sex. Perhaps the women who do not masturbate, and who are thus deprived of this early learning experience, are the same ones who do not have orgasms in sexual intercourse. This is exactly what Kinsey's data suggested — that women who masturbate to orgasm before marriage are more likely to have orgasms in intercourse with their husbands. For example, 31 percent of the women who had never masturbated to orgasm before marriage had not had an orgasm by the end of their first year of marriage, compared with only 13 to 16 percent of the women who had masturbated (Kinsey et al., 1953, p. 407). There seems to be a possibility, then, that women's lack of experience with masturbation in adolescence is related to their problems with having orgasms during intercourse.

It is interesting to note from the Kinsey data that boys and girls seem to learn about masturbation in different ways. Most males reported having heard about it before trying it themselves, and a substantial number had observed others doing it. Most females, on the other hand, learned to masturbate by accidental discovery of the possibility. Apparently communication about sexual behavior is not so free among girls as it is among boys, or perhaps girls are not so eager to pursue this information. At any rate, it appears that most males have learned to associate the genital organs with pleasure by the time of puberty, while many females have not.

Not only may women's relative inexperience with masturbation lead to a lack of sexual learning, but it may also create a kind of "erotic dependency" on men. Typically, boys' earliest sexual experiences are with masturbation. They learn that they can produce their own sexual pleasure. Girls typically have their earliest sexual experiences in heterosexual petting. They therefore learn about sex from boys. Their early learning experiences are with boys, and they learn that their sexual pleasure is produced by the male. As sex researcher John Gagnon commented:

> Young women may know of masturbation, but not know *how* to masturbate — how to produce pleasure, or even what the pleasures of orgasm might be. . . . Some young women report that they learned how to masturbate after they had orgasm from intercourse and petting, and decided they could do it for themselves. (1977, p. 152)

Experiences with masturbation — or lack of such experiences — then, may be very important in shaping female sexuality and making it different from male sexuality.

Of course, socialization forces on the female's developing sexuality are also important. Our culture has traditionally placed tighter restrictions on women's sexuality than it has on men's, and vestiges of these restrictions linger today. It seems likely that these restrictions have acted as a damper on female sexuality, and thus they may help to explain why some women do not masturbate or do not have orgasms.

One of the clearest examples of the differences in restrictions on female and male sexuality is the "double standard." The double standard says, essentially, that the same sexual behavior is evaluated differently, depending on whether a male or a female engages in it. An example is premarital sex. Traditionally in our culture, premarital intercourse has been more acceptable for males than for females. Indeed, premarital sexual activity might be considered a status symbol for a male but a sign of cheapness for a female.

These different standards have been reflected in behavior. For example, the Kinsey data, collected in the 1940s, indicated that over twice as many males (71 percent) as females (33 percent) had premarital sex. Apparently, society's message got through to young women of that era. Most of them managed to keep themselves chaste before marriage, while their male contemporaries tended to get the experience that was expected of them.

Generally, there seems to be less of a double standard today than there was in former times. For example, people now approve of premarital sex for females about as much as they do for males. In Hunt's sample, 82 percent of the men felt that premarital sex was acceptable for males when the couple is in love, and 77 percent felt that it was acceptable for females under the same circumstances (Hunt, 1974).

This change in attitude is reflected in behavior. A much higher percentage of women report having engaged in premarital intercourse now than in Kinsey's time. In the Hunt sample, among respondents aged 18 to 24, 95 percent of the males and 81 percent of the females had had premarital intercourse. Thus there is much less of a difference between females and males now than there was a generation ago.

As we noted in Chapter 6, *ambivalence* is an important theme in the psychology of women. In that chapter we discussed ambivalence about achievement and femininity. Sexuality is another area of ambivalence for women. Doubtless this ambivalence results from the kind of mixed message that females get from society. Beginning in adolescence, they are told that popularity is important for them, and being sexy increases one's popularity. But actually engaging in premarital intercourse can lead to a loss of status. The ambivalence-producing message is "Be sexy but don't be sexual."

Ambivalence toward sexual relations is reflected in the large number of unwanted pregnancies among unmarried women who were well informed about contraception (Stiller, 1966). For example, research in the 1970s indicated that of sexually active single girls, 75 percent claimed they used contraceptives not at all, or only occasionally ("Teen-Age Sex," 1972). The evidence shows that they failed to use contraceptives. Why? Taking a birth-control pill every day indicates that the woman thinks intercourse is a real possibility. For unmarried women, particularly those not involved in a long-term relationship, this is a difficult admission to make. Constantly being ready for sexual relations still suggests cheapness. In fact, the antipathy toward taking a daily measure against conception is apparently so great that it outweighs the undesirability of pregnancy. The woman would much prefer to believe that she was "swept off her feet," rather than the implied alternative, that she was expecting to have sex.

Research on the development of sexuality suggests that discussing gender differences in sexuality is too simple an approach. It is the developmental process of sexuality that differs for males and females (Kaplan and Sager, 1971). In a sense, males and females appear to move through the stages of sexual development in adolescence and adulthood in opposite orders. For males, adolescent sexuality is genitally focused with strong orgasmic needs — four to eight orgasms per day are not unusual. But by the time a man reaches fifty, emphasis has shifted away from genitally centered sensations to a more generalized, sensuously diffuse experience, and two orgasms per week are considered satisfactory. For the female, adolescent sexuality is diffuse and not genitally focused, with little emphasis on orgasm. Genital sexuality and orgasmic potential develop later, not reaching a peak until the thirties and forties. Orgasmic response in women is faster and more consistent in the forties than it is in the teens or twenties. It appears, then, that early male sexuality is genital and gradually evolves to a more complex, diffuse sensuous experience, while female sexuality begins as a complex, diffuse experience, and only later develops the genital component.

Fantasies   The psychoanalytic school has traditionally considered fantasies during intercourse as a sign of pathology. Some women further resist fantasies because they seem to be a sign of disloyalty to their partners. Hence, these fantasies have been considered rare, and have received little attention in research.

A recent questionnaire study of 141 adult women volunteers indicated that 65 percent fantasized during intercourse with their husbands (Hariton, 1973). An additional 28 percent reported occasional thoughts during intercourse that might be counted as fantasies, leaving only 7 percent of the sample indicating no fantasies at all. Statistically, then, it seems that it is the woman who does *not* fantasize who is abnormal!

The following are the ten most common fantasies listed in order of frequency:

1. Thoughts of an imaginary lover enter my mind.
2. I imagine that I am being overpowered or forced to surrender.
3. I enjoy pretending that I am doing something sick or forbidden.
4. I am in a different place like a car, motel, beach, woods, etc.
5. I relive a previous sexual experience.
6. I imagine myself delighting many men.
7. I imagine that I am observing myself or others having sex.
8. I pretend that I am another irresistibly sexy female.
9. I pretend that I struggle and resist before being aroused to surrender.
10. I daydream that I am being made love to by more than one man at a time. (Hariton, 1973)

The two most common themes are being with another man, and being overpowered. It should be noted that males and females share fantasies of common content; for example, fantasies of both may involve being dominated by a member of the other gender (Hunt, 1974).

Women who have fantasies during coitus are generally independent, impulsive, and nonconformist — all personality characteristics typical of creative people. Their fantasies do not appear to be signs of poor marital adjustment; on the contrary, they seemed to have better sexual relations than the nonfantasizers. This latter group, in contrast, were generally conciliatory, unassuming, nurturing, and affiliative (Hariton, 1973).

In previous sections, we have emphasized the need for interpersonal relationship as an important aspect of female sexuality. Here we see the other side of the coin, the woman's experience of her own, individual, creative sexuality.

There's more to female sexuality   According to a recent theory (Newton, 1971, 1973), women have at least three distinct sources of sexual satisfaction and are, therefore, "trebly sensuous." The theory states that at least three reproductive acts are included in female sexuality, all involving two people: coitus, parturition (labor, or giving birth), and lactation. The concentration on coitus as the only outlet for female sexuality is probably the result of research dominated by men, for whom coitus is the primary outlet.

The basic observation that led to this theory is the similarity of psychological and physiological responses in both childbirth and sexual intercourse (Newton, 1971, 1973). Breathing patterns, vocalizations, and facial expression are similar in both, although the distorted facial expression during childbirth has often been mistaken for an expression of pain. The upper portion of the uterus, as well as the abdominal muscles, contract rhythmically during both. The woman's typical position (missionary position) in intercourse as well as childbirth is similar — supine, with legs spread apart. In childbirth, as in coitus, the woman's actions become uninhibited, and she is oblivious to happenings in the surrounding environment. The flood of emotion following both intercourse and childbirth is also similar. It must be noted, however, that these are the reactions in undisturbed, undrugged childbirth. The alternative setting for childbirth in the United States, in which the woman is strapped down to a table and generally made to think that the whole experience will be ghastly, is certainly not conducive to making it a pleasurable sexual experience, any more than sexual intercourse would be pleasurable if the woman were strapped down and surrounded by a group of spectators who are strangers.

Another bit of evidence suggesting that childbirth is a sexually satisfying experience is an obstetrician's observation of clitoral engorgement in some of his patients during childbirth, beginning at the time of cervical dilation and lasting until the episiotomy is sewn (Newton, 1971). It is unfortunate that the pleasurable aspects of the childbirth experience have been so long denied.

Breastfeeding is the third kind of two-person sex that women experience, according to Newton. It involves a kind of very close, intimate contact between the child and mother, in which the infant stimulates an erotic region (the breast) in the mother.

Masters and Johnson (1966) have also reported that breastfeeding leads to various stages of sexual arousal, including orgasm. Unfortunately, this association between sexuality and the infant evokes considerable anxiety in many mothers, possibly because incest is suggested, and some even discontinue nursing as a result. Masters and Johnson also report an earlier return of sex drive and desire for intercourse after childbirth among women who are breastfeeding. The opposite process has also been noted; women who have recently had children and are lactating sometimes eject milk during sexual intercourse and orgasm.

Clearly, a common physiological process, involving both the nervous system and hormones, is mediating breastfeeding and sexual behavior. There are two basic processes involved in lactation: milk secretion, stimulated by lactogenic hormone (for example prolactin) from the anterior pituitary; and milk ejection, stimulated by oxytocin, from the posterior pituitary. The act of suckling stimulates both milk secretion and milk ejection via stimulation of the central nervous system, the signal passing through the hypothalamus, and then to the pituitary. Within thirty to ninety seconds after suckling begins, mammary-duct pressure rises and milk begins to flow. This results from the stimulation of the milk-ejection reflex, and is popularly called the "letdown" or "draught" (Turner and Bagnara, 1971).

It appears that the common hormone linking nursing and sexual arousal is oxytocin (Newton, 1971). It is probably secreted during sexual stimulation, and will therefore cause milk ejection if the rest of the woman's physiology is so adjusted; conversely, it is secreted during nursing, and may lead to sexual arousal and orgasm. Apparently nature has created a very functional mechanism here. The mother's mothering can be rewarded by considerable pleasure, if society will only permit it.

Having considered various aspects of normally functioning female sexuality, let us turn now to considering the problems that may occur in that functioning.

SEXUAL DYSFUNCTION AND THERAPY

The term *sexual dysfunction* refers to various disturbances or impairments of sexual functioning, such as inability to have an orgasm (orgasmic dysfunction), or premature ejaculation. Once again, we have Masters and Johnson to thank for investigating this field and pioneering in therapy for these problems.

Most authorities agree that the majority of cases of sexual dysfunction are psychogenic rather than organic (physical) in nature. But Masters and

Johnson have rejected most of the traditional notions about the psychological sources of the problem. They say

> Sociocultural deprivation and ignorance of sexual physiology, rather than psychiatric or medical illness, constitute the etiologic background for most sexual dysfunction. (1970, p. 21)

That is, sexual problems may not be symptoms of deep psychiatric disturbance, but may have simpler sources, such as educational deprivation. Therefore, Masters and Johnson have adopted a rapid treatment program, two weeks in duration, which has attained remarkable success.

Their treatment program has a number of unusual features. One is that it requires that both husband and wife participate in the therapy. Masters and Johnson maintain that there is no such thing as an uninvolved partner in cases of sexual dysfunction, even if only one person displays overt symptoms. For instance, a wife who does not experience orgasm is anxious and wonders whether there is anything wrong with her, or whether she is unattractive to her husband. The husband, on the other hand, while performing adequately, may wonder why he is failing to stimulate his wife to orgasm. Hence both partners are deeply involved. Realizing the reciprocal nature of sexual gratification, Masters and Johnson employ the practice of having both partners participate.

The major objective in their therapy is abolishing goal-directed sexual performance. Most people think that certain things should be *achieved* during sexual activity — for example, that the female should achieve or attain an orgasm. This emphasis on achieving leads to a fear of failure, which spells disaster for sexual enjoyment. Masters and Johnson therefore try to remove the individual from a spectator role in sex — observing her or his own actions, evaluating their success. Instead, the emphasis is on the enjoyment of all sensual pleasures. Patients use a series of "sensate focus" exercises, in which they learn to touch and to respond to touch. Patients are also taught to express sexual needs to their partners, which people generally are reluctant to do. For instance, the woman is taught to tell her husband in which regions of her body she enjoys being touched most, and how firm or light the touch should be. Beyond this basic instruction, which includes lessons in sexual anatomy and physiology, Masters and Johnson simply allow natural sexual response to emerge. Sexual pleasure is natural, sexual response is natural. After removing artificial impediments to sexual response, they find that people quickly begin joyful, "successful" participation in sex.

Another important feature of the Masters and Johnson work is that they have been quite careful to evaluate the success of their therapy, both during the two-week therapy session, and in follow-up studies for periods as long as five years after couples leave the clinic. Their success rate appears to be remarkable. Therapy is successful in approximately 75 percent of the cases that are treated at the clinic, and there is little recurrence of symptoms after leaving.

Let us now look at some specific examples of sexual dysfunction in females.

Orgasmic dysfunction   In "primary orgasmic dysfunction" the woman has had intercourse but has never experienced an orgasm. Masters and Johnson do not use the term "frigidity" because it has a variety of imprecise, negative connotations. Examples of some of the causes of orgasmic dysfunction in a woman are: (1) strong religious prohibitions that treat sex as dirty and sinful; (2) lack of development of emotional maturity; (3) inability to identify with her partner — she generally dislikes one or several of his characteristics; and (4) marriage to a sexually inadequate man (Masters and Johnson, 1970). In this last case, it is obvious how primary dysfunction in one partner can bring about dysfunction in the other partner — that is, the critical nature of the reciprocity of the relationship.

Masters and Johnson's assertion that the above factors cause orgasmic dysfunction has been challenged, however. In multiple samples of women, Fisher (1973) found repeatedly that orgasm consistency was unrelated to the following factors: the woman's psychological stability; her amount of "practice" with sex, or her husband's attitudes; her degree of femininity, or her hostility and dominance; her degree of religiosity; or her parents' attitudes toward sex. That is, the factors Masters and Johnson suggest promote orgasmic dysfunction do not in the Fisher study appear to be related to the consistency with which women do have orgasms. For example, the suggestion that orgasmic dysfunction is related to a family and religious background that treated sex as dirty is not borne out by the lack of correlation between orgasm consistency and parents' attitudes toward sex or strength of religious ties. The two factors that do emerge as related to orgasm capacity are fears of separation or loss in personal relationships, and father's lack of interest during childhood (Fisher, 1973).

In "situational orgasmic dysfunction," according to Masters and Johnson, the woman has orgasms in some situations, but not in others. Clearly in this case, there is no organic impairment of orgasm, since the woman is capable of experiencing it. The systematic nature of the situations in which the woman can and cannot experience orgasm often leads to an understanding if the psychogenic nature of the problem (Masters and Johnson, 1970). Sometimes a woman who has frequently experienced orgasm in intercourse with her husband is no longer capable of it. This may be related to a change in her identification with him. For instance, in one case a woman who strongly desired an increase in the family's social and economic status became sexually dysfunctional after her husband lost several jobs. Apparently she realized he would not accomplish what she wanted, and her disillusionment was channeled into her sexual response, or lack of it. A strong homosexual orientation can also be a source of situational orgasmic dysfunction. If a woman has had a long and significant homosexual relationship, particularly when she is young, she may be capable of experiencing orgasm in homosexual relations, but not in heterosexual ones. Some women simply have a low sexual tension, or little interest in sex, and experience orgasm very infrequently. Another kind of situational dysfunction is masturbatory orgasmic inadequacy, in which the woman cannot masturbate to orgasm (the reverse is much more common — women who can masturbate to orgasm, but cannot experience orgasm in heterosexual intercourse). This syndrome is frequently associated with guilt over masturbation.

The basic therapy technique Masters and Johnson use with these patients involves teaching them how to be sexual creatures in an appropriate psychosocial context. Because of the societal "double standard" that prohibits women from being honorable sexual beings, many women feel they need special permission for sex, or that it is only a duty to their husband. Naturally, this will inhibit their response. Therefore, Masters and Johnson see the overcoming of these inhibitions as their major task.

Vaginismus   Vaginismus involves a tightening or spasm of the outer third of the vagina, possibly to such an extent that the opening of the vagina is closed and intercourse becomes impossible. Factors in the woman's history that seem to cause this condition include marriage to an impotent man, family background in which sex was considered dirty and sinful, a previous physical assault, and long experience of painful intercourse due to a physical problem (Masters and Johnson, 1970).

In therapy, Masters and Johnson find it quite important to demonstate to both husband and wife the reality and nature of the vaginal spasm, of which they are frequently unaware. The treatment consists mainly of using vaginal dilators of progressive size to enlarge the opening. In cases where physical problems seem to be the source, treatment of these problems often seems to help the emotional problems.

Painful intercourse   Painful intercourse or *dyspareunia* may be organic or psychogenic in origin. Too often, the woman's complaints of pain are dismissed, particularly if the physician cannot find an obvious physical problem. However, this is a serious condition, and should be treated as such. When pain is felt in the vagina, it may be due to failure to lubricate, to infection, to special sensitivity of the vagina (such as to the contraceptives being used), or to changes in the vagina due to age. Pain may also be felt in the region of the vaginal outlet and clitoris, or deep in the pelvis. In this latter case, the causes may be infection, or tearing of the ligaments supporting the uterus, particularly following childbirth.

In summary, Masters and Johnson have developed a therapy program for treatment of sexual dysfunctions. They have treated women most commonly for orgasmic dysfunction and painful intercourse. Their treatment program is a behavioral one, de-emphasizing psychodynamic interpretations of sexual problems and emphasizing direct, simple changes in sex behavior. They stress that intercourse is not an achievement or performance situation, but rather an experience of sensations to be enjoyed. The success of their therapy program has been impressive.

New therapies for women's sexual dysfunctions   The incidence of women who have problems having orgasms, particularly in intercourse, is so high that it seems that this pattern is well within the range of normal female sexual response. It is questionable whether it should be called a dysfunction, except insofar as it causes unhappiness for the woman. With the growing awareness of the frequency of this problem have come a number of self-help sex therapy books for women, one of the best being Lonnie Garfield Barbach's *For Yourself: The Fulfillment of Female Sexuality* (1975; see also Heiman et al., 1976).

A common recommendation of Barbach and other therapists (e.g., LoPiccolo and Lobitz, 1972) is that pre-orgasmic women practice masturbation in order to increase their capacity for orgasm. The idea is that women must first explore their own bodies and learn how to bring themselves to orgasm before they can expect to have orgasms in heterosexual intercourse. As noted earlier in this chapter, many women have not had this kind of practice, and sex therapists recommend that they get it.

Another exercise that is recommended is the *Kegel exercises* or *pubococcygeal muscle exercises* (Kegel, 1952). The pubococcygeal (PC) muscle runs along the sides of the entrance of the vagina. Exercising this muscle seems to increase women's sexual pleasure by increasing the sensitivity of the vaginal area. This exercise is particularly helpful to women who have had the PC muscle stretched in childbirth or who simply have poor tone in it. The woman is instructed first to find the PC muscle by sitting on a toilet with her legs spread apart, urinating, and stopping the flow of urine voluntarily. The muscle that stops the flow is the PC. After that, the woman is told to contract the muscle 10 times during each of six sessions per day. Gradually she can work up to more.

GENDER SIMILARITIES

In previous chapters we have stressed gender similarities in psychological processes. There are also great gender similarities in sexuality. A few decades ago, at the time of the Kinsey research, there were marked gender differences in several aspects of sexuality. However, more recent research shows that these differences are greatly decreased, or even absent now.

For example, according to Kinsey's data collected in the 1940s, 71 percent of males, but only 33 percent of females had premarital intercourse by age 25 (Kinsey et al., 1953). There was, at that time, a marked gender difference in premarital sexual activity. However, data on the youngest (18 to 24) age group in the Hunt survey (1974) indicate that 95 percent of males and 81 percent of females had had premarital intercourse. The data, then, indicate that in the future nearly everyone, both female and male, will engage in premarital intercourse. Thus the general trend seems to be toward gender similarities in sexuality.

13

LESBIANISM AND BISEXUALITY

Between man and woman love is an act; each torn from self becomes other: what fills the woman in love with wonder is that the languorous passivity of her flesh should be reflected in the male's impetuosity; the narcissistic woman, however, recognizes her enticements but dimly in the man's erected flesh. Between women love is contemplative; caresses are intended less to gain possession of the other than gradually to re-create the self through her; separateness is abolished, there is no struggle, no victory, no defeat; in exact reciprocity each is at once subject and object; sovereign and slave; duality becomes mutuality.

SIMONE DE BEAUVOIR, The Second Sex

With the sexual revolution and the feminist movement has also come the rise of gay liberation. The gay liberation movement can probably be counted as dating from June 1969, when, in response to police harassment, homosexuals rioted in Greenwich Village in New York. Lesbians have sometimes been united with the women's movement and sometimes in conflict with it. Radical lesbians argue that to be truly liberated, women must become separatists, that is, they must stay separate from men. Among other things, this would argue *against* heterosexuality and *for* lesbianism. More moderate lesbians join in working for the moderate goals of the women's movement, such as an end to job discrimination. It is clear that a discussion of women today would be incomplete without a discussion of lesbianism.

THE EXPERIENTIAL WORLD
OF THE LESBIAN

We shall try in the following section to understand the lesbian experience, to understand how lesbians think and feel. Historically, there has been little written information on this topic. Social stigmas were so great that lesbians were unable to acknowledge their own lifestyle for fear that they would then be the objects of discrimination. With the recent liberalization of attitudes toward homosexuality, some lesbians have stepped forward to openly acknowledge, indeed proclaim, their sexual preferences. Accompanying this trend toward openness are a number of published accounts of the lesbian experience (see particularly Martin and Lyon, 1972).

We must keep in mind that describing lesbians as a group engenders the same error that occurs when we collectively describe any group. That is, lesbians are as varied and differ as much among themselves as do heterosexual women or men. In addition, it is likely that the lesbians about whom we know the most from research are those who for one or many reasons find their way to the clinician in order to stabilize their adjustment. Therefore they may provide a distorted view of lesbianism. Nevertheless, we can attempt to construct a picture of what it is like to be a lesbian on the basis of reported clinical and research materials from such persons as Charlotte Wolff (1971) and from experiential accounts such as those of Martin and Lyon (1972).

Certainly society's persecution of homosexuals is a part of the experience of lesbians. There are numerous documented cases of women being fired from their jobs or dishonorably discharged from the armed forces upon disclosure of their sexual preferences (Martin and Lyon, 1972). The lesbian must live with the knowledge that this might also be her fate if her lifestyle becomes known, and a generalized paranoia (probably justified) may result. The alternative is to publicly deny her lifestyle. She must then role-play a denial of that which is so important to her. Fears of discovery and ostracism persist, and may lead her to question, at some level, the acceptability of her choice. Certainly the role-playing, leading a double life, requires great emotional energy. Thus the beauty and emotionality she finds in sharing life with another woman is constantly overlayed by "fear of the other" (Wolff, 1971, p. 117).

A subtler result of society's persecution is the prohibition against lesbians having children. In most states it is illegal for lesbians to adopt children, and lesbianism may be grounds for a father regaining custody from a lesbian mother of children they had when married. Yet many lesbians desire children, and these restrictions may be a great source of sadness to them. There is currently a move in several states to modify some of this discrimination against lesbians, which will help to ease at least one strain on them.

Yet, lest the picture look overwhelmingly negative, the nature of homosexual love between women is, at its core, basically romantic and idealistic. A homosexual woman lives almost an idyllic love relationship with her partner, with more intense emotion and imagination than the typical heterosexual relationship (Martin and Lyon, 1972). So much is risked for the relationship that the sharing is more intense and sensuous and is necessarily more central to her existence than is the relatively unrisky heterosexual love. Further, emotional resources are not so divided as they would be with care and attention to children; this makes the commitment to the partner more focal and profound. And yet, within the commitment, there may also be unrealistic expectations and intense demands made of the partner, leading to hurt and disappointment. Thus, lesbian romantic love is all-encompassing and "deadly serious" (Wolff, 1971, p. 110). Indeed, the term "homoemotional" may be preferable to "homosexual" in describing lesbian life, de-emphasizing the sexual aspects of the relationship and emphasizing the emotionality that is more central (Wolff, 1971).

The realization that lesbianism is primarily defined by the direction of an emotional commitment to another female may also help to dispel some other misconceptions regarding lesbianism. A common stereotype is that lesbians play butch-femme roles — that one takes the male role, the other the female. In fact, such role-playing, while it does occur, is far from typical. Martin and Lyon suggest that it is generally characteristic of young and inexperienced lesbians who are trying to define their new lifestyle in the only terms they know, that of heterosexual relations. Lesbian role-playing has all the pitfalls of heterosexual relations (inequality of status in decision making, dominance-submissiveness), and is generally not retained as the relationship progresses. Such role-playing is even less common today, as feminist lesbians reject traditional masculine/feminine roles. A related misconception is that the lesbian is extremely mannish, with short hair, dressed in a business suit or black leather. It is quite important to make a distinction between gender identification and choice of sexual partner. Most lesbians have a female identification — that is, they are quite definitely women; they dress and behave like women; but they simply choose to direct emotional, sexual love toward other women. Indeed, a large proportion of them have had heterosexual relations, and many are or have been heterosexually married. According to the Kinsey data, about 13 percent of all females have had at least one homosexual experience leading to orgasm, but less than 1 percent of all females are exclusively homosexual throughout their lives.

Psychologist Anne Peplau and her colleagues (1978) have studied the nature of lesbian relationships based on lengthy questionnaires administered to 127 lesbians recruited through feminist and gay organizations in Los Angeles. They found a number of interesting results, and concluded that two fundamental values were related to the nature of lesbian relationships: attachment to the partner and personal autonomy. That is, lesbians vary in the extent to which they want a strong attachment to the partner, emphasizing emotional closeness, love, and security, and the extent to which they want personal independence. These two values are related to the kind of relationship that is formed. The feminist lesbians tended to emphasize the personal autonomy value.

The length of the longest lesbian relationship these women had had ranged from one month to 25 years, with a median of 2.5 years. In describing their current relationship, most of the women reported it as being close and loving. About 75 percent reported that they and their current partner were "in love." There was a high degree of satisfaction with the relationship (mean of 7.1 on a 9-point scale). There was also a great deal of satisfaction with the sexual aspects of the relationship. Over 70 percent of the women said that they almost always experienced orgasm when having sex with their partner. In regard to power in the relationship, the majority said that they and their partner shared equally in power. Peplau and her colleagues concluded that lesbians can and do form committed, satisfying relationships.

Having considered the nature of the lesbian experience and relationships, let us proceed to see what various psychological theories have to say about the nature of lesbianism and its development.

THEORETICAL VIEWS

The psychoanalytic view   Sigmund Freud was one of the first medical therapists to attempt the treatment of a homosexual woman. He was not optimistic about altering behavior, but argued that the best to be accomplished would be the understanding of the psychic mechanisms involved.

FIGURE 13.1

Lesbians can and do form satisfying, long-term relationships.

Source: Photo by Eric A. Roth, © 1978. / The Picture Cube.

Nevertheless, his first comprehensive statement regarding homosexuality was given in 1910 in a classic paper, "Three Essays on the Theory of Sexuality," with additional revisions and insights in subsequent papers, "The Psychogenesis of a Case of Homosexuality in a Woman" in 1920, "Some Psychical Consequences of the Anatomical Distinction Between the Sexes" in 1925, and "Female Sexuality" in 1931.

Freud considered human beings to be bisexual in nature. In this assertion, he recognized that all humans are capable of homosexual behavior. According to Freud, the sources of sexual pleasure in the young are many and diffuse. With time there is increasing specificity in terms of *object choice*. That is, with time the child manifests increasing specificity in the body zone and object capable of eliciting pleasure.

At about age three, the boy encounters the Oedipal complex. In the positive component of the complex, the mother is a love object for the boy and the father is the object of ambivalence. In resolving the Oedipal complex, the boy comes to identify with his father. A *negative Oedipal complex* occurs when the shift to identification with the father is not made, and the boy continues his initial identification with the mother, wanting (like the mother) to be loved by the father. According to Freud, people never really completely shed themselves of this negative component, but homosexual people remain fixated on it.

Freud initially viewed these psychological mechanics as highly similar for boys and for girls. It was some years before the gap between the logic of the theory and the realities of female development disposed Freud to a revised version of normal and abnormal sexual development in women. He finally recognized that the boy's Oedipal development was far simpler than the girl's. The boy retains his original love object (mother), merely substituting another female for the original. For the girl, the mother is naturally the original love object (because the mother is the primary source of pleasure and pain relief to all children), but the father must become the object. Thus presumably the negative Oedipal situation for the girl — in which she continues to love the same gender parent, the mother — may well be more intense, last longer, and not be resolved. According to Freud, in the normal condition the girl recognizes the loss of the prized penis, views herself as mutilated, and though identified with the mother, blames the mother for her loss. So her identification with the mother is fused with contempt and rivalry. In this condition, then, she rejects the mother and adopts the father as a love object and wishes to have a baby by him as a substitute for the longed-for penis. When she realizes that the wish cannot be fulfilled, she reverts to her identification with the mother and femininity, with the father-substitute male being the object choice — that is, choosing the male as a sexual partner. The lesbian alternative, according to Freud, occurs when the negative Oedipal component persists, so that mother, and later other women, are the object of love. The masculine component of the woman's personality is retained and the object choice is homosexual.

Freud speculated that the basis for homosexuality in men and in women may well be a matter of self-love or narcissism. The outcome, then, is to love the self, and to seek a same-gender person, who resembles the self, for a sex partner. From this perspective we may be seeing a positive aspect of lesbian development. A problem with "normal" female development is that many women end up with low self-confidence and low regard for other women. Lesbian development may be an alternative in which the self and the female can be loved and valued.

A psychoanalytic variant   In her book *Love Between Women* (1971), Charlotte Wolff provides a variant of the psychoanalytic model based on her research with nonpatient lesbians. Her theory of gender-role development in women emphasizes the normal, intense attachment of the young girl for her mother, where the mother is seen as all-powerful and godlike. It is not long before the developing female realizes that the mother values males more highly than females in a man-valuing society, and that her chances of getting her mother's love are less than her father and brother have. The most important effect of all this is the perception that mother values her own gender less, which leads the developing young girl to be insecure about her own value.

In a sense, then, the mother gives a second-rate status to the young girl. At this point the girl may choose to pursue one of two strategies for dealing with this situation: she may strive to be a very feminine female, ingratiating herself to the mother (the heterosexual course); or she may seek to become like the superior gender, becoming masculine and competitive (the lesbian course). More commonly, she chooses the first course of action, becoming like the mother and emulating those many aspects of femininity that the mother models. Wolff maintains that in such a maneuver, the behavior has a two-fold motive: to attract the male and to outdo the depriving mother. And if she cannot come first with the mother, she can, by being feminine, cultivate the rewards of coming first with the father and other males.

Note then that in this conceptualization, the female's first choice is mother's love. Her attraction to the male is a secondary choice in the face of an inability to get mother's love. As Wolff sees it, "The love a man can give her is bound to fall short in essentials, which only a mother can provide" (p. 71). Thus the girl is not only insecure, but lonely. She combats this loneliness through a community of feminine relations that are more intimate than those with males, namely with other girls, sleeping in the same bed, holding hands — all lacking sexual intimacy but emphasizing contact. But the heterosexual woman's existence must always continue to be somewhat lonely. Further, the typical heterosexual woman remains infantile, trying to please the father and then the lover and husband.

The homosexual woman, on the other hand, has chosen a different strategy and therefore need not play such games. She fights and strives for equality with men in order to be worthy of her mother's love, which is the core of her striving. "Emotional incest with the mother is indeed the very essence of lesbianism" (p. 72). Further, there is a suggestion that males are basically alien to the lesbian. Wolff found that many of the lesbians she studied had a history of a father who was absent for a substantial period during their childhood — for example, during the war. Such girls grow up in a basically feminine world in which males are strange and alien. Thus, according to Wolff's view, lesbianism arises from the girl taking a masculine, competitive strategy to deal with the insufficiency of her mother's love.

Wolff's theory rests on the somewhat tenuous assumption that the mother is the girl's only real love object, that she continues to seek the mother's love throughout life, and that males are loved or manipulated only as a substitute. Further, Wolff commits an error similar to Freud's in confusing gender identity with choice of sexual partner — that is, she assumes that lesbian development leads to masculinity. Yet empirical research shows that lesbians generally have a feminine identification, and that they may be aggressive and competitive, or passive and shy, just as may heterosexual women. Wolff assumes that all lesbians enter into direct competition with males — again, that they are masculine. Nonetheless, her theory and research give some insights into the emotional and love aspects of lesbianism.

The behaviorist model   A behaviorist approach (for example Bermant, 1972; Ford and Beach, 1951) emphasizes the point that all animals up to and including humans display or are inherently capable of homosexual activities. Studies of natural behaviors in lower animals confirm the notion that homosexual activities are not at all uncommon and may even be the expression of the normal developing sex drive, some retained throughout life, some preadaptive to adult "mature" sexual behavior. Thus, animals appear to be bisexual in that the environment may have a great influence on whether one or another choice of sex partner is made. In some primitive cultures, a male may be the appropriate sex partner for a young male, while in his adulthood the accepted partner may be a female (Mead, 1961).

Therefore humans may have no inborn preference for the opposite gender as an appropriate sex partner, but the nature of conditioning and socialization channels this disposition. That is, cultural pressures channel a generalized drive in a culturally prescribed direction. Ford and Beach (1951) in their classic work on sexual behavior in humans and animals give detailed evidence of the bisexual inheritance of humans that tends to confirm the above notion. One might conclude that heterosexual behavior is an acquired, that is, a learned, state of being. The behaviorist view points out that heterosexual development is actually far more chancey than most people realize. We should ask not only "Why do homosexuals and lesbians develop?" but also "Why do heterosexuals develop?"

The behaviorist view, then, is that humans have a general pool of sex drives that may, depending on experience and circumstance, be channeled in one direction or another, into heterosexuality or into homosexuality. One problem with this view is that it asumes that the mechanisms of male homosexual and female homosexual development are similar. This would seem unlikely in view of the different experiences and status of men and women in our culture, a point more adequately acknowledged in the psychoanalytic theories. On the other hand, the behaviorist model readily accommodates lesbianism as a normal form of behavior in contrast to the psychoanalytic theories, which treat it as deviant or compensatory.

Existentialism and lesbianism   Existential philosophy maintains that anyone can change one's self view and view of the world at any time, and can thus profoundly alter the course of one's life — that humans are always free to reappraise their own condition and to take some action to alter it. People need not rely forever on the "crutches" of morals, social expectations, and past habits, but can in their own lives think for themselves and disavow all those things that they have been in the past. The only dictum is that humans should be authentic, and *authenticity* demands that one accept full responsibility for one's actions.

The existentialist who has commented most on lesbianism is Simone de Beauvoir (1952). Exemplifying the existentialist theme, she insists that: "The truth is that homosexuality [lesbianism] is no more perversion deliberately indulged in than it is a curse of fate. It is an attitude *chosen in a certain situation* — that is at once motivated and freely adopted" (p. 398, italics the author). She views female homosexuality not as a compensatory condition of life, but as an instance of self-reappraisal and choice. Further, Beauvoir is in accord with the modified psychoanalytic position of Wolff (1971, p. 74) that all women have a natural homosexual component. Thus, lesbianism from this viewpoint is merely the reflection of conscious choice and a willingness to accept the responsibilities for such a choice. Beauvoir attacks the psychoanalytic position that lesbianism is inauthentic, an infantile fixation or masculine protest. (According to Wolff, however, such a criticism is not valid since in his "Three Essays," Freud did, indeed, declare homosexuality in humans as a normal condition, not a neurosis.)

The existential thesis helps to describe the elements required to give one's love to another of the same gender. Thus, a woman who enters upon heterosexual relations enters upon a social contract society expects and reinforces. It appears to require much greater, not less, emotional strength and conviction (authenticity) for a woman to enter upon a homosexual relationship, risking social rejection. So, according to the existentialists, in some sense it requires a much more integrated woman, emotionally, socially, and intellectually, to hazard the risks of social ostracism in order to consciously choose a relationship such as this. Indeed, it may require not less, but far more intense emotional strength, to do so. Thus, intense emotion appears to be both risk and reward for the lesbian much more than for her heterosexual counterpart.

Such a choice brings with it the risk of alienation from the opposite gender and society in general. If a woman seeks to be, in this realm as well as in nonsexual roles, what she feels is most important for her, she inevitably encounters pain and rejection. By the nature of her choice, the lesbian has a bond with all other women who make the same choice: the rejection of the status of woman provided by a male-valuing society. The "normal" woman making the heterosexual choice eases her conscious burden, meanwhile requiring even greater emotional strength in order to become an independent, achieving woman. So, in the existential thesis, the woman who chooses heterosexuality gives up, inhibits, or denigrates her authentic self to live "amicably" in the existing system. Finally, the thesis argues that this choice is an emotional choice, not a sexual one, in that the lesbian emotionally, not necessarily sexually, rejects the male. Heterosexual sex, then, is not offensive or alien to her; it is emotional love that she can share only with another woman, not sexual intercourse. The sex act is secondary for her, and the love-emotional-sex constellation is primary, and reserved for another woman.

The language of existentialism remains at the level of conscious choice and authenticity, words difficult to define precisely. It is a language unsatisfying to the psychologist because it gives little insight into the development or meaning of lesbianism; indeed, the existentialist rejects the notion that a homosexual choice of sex partners is rooted in previous experiences, insisting instead that it is simply a matter of free choice. On the other hand, the existentialist position does treat lesbianism as a legitimate, normal form of behavior.

LESBIANISM: NORMAL OR ABNORMAL?

The majority of Americans disapprove of homosexuality and view it as abnormal. In a 1970 study conducted by the Institute for Sex Research, two-thirds of the respondents regarded homosexuality as "very obscene and vulgar" (Weinberg and Williams, 1974). In a 1969 Harris poll, 63 percent of Americans considered homosexuals harmful to American life. What scientific evidence is there regarding whether homosexuality is abnormal?

To answer this question, we must first define what we mean by "abnormal." A variety of definitions are possible (Hyde, 1979). The one that seems most appropriate here is that a sexual behavior is abnormal if it is associated with poor psychological adjustment and the person is unhappy about it.

The massive research of Kinsey and his colleagues (Kinsey et al., 1948, 1953) contributed to destroying simplistic classifications of sexual behaviors as normal or abnormal. Many behaviors that were thought to be rare perversions turned out in reality to be fairly common. A good example is male homosexuality, long thought to be a deviant form of behavior; in fact, it is engaged in by substantial proportions of males. Kinsey found that about 60 percent of all males had some form of homosexual experience before adulthood; about 37 percent of all males had at least one adult homosexual experience leading to orgasm. Indeed, many men who engage in homosexual activities are respectable, middle-class citizens, and many are married (Humphreys, 1970). In view of such statistics it is difficult to view the behavior as deviant.

Empirical research also supports the view that lesbianism is not a deviant form of behavior (see review by Rosen, 1974). First, it is important to note that much of the early research on lesbian adjustment used lesbians who were patients in psychotherapy as subjects. The use of such a subject pool was not surprising, since they were easy to recruit, and, with the assumption that lesbianism was an abnormal form of adjustment, the researcher could rationalize the sampling techniques by saying that the "typical" lesbian would be in therapy.

In view of the subjects, it is not surprising that some of these early research efforts did find abnormal personality characteristics in lesbians. However, a major breakthrough occurred with the advent of research on nonpatient lesbians, recruited through homophile organizations or newspaper ads. Such studies have generally found that lesbians do not differ psychologically from control groups of heterosexual women in any consistent ways, with the one exception of their choice of sex partner. For example, lesbians could not be distinguished from heterosexual women on the basis of projective test performance, although there was some evidence that the lesbians were more likely to have a hostile-fearful conception of the female role (Armon, 1960). While the results of one study indicated that a nonclinical group of lesbians were higher in neuroticism than a comparison group of heterosexuals (Kenyon, 1968), another study indicated that lesbians and heterosexuals did not differ in neuroticism (Hopkins, 1969). Similar results, in which lesbians and heterosexuals did not differ, were obtained in several other studies (Freedman, 1968; Saghir and Robins, 1971; Siegelman, 1972). While Saghir and Robins found that depression, suicide attempts, and alcohol abuse were more common among nonpatient lesbians than among heterosexuals, such differences were not found in another study (Asimos and Rosen, unpublished, reported in Rosen, 1974). No differences in adjustment as measured by the MMPI were found between a group of single homosexual women and single heterosexual women (Oberstone and Sukoneck, 1977). And in another study, lesbians had significantly higher self-esteem than college women (Spence and Helmreich, 1978).

Thus the assumption that lesbianism is an inadequate form of adjustment is not supported by the available data and, as Rosen concludes, "The only difference between the lesbian and other women is the choice of love object" (1974, p. 65). The comparative absence of psychological disturbance among lesbians is even more remarkable in view of the social pressures to which they are subject. The notion that lesbianism, and homo-

TABLE 12.1.   Percentages of lesbians and unselected female college students in the four gender-role categories (discussed in Chapter 4)

	Gender Role Category			
	Androgynous	Feminine	Masculine	Undif-feren-tiated
Lesbians	33	13	22	32
College women	27	32	14	28

Source: Spence and Helmreich, 1978, pp. 53, 67.

sexuality more generally, is an adequate form of adjustment is reflected in a recent decision of the American Psychiatric Association to remove the term "homosexual" from its official list of diagnostic nomenclature.

In a recent study the gender-role identities of lesbians were examined, using the categories of androgynous, feminine, masculine, and undifferentiated discussed in Chapter 4 (Spence and Helmreich, 1978). The results, in comparison with college women, are shown in Table 12.1. It is true that a relatively low percentage of lesbians fall into the feminine category. We also find corresponding increases in the androgynous and masculine categories, and a slight increase in the undifferentiated category. The largest group of lesbians fall into the androgynous category. Given our earlier conclusions about androgyny being mentally healthy, this is a further indication that lesbianism is a healthy form of adjustment.

RESEARCH ON THE GENESIS OF LESBIANISM

Having tried to understand the nature of lesbian development through both experiential and theoretical approaches, we must next bring these ideas to the test by comparing them with the available empirical data on the life histories and family backgrounds of lesbians to see what factors appear to predispose a woman to choose another woman as her sexual and love partner.

One of the largest studies of lesbians and their developmental histories is that of the psychiatrist Charlotte Wolff (1971). She studied more than a hundred nonpatient lesbians, comparing them with a control group of women matched for family background, profession, and social class. Her research used clinical interviews, questionnaires, and autobiographical materials. In brief, her results suggest that the relationship with the mother has a strong influence on the sexuality of the developing young girl. Mothers of lesbians were significantly higher on destructive maternal attitudes; they tended to be either indifferent or neglectful. In addition, they tended to be more ambivalent toward the daughter. "The overall picture of the mother in the lesbian group suggests immaturity and unreliability" (p. 149). Additionally, neglect frequently was accompanied by the mother's avowed preference for the girl's brother. Family instability was relatively common, with a high degree of parental discord and frequently divorce. In contrast, the family life of the control subjects was characterized as sound, caring, and protective. There were more stepfathers present in the families of lesbians, which often gave rise to traumatic experiences that further drove the subject to rejection of male figures. The sibling structure of the family is also of interest, lesbians more often being only children or first-born children, with intense passion directed to the mother, and as a result, severely frustrated by her rejection of them. The majority of lesbians had wished to be a boy when they were young, and tomboyism was widespread among the homosexual girls in contrast with the controls. However, as adults lesbians did not wish to be men, suggesting a basic female identification. They manifested a willingness or desire to accept the homosexual role, implying comfort in that role, rather than to imitate the role of heterosexual relationships. It is not surprising that many lesbians were hostile to males, and specifically to their younger brothers whom they envied and had to care for while growing up.

In sum, then, Wolff's research indicates that the family is important in the development of lesbianism, and that the rejecting or indifferent mother may be particularly important. However, it should be emphasized that while such factors may be statistically more common in the families of lesbians than in the families of controls, they may be far from typical for lesbians. For example, while mothers of lesbians were more frequently indifferent or negligent, indifference was characteristic of only 27 percent of the mothers of lesbians (as compared with 10 percent of mothers of controls), and negligence was characteristic of only 10 percent of the mothers of lesbians (with 0 percent for controls) (Wolff, 1971, p. 273). Thus, maternal indifference or negligence is more common among lesbians than among controls, but was experienced by only a minority of lesbians.

Saghir and Robins (1973) in similar research found that as children lesbians had more frequently been tomboys and wished they could be boys. The gender ratio of their siblings showed an unusually high proportion of males. We question Saghir and Robins' suggestion that tomboyism is a precursor of lesbianism, however (Hyde, Rosenberg, and Behrman, 1977). This view attempts to reinforce the stereotype that the lesbian is masculine or boyish, which confuses the concepts of gender identity and choice of sexual partner. In our own samples of the general population, we have found that tomboyism is quite typical of girls — in several samples, the percentages of women claiming to have been tomboys in childhood range from 51 to 78 percent. Thus, tomboyism appears to be typical in female development, not just in pre-lesbian development.

There have been numerous other speculations as to the factors causing lesbianism (Romm, 1965; Wilbur, 1965; Martin and Lyon, 1972). As Rosen summarizes them, they include

> fear of growing up and assuming adult responsibilities; fear of dominance and destruction; fear of rejection; fear of the opposite sex; fear of castration and of the penis; the desire to conquer and possess the mother; neurotic dependency; heterosexual trauma (including rape); seduction in adolescence by an older female; first sexual experience with someone of the same sex and finding it pleasurable; tomboy behavior in early childhood; prolonged absence of the mother; masturbation with a resulting clitoral fixation; social factors (such as heterosexual taboos and unisexual, all female, groups); and physical factors (genetic, constitutional, and endocrine abnormalities). (1974, p. 8)

With regard to the last possibility, that of physical factors, research has consistently failed to find anatomical or genetic differences between lesbians and comparison groups of heterosexual women (Wolff, 1971; Marmor, 1965). While there have been numerous attempts to document hormonal differences between male homosexuals and heterosexuals — and the attempts have generally been unsuccessful or not replicatable — we know of only one similar attempt to document such differences between lesbians and heterosexual women. There was some suggestion of hormonal imbalance among lesbians who had higher testosterone and lower estrogen levels than a comparison group of heterosexual women (Loraine et al., 1971; see also Dörner, 1969). These results should be viewed cautiously, however, until they are replicated. Given the available research, it would seem dangerous to conclude that lesbianism is a result of simple biological determinants.

Perhaps the failure of research to uncover a consistent single "cause" of lesbianism is a result of the fact that there is no single cause, just as there is no single "lesbian personality." Variability among lesbians is great, and they come in all sizes, shapes, and personality types, just as do heterosexuals. What we are saying is that "lesbian" is not a homogeneous category, although we have been misled into thinking it is because of the superficial similarity that all lesbians prefer women as lovers. Since the category is nonhomogeneous, a single cause would not be expected. Throughout this chapter we refer to "lesbianism," using a single label with the understanding that it refers to a collectivity of behaviors, experiences, and developmental processes.

If there is a single factor in development that most frequently has major importance, it appears to be the nature of the first sexual experience — lesbianism may result if the experience is with a male and is unpleasant, or if it is with a female and is very pleasant (Rosen, 1974). Nonetheless, while such an etiology may be common, lesbianism may also arise in a variety of other ways. Indeed, it has been recommended that we stop using the term "homosexuality" and substitute "homosexualities" (Bell,

1974), in order to recognize more adequately the diversity and heterogeneity of the category. Such a view helps to make sense out of the finding that factors such as maternal neglect and indifference are more common among lesbians than among controls, but that they are still relatively rare for lesbians — maternal indifference and neglect may contribute in the development of lesbianism in some cases, but not in others.

DIFFERENCES BETWEEN GAY WOMEN AND GAY MEN

Theorists frequently refer to homosexuality as if it were a unitary phenomenon, there being no difference between male and female homosexuality (or else male homosexuality being the only phenomenon of interest or concern). The interesting question arises as to whether these two phenomena are in fact different.

There do appear to be some differences between male and female homosexuality. First, as we have seen, the lesbian appears to place primary emphasis on the emotional aspects of her relationship, while the male homosexual emphasizes the sexual aspects. Second, male homosexuals frequently have many different sex partners, while lesbians more often form long-term relationships (Loney, 1972). In one study of female and male homosexuals, the males reported a median (average) of 75 different partners, contrasted with a median of 5 for the females; 56 percent of the men had had 50 or more partners, but only 5 percent of the women had had that number (Schafer, 1977). In another study, 64 of the 65 gay women interviewed said they preferred a stable, long-term relationship (Hedblom, 1972). Third, bisexuality is more characteristic of lesbians and exclusive homosexuality less common than among male homosexuals. According to Kinsey data, by age 45 about 13 percent of all women and about 37 percent of all men have had a homosexual experience to orgasm; lesbianism is therefore less frequent than male homosexuality. But exclusive homosexuality is even less common among women. Kinsey estimated that only about 1 to 3 percent of all women are exclusively homosexual, as compared with about 3 to 16 percent of all men. Most lesbians, then, are bisexual or have had at least some heterosexual experience, while a substantial proportion of male homosexuals are exclusively homosexual (Kinsey et al., 1953, pp. 487–488).

Developmentally, the two phenomena probably arise in different ways, although there is little research available to document the nature of the differences. Gordon Bermant (1972), articulating a behaviorist position, constructed a developmental theory to account for the higher frequency of male, as compared with female, homosexuality. His basic observation was that homosexuality and a variety of other "inappropriate" sex behaviors ("inappropriate" referring to anything other than heterosexual coitus, and therefore including masturbation and homosexuality) are more frequent among males than among females in all species. He argues that in the male, physical sexuality develops before cognitive structures are sufficiently mature for the boy to have acquired the concept that the appropriate partner is one of the opposite gender. The boy therefore engages in homosexual behavior not knowing that it is inappropriate. The cognitive structures of the girl, on the other hand, mature earlier than her physical sexuality, so that she understands the appropriate object choice before she is confronted with arousal. She is therefore less likely to make the homosexual "mistake."

In sum, according to our descriptions, male and female homosexuality appear to be similar only in a superficial sense. The differences between the two are logical consequences of psychological differences between the genders and differences in their developmental experiences. Indeed, while it has been found that one's gender is a fairly good predictor of a number of psychological characteristics, one's homosexual status is not (Bell, 1973). That is, as we have seen, there are substantial gender differences among adults on a number of psychological variables such as aggression; one's gender will therefore be a fairly good predictor of one's score on these variables. But whether one is a heterosexual or a homosexual does not predict one's score. Therefore, a lesbian is probably more like a heterosexual woman than she is like a homosexual man. Her identity is first as a woman and only second as a homosexual.

BISEXUAL WOMEN

Bisexuality has become rather chic in recent years, particularly on the East and West coasts, and many large cities now have "bi" bars and discos. Because the topic and research on it are new — although the behavior certainly is not — our discussion will be relatively brief.

Bisexuality refers to having sexual relations with both males and females. As noted earlier, using this definition, bisexuality is actually more common than is exclusive homosexuality. For example, Kinsey found the following percentages of women to have had more than incidental homosexual experience: 6 to 14 percent of unmarried women, 2 to 5 percent of married women, and 8 to 10 percent of previously married women (Kinsey et al., 1953). The comparable statistics for exclusive homosexuality were 2 to 6 percent, 1 percent, and 1 to 6 percent, respectively.

In the absence of more systematic psychological research, the case of Joan, a bisexual woman, is offered to illustrate the life experience of a bisexual woman. One interesting fact that emerges from such cases is that women often become bisexual after a long history of exclusive heterosexuality or exclusive homosexuality, at relatively late ages (Blumstein and Schwartz, 1976).

CASE HISTORY OF JOAN,
A BISEXUAL WOMAN

Joan, a professional woman in her middle thirties, considered herself exclusively heterosexual until about four years ago. Until that time she had never had homosexual fantasies or feelings, but she had been generally liberal about "sexual alternatives" and believed in equal rights for homosexuals. Four years ago, however, Joan became active in the women's liberation movement and developed closer friendships with some of the women with whom she worked. None of these relationships was sexualized, but her curiosity was aroused by sexual possibilities with women. Her approach to her own potential homosexual behavior was at this time still more intellectual than emotional and was not accompanied by graphic fantasies or feelings of attraction to other women whom she might meet or see in public.

During this period, Joan met another woman in her profession whom she found both intellectually and socially attractive. Vivian was also heterosexual, but she had had a few homosexual experiences. The relationship between the two women became closer, and during an exchange of confidences Joan learned that Vivian had had sexual experiences with women. At this point, Joan began to have sexual fantasies involving Vivian and began to be more overtly physical toward her, but she never crossed the bounds of female heterosexual friendship. The relationship intensified, and intimate discussions about sexuality turned to the possibility of sex between the two women. After about six months of such discussions, they slept together, first having overcome their initial worries concerning the effect that any guilt feelings about their "experimentation" might have on their friendship.

After the first successful sexual experience, Joan and Vivian repeated it approximately once every month for over a year. Vivian, however, continued to think of herself as a heterosexual, while Joan began to feel that she was in love with her friend and to want a more committed relationship. Joan stopped sleeping with Vivian when she realized that Vivian did not agree with her terms for the relationship. The two remained close friends, but Joan looked for someone else who might wish to share a committed relationship. She eventually fell in love with another woman, and an intense romantic and sexual relationship continued for two years. At the present, Joan is unsure of what sexual label to apply to herself, but she prefers "bisexual." At the time of her interview, she had both a male and a female lover.

Source: Philip W. Blumstein and Pepper Schwartz. "Bisexual Women." In J. P. Wiseman, ed., *The Social Psychology of Sex* (New York: Harper & Row, 1976), pp. 156–157.

Sociologists Philip Blumstein and Pepper Schwartz (1976) have conducted interviews with bisexual women. On the basis of these interviews, they concluded that a number of factors contributed to a woman with a lesbian history moving toward bisexuality. Most lesbians — probably

50 to 80 percent (Hedblom, 1973; Saghir and Robins, 1973) — have had at least some heterosexual experience, including intercourse. When these are recalled as pleasurable it is reasonable to return to them later in life. Another factor is all of the social rewards in our society that go with a heterosexual lifestyle, including having a husband and children. Bisexuality can be a way of avoiding the social ostracism that lesbians must often face, while still engaging in some lesbian activity. On the other hand, some forces discourage the movement from lesbianism to bisexuality. Many lesbians receive their major emotional support in a lesbian community, and they stand to lose this if they adopt bisexuality. Some lesbians view bisexual women with suspicion or downright hostility.

Blumstein and Schwartz feel that a number of factors contribute to heterosexual women moving in a bisexual direction. They believe that women learn, as part of learning how to compete with women in being attractive to men, what is attractive in other women. They thereby become aware of erotic qualities in other women. Further, women are more permitted to be emotionally and physically expressive toward each other in our society, once again making a move towards bisexuality easier. As part of the more liberated sexual standards in recent years, some people experiment with having sex in groups of more than two persons at once, allowing an opportunity to experiment with lesbianism. Finally, the women's movement has created an environment that is relatively supportive of lesbianism, and some heterosexual women decide to experiment with lesbianism, and thereby become bisexuals, out of feminist convictions.

IN CONCLUSION

We have attempted an understanding of the nature of lesbianism based on the assumption — which appears to be supported by the available data — that it is a normal form of behavior. The accounts of the lesbian experience emphasize that her bond with another woman may be more emotional than sexual. She also experiences many conflicting pulls in her life — the pleasure and satisfaction of her bond with another woman, yet the ever-present tensions created by society's disapproval of homosexuality; the need to play roles in public; the fear of discovery; the strain of living in two worlds. Theoretical views of the nature of lesbianism are varied. Psychoanalytic theory sees it as an outcome of a persisting negative Oedipal complex, so that the woman continues to love her mother, and later other women, throughout her life. Wolff's neoanalytic theory sees lesbianism as a continued competition with males for the mother's love, which the lesbian was deprived of as a child. Behaviorism stresses that sex drive is a generalized drive that is channeled toward one or another object through experience and circumstance; thus both heterosexuality and homosexuality are learned. Existentialism does not concern itself with the developmental origins of lesbianism, but instead treats it simply as a free and legitimate choice. Research on the development of lesbianism suggests that there is probably no one single causal factor, although the nature of the first sexual experience may be important. Finally, we argued that male and female homosexuality are different in nature as a logical consequence of psychological differences between females and males.

Research on lesbianism is in its infancy, and the conclusions we draw must be tentative. Certainly the nature of reasearch on lesbianism is changing as we shed the assumption that it is a form of pathology. We now no longer seek to find what disturbances in development would create such a perversion; instead, we ask what developmental factors would lead a woman to choose heterosexuality or homosexuality or bisexuality. And just as surely, with society's increasing acceptance of lesbianism, the nature of lesbianism will change, presumably as many of the tensions are removed from it. Indeed, in the future we may even come to consider lesbianism preferable to heterosexuality. As Szasz provocatively suggests:

> We might even advocate homosexuality over heterosexuality: this choice could be supported as a contraceptive technique, especially for women intellectually or artistically gifted, for whom the value of traditional feminine heterosexuality is a barrier to achievement. (1965, p. 137)

14

VIOLENCE AGAINST WOMEN

Rape is a crime against the person, not against the hymen.

DEENA METZGER, The Rape Victim

Rape is one of the most important topics in the women's liberation debate. Feminists assert that rape is one of the ways that men exercise power and control over women (e.g., Brownmiller, 1975). With feminist attention to the topic, rape has "come out of the closet"; in the span of a decade, it has gone from being the secret that no woman would tell, to being the topic of television specials. More recently, attention has been drawn to the plight of battered wives. This topic, too, has moved from being something a woman felt she should hide, to being a topic of public debate.

This chapter is about violence against women as seen in rape and wife-beating. A discussion of all aspects of these problems (e.g., legal, self-defense) is beyond the scope of this book. Here we will concentrate on the psychological aspects.

THEORETICAL VIEWS
OF RAPE

To provide a perspective for the discussion that follows, we can distinguish among three of the following major theoretical views of the nature of rape (Albin, 1977):

1. Victim-precipitated — This view holds that a rape is always caused by a woman "asking for it." Rape, then, is basically the woman's fault. This view represents the tendency to "blame the victim."
2. Psychopathology of rapists — This theoretical view holds that rape is an act committed by a psychologically disturbed man. His deviance is responsible for the crime occurring.
3. Feminist — Feminist theorists view rapists as the standard (normal) product of gender-role socialization in our culture. They deemphasize the sexual aspects of rape and instead view rape as an expression of power and dominance by men over women.

You personally may subscribe to one or the other of these views. It is also true that researchers in this area have generally based their work on one of these theoretical models, and this may influence their research. You should keep these things in mind as you continue to read the rest of this chapter.

ATTITUDES TOWARD RAPE

Psychologist Hubert Feild (1978) has investigated attitudes toward rape among police, rapists, rape-crisis counselors, and citizens from the general population. He began his research by constructing a paper-and-pencil questionnaire that would measure people's attitudes toward rape on a number of different dimensions. Items were ranked on a scale from one (strongly agree) to six (strongly disagree) and consisted of statements such as "A woman should be responsible for preventing her own rape." Once Feild had developed this attitude scale, he administered it to people from the groups listed above. He obtained a number of interesting results.

In general, there was strong agreement with the following statements: "A woman can be raped against her will," and "A woman should feel guilty following a rape." There was strong disagreement with "A raped woman is a less desirable woman"; "If a woman is going to be raped, she might as well relax and enjoy it"; "Most women secretly desire to be raped"; "It would do some women some good to get raped"; " 'Nice' women do not get raped"; and "Rape serves as a way to put or keep women in their 'place.' " On the other hand, people on the average were fairly neutral (ratings around 3.5) on items such as "Women provoke rape by their appearance or behavior" and "The reason most rapists commit rape is for sex."

There were a number of gender differences in attitudes toward rape, as might be expected. Men indicated to a significantly greater extent that it was a woman's responsibility to prevent rape, that punishment for rape should be harsh, that victims precipitate rape through their appearance or behavior, that rapists are mentally normal, that rapists are not motivated by a need for power over women, that a woman is less attractive as a result of being raped, and that women should not resist during rape. It was also true that attitudes toward rape were correlated with attitudes toward women.

Comfortingly, there was a significant difference between rapists and rape-crisis counselors in their attitudes toward rape. Convicted rapists were more likely to endorse the following views: rape prevention is primarily a woman's responsibility; rape is motivated by a desire for sex; victims are likely to precipitate rape through their appearance or behavior; and rapists are not mentally normal.

Distressingly, however, police officers' views of rape were more similar to the rapists' than they were to the counselors'. No significant differences were found between police and rapists on most dimensions. It was also true that citizens from the general population had attitudes more like those of rapists than those of counselors. The citizens generally seemed to hold a negative view of rape victims.

THE RAPE VICTIM[1]

Psychological responses of the rape victim   A major program of research on rape victims has been done at Boston City Hospital by Ann
Wolbert Burgess, a nurse, and Lynda Holmstrom, a sociologist (Burgess
and Holmstrom, 1974a, 1974b). They have found that rape is a time of
crisis for a woman and the effects on her adjustment may last for six
months or more. Based on a study of 92 victims of forcible rape, Burgess
and Holmstrom documented the existence of a *rape trauma syndrome*,
which refers to the emotional changes that a woman undergoes following
a rape or an attempted rape.

The rape trauma syndrome progresses in two phases: an acute phase
and a long-term reorganization phase. The *acute phase* begins immediately after the rape and generally lasts for several weeks. During the first
few hours following the rape, women have a wide variety of emotional
reactions that may be classified into two basic categories: an expressive
reaction, in which the woman cries and expresses fear, anger, anxiety, and
tension; and a controlled reaction, in which the woman apparently masks
her feelings and appears calm and composed or subdued.

The women studied by Burgess and Holmstrom reported many physical reactions during the acute phase. Some of these were direct results of
the bruises and cuts they had received during the scuffle. Some women
were forced to have oral sex and suffered irritation or damage to the
throat. Rectal bleeding and pain were reported by the women who had
been forced to have anal intercourse. Various irritations of the genitals
were also common, as were symptoms of tension such as headaches, sleep-
lessness, and a feeling of jumpiness. Women also reported stomach pains
and nausea.

Emotional reactions varied widely, ranging from fear, humiliation, and
embarrassment to anger and a desire for revenge. Two feelings were especially prominent: fear and self-blame. Many women reported an over-
whelming fear of physical violence and said that they had believed they
would be murdered during the attack. These feelings of fear sometimes
persisted long after the rape had taken place. Self-blame also occurred,
with the woman spending hours agonizing over what she had done to
bring on the rape or what she might have done to prevent it: "If I hadn't
worn that tight sweater, . . ." "If I hadn't worn that short skirt, . . ."
"If I hadn't been stupid enough to walk on that dark street, . . ." "If I
hadn't been dumb enough to trust that guy, . . ." This is an example of a

---

[1] Portions of the material that follows on rape are adapted from *Understanding Human
Sexuality* by Janet S. Hyde. © 1979 by McGraw-Hill Book Co. Used with permission
of McGraw-Hill Book Co.

tendency, on the part of both the victim and others, to "blame the victim."[2]

The acute phase is followed by a *long-term reorganization phase*. The rape creates a major disruption in the woman's life. For example, some women are unable to return to work after being raped, particularly if the rape occurred at work (Brodsky, 1976). They may quit their jobs and remain unemployed for some time. Many of the women studied by Burgess and Holmstrom moved during the long-term reorganization phase, sometimes several times; many also changed their telephone number, and some got an unlisted number. These actions seemed to result from a fear that the rapist would find them and attack them again. Some women who had been raped indoors developed fears of being indoors, and some who had been raped outdoors developed fear of being outdoors. Sexual phobias were also common. The women's normal sexual lifestyles were often severely disrupted for long periods. For example, one woman reported, five months after being raped, "There are times I get hysterical with my boyfriend. I don't want him near me; I get panicked" (Burgess and Holmstrom, 1974a, p. 984). In some cases, it may be years before the victim returns to a normal lifestyle and is able to cope with the crisis she experienced.

If a woman reports the rape and decides to press charges, the police investigation and the trial itself may be further crises for her. She must recall the traumatic experience in detail. The police and the courts have a history of callous or even abusive treatment of rape victims. The woman may be offered little sympathy, and the police may adopt a cynical attitude, suggesting that she agreed to have sex but then changed her mind afterward. The attitudes of the police are not too surprising, growing up as they did in a culture that abounds with stereotypes about women, including the one that says that rape is only a situation in which a woman changed her mind. Of course, not all police officers have been guilty of such cynicism, but too many victims report treatment like this:

> They finally told me they thought I was lying. They said I'd probably been having sex with my boyfriend and probably was afraid I was pregnant. They also theorized that my boyfriend had set me up for it. They wanted to know if he'd ever asked me to have relations with his friends. (Brownmiller, 1975, p. 366)

Or this:

> I went to the police station and said, "I want to report a rape." They said, "Whose?" and I said, "Mine." The cop looked at me and said, "Aw, who'd want to rape you?" (Brownmiller, 1975, p. 364)

---

[2] In fact, however, in 71 percent of the cases, the rapist planned the rape ahead of time (Amir, 1971); it is therefore difficult to believe that it was the victim's fault.

Beyond these anecdotal reports, we have more solid scientific evidence of negative attitudes of the police in the study by Feild discussed earlier in this chapter.

The defense lawyer, in attempting to defend the rapist, may try to make it look as if the victim was actually the criminal — that she seduced him and later decided to call it rape, that she is a slut and therefore cannot be raped, and so on. She may be questioned about her prior sexual experiences, the idea being that if she has had premarital or extramarital sex, she is promiscuous and cannot be raped. As one woman expressed it:

> They trotted out my whole past life, made me go through all these charges, while he just sat at the defendant's table, mute, surrounded by his lawyers. Of course that was his right by law, but it looked like I was the one who was on trial. (Brownmiller, 1975, p. 372)

Recently some states have passed "reform" evidence laws, which do not permit the woman's previous sexual experience (except with the alleged rapist) to be a topic during a trial for rape.

Recently, perhaps partly as a result of several excellent television programs dramatizing the plight of the woman who has been raped, many police departments have tried to change their handling of rape victims. Some even have special "rape squads" composed of women police officers who record the woman's story and investigate the case; this spares the woman the embarrassment of describing the incident to a man.

It also appears that the victim's sense of guilt over the crime contributes to the trauma she experiences. According to a specialist in criminal psychiatry, "The victim who is beaten into almost senselessness may suffer far less emotional trauma than the woman who submits to rape when her life is threatened" (Brussel, 1971, p. 30). That is, emotional non-involvement between the victim and the criminal helps the victim adjust better afterward. The woman who is beaten unconscious is much less likely than the woman who escapes with only minor scratches to have others imply (or to think in her own mind) that she brought on the attack or that she cooperated or enjoyed it.

To say the least, then, rape is an extremely traumatic experience for many women, and it may have effects lasting six months or more after the attack. In view of this, Burgess and Holmstrom emphasize the need for counseling for rape victims. The counselor provides support and encourages the victim to vent her feelings. The counselor should be with the victim during the hospital stay and while the police are questioning her, and then should provide follow-up counseling; the counselor should also be with the woman during the court procedures since, as has been noted, they can be extremely traumatic.

Silent rape reaction   Burgess and Holmstrom (1974a) have also documented the existence of a phenomenon they call the "silent rape reaction."

Probably the majority of rapes (experts say 80 percent) are not reported. Not only do some women fail to report the rape to the police, but they also do not tell anyone about it. They, of course, experience the same problems of adjustment that other rape victims do, but they have no way of expressing or venting these feelings. People who do counseling or psychotherapy should be aware of this syndrome. For example, a woman may come for counseling complaining of quite different problems — perhaps inability to have orgasms or anxiety and depression — when her real problem is that she has been raped but is unable to talk about it. Symptoms of this silent rape reaction are similar to those associated with the rape trauma syndrome, described above. Such women should be gently helped to begin to talk about the experience so that they can start to deal with it.

THE RAPIST

The typical rapist   What is the profile of the typical rapist? The basic answer to that question is that there is no typical rapist. Rapists vary tremendously from one to the next in occupation, education, marital status, previous criminal record, and motivation for committing the rape. To deal with this diversity, some scientists have attempted to develop typologies of rapists (ways of classifying them). These will be discussed in the next section.

A few generalizations can be made about rapists. Most are young. According to the FBI *Uniform Crime Reports*, 61 percent are under 25. Many have a tendency to repeat their offense (Cohen et al., 1971). It is also true that most rapists are not murderers (Selkin, 1975). Probably only about one rape in 500 is accompanied by a murder (Brownmiller, 1975).[3] This statistic is important for women who wonder how best to react in a rape situation. Statistically, although the rapist may threaten the woman with violence or murder, he is unlikely to carry through on this and is only using the threat to get her to submit. This may encourage women to resist the attacker rather than to submit to him.

A typology of rapists   In an attempt to deal with the diversity in the personalities and approaches of rapists, psychiatrist Murray Cohen and his colleagues (1971) have developed a typology or scheme for categorizing rapists. The typology is based on the motivation of the rapist for committing the crime, in particular whether he was motivated by sex or by aggression. According to this typology, there are four kinds of rapists: the

---

[3] If anything, this is probably an overestimate of the number of rapes that end in murder, since rape-murders are invariably discovered, whereas the rape in which the woman escapes with minor scratches is likely to go unreported.

aggressive-aim rapist, the sexual-aim rapist, the sex-aggression-fusion rapist, and the impulse rapist.

The *aggressive-aim* rapist is motivated by a desire to hurt his victim. Sex has little to do with the act for him, except insofar as he uses sex to hurt his victim. Aggressive-aim rapists may try to damage the victim's breasts or genitals, or they may painfully insert objects into the woman's vagina.[4] Their emotional state during the rape is anger, and their victims are typically strangers. They often have a stable work history, with the work being in a very "masculine" occupation such as that of truck driver or machinist. Rapists in this category are often married, but they have a history of irritating or even violent relationships with women.

The *sexual-aim rapist* is quite different. For him the motivation for the rape is clearly sexual. Generally, he uses a minimal amount of violence and aggression — only what is needed to accomplish his sexual aim. During the act, he is highly sexually aroused and is fully aware of what he is doing. The act is not impulsive. He has lived through it many times in a fantasy in which the woman first protests but then submits; he shows great skill in his sexual performance, and she is so pleased that she falls in love with him. He has a history of poor sexual adjustment. As a child and early adolescent he may have shown signs of voyeurism, exhibitionism, and fetishism; adequate heterosexuality was present only in fantasy. In adolescence he became increasingly shy, lonely, and passive. He is characterized by low self-esteem and is simply incapable of forming mature relationships. He often releases his victim if she resists. Fighting back against such a rapist may thus be quite effective and probably involves little danger.

The *sex-aggression-fusion* rapist appears to be motivated by sadism. For him, violence is necessary in order to experience sexual excitement. Indeed, he may be unable to get an erection unless the woman resists. Rapist-murderers are an extreme version of this type; most sex-aggression-fusion rapists use violence only to become aroused, and they employ no further aggression once the act is over. This type of rapist may also project his own confusion of sex and aggression onto his victim, saying that women like to be roughed up. While he may be married, there is often a history of marriages and divorces, and he appears uncommitted to any of the marriages. His personality is similar to that of the psychopath; he has a history of antisocial behavior, an inability to form stable relationships, a noncaring attitude toward others, little control over his impulses, and no feelings of guilt over his behavior. He may have had a history of aggressive behavior toward younger children, peers, and animals even before he reached puberty. This type of rapist is clearly the most dangerous, but fortunately he is also the rarest.

---

[4] It is clear from the statistics that intercourse is not always the goal of the rapist. In one study, vaginal intercourse occurred in less than half the rape cases investigated (Selkin, 1975).

Finally, the *impulse* rapist has neither a sexual nor an aggressive motive. Rather, he commits the rape on impulse. For example, he may be involved in robbing an apartment when he notices that it is unoccupied except for one woman who is asleep in her bed. He sees the opportunity for rape, and he seizes it. He does it simply because it gives him satisfaction. This type has also been called the *predatory* rapist (Selkin, 1975).

The date rape   Though often not categorized as rape, some acts of coitus on dates involve a great deal of force and could at least be called *sex aggression.*

Incidents of this type were investigated by Eugene J. Kanin (1969; see also Kanin and Parcell, 1977). He began by contacting a random sample of unmarried male university students; 95 percent cooperated. Of those who responded, 25 percent reported having performed at least one act of sex aggression, defined as making a forceful attempt at coitus to the point of being disagreeable and offensive to the woman, with the woman responding by fighting or crying, for example. The 87 males who had engaged in such acts reported 181 episodes with 142 females.

The incidents of sex aggression were not confined to cases of casual bar pick-ups. They occurred in every degree of involvement, from pick-ups and first dates to couples who dated regularly or were pinned.

In some cases, the sex aggression appeared to result from female-male miscommunication. There is a saying among males that "When she says 'no,' she really means 'yes.'" How, then, is a woman supposed to say "no" when she really means it? Such confused communication patterns between men and women can contribute to the date rape, as described in the following example:

> I picked up M and she suggests we go and park and "talk." Talk shifts to "old times." I move over and kiss her. One thing leads to another and I am petting her breasts. M begins to complain about her girdle and removes it. The pace increases to the point where I try to lay her down on the front seat of the car. She resists and I keep going until she suddenly starts fighting and screaming at me. I finally told her to shut up and took her home. She was really sore. (Kanin, 1969)

In this case, the man doubtless interpreted the woman's taking off her girdle as an invitation to intercourse, while she probably in fact took it off because it felt very uncomfortable.

In some cases, miscommunication and misunderstanding are so great as to be nearly unbelievable. For example, some rapists have been reported to ask, after the rape, whether the victim had an orgasm (see, for example, the case reported by Anonymous, 1975).

In other cases, the rape appears to be a way for the man to exert social control over the woman. For example, sex aggression was apparently used by some men to punish women whom they perceived as being "teases" or "gold diggers."

Other factors also appeared to contribute to cases of date rape; however, the more important point is that such incidents were not found to be rare.

Recent attention has focused on a related phenomenon, *marital rape*. One of the most important first steps in dealing with it will be a legal one, namely, designating it as a crime. Currently, American laws do not acknowledge that rape can occur between husband and wife. This is a topic deserving of psychological research as well.

Sex and aggression   Psychologists Seymour Feshbach and Neal Malamuth (1978) have done a series of studies on the link between sex and aggression. These studies may provide us with some clues about how forces in our society encourage rapists, and what might be done to remedy this situation.

In one of their typical experiments, they exposed subjects (college students) to an erotic film or written story. Afterward, they gave the subjects an opportunity to act aggressively by allowing them to shock a "subject" (really a confederate of the experimenters') for making errors in a guessing game. The amount of shock the subject administered was used as an index of aggression. The results indicated that subjects who were sexually aroused from seeing a film showed significantly more aggression than a control group who had seen a neutral film.

In explaining this phenomenon, Feshbach and Malamuth believe that it is not a simple link between sex and aggression, with sexual arousal causing increased aggression. Instead, they believe the link is in the fact that our society has taboos on both sexual and aggressive behavior. When the taboo on one is lifted, it tends to lift the taboo on the other. As the researchers commented, "By showing the erotic film, we communicated the unspoken message that 'taboo behavior like sex is okay.'"

Other studies have also shown that the effect can work in the reverse direction — that is, by giving subjects permission to be aggressive, they can become more sexually aroused. However, aggressive behavior that is stronger and more deviant can interfere with sexual feelings. Generally, reading about a rape inhibited the sexual responses of both men and women. However, there was some variation depending on the content of the passage, in particular whether the victim was described as being in pain and whether she finally succumbed and enjoyed the act. For women, strong pain cues inhibited sexual arousal, regardless of whether the woman finally gave in. For men, however, the theme of the woman getting aroused in the end, despite the pain and violence of the rape, led them to increased arousal. Indeed, there was some evidence that men identify with the rapist and consider his behavior within their own potential range. When asked how likely they would be to behave as this man did under the same circumstances, 51 percent responded that they might do it if they were assured that they would not be caught.

While not opposed to pornography *per se*, Feshbach and Malamuth argue strongly that sadomasochistic pornography, in which violence and sexual arousal are shown together, can be harmful. In particular, it may help to form a conditioned association between sexual arousal and violent responses. In an analysis of five years of pictures and cartoons in *Playboy* and *Penthouse*, they found that the amount of sexual violence increased each year. There is cause for concern about this because, if they are correct, combining sex and aggression and showing it to men may lift some of their inhibitions against rape.

GENDER-ROLE SOCIALIZATION AND RAPE

Female socialization: creating rape victims   How do women become victims of rape? In this section we will discuss the notion that many of the qualities for which females are socialized make them vulnerable to rape (Russell, 1975; Weis and Borges, 1973).

For example, according to gender-role stereotypes, weakness is feminine, while strength is masculine. The stereotype of weakness is compounded by the lack of athletic training that females generally receive, compared with males. As a result, many women think of themselves as being physically weak, and, because they lack training and do not exercise, they may actually be weak. This weakness is symbolized in many ways, as when men open doors for women or carry heavy bundles for them. To expect a person who needs such assistance to fight off a 220-pound attacker would be silly. Thus, the weakness and passivity for which females are socialized contribute to making them rape victims.

Females are also socialized for nurturance (taking care of others) and altruism (paying attention to the needs of others rather than one's own needs). The woman who has been socialized to be nurturant and who spends her days expressing her gentleness toward her children can scarcely be expected to attempt to gouge out a man's eyes with her fingernails, as some self-defense experts advise. Female altruism has an ironic effect in the rape situation. Some women report the rape but then choose not to press charges because they say they are afraid that the rapist might have to go to jail for a long time[5] or that his reputation will be ruined. Thus, the victim may adopt a nurturant, altruistic attitude toward her attacker, considering his needs and feelings first.

---

[5] Those who worry about condemning a man to a long jail sentence may be interested to know that the average convicted rapist spends less than four years in jail for the offense (Brownmiller, 1975).

The feelings of altruism that lead to nonreporting are magnified by the fact that, in nearly half the cases, the victim knows her attacker at least casually. Statistics indicate that in 53 percent of all cases, the attacker is a total stranger. However, in 30 percent of all cases, the woman and the rapist are slightly acquainted; in 7 percent, they are relatives (father and daughter, brother and sister, uncle and niece, etc.); and in 3 percent, they are not related but have had a previous close association (Mulvihill et al., 1969).

Females are also socialized for a group of qualities that might be called collectively "being ladylike." Ladies, for example, do not make scenes. To fight off a rapist, of course, one needs to make a scene, but many women may be inhibited from screaming or engaging in a rough scuffle because that is not ladylike behavior. Ladies are also neat and clean and pretty. Some women, immediately after a rape, go home to shower, wash their hair, and change their clothes; then they proceed to the police station. While their emotional need to get themselves clean is understandable, they have destroyed most of the evidence of the crime, and the skeptical reaction of the police is not surprising. If you look neat and clean and pretty, it is hard to believe that you have just been raped.

Children, and girls especially, are taught to fear sex crimes. They are told never to accept rides with strange men or to take candy from them. Yet the exact nature of the potential danger remains unknown, and so the girl may build up an exceedingly great dread of a mysterious crime, perhaps thinking that it would be the worst thing that could ever happen to her. Thus, when she is attacked, she may be immobilized with fear. She freezes and is unable to wage an effective counterattack.

The reader can probably think of other examples of qualities that females are socialized for that contribute to making them rape victims. However, the important point is that conformity to traditional standards of femininity makes women more vulnerable to rape, at least when they are in a situation in which a man intends to rape them (Russell, 1975).

Male socialization: creating rapists   The parallel argument to the one above is that males are socialized for characteristics that contribute to making them rapists (Russell, 1975; Weis and Borges, 1973).

Aggression, dominance, power, and strength are considered to be manly. Having been socialized to be aggressive, it is not surprising that men commit the aggressive crime of rape. Further, rapists may themselves be victims of our culture's confusion of sex and aggression. For example, we often refer to the male as playing the "aggressive" role in sex, suggesting that sex is supposed to have an aggressive component. As noted above, sex and aggression are also combined in the sadomasochistic pornography that is so common. The rapist's confusion of sex and aggression reflects a confusion existing in our society.

It may be, then, that rape is a means of proving masculinity for the male who is insecure in his role. For this reason, the statistics on the youthfulness of rapists make sense; youthful rapists may simply be young men who are trying to adopt the adult male role, who feel insecure about doing it, and who therefore commit a rape as proof of their manhood. Further, heterosexuality is an important part of manliness. Raping a woman is a flagrant way to prove that one is heterosexual. Interestingly, some rapists have a history of passivity, heterosexual inadequacy, and being called "queers" or "pansies" by their peers in adolescence. Rape may seem to them to be a way of establishing their heterosexual manliness.

Further support for this viewpoint comes from the fact that, in one study, 43 percent of rapes were committed by pairs or groups of men (Amir, 1971). Often in such cases the men or boys appear to be vying to prove their masculinity (Blanchard, 1959), and rape is a way of accomplishing that.

FIGURE 14.1

Karate demonstration at International Women's Day, March, 1973. Many experts feel that women should learn self-defense skills as a way of combating rape.

Source: Photo by Elizabeth Hamlin / Stock Boston.

The wider impact of rape   To this point, the discussion has centered on rapists and the impact of rape on the victim. But rape has much broader ramifications in our society, and it affects many people besides the victim. Most women perform a number of behaviors that stem basically from rape fears. For example, a single woman is not supposed to list her full first name in the telephone book, since that is a giveaway that she is alone. Rather, she should list a first initial or a man's name. Many women, when getting into their car at night, almost reflexively check the back seat to make sure that no one is hiding there. Most college women avoid walking alone through dark parts of the campus at night. At least once in their lives, most women have been afraid of spending the night alone. If you are a woman, you can probably extend the list from your own experience. However, the point is that most women experience the fear of rape, if not rape itself.[6] In addition, this fear restricts their activities.

There are also probably some bad consequences for society at large. Surely it is not pleasant for the average man to be viewed by a woman as a potential rapist. Further, there are probably effects on husbands of raped women, although these have yet to be studied.

BATTERED WIVES[7]

One solution that some people propose to the rape problem is for women simply to stay home, off the streets. However, the data indicate that a woman may actually be less safe in her own home than on the street. The following statistics give some indication of the extent of the problem (Martin, 1976):

- In Atlanta, Georgia, 60 percent of all police calls on the night shift are domestic disputes.
- In 1974, Boston police responded to 11,081 family disturbance calls, most of which involved physical violence.

---

[6] Actually, statistics indicate that the chances of being raped are higher than you might think. *Psychology Today* (January 1975) did a sample calculation of the chances that a female resident of Los Angeles would be the victim of a rape attempt at some time in her life. Using the number of reported rapes and rape attempts in 1972 (2205) and the conservative estimate that 50 percent of all rapes go unreported, the magazine estimated the chances that a woman in Los Angeles would be the victim of a rape attempt at some time during a 30-year period to be about 1 in 10. The rape rate in Los Angeles, of course, is higher than rape rates in some other areas of the country, but the statistic is nonetheless disturbing.

[7] Battering can occur in situations other than marriage; examples are a divorced or separated couple in which the husband returns to beat the woman, or couples who are simply living together. To simplify the terminology, we shall refer to "battered wives." It is also true that in some cases it is the wife who beats the husband. However, when the violence is physical but not homicidal, the greater physical strength of the male means that far greater damage is done in wife-beating than in husband-beating (Steinmetz, 1977). Our focus here will be on wife-beating rather than on husband-beating.

— Women are the ones who need help most of the time in these disturbances. About 75 to 95 percent of the complaints in domestic disturbances are filed by women.

— In order to get a control group for his study *The Violent Home,* Richard Gelles (1974) interviewed 40 neighbors of known violent families. Of these supposedly "nonviolent" families, 37 percent had experienced at least one incident of violence, and for 12 percent, the violence was a regular occurrence.

— About one-third of female murder victims in California in 1971 were killed by their husbands.

It is only recently that the topic of battered wives has been brought to the attention of the public, and thus it is a topic that has received less research than rape. In fact, wife-beating has a long history, and at many times has been considered a legitimate form of behavior, a logical extension of the roles of men and women. For example, in the sixteenth-century France, the Abbé de Brantôme, although reluctant to speak against the teachings of the Church, felt compelled to ask, "But however great the authority of the husband may be, what *sense* is there for him to be allowed to kill his wife?" (Davis, 1971, p. 261). In Russia during the reign of Ivan the Terrible, the state church supported such practices by issuing a Household Ordinance that detailed how a man might most effectively beat his wife (Mandel, 1975, p. 12). Probably the first contemporary book exposing the topic was *Scream Quietly or the Neighbors Will Hear,* by Erin Pizzey (1974), who has opened a shelter for battered women in England.

ATTITUDES TOWARD MARITAL VIOLENCE

Several recent surveys indicate that a surprisingly large number of Americans approve of some violence in marriage, and that acceptance of such practices is actually stronger in the middle class than the lower class. In one sample of American adults, 25 percent approved of husband-wife battles. Among grade-school graduates, 17 percent approved, but 32 percent of college graduates approved (cited in Martin, 1976, p. 19). A Harris poll done in 1968, based on interviews with a representative national sample of 1176 adults, showed that one-fifth approved of slapping one's spouse on "appropriate" occasions (Stark and McEvoy, 1970). It would be interesting to know how the respondents construed the term "slap," and whether they would have answered differently had the term been "beat" or "hit."

Insofar as there is social approval of marital violence, the abused woman's situation worsens. It is difficult for her to complain about her crisis if people do not view it as such.

THE BATTERER:
PSYCHOLOGICAL ASPECTS

What kind of man beats his wife? As with the rapist, we can give no profile of the "typical" wife beater. Such men are found in all social classes and in a wide variety of occupations. Contrary to stereotypes, the wife-batterer is not always an unemployed man in the lower class (Martin, 1976). One woman, whose physician husband beat her, said that he was "a general practitioner and while at medical school was an amateur boxer, so he had plenty of brawn as well as brain, plus enough money to keep him well-supplied with as much whiskey as he wanted." (Martin, 1976, p. 45).

Within this diversity, a few factors do emerge as common among wife batterers. Drugs, particularly alcohol, are common problems among wife beaters, and they are often being used at the time of violent incidents. In one study of women seeking help from an abused women's crisis center, 85 percent reported that their violent husbands had either alcohol or other drug problems (Roy, 1977b). Of the men who drank occasionally, 80 percent beat their wives only while under the influence of alcohol. Some authorities, however, feel that the effects of alcohol in family violence have been exaggerated (Martin, 1976). In our society, we believe that people do things that are "out-of-character" while they are drunk, and thus drunkenness can become a kind of excuse for the batterer and his victim, disguising what is really happening.

It does appear that wife-batterers come from violent families. In one study, 81 percent of wife-beaters had either been abused as children or had witnessed their father beating their mother (Roy, 1977b). Thus violence in families may perpetuate itself from one generation to the next.

In an attempt to describe the diversity of types of men who seriously assault their wives, one study of men who had been arrested for such assaults found that there were five different personality types among these men (Faulk, 1974): (1) Dependent and suspicious — The husband is extremely jealous and the violence arises from this; (2) Violent and bullying — These men use violence to solve problems in many areas of their lives including their marriages; (3) Dominating — These men have a great need to be dominant over their wives, and apparent insubordination could lead to violence; (4) Dependent and passive — In this case the wife appears to dominate the relationship, and violence occurs after prolonged poor treatment from her; and (5) Stable and affectionate — In this group, the men appear to have a long-term, affectionate relationship with their wives, and violence occurred during an episode of psychological disturbance, typically depression.

The violent episode is often preceded by an argument. According to one study, the following are the four most common areas of disagreement when wife-beating occurs: arguments over money, jealousy, sexual problems, and alcohol and other drugs (Roy, 1977b).

THE BATTERED WOMAN: PSYCHOLOGICAL ASPECTS

Battered women, just like their husbands, are a diverse group, varying in social class, education, and occupation. Compared with the 81 percent of wife-beaters who came from violent homes, however, only 33 percent of battered women were abused as children or witnessed their father beating their mother (Roy, 1977b).

One of the most interesting questions to ask about battered women is, Why do they stay? Many of these women endure years of repeated beating. Often to the frustration of crisis counselors, a battered woman who has left her husband may return to him. The following were the five most common reasons given for staying by battered wives, listed in order from most to least frequent: (1) hope that the husband would reform; (2) having no other place to go; (3) fear that there would be reprisals from the husband; (4) concern about the children (they need a father, can't support them herself, etc.); and (5) economic dependence (can't support herself) (Roy, 1977b). Although a psychoanalyst might think that these women are masochistic, the reasons listed above more often reflect stark practical and economic factors, such as not being able to support oneself and having no place else to live.

Beyond this, there is little research available on the psychological characteristics of the battered woman. The letter from a battered woman at the end of this chapter is offered as providing more psychological insights than scientific research has yet achieved.

THE CHILDREN

In addition to the effects on the battered woman, it is also important to consider the effects on the children. These effects fall into two categories. First, the man who beats his wife is likely to abuse his children. In one study of battered wives, 45 percent reported that the husband also assaulted the children (Roy, 1977b). In a study of battered women in England, 54 percent said that their husband also committed acts of violence against the children (Gayford, 1975). Second, even if the man does not abuse the children, one must consider the effects on the children of watching their father beat their mother. Those effects have not been precisely documented, but, as noted earlier, wife-beaters frequently come from such families.

WHAT CAN BE DONE?

The problems of battered women are complex, and no single measure is likely to solve them. If violence in American society could be reduced in general, that would probably help to a certain degree. Some of the problems of battered women, however, are special and require special solutions. One solution is providing refuge houses. These houses provide the woman with a safe place to go (one of her most immediate needs), with emotional support from those around her, and possibly with job counseling and legal advice. A number of these houses have been founded in the United States, such as the Women's House in St. Paul, Minnesota; Rainbow Retreat in Phoenix, Arizona; and Haven House in Pasadena, California (Martin, 1976).

Community social services are also needed to deal with the problem of wife-beating. Crisis hotlines are important so that the woman can get immediate help. In addition, counseling services for the batterer, the victim, and the children are needed. Feminist therapy (see Chapter 7) should be particularly helpful to the battered woman.

Self-defense training for battered women has been recommended by some experts (e.g., Martin, 1976). The woman who is an expert in karate or some other system can offset the greater strength of her husband and assertively discourage his attacks.

Legal and police reform are also important (e.g., Roy, 1977a; Martin, 1976). One problem is that the American legal system has considered the family and home to be sacred, and has been loath to interfere with them in any way. Somehow the police officer who intervenes in a "family" fight is viewed as violating the sanctity of the family. Police officers are often unwilling to arrest a husband for assault unless the officer has actually witnessed the attack, which is rare since the police are usually called after the fact. A simple solution is for the woman to make a citizen's arrest, but women are often not aware that they can do this, and the police neglect to inform them of this option.

At least some of the blame must also rest with traditional gender roles and socialization. Wife-beating, after all, is a way of being dominant and thereby of fulfilling the male role. And staying with such a husband is consistent with the submissiveness for which women are socialized. Reforms in gender roles, socialization, and education, therefore, might be expected to help remedy this situation.

IN CONCLUSION

In this chapter we reviewed psychological research on rape and wife-battering. Not only are these two both areas of violence toward women in our society, but they are further linked because both appear to be means by which men express power and dominance over women. Finally, there is evidence that rape and wife-battering are outcomes of gender-role socialization patterns in our society. In thinking about how socialization practices should be revised, it is important to keep these two phenomena in mind.

A LETTER FROM A BATTERED WIFE

I am in my thirties and so is my husband. I have a high school diploma and am presently attending a local college, trying to obtain the additional education I need. My husband is a college graduate and a professional in his field. We are both attractive and, for the most part, respected and well-liked. We have four children and live in a middle-class home with all the comforts we could possibly want.

I have everything, except life without fear.

For most of my married life I have been periodically beaten by my husband. What do I mean by "beaten"? I mean that parts of my body have been hit violently and repeatedly, and that painful bruises, swelling, bleeding wounds, unconsciousness, and combinations of these things have resulted.

Beating should be distinguished from all other kinds of physical abuse — including being hit and shoved around. When I say my husband threatens me with abuse I do not mean he warns me that he may lose control. I mean that he shakes a fist against my face or nose, makes punching-bag jabs at my shoulder, or makes similar gestures which may quickly turn into a full-fledged beating.

I have had glasses thrown at me. I have been kicked in the abdomen when I was visibly pregnant. I have been kicked off the bed and hit while lying on the floor — again, while I was pregnant. I have been whipped, kicked and thrown, picked up again and thrown down again. I have been punched and kicked in the head, chest, face, and abdomen more times than I can count.

I have been slapped for saying something about politics, for having a different view about religion, for swearing, for crying, for wanting to have intercourse.

I have been threatened when I wouldn't do something he told me to do. I have been threatened when he's had a bad day and when he's had a good day.

I have been threatened, slapped, and beaten after stating bitterly that I didn't like what he was doing with another woman.

After each beating my husband has left the house and remained away for days.

Few people have ever seen my black and blue face or swollen lips because I have always stayed indoors afterwards, feeling ashamed. I was never able to drive following one of these beatings, so I could not get myself to a hospital for care. I could never have left my young children alone, even if I could have driven a car.

Hysteria inevitably sets in after a beating. This hysteria — the shaking and crying and mumbling — is not accepted by anyone, so there has never been anyone to call.

Source: Excerpted from *Battered Wives*. Copyright © 1976 by Del Martin. All rights reserved. Published by Glide Publications, Inc., 330 Ellis Street, San Francisco, CA 94102 ($7.95). Used with permission.

My husband on a few occasions did phone a day or so later so we could agree on the excuse I would use for returning to work, the grocery store, the dentist appointment, and so on. I used the excuses — a car accident, oral surgery, things like that.

Now, the first response to this story, which I myself think of, will be "Why didn't you seek help?"

I did. Early in our marriage I went to a clergyman who, after a few visits, told me that my husband meant no real harm, that he was just confused and felt insecure. I was encouraged to be more tolerant and understanding. Most important, I was told to forgive him the beatings just as Christ had forgiven me from the cross. I did that, too.

Things continued. Next time I turned to a doctor. I was given little pills to relax me and told to take things a little easier. I was just too nervous.

I turned to a friend, and when her husband found out, he accused me of either making things up or exaggerating the situation. She was told to stay away from me. She didn't, but she could no longer really help me. Just by believing me she was made to feel disloyal.

I turned to a professional family guidance agency. I was told there that my husband needed help and that I should find a way to control the incidents. I couldn't control the beatings — that was the whole point of my seeking help. At the agency I found I had to defend myself against the suspicion that I wanted to be hit, that I invited the beatings. Good God! Did the Jews invite themselves to be slaughtered in Germany?

I did go to two more doctors. One asked me what I had done to provoke my husband. The other asked if we had made up yet.

I called the police one time. They not only did not respond to the call, they called several hours later to ask if things had "settled down." I could have been dead by then!

I have nowhere to go if it happens again. No one wants to take in a woman with four children. Even if there were someone kind enough to care, no one wants to become involved in what is commonly referred to as a "domestic situation."

Everyone I have gone to for help has somehow wanted to blame me and vindicate my husband. I can see it lying there between their words and at the end of their sentences. The clergyman, the doctor, the counselor, my friend's husband, the police — all of them have found a way to vindicate my husband.

No one has to "provoke" a wife-beater. He will strike out when he's ready and for whatever reason he has at the moment.

I may be his excuse, but I have never been the reason.

I know that I do not want to be hit. I know, too, that I will be beaten again unless I can find a way out for myself and my children. I am terrified for them also.

As a married woman I have no recourse but to remain in the situation which is causing me to be painfully abused. I have suffered physical and emotional battering and spiritual rape because the social structure of my world says I cannot do anything about a man who wants to beat me. . . . But staying with my husband means that my children must be subjected to the emotional battering caused when they see their mother's face or hear her screams in the middle of the night.

I know that I have to get out. But when you have nowhere to go, you know that you must go on your own and expect no support. I have to be ready for that. I have to be ready to support myself and the children completely, and still provide a decent environment for them. I pray that I can do that before I am murdered in my own home.

I have learned that no one believes me and that I cannot depend upon any outside help. All I have left is the hope that I can get away before it is too late.

I have learned also that the doctors, the police, the clergy, and my friends will excuse my husband for distorting my face, but won't forgive me for looking bruised and broken. The greatest tragedy is that I am still praying, and there is not a human person to listen.

Being beaten is a terrible thing; it is most terrible of all if you are not equipped to fight back. I recall an occasion when I tried to defend myself and actually tore my husband's shirt. Later, he showed it to a relative as proof that I had done something terribly wrong. The fact that at that moment I had several raised spots on my head hidden by my hair, a swollen lip that was bleeding, and a severely damaged cheek with a blood clot that caused a permanent dimple didn't matter to him. What mattered was that I tore his shirt! That I tore it in self-defense didn't mean anything to him.

My situation is so untenable I would guess that anyone who has not experienced one like it would find it incomprehensible. I find it difficult to believe myself.

It must be pointed out that while a husband can beat, slap, or threaten his wife, there are "good days." These days tend to wear away the effects of the beating. They tend to cause the wife to put aside the traumas and look to the good — first, because there is nothing else to do; second, because there is nowhere and no one to turn to; and third, because the defeat is the beating and the hope is that it will not happen again. A loving woman like myself always hopes that it will not happen again. When it does, she simply hopes again, until it becomes obvious after a third beating that there is no hope. That is when she turns outward for help to find an answer. When that help is denied, she either resigns herself to the situation she is in or pulls herself together and starts making plans for a future life that includes only herself and her children.

For many the third beating may be too late. Several of the times I have been abused I have been amazed that I have remained alive. Imagine that I have been thrown to a very hard slate floor several times, kicked in the abdomen, the head, and the chest, and still remained alive! What determines who is lucky and who isn't? I could have been dead a long time ago had I been hit the wrong way. My baby could have been killed or deformed had I been kicked the wrong way. What saved me?

I don't know. I only know that it has happened and that each night I dread the final blow that will kill me and leave my children motherless. I hope I can hang on until I complete my education, get a good job, and become self-sufficient enough to care for my children on my own.

15

BLACK WOMEN AND WOMEN AS A MINORITY GROUP

We are the women whose hair is compulsively fried, whose skin is bleached, whose nose is "too big," whose mouth is "too big and loud," whose behind is "too big and broad," whose feet are "too big and flat," whose face is "too black and shiny," and whose suffering and patience is too long and enduring to be believed.

ABBEY LINCOLN

We must confront a serious problem: Much of what we have referred to as "the psychology of women" is, in reality, a psychology of white, middle-class, American women. But is the femininity-achievement double-bind, of low expectation for success, a phenomenon inherently part of womanhood? When we consider other groups of women, in particular black women, it becomes immediately apparent that the complex social forces acting on them are so different that their psychology is probably also different. Among these forces are poverty, discrimination, variations in family structure (the extended family, more frequently absent fathers), more frequent necessity for them to hold a job, evaluation of their appearance by white standards of beauty, and identification with the Black Power movement. What impact do all these forces have on the psychology of black women?

While it is interesting to explore subcultural variation in the psychology of women, we do not wish to treat the psychology of black women as being of interest only insofar as it represents a deviation from white norms. It has an intrinsic interest and integrity of its own. Indeed, some writers have suggested that black culture has progressed further than white culture and that the trend may be for whites to become more like blacks. Thus the psychology of black women may have important implications for the psychology of women in general, and particularly for the psychology of women in the future.

Parenthetically we should note that we originally intended this to be a chapter on minority-group women. In researching the chapter, it quickly became apparent that there simply was not sufficient research available to be able to make any conclusions about the psychology of minority-group women other than blacks. Certainly here is a large body of potential research sorely in need of attention. In addition, the amount of research on black women is not large; the reader should keep in mind that many of the conclusions we draw in this chapter are based on only a limited amount of data and therefore should be accepted only tentatively, awaiting further research.

A very fundamental problem in much of the research to be cited is the confounding of race and social class. Because blacks tend to be over-represented in the lower class and whites in the middle class, it is generally not clear whether differences between blacks and whites should be attributed to race differences or to social-class differences. Research techniques generally have not been powerful enough to conquer this ambiguity. The reader should keep in mind that much of what we call race differences may actually be due to social-class differences.

BLACK WOMEN

Gender roles   A singularly important input into the gender identity of any woman comes from the gender roles prescribed for her by her culture or subculture. So we begin our discussion of the psychology of black women by looking at these roles. The constellation of gender roles for black women seems to differ in important ways from that of white women. Gender role for black women involves multiple roles — worker, head of household, mother, lover. Most notably, the traditional white middle-class feminine gender role — that of full-time housewife and mother, with an attending definition of one's identity almost exclusively in terms of these gender roles — has been denied to the black woman because of economic necessity. Allowing women to be economically unproductive is a luxury of the modern middle class. Because black women have not been permitted this luxury, they have taken on other gender roles and found alternative definitions of womanhood. This was expressed with a brilliant clarity by Sojourner Truth at a Women's Rights Convention in the 1800s:

> Dat man ober dar say dat women needs to be helped into carriages, and lifted ober ditches, and to have de best place every whar. Nobody ever help me into carriages, or ober mud puddles, or gives me any best places . . . and ar'nt I a woman? Look at me! Look at my arm! . . . I have plowed and planted, and gathered into barns, and no man could head me — and ar'nt I a woman? I could work as much and eat as much as a man (when I could get it), and bear de lash as well — and ar'nt I a woman? I have borne thirteen children and I seen 'em mos' all sold off into slavery, and when I cried out with a woman's grief, none but Jesus heard — and ar'nt I a woman? (*Abolitionist*, 1831)

Black women have had to define their identity, including their gender identity, in terms of roles other than housewife-mother. Although motherhood is still a prime gender-role definer, they have taken on additional roles, such as worker and head of household. Black women generally expect that they must hold paying jobs as adults (Kuvlesky and Obordo, 1972), and this has important consequences for their educational and occupational attainments, as we shall see in later sections.

The role of the black woman as head of household has received a great deal of publicity under the name of *black matriarchy*, suggesting that the black female has greater power than the male in the black family and culture. The high frequency with which black households, as compared with white households, are headed by females is usually given as evidence for this phenomenon. In 1974, 34 percent of all black households were headed by females, compared with 10 percent of white households (Clay, 1975). This in turn seems to be the result of three factors: the obstacles black men have encountered in seeking and maintaining jobs necessary to support their families; the rules of the welfare system, which make it financially desirable for the man to live separately from his family; and the greatly disproportionate gender ratio (number of males to number of females) among blacks. While there are more white women than men (about 98 adult males to 100 women), the ratio is even more imbalanced for blacks (in 1970, about 91 men to 100 women), so that there are just not enough men to go around (Jackson, 1973; Malina, 1973). On the other hand, the emphasis on matriarchal domination of black society ignores the fact that if 34 percent of black households are headed by females, then surely 66 percent must be headed by males or by males and females jointly. Thus, the female head of household, while more frequent in black than in white society, is far from typical for blacks.

Other studies have not looked at the simple notion of head of household in determining matriarchy or patriarchy, but rather have tried to assess more subtle patterns of *spouse dominance* by looking at the ways in which couples solve problems (such as child care and purchasing). The emerging conclusions from this research are that there are no race differences in spouse dominance patterns — the equalitarian pattern is by far the most common one for both blacks and whites (see review by Jackson, 1973). Interestingly, husbands tend to be more dominant when the wife works, a parallel also noted for white working women (Hartley, 1960). Also, matriarchy and patriarchy seem to be more common among the lower class, although even here, equalitarianism is probably quite common. There are also regional variations: in the South, lower-class, intact black families are more frequently patriarchal than whites, while in the North, the reverse pattern seems to hold.

Since black women seem to asume "male" roles with some frequency — worker and head of household — the question arises as to whether their status in the black community might be higher than the status of white women in the white community. In fact, the term "black matriarchy" seems to imply that the black woman enjoys higher status than the black man. However, some simple income figures will correct this notion. Statistics from the Women's Bureau of the United States Department of Labor show that in 1976 minority women had the lowest average wage of any of the race-gender groups (U.S. Department of Labor, 1978):

White males	$14,071
Minority males	$10,496
White females	$8,285
Minority females	$7,825

(Notice that minority males still make more than white females.) Hence, the most accurate statement seems to be that black women enjoy higher status within their community than white women do in theirs, but it is questionable whether their status is higher than that of black men (Jackson, 1973).

Indeed, some scholars (such as Ladner, 1971) argue that the extent of black matriarchy, with attending psychological castration of the black male, has been magnified out of all proportion in the writings of social scientists. The strengths of black women, standing in sharp contrast to the passivity of white women, have been misinterpreted as being dominance. In addition, the importance to the black woman of the emotional and financial support of "boyfriends" has generally been ignored. Certainly problems arise in research in this area as a result of evaluating black behavior by white standards. At the very least, the term "black matriarchy" oversimplifies the complex relationships between black men and women.

In terms of development, black girls appear to assume the adult female role much earlier than do white girls (Ladner, 1971). The white middle-class luxury of a protected, carefree childhood is generally not available to poor black girls, who may move into womanhood in early adolescence. They learn to relate to boys as sexual persons at an earlier age than do white girls (Broderick, 1965; Ladner, 1971). Adolescent black girls may have a baby in order to define themselves as responsible adults — that is, in order to define their womanhood — although premarital pregnancies are generally avoided by the upwardly mobile black girl. It appears, then, that womanhood is defined, and the role assumed, much earlier for black girls than for white girls.

The roles assumed by an aging black woman also seem to differ somewhat from those for aging white women. The sense of uselessness and lack of role suffered by many aging whites does not seem so common among blacks. The extended-family structure characteristic of blacks provides a secure position and role for the elderly. The "granny" role is a meaningful and valued role for the elderly black woman (Bart, 1971) — helping to care for young grandchildren, giving advice based on experience. It seems that old age can be assumed with dignity by the black woman.

Gender roles, then, are defined somewhat differently for black Americans than for white Americans. Gender-role definition for blacks may not be exclusively a result of the experience of slavery and subsequent racial oppression, but actually may have earlier roots in the African heritage (Ladner, 1971; Dobert, 1975). Two characteristics of the African female role were perpetuated in slavery: (1) an important economic function; and (2) a strong bond between mother and child. African women have traditionally been economically independent, functioning in the market place and as traders. Black women continue to play this important economic function in the family to the present day. Mother-child bonds also continue to be extremely important in the structure of black society.

The black woman as mother   The black woman's role as mother certainly occurs in the context of, and is influenced by, the structure of the black family. We have already noted that black women are more frequently heads of households. It appears that the mother role among blacks has correspondingly adapted to this difference in family structure, and further, that this adaptation has been successful (Rhodes, 1971).

Talcott Parsons has made the distinction between male roles as being *instrumental* and female (mother) roles as being *expressive* (Parsons, 1942; Parsons and Bales, 1955; see Chapter 16). It has been noted, however, that lower-class black mothers seem to play dual instrumental-expressive roles to their teenage sons (Nobers, 1968). These women appeared to provide adequate role models for their sons, making up for the absence of their fathers. White mothers in the same sample, on the other hand, were more exclusively feminine-expressive in their role orientations. Further, the absence of fathers for preschool black boys may not be as much a problem as the literature suggests it is for white boys (Williams, 1969), probably because the black woman is capable of being both mother (expressive) and father (instrumental) to her sons. Black mothers without husbands appear to function much more effectively than do white mothers with absent husbands (Hartnagel, 1970).

Self-concept and identity   The traditional psychological literature indicates that blacks, like white women (presumably as a result of similar patterns of oppression and its psychological consequences), have negative self-concepts, or a low sense of self-esteem. Experiments several decades ago showed that black children rejected dolls with dark skin in favor of those with light skin, presumably indicating a corresponding self-rejection (Clark and Clark, 1947; for recent reviews, see Banks, 1976; Williams and Moreland, 1979). The implication is that blacks had introjected the negative valuation of themselves held by the dominant white culture. However, it seems quite possible that the complex of social changes in the last decades, particularly the Black Power movement, with its emphasis on black pride and "black is beautiful" has made real improvements in black self-concept. Hence, although many of the studies we cite may appear to be contradictory, in reality they represent a change over time in the self-esteem of black people.

For black women, physical appearance and beauty may have been particular sources of low esteem. American standards of beauty, which emphasize light skin, straight hair, and shapely legs, apparently were assimilated by blacks so that the black woman was in the position of valuing a kind of beauty she would never have (Grier and Cobbs, 1968).

For example, Americans (including, for many years, black Americans) valued light-colored skin highly. Black women, then, on the average, must be less attractive than white women, and very black women must be very ugly. It is hard for many whites to grasp the intensity of the value blacks attached to skin shade. Perhaps these quotes taken from an autobiography written by a black woman will convey some of this intensity. After explaining that both of her parents and her twin brother had much lighter skin than she, she wrote:

People were always haunting me about the color of my skin. It wasn't enough that the white people would reject me because of it. I had to be rejected by my own people as well. People were always making bets on . . . my skin color. When I was in elementary school one teacher bet another teacher (right in front of my face) that I wasn't as good-looking as my twin brother. The two teachers had found out from one of the students in the class that Don and I were twins. Obviously they found this so hard to believe that they were going to actually let the class vote on who looked the best Don or Donna. Luckily for me, my pride wasn't shattered because the other teacher looked into my eyes and saw how hurt I felt and he then refused to accept the bet . . . As a child I was made aware that black is bad and I grew to hate myself for not being born with a lighter skin shade. The lighter you were the more you were accepted.[1]

The eagerness with which many black women have endeavored to bleach their facial skin, sometimes leading to burns and serious disfiguration, also attests to the high value placed on light skin and the low value placed on natural appearance.

Weight has also been a problem for black women (but not so much so for black men). While black girls from six to ten years old are more frequently thin than white girls, by the age of fourteen to eighteen, twice as many black as white girls were classified as obese (Rauh et al., 1967).

The "black is beautiful" motto was well-chosen for black women, and presumably it is bringing about a more positive sense of self as it replaces the culturally conditioned low valuation of the black woman's natural physical appearance. The Black Power movement has placed an emphasis on getting more black women in television commercials, on stage, and working as models. This points up the possibility that problems relating to beauty for black women may have resulted not only from devaluation of black characteristics, but also from an absence of attractive gender-role models. That is, the rejection by blacks of white standards of beauty as normative is not sufficient — blacks must develop their own sense of what it means to be beautiful — and certainly black actresses and models will be instrumental in conveying these standards and aspirations to other black women.

Recent years have seen an increase in systematic psychological studies on gender and race differences in self-esteem (for reviews, see Baughman, 1971; Christmas, 1973). Traditional research would have led one to expect that blacks — and particularly black women, because of the "double jeopardy" situation (Beal, 1970) of being both black and female — would have lower self-esteem than whites. However, research findings have been quite contradictory. Black children in essentially segregated schools had

---

[1] From a student essay for a psychology of women course, paraphrased and with names changed.

higher self-esteem than whites, and females were higher than males, so that the order, from highest to lowest self-esteem, was: black girls, black boys, white girls, white boys (Wendland, 1967). Race differences appeared to be of larger magnitude than gender differences. On the other hand, other investigators have found boys and whites having higher self-esteem, so that black girls had the lowest self-esteem of any race-gender group (Bridgette, 1970; Carpenter and Busse, 1969). Yet another investigator found no gender differences in self-concept among Southern rural black high school students (Blair, 1972). In the midst of social changes aimed at improving the self-concept of blacks in general, and of women in particular, it is not too surprising that these studies, over time and in different geographical locations and in the midst of desegregation, should obtain different results. At any rate, it is not at all clear from the empirical data whether the low self-esteem thought to be characteristic of black women actually exists.

Strength and adaptation   The apparent tragedy of the black woman — poverty, the victim of both racial and sexual oppression, welfare mother, managing a fatherless household, former slave — has often led to romanticizing her plight. While this is certainly one aspect of the black woman's condition, it leads one to ignore the immense strengths and coping abilities black women have cultivated so well. Historically, black women have frequently exerted leadership roles in resisting poor treatment from whites and were often experts at waging psychological warfare. Lerner (1972) recounts an amusing example that illustrates this point well:

> Not long ago I heard some Negro women talking of old times over their sewing. One said . . . "I couldn't read, but my uncle could . . . I was waiting-maid, an' used to help missis to dress in the morning. If massa wanted to tell her something he didn't want me to know, he used to spell it out. I could remember the letters, an' as soon as I got away I ran to uncle an' spelled them over to him, an' he told me what they meant."
>
> I was attracted by this, and asked if she could do this now.
>
> "Try me, missis; try me an' see!" she exclaimed. So I spelled a long sentence as rapidly as possible, without stopping between the words. She immediately repeated it after me, without missing a letter.
>
> The children of this woman were amongst the first to enter a freedman's school during the war. They took to books as ducks take to water.[2]

This black woman, while feigning ignorance, was actually managing to get a great deal of information from the whites through her own clever-

---

[2] From E. Botume, *First Days Among the Contrabands* (Boston: Lee & Shepard, 1893), pp. 29–30.

ness, a quality she cultivated in her children as soon as opportunities were available.

While acknowledging that many blacks may have experienced feelings of inadequacy as a result of judging themselves on the basis of white standards, it is possible then, that the results have not been as psychologically devastating as some have suggested. Black women have developed mechanisms for coping with their situation. For example, in interviews with adolescent black girls in a housing project, when asked what it meant to be a poor black girl, some replies were

> I feel good as a Negro. I think that we have special rights as everyone else because you know Thomas Jefferson said every man was created equal and I think that just being a Negro doesn't mean we can't have the finer things of life just as the white person does.

> I'm very fond of being a Negro because Negroes have much talent. . . . I was kind of glad to see that we have one Negro in the White House working and they can sing and dance, and do things just as well as white people can. I don't mind being poor . . . because I'm getting along and it doesn't matter to me . . . I think my friends feel the same because I never hear any of them say anything like "I wish I was white." . . . To me a Negro knows how to have fun. (Ladner, 1971, pp. 88–89).

Instead of feelings of low self-esteem and inadequacy, there appears to be a remarkable feeling of pride and adjustment. Ladner concludes "Thus, there was no evidence of low self-esteem and severely damaged psyches among these young ladies" (1971, p. 91). Black women, then, have developed surprisingly adaptive psychological resources and coping mechanisms to deal with their situations, beginning in the days of slavery and continuing to the present.

Further evidence of the strengths of the black woman comes from research showing that black mothers without husbands function much more effectively in rearing their children than do white mothers experiencing father absence (Hartnagel, 1970). This seems related to our earlier observations that black women are capable of playing dual instrumental-expressive roles for their children. Apparently the stresses placed on black women have effectively functioned to yield adaptive psychological results.

Abilities, achievement, and motivation   If decades of deprivation have resulted in successful adaptations to the social system, in what ways, if any, is this reflected in the abilities, school achievements, and motivation of black females? Once again, the strengths of black women are striking.

The best information on this point is Baughman and Dahlstrom's (1968) massive study of gender and race differences. They found a small gender difference among blacks in general intelligence (IQ) favoring females. But on the basis of the size of the difference and of comparison with other studies, they concluded that there are no gender differences among blacks in general intelligence (Baughman, 1971). The result, then, is similar to that for whites (Chapter 8). On the other hand, there do seem to be some gender differences among blacks on special abilities as measured by the Primary Mental Abilities Test (PMA). Black girls do better than black boys at all age levels except age ten on both Verbal Meaning and Number Facility. Interestingly, the well-documented, consistent gender differences in spatial ability (Chapter 8) do not appear to hold for blacks. The spatial relations subtest of the PMA showed no gender differences at any age level for blacks.

In terms of school achievement, research seems to show that black girls consistently achieve more than black boys at every age level (Baughman and Dahlstrom, 1968). In fact, the gap between the performance of black girls and white boys, particularly at upper-age levels, is small — black girls actually do better than white boys on spelling. To this point, the developmental parallels in achievement and abilities for black girls and white girls are apparent.

In the absence of gender differences in general intelligence, Baughman and Dahlstrom attributed the observed gender differences in scholastic achievement to higher motivation on the part of black females. In fact, the consistent findings from a large body of research literature are that black females have higher aspirations, more achievement motivation, and greater plans and expectations (that are more likely to be carried out) than do black males (Kirkpatrick, 1973). A survey administered to students in North Carolina indicated that black girls aspired to professional or technical occupations more frequently than did white girls (Thorpe, 1969). Nonetheless, black women's career aspirations appear to be constrained by gender roles; as professionals, they are found mainly in feminine areas such as teaching, social work, and nursing (Murray and Mednick, 1977).

Further information comes from Horner's (1970b) research on the motive to avoid success. As we indicated in Chapter 8, the motive to avoid success is shown in the response to projective tests given by high-achieving women. However, among blacks, this fear-of-success imagery is found most often among males, as can be seen from this comparison by race and gender of percentage of subjects showing fear-of-success imagery:

white men 10%   black men 67%
white women 64%   black women 29%

(see also Murray and Mednick, 1977). Despite the double jeopardy of being both black and female, the black woman seems to have maintained her motivation better than either black men or white women.

These results were essentially confirmed in a study in which it was found that black college women exhibited fewer motive-to-avoid-success responses than did white college women (Weston and Mednick, 1970). Contrary to expectations, lower-class black women did not exhibit fewer such responses than middle-class black women — the level was about the same for both groups. In explaining the result, the investigators concluded ". . . intellectual mastery is not threatening and professional achievement may in fact not lead to rejection by the [black] male" (1970, p. 290). This suggests that the structure of black society is such that achievement is not in conflict with femininity and therefore does not threaten female gender identity; indeed the structure of black society may actually encourage women to achieve.

In Chapter 8 we discussed results indicating that women — at least white women in competitive situations — have patterns of casual attributions and expectations for success that differ from men's. There is some evidence that black women have a pattern different from white women (Murray and Mednick, 1977). For example, white women with high achievement motivation tend to attribute their successes to effort rather than to ability (Frieze, 1975). However, black women tend to attribute their successes both to their effort and to their ability, in a manner similar to men (Weiner & Kukla, 1970; Kukla, 1972). Once again, this might be explained by achievement being more gender-appropriate for black women than it is for white women.

Black professional women   By virtue of school achievement and motivation, the black woman should be well equipped to enter high-status, professional occupations. And, indeed, she has, to an impressive extent. For example, in 1974, of the fifteen women in the United States House of Representatives, 3 (20 percent) were black (blacks constitute about 11 percent of the American population). The 1960 census showed that 7.2 percent of the black female labor force was in professional occupations, as compared with 3.1 percent of the black male labor force (Bock, 1969). Compared with white women, black women have also done well: in 1960, 6 percent of white physicians were women, but 10 percent of black physicians were women; 3 percent of white lawyers were women, while 8 percent of black lawyers were women (Epstein, 1973b). But while black women constitute impressive percentages of professionals, their absolute numbers are nonetheless small. According to the 1960 census, there were a total of 222 black female attorneys and 487 physicians in the United States; this number is increasing rapidly (in 1970, there were 497 lawyers and 1855 doctors), but the absolute numbers are still small.

Black women, then, have contributed much more at high occupational levels than would be predicted on the basis of their race and gender. One rationale advanced to explain their success is the "farmer's daughter effect" — black women have had greater access to the upper echelons of the white world than have black men because they were less feared sexually and less threatening occupationally (Bock, 1969). In addition, it is thought that black families have often given preferential treatment and made more sacrifices for their daughters', rather than their sons', education (Lerner, 1972; this idea has been called into question by Jackson, 1972). This favoring of the female could be due to two factors: a realization that black women have access to better jobs than black men do, and an assumption that the black woman will have to work at some job as an adult, not being allowed the white-middle-class luxury of exclusive house and child care. If work outside the home is inevitable, then one is motivated to prepare oneself for a worthwhile occupation. Recall that black girls aspire to professional and technical occupations more frequently than white girls do (Thorpe, 1969).

Epstein (1973b) has conducted perhaps the most intensive psychological–sociological research on black women professionals, using a sample of 31 black female professionals in New York. Several common biographical themes emerged among these highly successful black women. A large proportion (over one-third) of the women in the sample were of West Indian extraction. They seem to have been reared according to the Protestant ethic of American immigrants, with middle-class values (if not standard of living) and strong emphasis on "getting ahead." All 31 of these black women uniformly reported that their families had supported them in their striving for education. In contrast to the white women professionals, the black women never considered dropping their career ambitions once they had begun. And finally, they generally seem to have had mothers who were good models of instrumental behavior. Only four of the thirty-one subjects reported that their mothers had not held jobs outside the home. Apparently they learned an image of woman as "doer," capable of coping with the outside world — and they continued this image themselves.

The psychological characteristics of these women were also interesting, particularly in their contrast to those of white women professionals. In general, the black professional women seemed to show much less self-hatred and more self-confidence than their white counterparts. In addition, the black women had a higher regard for other female professionals — some white women indicated doubts about their female colleagues' competence.

In general, these black female professionals showed much less ambivalence about combining the worker and mother roles. Blacks do not assume that marriage will lead to a woman's withdrawal from the labor force, and most black women hold jobs outside the home. Hence blacks do not perceive marriage and motherhood as incompatible with work as many whites do (Murray and Mednick, 1977), and black women are not forced into a double-bind, ambivalent situation. Black women professionals seemed much less anxious about their children than whites were. The black female professional benefits from the tradition of the extended family, so that she has relatives to help with care of her children while she pursues her career, unlike the white female professional, who must generally bear this burden alone.

The marital patterns of these women are also interesting. The general pattern among white women professionals of being married to another professional in the same field is unlikely for blacks, since there are fewer black male than black female professionals and the chance of finding one in the same field is even slimmer. Therefore a substantial number of the women in this sample were unmarried, or were married to men lower in occupational status than themselves. This seemed to create some marital tensions. On the other hand, black women were also less likely to slip into the white professional woman's pattern of seeing her own career as subordinate to her husband's. In addition, the black women were not subject to the constant demoralizing temptation to quit work and let their husbands support them, since they generally could not maintain middle-class standards of living on their husband's earnings alone. The women in Epstein's sample also had a very low fertility rate, as is true of upper-class blacks in general.

Epstein's explanation of the apparent paradox of the black female professional, subject to double prejudice, being more successful than either her race or gender would predict, is similar to some of the reasoning outlined above. Some of the women she interviewed said they believed they had succeeded where black men had failed because they faced less discrimination. About a third of her subjects subscribed to the notion that black men were a threat to white men. Black women, comparatively, are less threatening, and therefore have more access to and less discrimination in the white world. Epstein (1973a) has also suggested that positive effects may result from a doubly negative (black/female) status. For example, two statuses in combination may form a new status category that has no established "price" because it is unique. An employer may know how he pays blacks and how he pays women, but what does he do when confronted with a black woman? Because her status is unique, she may be in a better bargaining position to set her own value. Further, her unique position may encourage her to experiment with alternative life-styles.

The double-bind theme   We have suggested that one of the chief factors in female personality is the double-bind, in which femininity and achievement are perceived as being incompatible. The discussion above would seem to indicate that black women are less likely to encounter this double-bind, that achievement seems quite compatible with gender-role expectations for them. However, the black woman is not completely free from double-binds, and here we will discuss some of them.

It is striking that black women have generally shown a lack of interest in the women's movement. Presumably this is because black women feel racial oppression much more keenly than they do sexual oppression, and

FIGURE 15.1

Black women have achieved more in the professions than either their race or their gender would predict.

Source: Photo by Constantine Manos / Magnum.

therefore identify with the Black Power movement more than the women's movement. It seems quite possible that the black woman is being put in a double-bind situation here. Certainly if the oppression of women is not attacked, the abolition of racial oppression alone will not lead black women to utopia. And yet many males in the Black Power movement suggest that black women who identify with the women's movement are betraying their race — a double-bind, indeed. Militant black women have recently recognized this problem — that striving for middle-class status for blacks may not be totally satisfactory:

> A woman who stays at home, caring for children and the house, leads an extremely sterile existence. . . . Black women were never afforded such phony luxuries.

> It must also be pointed out at this time, that black women are not resentful of the rise to power of black men. We welcome it. We see in it the eventual liberation of all black people from this oppressive system of capitalism. Nevertheless, this does not mean that you have to negate one for the other. This kind of thinking is a product of miseducation; that it's either X or it's Y. It is fallacious reasoning that in order for the black man to be strong, the black woman has to be weak.

> Those who are exerting their "manhood" by telling black women to step back into a submissive role are assuming a counterrevolutionary position.
>   (Beal, 1970, pp. 341–344)

It does seem that black women are in a double-bind in that their search for rights as women is perceived to be in conflict with their search for rights as blacks; the two, of course, need not be antagonistic, but could well be complementary, as could achievement and femininity for white women.

In a sense, the lesser participation of black women in the women's movement highlights a more general source of ambivalence for the black woman, the conflict between white standards and black standards, the conflict between the values of the dominant culture and her own culture (Ladner, 1971). The issues raised by the women's movement do not seem relevant because they are problems in white culture, and other problems are much more salient to blacks. The "battle of the sexes" may seem a rather luxurious pastime to the black woman by comparison with the stark realities of unemployment and poverty.

Another seeming double-bind for black women is in the area of sexuality and reproduction. Black leaders have for some time opposed the use of modern methods of birth control and abortion, saying that it represents genocide, a way for whites to decimate blacks by preventing their reproduction. However, one cannot help but wonder whether this is not so much the position of blacks as it is of black males. Black women must ultimately bear and rear the children, and surely must have some feelings on the issue. Research shows that modern black women do not value large families (Bernard, 1966). Mothers of kindergarten-age children were asked whether they had been pleased when they discovered they were pregnant with the child. Of the black mothers, 59 percent replied no, as compared with 23 percent among the white mothers (Baughman and Dahlstrom, 1968). Once again, the black woman seems to be in a double-bind in which birth control, which may seem desirable to her as an individual and as a woman, is seen as being incompatible with her racial loyalties.

The ambivalence of black women toward sexuality and reproduction also seems to be conveyed to their daughters. Black mothers seem to offer information on reproduction to their daughters less frequently than do whites. In one study it was found that 63 percent of black girls aged eleven to eighteen had been prepared for menstruation, as compared with 76 percent of white girls, and that very few of the black girls had been informed by their mothers (Henton, 1961). Many black adolescent girls who have become pregnant appear to have done so because contraceptive information was unavailable to them (Furstenberg, 1971). Apparently black mothers hide contraceptive information from their daughters, hoping to prevent their sexual activity. Unfortunately, instead of preventing sexual activity, it seems to promote pregnancy. Once again, this seems to be a manifestation of the black mother's ambivalence to sexuality, another instance of a double-bind for her.

These ambivalences are clearly expressed in the following excerpt from an autobiography by a black woman:

> Recently it dawned on me that the reason a former boyfriend and I had to call it quits was because he felt intimidated by the fact that I am a college student whereas he works in the steel mill six days a week. Anytime I used a word not in his vocabulary he would ask me to "break down that college term." I sincerely doubt that my vocabulary had increased so noticeably in a few quarters. Actually I had been talking the same all the time but we were on the same educational level before. Here is an example where I felt that my identity was more important than playing a sex determined role in which I would watch that I only used five letter words so that I could humor his male ego.
>
> Humoring an ego is not the same as helping a person discover that he has one. Here is the dilemma the Black woman finds herself in. Where does she draw the line between denying herself and helping her man? . . . My sexual identity I believe is typical of other black educated women who discovered that there is such a think as a sexual identity and struggle with themselves trying to define one. The black woman doesn't want to be used yet she doesn't want to use anyone of the opposite sex. She realizes that her strong, overbearing matriarchal nature must step aside so that the black man can find and utilize himself. Yet she knows she cannot step behind him because she wants to maintain her identity as a person, also. So, the black woman desires to walk beside her man and it is a truly difficult task especially for an educated black woman.[3]

---

[3] From a student essay for a psychology of women course, paraphrased.

Therefore, it seems reasonable to conclude that, while the femininity-achievement double-bind is salient for white women, black women have their own version of the double-bind, in the areas of sexuality, reproduction, and racial versus gender identity.

WOMEN AS A MINORITY GROUP

In 1951, sociologist Helen Hacker wrote a paper in which she pointed out a number of striking sociological and psychological parallels between blacks and women. These are summarized in Table 15.1. There is good reason to think that women have many of the sociological and psychological characteristics of a minority group. Because of obvious physical characteristics, neither blacks nor women can hide the respective facts of their race or gender. Stereotypes and discrimination against both have relegated them to inferior job status. And so the list goes.

TABLE 15.1. Some Parallels Between Blacks and Women

1. High social visibility
   a. skin color; secondary sex characteristics
   b. clothing — "flashy" clothes; dresses
2. Ascribed psychological characteristics
   a. inferior intelligence; few geniuses
   b. more free in instinctual gratifications; emotional, childlike
   c. threatening sexuality — virility of black male; woman as temptress
   d. general stereotype of inferiority
3. Behaviors used to "cope"
   a. deferential manner
   b. apparent need for directions — fake shows of ignorance; pretended helplessness
   c. sensitivity to methods of outwitting dominant group; dominant group's susceptibility
4. Rationalization of status
   a. are all right in their place
   b. myth of contented black; contented housewife
5. Discriminations
   a. limitations on education
   b. jobs — confined to traditional jobs; barred from being supervisors; their competition feared; no family precedents (role models) for higher education
   c. little political power
6. Resulting psychological problems
   a. roles not clearly defined; roles conflicting
   b. conflict between achieved and ascribed status

Source: After Hacker, 1951.

We are most interested here in the psychological parallels, the commonalities between minority-group psychology and the psychology of women. First, there are certain parallels in ascribed psychological characteristics — that is, in stereotyped notions of the ways blacks and females behave. Both groups are believed to have inferior intelligence and to be incapable of producing outstanding persons; both groups are supposed to have little control of their impulses (immature superego!); and both groups are seen as sexually threatening.

There are also parallels in the true, not ascribed, psychological characteristics that blacks and women share, which may be seen as common products of similar relegation to inferior status. Perhaps most striking of these is the self-rejection and low self-esteem that has long been a common characteristic of minority groups (Adelson, 1958, pp. 486–489; Allport, 1954; Simpson and Yinger, 1965, pp. 227–229; Lewin, 1941). In Chapter 8 we looked at the experiment by Goldberg (1968) which showed that females value the work of a female less than that of a male. Women devalue the work of other women and, by implication, devalue themselves.

It would appear that both blacks and women, then, hold members of their own race or gender and by implication themselves, in low esteem. On the other hand, we noted in our discussion of black women that much of the low self-esteem of blacks may be changing as a result of black pride, the emphasis on "black is beautiful," and so forth. White women are not nearly so far along in their own personal advancement.

Attacking the psychological handicaps of self-rejection and low self-esteem is clearly essential in any attempts at improving the status of women or minority groups. Perhaps the most important achievement of the women's movement has been the establishment of consciousness-raising groups in which this very problem is attacked and in which women attempt to improve their attitudes toward and relations with other women and with themselves.

Simone de Beauvoir (1952) has expressed many of the underlying parallels between minorities and women in her concept "the Other." Men see themselves as the Subject, the One — women then become the Other.

> Thus it is that no group ever sets itself up as the One without at once setting up the Other over against itself . . . In small-town eyes all persons not belonging to the village are "strangers" and suspect; to the native of a country all who inhabit other countries are "foreigners"; Jews are "different" for the anti-Semite, Negroes are "inferior" for American racists, aborigines are "natives" for colonists, proletarians are the "lower class" for the privileged. (Beauvoir, 1952, p. xviii)

And so both blacks and women are an out-group, perceived as "the Other" by whites and by men.

We are also becoming aware in this country that there is a great deal of discrimination against the elderly and that, in a sense, they form yet another minority group. There are some striking parallels between the psychology of the aged and the psychology of women. Both the elderly and women — as well as other minorities — frequently suffer from having no paying job, which can contribute to feelings of worthlessness and low self-esteem. Both the elderly and housewives are confronted with large amounts of unstructured time, which is exhilarating to some, but extremely difficult for others. With further research on the psychology of aging, more parallels may emerge.

There is one notable flaw in the parallel between women and other minority groups. Most minority groups are "colonized" — that is, they live together with others of their group apart from the larger society, as in a ghetto. Women, however, are not colonized, since they live intermingled with men. Colonization has both positive and negative aspects. Among the negative, it results in various forms of environmental disadvantage such as inadequate housing. Women, on the other hand, share the life-style of their husbands. But a positive aspect of colonization is that it promotes the cohesion and identity of the group, which is certainly important as a first step in raising the group's status and self-esteem. Probably because of their lack of colonization, women have only recently come to identify themselves as an oppressed group; even now the identification is far from complete.

SOME CONCLUSIONS — IN THE MIDST OF SOCIAL CHANGE

So often in this chapter we have been forced to reconcile apparently contradictory results from two different pieces of research by saying that social change accounted for the differences. That is, two contradictory studies may both be accurate descriptions of reality — only one describes reality before a complex of social changes including the Black Power movement, the other during or after it. On the other hand, we actually have few studies demonstrating that such changes have indeed occurred. This has introduced a certain awkwardness into our descriptions of the psychology of black women, because of the necessity of describing some "traditional" phenomena, and their "new" versions. On a more positive note, one cannot help but be impressed with the apparent potential for improving the psychological state of a group by means of social change.

There seems to be a great potential for the emerging disciplines of black psychology and psychology of women to be complementary, that is, mutually beneficial to each other. The psychology of women may take several cues from black psychology, especially from the psychology of black women. First, women might follow the example of blacks in attacking the problem of self-rejection directly. Emphasis needs to be put on female as good and worthwhile and valuable. The women's movement has stressed the importance of women having rights equal to those of men, but an equally important drive should be to emphasize that women's roles, such as motherhood, are valuable. Otherwise the low self-confidence of the housewife may simply be compounded. A second cue women may take from blacks is that role redefinition actually seems to be feasible. Blacks have demonstrated, for example, that family organization can adapt to women working, and that in fact actual psychological benefits may result for the woman. Blacks have demonstrated that occupational achievement need not be incompatible with femininity.

Conversely, black psychology may benefit from some of the insights of the psychology of women, which is now largely a psychology of middle-class white women. In particular, blacks seem in imminent danger of having among them a lot of middle-class women. While this may represent great improvements economically and socially, it also carries with it the danger that black women, in becoming middle class, will develop the psychological problems of their white sisters — low self-confidence, motive to avoid success, depression, to name a few. Indeed, it almost seems that black leaders advocate the advent of these phenomena. For example, the first sentence in Grier and Cobbs's chapter, "Achieving Womanhood," in their book *Black Rage* is: "In the world of woman an abundance of feminine narcissism is not only a cheerful attribute but a vital necessity to emotional well-being" (1968, p. 32). While surely a certain amount of narcissism is an improvement over the feelings of the self as ugly, which black women may have traditionally endured, emphasis on narcissism can lead to an overvaluation of the external self and little cultivation of one's own inner resources. At a time when many women feel that Freud's description of women as narcissistic is an insult, Grier and Cobbs's opening sentence seems strange indeed. Black women and blacks in general may want to guard against the Black Power movement achieving better jobs for black men and only more cosmetics for black women. The potential for negative psychological change is indicated by a study that found that the motive to avoid success is frequent among black college women who endorse black militant attitudes (Puryear and Mednick, 1974). On the other hand, the study by Weston and Mednick (1970) cited earlier suggests that black women in the middle class may not assume some of its psychological pitfalls such as the motive to avoid success.

One tempting game of speculation to play is "who's got it worse" — black women, or white women? Certainly in terms of the cold realities of life, one could well make the argument that black women have it much worse — poverty, inadequate housing, the necessity for raising children without the help of an adult male. Yet, one could also make the argument that, in a psychological sense, it is white women who are disadvantaged.

Black females seem in some ways better equipped to take advantage of the opportunities arising from drives for equal opportunity, not having the handicap of the femininity-achievement incompatibility. In fact, some authors (such as Jackson, 1973) have suggested that black family structure is actually *ahead* of white family structure — perhaps by as much as 100 years — in adapting to existing social conditions. Statistics on marital status and illegitimacy rates indicate that whites are becoming more like blacks. White women in growing numbers are having children out of wedlock, and premarital sex is on the rise among whites (both trends of whites behaving more like blacks) (Ladner, 1971). A social structure that permits women to achieve occupationally and to still hold a wife-mother role would seem very attractive, indeed necessary, in view of apparent current social trends. Perhaps blacks have pioneered in creating such a structure.

Some data bearing on this point come from a study that found that black males and black females did not differ significantly in their conception of the "ideal woman," while there were significant differences between white males and white females (Steinman and Fox, 1970). Black males and females preferred a balancing of self-actualizing and family orientations for women. White males shared this view, but white females *expected* white males to demand nearly exclusive family orientation from them. Black males and females also showed greater similarity in their expectations about gender roles in marriage and child rearing than did white males and females. Apparently blacks have managed a greater harmony among the various roles demanded of women. Certainly this is a direction in which one hopes whites can also move.

16

CROSS-CULTURAL PERSPECTIVES ON THE FEMALE ROLE

The differences between the two sexes is one of the important conditions upon which we have built the many varieties of human culture that give human beings dignity and stature. In every known society, mankind has elaborated the biological division of labour into forms often very remotely related to the original biological differences that provided the original clues . . . Sometimes one quality has been assigned to one sex, sometimes to the other . . . Some people think of women as too weak to work out of doors, others regard women as the appropriate bearers of heavy burdens, "because their heads are stronger than men's." . . . In some cultures women are regarded as sieves through whom the best-guarded secrets will sift; in others it is the men who are the gossips.

MARGARET MEAD, Male and Female

Margaret Mead's classic studies of three New Guinea tribes informed Americans of an important fact: not every society has the same gender roles as ours. Her research and that of others is important in demonstrating the extent to which gender roles and the personality and behavior of women are shaped by cultural, rather than biological, forces. It is this research that we shall consider in this chapter.

In doing so, we are shifting to the anthropological and sociological perspective. The basic method of the anthropologist is to explore various phenomena, such as gender role, across different cultures, often cultures quite different from our own. Such an approach has a number of advantages. Most importantly, it points out the enormous cultural variations in gender role. Sometimes the roles assigned to men and women are so different from what we expect from our ethnocentric perspective that we would not have been able to imagine an actual culture so different from our own. Knowledge of these cultural variations challenges our beliefs about what is "natural." For example, in some cultures women are more aggressive than men. This strongly challenges our notion that the unaggressive passivity of American women is "natural," a result of biological givens.

Another important advantage of the anthropological approach is that it may uncover universals in gender role, features of gender role that hold in all existing human cultures. Such pancultural phenomena may be the result of biological determinants (for example, childbirth and breast-feeding are behaviors of which only women are capable) and will suggest the limits beyond which society cannot transcend biology.

An alternative explanation of universals in gender-role assignment is that they arise from universal experiences, as opposed to universal biological endowment. For example, a universal human experience is that of being fed by the mother in infancy, in most cases by breast-feeding. Such a universal human experience may lead to universal qualities in gender role.

The discovery of such cross-cultural universals is a very powerful piece of scientific information. It is quite a different matter for the layperson to say, "of course there are gender differences and there always will be," than for the anthropologist to say that in all known human cultures, gender differences are elaborated in some fashion (Mead, 1949). In sum, the anthropologist looks for both differences and similarities — for variations in gender role cross-culturally, and for cross-cultural similarities or universals in gender role.

As a way of clarifying the anthropological perspective, Angrist (1969) has made a useful distinction in terminology that helps to illuminate some of the differences in approach between the present chapter and that of the previous ones. Anthropologists generally study gender role in terms of *position*. That is, gender role is seen as a position, or location, in a social system, in particular in the division of labor by gender. Psychologists look at gender roles in terms of *behavior* — that is, they study gender differences in behavior, sometimes attributing such differences to biological causes. Sociologists study gender role mainly in terms of *relationships*, stressing the individual's interactions with others and the socialization process through which roles are acquired. While psychologists, then, look at gender differences in behavior, anthropologists concentrate on the way the society apportions tasks on the basis of gender, and sociologists emphasize the socialization process. Another way of stating the contrast in perspective is that psychologists tend to look at gender differences and gender role in terms of personal characteristics, while anthropologists define gender role in terms of cultural processes. From the anthropological perspective, gender differences are not characteristic of individuals, but rather represent culturally transmitted patterns of behavior determined by the society.

In this chapter we shall examine cross-cultural variations in gender role, particularly in the female role, and see how these roles are acquired. An implicit motive is to consider to what extent the psychology of women considered so far in this book is really specific only to middle-class America. And finally, we want to consider the current process of social change in gender roles, in particular by examining "progressive" cultures such as those of Scandinavia, Israel, and the Soviet Union to see how gender roles can be modified in a modern, technological age.

GENDER ROLE ACROSS CULTURES

Variations across cultures   The variations in gender role from one culture to the next are remarkable. The reality of this cross-cultural diversity in gender roles may become apparent if we examine in detail some cultures whose gender roles are quite different from our own. Margaret Mead has documented some of the most interesting examples.

The Arapesh are a mountain-dwelling people in New Guinea, observed by Mead in the 1930s (Mead, 1935). The Arapesh do not expect or believe that there should be gender differences in temperament (personality). Their children are reared accordingly, so that as adults they do not display any major gender differences in personality. In the Arapesh community everyone is expected to be loving and caring (what we would call "feminine" traits). Even bartering is referred to as "giving gifts." Male aggression is almost nonexistent — there is no headhunting and little warfare, and males are as nurturant as females. In fact, the Arapesh are so unable to understand murder that, in the rare instances when a murder does occur, they explain it as being an accident or a case of a person defending a relative. The Arapesh have an interesting custom in which a young male takes a bride when she is about ten years old. They live together as brother and sister and do not have sex for several years. Meanwhile he brings food to her and cares for her, what they call "growing" his bride. In this society both males and females have the personality characteristics expected of American females — gentleness, nurturance, responsiveness, cooperativeness, willingness to subordinate the self to the needs of others. As an aside, female orgasm appears to be virtually nonexistent among the Arapesh (Mead, 1935); perhaps their extreme passivity is antithetical to female sexual response.

In distinct contrast to the Arapesh is another New Guinea society, the Mundugumor, who are headhunters (Mead, 1935). Hostility, hatred, and suspicion are the dominant personality characteristics among these people. Nurturance, including maternal nurturance, is a virtually unknown trait and everyone, including females, is supposed to be aggressive. Sexual foreplay includes violent scratching and biting, sometimes to the point of drawing blood, breaking the partner's jewelry, and ripping the grass skirt. The Oedipal conflict has essentially been institutionalized in this society, since inheritance passes from mother to son and from father to daughter, creating a great deal of rivalry and strife between siblings and between parents and children. It is not surprising that babies born into such a hostile environment would experience socialization forces and modeling that would channel them into the expected adult personality. At any rate, we see here a society in which females and males are expected to have similar personalities, the common expectation being almost a caricature of the personality expected of the American male.

These cultural variations in gender roles and personality call into serious question the notion that gender differences in nurturance or aggressiveness are biologically determined. Certainly biological differences between males and females are the same in New Guinea as they are in the United States. From these data it is clear that humans can be socialized to have few gender differences in personality. And further, apparently females can be socialized to be passive, as in the United States, extremely passive, as among the Arapesh, or extremely aggressive, as among the Mundugumor.

Cross-cultural universals   While the variations across cultures in personality and role expected of females and males are nearly infinite, there do seem to be two principles that hold universally. First, every known society recognizes and elaborates gender differences (Rosaldo, 1974). There is no society that treats males and females identically; there is always some distinction, whether in personality, division of labor, clothing, or even supernatural manifestations. Second, the male role, whatever it is, is always valued more (Mead, 1935; Rosaldo, 1974). For example, in some parts of New Guinea, the women grow sweet potatoes and the men grow yams; but yams are the prestige food, the food used in important ceremonies. Even in this case where the labor of females and males is virtually identical, what the male does is valued more.

Historical origins of roles   How can one explain the two universal principles mentioned above? According to many anthropologists, the explanation is as follows: In primitive times, the performance of certain functions — hunting, food gathering, childbearing — was a necessity. Men's greater strength and muscle-to-fat ratio, women's childbearing capacity and attending lesser mobility, and other physical gender differences provided biological bases for the division of labor between men and women. Capitalizing on the obvious physical differences between women and men might well have been the simplest and most economical basis for division of labor. Following this basic logic, one theoretical view is that males, because of their greater muscular strength, assumed the hunting role and seized the power in the society (D'Andrade, 1966); their control of power persists to the present. Another argument is that women, because of their childbearing and nursing functions, were more restricted in their wanderings, tending to stay near the home. Therefore, women assumed domestic (close to the home) roles, while men assumed public (away from the home, in contact with many people) roles (Rosaldo, 1974; Sullerot, 1971); to the present day, we continue to believe that women should work "inside," men should work "outside" (Bird, 1968, see Figure 16.1). Authority and political power can be obtained only through public roles, and hence the male role is more valued and more powerful. Once again, this logic also explains why the female role has less power and value.

Whatever the precise historical origin of the differentiation in roles, human culture advanced and human control over the environment increased enormously. Yet gender roles based on physical differences persisted. In our technological age of labor-saving inventions, physical strength is no longer of major importance, yet gender-role division based on gender differences in physical strength persists. These roles have probably persisted simply because the roles were known and comfortable, and because any serious efforts to reassess or change them seemed to people to be extremely threatening. Gender roles, even when they no longer bear any consistent relationship to physical gender differences, are still a way by which humans create order out of the chaos of human existence. In sum, primitive conditions probably brought about an assignment of roles and behaviors fairly directly linked to physical characteristics. Such a relation between biology and role has long since vanished, but the allocation of roles persists.

Multiplicity of gender roles   Cross-cultural studies also provide impressive evidence of the complexity and multiplicity of gender roles. In our own culture, we tend to expect only two gender roles, the male role and the female role, much as we hold a typological conception of masculinity and femininity (Chapter 4). However, cross-culturally, we find that gender roles are much more varied. Mead (1961) enumerates eleven formal gender roles that are available. These include married females who bear children; married males who beget and provide for children; adult males who do not marry and beget children but who exercise some prescribed social functions involving celibacy, sexual abstinence, and renunciation of procreation; adult males who assume female roles; adult females who maintain themselves economically by the exploitation of sex relationships with extramarital partners; adult females who assume male roles including transvestism, and so on. Clearly there is a tremendous variety of gender roles cross-culturally. This enumeration suggests that there are in fact more than simply two gender roles in the United States.

Gender role generally involves multiple roles (Angrist, 1969). For example, the typical adult American female role involves, at the very minimum, the wife role and the mother role, and may include roles such as volunteer worker, professional, daughter, grandmother, and so forth. A given individual then does play a variety of gender roles (not to mention other roles) at different stages of the lifespan, or even at a single time. Unfortunately, two roles held simultaneously may sometimes be in conflict, and success in one role may imply defeat in another. This is apparent in the conflict experienced by college women between the "modern," achieving role and the traditional feminine role, both of which are expected of the college woman (Komarovsky, 1946). Adequacy or "success" in gender role, as judged by the individual and others, tends to be very important to people. Given the complex constellation of roles involved in gender role, "success" may be a difficult and complex thing.

In summary, the variability in gender roles cross-culturally is enormous. This constitutes important evidence that gender differences in behavior are cultural or social, rather than biological, in origin. In addition to the variability, two universal principles emerge: all known societies have gender roles, and the male role, whatever it is, is always valued more. These two phenomena probably arise from a prehistoric division of labor on the basis of physical gender differences. Finally, we have seen that gender role involves a complex constellation of roles.

GENDER-ROLE SOCIALIZATION

How is it that individuals come to behave appropriately in their culturally-prescribed role? The answer is found in what psychologists would call the developmental process and what anthropologists and sociologists would term the process of gender-role socialization.

According to the view of anthropologists, anticipatory socialization for male and female roles begins at birth with gender designation. That is, if a baby is female, society assumes that as an adult she will occupy the female role. From the time of her gender designation at birth, she is subjected to socializing influences to assure that she will behave appropriately in that role in adulthood. In societies in which a larger number of formalized gender roles are available, children are watched carefully to determine what role might ultimately be embraced. For example, since bravery is a determining quality for males among Plains Indians, a timid male child may be assigned the role of transvestite. Children are socialized, then, for congruence with their anticipated gender role. The agents of socialization are not only the parents, but also other adults and peers. Thus the community establishes patterns of behavior and employs educational techniques for assuring that individuals will perform these behaviors. Presumably once the initial pattern of gender-role behavior is established, the maintenance of gender-appropriate patterns becomes self-sustaining. After finding out how reinforcing it is to perform the appropriate gender role, the child subsequently internalizes the role as part of his or her identity.

The forces of gender-role socialization are apparent even in modern American culture. At birth, little girl babies are dressed in pink while little boy babies are dressed in blue. Later, little girls must at least occasionally wear dresses. Toys and games are gender-typed. Girls receive dolls, doll houses, and tea sets for presents; boys get trucks, erector sets, and baseball gloves. Clearly the accompanying differences in play activities represent a kind of anticipatory gender-role socialization — playing with dolls prepares one to be a mother, while playing with trucks, erector sets, and baseball gloves prepares one for exciting masculine jobs. A division of labor based on gender may begin early in the home. Girls may be expected to wash dishes and help with the cooking, while boys are assigned to take out the garbage and mow the lawn. Already the feminine sphere of influence has become inside, internal, in the home, while the male operates on the outside. Available role models differ for boys and for girls and constitute a further force of gender-role socialization. For example, children's readers portray quite distinct ideas about what males and females can and cannot do (Women on Words and Images, 1972; Weitzman et al., 1972 — see Chapter 6). Of course, there has been a trend in the United States in the last decade to diminish gender-role socialization and to encourage children to aspire to nontraditional careers. But assumptions about gender roles remain powerful, if sometimes nonconscious, and gender-role socialization forces persist even today, though perhaps in subtler form than they did a generation ago (Bem and Bem, 1970). The more general point is that, in our society as in others, the forces of gender-role socialization are designed to mold children so that they will behave as adult males and females are expected to behave.

The anthropological position generally argues for *cultural functionalism.* That is, children are trained into the kind of personality that is functional for the adult life of the society and necessary in order for a particular way of life to continue (Barry, Bacon, and Child, 1957). In order for a particular culture to persevere, certain rituals, social institutions, customs, and taboos are institutionalized. Roles and socialization procedures are thus directed to this end, serving the continuing necessary functions of the society. Gender roles and gender-role socialization procedures are necessary for the perpetuation of the society, the way of life of the culture (Rosenberg, 1971).

Gender-role socialization is also an efficient practice (Dornbusch, 1966). Training children for different functions, depending on their biological gender, removes the necessity for training all children in all types of activity. Just as gender role is an efficient division of labor, so gender-role socialization is an efficient means of allocating specialized training.

For the most part, gender-role socialization practices are as diverse cross-culturally as are gender roles. However, just as there were some universal patterns in gender roles cross-culturally, so there are also some universal trends in gender-role socialization practices. In a classic study, Barry, Bacon, and Child (1957) surveyed 110 cultures, mostly preliterate. They found that most cultures do not socialize for gender differences during the infancy period. During childhood, the widespread pattern cross-culturally is to reward nurturance, obedience, and responsibility in girls and achievement and self-reliance in boys. While this pattern is by far the most common, there are a few societies where the pattern is reversed or where gender differences are minimized. The amount of gender differentiation appeared to depend on the social structure of the society and on its environmental pressures. In particular, socialization for the greatest number of gender differences occurs in economies where superior strength is important, and therefore also the superior development of motor skills requiring strength, which is characteristic of males. Gender differences are also large in societies where the family structure is a large group with cooperative interaction. A great deal of division of labor by gender is therefore practical.

These results provide support for the position of cultural functionalism, in that they show how certain functions of the society, such as hunting large animals, must be performed, and how gender roles, such as courage and aggressiveness in males, are socialized so that there will be individuals to perform the required functions. The results also suggest that current trends toward decreasing gender differences in socialization practices in our own culture are probably related to changes in social structures, most notably to the decreased importance of physical strength and the prevalence of the nuclear family.

In sum, gender roles are perpetuated in society through the socialization process. Gender roles and socialization practices vary greatly from one culture to the next, although some general patterns emerge.

In order to make sense out of the diversity of gender roles and socialization practices and the presence of some universal phenomena, we shall next consider the two theoretical views of the nature of gender roles put forth by Talcott Parsons and David Bakan. Both attempt some generalized understanding of the universal nature of gender roles cross-culturally.

THE VIEW OF TALCOTT PARSONS

Talcott Parsons is an eminent sociologist whose theorizing represents a fusion of psychoanalytic theory with sociological theory. He postulates stages of psychosexual development (oral, anal, phallic, and genital) as does psychoanalytic theory, but he also emphasizes the importance of social interactions and the socialization process.

Articulating a sociological viewpoint, Parsons maintains that certain functions must be performed in order for group life to continue; these functions are differentiated along an *expressive-instrumental* dimension. He uses the term "expressive" to refer to concerns with internal affairs of the system — the maintenance of integrative, harmonious relations among the members. The term "instrumental" refers to a practical concern for the relations between the system and the outside world (Parsons and Bales, 1955). Both expressive and instrumental functions must be performed in order for the group to continue to function.

From the social-psychological perspective, Parsons has applied results from the analysis of small-group functioning to the case of the family (Parsons and Bales, 1955). Thus the nuclear family is viewed as a small group in which typical specializations of function occur — for example, one person becomes the "idea" person (the instrumental function) while another person becomes the "likable" person (the expressive function). This specialization of function corresponds roughly to the division of gender roles.

The nuclear family is thus a particular case of group life in which instrumental and expressive functions must be accomplished. In the nuclear family, one major axis of group life, gender (female and male, or expressive and instrumental) is conjoined with the other major axis of group life, generation (parent and child, or superior and inferior). Presumably there is no known social system that fails to discriminate among these four cardinal roles: *generation* as a main axis of superior-inferior or power differentiation of roles; and *gender* as the main axis of the instrumental-expressive distinction in roles.

According to Parsons' view, gender role becomes associated with the instrumental-expressive distinction (female as expressive, male as instrumental) primarily as a result of the childbearing and child-rearing functions of the female. The childbearing and nursing functions are biologically assigned to the female, and the child-rearing function, while culturally assigned, seems to be a near-universal extension of these biological functions. Thus in the nuclear family, the relation of the mother to the small child, an expressive, within-system function, is a very basic relationship. This establishes a presumption that the man, who is exempted from these biological functions (and generally from child rearing as well), would specialize in the alternative instrumental (between-systems) direction. Thus, as Parsons sees it, the necessary functions of any social group are, in part, an extension of the biological functions of males and females.

In terms of his developmental model, the instrumental-expressive distinction is somewhat more complex. The mother is initially not only expressive, but also instrumental with the infant. At some later point, when the child is approximately five years of age, the mother relinquishes the instrumental aspects of her relationship with the child, becoming primarily expressive and feeling. The father assumes the instrumental function, bringing the child into recognition of the world beyond the nuclear family. That is, he teaches the child the values of the larger society (for example, achievement orientation), thereby bridging the gap between the family and society. These forces result in the child's recognizing and internalizing his or her gender role — for the boy, relinquishing the natural expressive relationship with the mother and identifying with the masculine-instrumental role represented by the father; for the girl, identifying with the feminine-expressive role, continuing the primary attachment to the mother. Thus all young children, through these presumably universal dynamics, acquire the gender roles necessary for any group to function.

Evaluating Parsons' theory   There have been some attempts to confirm or disprove Parsons' theoretical view of the nature and origin of gender roles with empirical data. His general role division appears to hold across many cultures. In examining 75 primitive societies, there was a preponderance of instrumentalism in the father role and in no case was the mother's role more instrumental than that of the father (Zelditch, 1955). An analysis of the behavior of twelve mixed-gender juries indicated that men were directed toward the task, while the behavior of the women emphasized socio-emotional aspects, particularly tending to react to the contributions of others (Strodtbeck and Mann, 1956). The authors concluded that gender-typed differentiation of function in social groups can be demonstrated, another apparent confirmation of Parsons' view (although there is an awfully big jump from jury behavior to family roles).

On the other hand, several studies failed to confirm Parsons' ideas (see review by Sherman, 1971). For example, observations on 33 families indicated that the instrumental-expressive distinction characterized different activities performed by the parents at different times and under different circumstances, rather than being a major division of labor by gender (Machotka and Ferber, 1967). It is difficult to reconcile these conflicting results. Perhaps the instrumental-expressive distinction is valid, but the functions are not unique to one gender or the other.

In many ways, Parsons' theory does not represent a major departure from traditional views, particularly psychoanalytic theory. It still emphasizes the importance of the family, as opposed to the broader society (although somewhat more recognition is given the latter), as the major socializing influence. It also retains the assumption that early childhood is the primary period of gender-role development. As such, it does not recognize the importance of peers, of schools, or of late-occurring experiences.

Brim (1957, 1958, 1960) has attempted to expand this theoretical system to include other life influences. He argues that gender role acquisition is a persisting, ongoing life process that extends beyond the early years and is subject to the influence of peers, teachers, and many other individuals. Hence he sees gender-role learning as a continual process influenced by continuing interactions with others.

Slater (1961) has provided an excellent critique of Parsons' theory. Parsons states that parental roles must be differentiated along the expressive-instrumental dimension in order for the child to acquire a proper gender-role identification. But empirical data show that the more differentiated the roles of the parents, the more the problems of adjustment in the child. Slater also questions Parsons' assumption that expressiveness and instrumentalism are opposite ends of a single continuum (as we questioned the unidimensional, bipolar conceptualization of M-F, Chapter 4). Parsons' assumption would imply that the more expresive the mother, the less instrumental she would be; that is, expressiveness and instrumentalism should be negatively correlated. But available data from small-group studies actually indicate that there is a positive correlation between expressiveness and instrumentalism. Further, Slater points out that parents may differ considerably in their salience, a fact neglected by Parsons. For most children the mother is considerably more salient than the father, and she is both more expressive and more instrumental toward the child than he is. Most fundamentally, Slater questions Parsons' assumption that role differentiation for parents is functional in modern American society.

Kate Millett (1969) has criticized Parsons' work, seeing it as another instance of sexual politics, in which the social sciences perpetuate gender inequality. In particular, she suggests that Parsons simply uses complex academic jargon — terms like "expressive" and "instrumental" — to dull the obvious implications of a theory that rationalizes functional differences between women and men as being due to biological forces. She further criticizes Brim's (1958) extensions of Parsons' work, in which he categorized various personality traits as belonging to the instrumental or the expressive role. The results are reminiscent of the work on clinicians' judgments of mental health for males and females (Chapter 7). Socially desirable traits such as curiosity, originality, and ambition are assigned to the instrumental (male) role, while undesirable traits such as quarrelsomeness, revengefulness, exhibitionism, and jealousy are assigned to the expressive (female) role.

While Millett's criticisms are well taken, Parsons' assertion that the expressive-instrumental differentiation of gender roles arises from the mothering function is probably not an attempt by him to rationalize or perpetuate stereotyped gender roles. Instead, it represents a recognition that care of small infants is almost universally assigned to females. While ideally we may claim that child rearing is a culturally, rather than biologically, assigned behavior, the fact is that it is almost invariably assigned to the female, probably simply because the assignment is convenient. Those who look for change in woman's role might do well to recognize the intransigence of human cultures on this point; the child-rearing function, while culturally assigned, is not arbitrarily assigned but is an extension of the nursing function. This is not to say that this role allocation is not modifiable, but rather to point out that such change will meet with resistance. Historically and cross-culturally, convenience seems to have triumphed over idealism in gender-role allocation. On the other hand, child-care in most societies — except the American and European ones we are familiar with — is not solely the duty of the child's mother (Rosenblatt and Cunningham, 1976). Often older children, men, or the elderly are assigned to help with this duty.

Anthropologist Nancy Chodorow (1974) expands on this theme of the importance of women's child-rearing role to provide an explanation of some of the universal qualities of gender differences in personality. She argues that women's universal mothering role has effects on the personality development of girls and boys as well as on the relative status of men and women (recall that the male role is universally more valued). Early in development, the mother-infant bond is primary for both girls and boys. For the girl, in the process of development and gender-role identification, attachment to the mother continues. The female personality is thus defined in terms of relation to other people. But for the boy, this attachment to the mother must be broken. Thus, masculinity is defined in terms of denial of attachment and dependency, and further involves repression and devaluation of femininity. Chodorow suggests that to modify the inevitability of these gender differences, fathers must participate in child rearing, thus allowing boys and girls to form early attachments to both males and females.

In summary, Parsons argues that expressive and instrumental functions must be performed in order for a society to function properly. Because of the primacy of the mother-infant relationship, the female assumes the expressive function, leaving the male to assume the instrumental function. From this perspective, gender-role socialization is seen as a process that insures the continued filling of roles necessary for society.

THE VIEW OF DAVID BAKAN

David Bakan, a psychologist, has proposed an intriguing theory that in some ways parallels Parsons' view. According to Bakan's conceptualization, two fundamental modalities are characteristic of all living forms: *agency* and *communion* (Bakan, 1966). "Agency" describes the organism as an individual and manifests itself in self-protection, self-assertion, and self-expansion. "Communion" describes the individual organism in relation to the larger group and manifests itself in feelings of cooperation. Empirical research by Jeanne Block (1973; see also Carlson, 1971b) suggests that communion is emphasized in the socialization of girls, while agency is emphasized for boys. As she states:

> Little boys are being taught to control the expression of feelings and affects, while assertion and extension of self are abetted. Little girls are being taught to control aggression, including assertion and extension, while being encouraged to regard the inner, familial world as the proper sphere of their interest. Communion is emphasized in the development of girls but is explicitly discouraged in boys. (1973, p. 515)

Hence it is apparent that as a child develops, the agency-communion differentiation becomes associated with gender roles just as does the instrumental-expressive distinction — females are characterized by communion, and males by agency.

But Bakan's theorizing goes one step further. According to his view, the fundamental task of the developing organism is to combine agency and communion — that is, a well-developed, mature human will possess qualities of both. Mature, healthy development requires a balance of the two since either, by itself, may be disastrous. The well-integrated personality will be androgynous, including both "male" and "female" characteristics, a viewpoint that is similar to Bem's (see Chapter 4). Or, as Block puts it:

> For men, the integration of agency and communion requires that self-assertion, self-interest, and self-extension be tempered by considerations of mutuality, interdependence, and joint welfare. For women, integration of communion with agency requires that the concern for harmonious functioning of the group, the submersion of self, and the importance of consensus characteristics of communion be amended to include aspects of agentic-self-assertion and self-expression — aspects that are essential for personal integration and self-actualization. (1973, p. 515)

In summary, Bakan sees organismic functioning as differentiating into two modalities, agency and communion. These modalities become associated with gender roles in that boys are pressed to develop qualities of agency while girls are encouraged to develop qualities of communion. The mature personality, however, requires integration of both agency and communion.

"PROGRESSIVE" CULTURES

Anthropologists have traditionally relied on the study of primitive cultures for a better understanding of phenomena such as gender roles. We shall depart from this traditional approach by considering some contemporary societies, such as Scandinavia, the Communist countries, and Israel, which represent radical experimentation with gender roles. In doing so, we have several purposes. First, a study of women's roles in these "progressive" cultures is intrinsically interesting. And second, such cultures may give us a preview of the future of gender roles in the United States, which may in turn be useful in social planning.

Scandinavia   Numerous reports have appeared in the news media regarding the radical changes in sexual standards and gender roles occurring in the Scandinavian countries. Research on current attitudes toward gender roles and behaviors, based on interviews conducted with more than 400 persons in Helsinki in 1966, indicates that, while a relatively high percentage of Finnish women hold jobs outside the home (49 to 77 percent, depending on social class), women and men are expected to hold jobs in traditional fields, and women have generally not gained entry into high-status occupations (Haavio-Mannila, 1967). Traditional division of labor is most persistent in the family, despite the fact that about two-thirds of the women work outside the some. Women express dissatisfaction over this arrangement, in fact more dissatisfaction than over their lack of occupational status. Apparently, official norms for gender equality are better followed in public than in private life. This study suggests that current changes in gender roles in the United States must include not only legislation regulating labor outside the home, but also a considerable reorganization of family structure and responsibilities.

Studies of gender roles in Norway (Holter, 1970) indicate trends similar to those in Finland. It appears that in these countries people's actual behavior lags behind legislation, a situation opposite to that of the United States, where legislation has lagged behind trends toward equality in behavior.

The Soviet Union   Reports on the current status and roles of women in the Soviet Union are also interesting. Unlike American women, who represent a reserve labor force that is pressed into service in times of need (World War II) and at other times is told to return to the home, Soviet women are an integral part of the labor force. This is partly a result of the greatly disproportionate gender ratio in the Soviet Union owing to the death of so many men in World War II. Indeed, in 1959, about 30 million women were in the labor force, as compared with only about 19 million men. A frequently cited and quite impressive statistic is that two-thirds of all Soviet physicians are women. Certainly this is striking evidence that women are quite capable of being physicians, and that the lack of female physicians in the United States is largely a result of cultural factors. On the other hand, while the representation of women in the Soviet labor force is high, they are still underrepresented in directive, managerial, decision-making, and executive positions. In addition, the physician role is not as highly valued as it is in the United States. Thus, while women constitute an integral part of the labor force, they appear not to have achieved completely equal status with males (Field and Flynn, 1968).

The most distressing part of the report on Soviet women is the "double duty" most of them perform (Field and Flynn, 1968). While participation in the labor force is normative and encouraged by the government, women have also retained their domestic responsibilities. Indeed, the government has encouraged large families in order to compensate for the losses of World War II. Thus the Soviet woman is caught working at a full-time job yet retaining the responsibilities of full-time housewife and mother. This seems to have caused considerable stress both physically and psychologically. Life expectancy statistics give some indication of the magnitude of this stress. Currently in the United States the life expectancy for the female is three years longer than that of the male (approximately 72 years for males, 75 years for females). In the Soviet Union 65 years ago, the life expectancy for females was two years *less* than that for males; and currently in the Soviet Union, the life expectancy for females is eight years less than that for males (Sullerot, 1971). Psychological stress results from the female role being poorly defined, ambivalent and conflicting, yet demanding. Studies indicate that Soviet men have twice as much spare time as Soviet women. From this report, it appears that Soviet women are working harder and dying younger.

China   In Communist China the government ideology has stressed that all women must be part of the labor force (Huang, 1963). Indeed, women who attempt to stay exclusively in the home to care for their husband and children are frequently the object of public ridicule. An interesting shift in values has occurred. In the United States, we tend to think of the woman who holds a job outside the home as being somewhat selfish, the woman who stays at home caring for her children as being selfless. In Communist China, ideology dictates that the opposite is true. The woman who labors outside the home is seen as being selfless in her service to the state, while the woman who attempts to remain in the home is thought to be selfish and hedonistic, pursuing personal pleasures while sponging off others. Chinese women seem to have obtained some relief from familial roles with the lowering of the birth rate (it is currently substantially below two children per family), and with more adequate communal child care facilities. Nonetheless, one is left with the impression that there has merely been a shift from overcommitment to husband and children to overcommitment to the state.

There are some lessons to be learned from this examination of the changing role of women in these two Communist countries. They both indicate that increased entry of women into the labor force, by itself, does not necessarily indicate an improvement in the lifestyle of women. At least three other conditions need to be met. First, women need to be represented at upper occupational levels, particularly those involving policy making, so that they can be involved in making decisions regarding the status of women. Second, reorganization of family responsibilities must accompany the entry of women in the labor force, as we saw particularly in the Soviet case, and also in the Scandinavian report. Without such

FIGURE 16.1

The kibbutz includes communal child care, freeing women for other roles.

Source: Photo by Leonard Freed / Magnum.

reorganization, the woman is subject to considerable stress. And finally, women must retain the option of occupational choice, including the option to be a full-time housewife. Otherwise, as is apparent in the case of Communist Chinese women, the female role remains restrictive.

Israel   Perhaps the most purposeful attempt to modify gender roles in the direction of equality is that of the *kibbutz* in modern Israel. Living is entirely communal; the group, rather than individuals or families, owns the property. Achieving equality for women was a major factor in structuring the kibbutz, so communal dining and child care were provided. Women were to participate equally in all facets of life, including army service. The idea was that, if women could be freed from washing clothes and cooking meals, they would be able to participate in "productive" work — such as farming or construction — and thereby become equal to men. A great deal of research has been devoted to studying the gender roles resulting from this grand experiment (see Spiro, 1956; Rabin, 1970; Rosner, 1967; Mednick, 1975).

Kibbutz people (*kibbutzniks*) generally subscribe to the belief that women and men are equal in abilities and skills (Rosner, 1967). Despite these ideals, however, recent studies show that there has been a definite reversion to traditional roles. For example, psychologist Martha Mednick (1975) interviewed a random sample of kibbutzniks from 55 settlements, 400 original settlers and 918 second-generation adults. She found that women were back at the service jobs in the kitchen, laundry, and schools. Many second generation women seemed to yearn for traditional ways.

The problem in the kibbutz seems to be that the jobs the women do are not valued as highly as those the men do (Mednick, 1975). The kibbutz places a high value on "productive" work; services, such as child care, are not economically productive. Therefore, although everyone recognizes that they must get done, they are not prestigious. Once again, though by a somewhat unusual path, women find themselves in the low-status occupations.

The results of the kibbutz experiment, however, are not necessarily due to biological urges and instincts reasserting themselves. Mednick (1975) believes that a number of situational factors may have contributed to the failure of the experiment in equality. First, the founding ideologies were not quite so egalitarian as they sounded. Women were to have the "privilege" of doing male jobs, and to be "relieved" from female jobs in order to do so. There was no corresponding "privilege" for men to do women's jobs. The problem is that "male" jobs were regarded as prestigious, and it was a privilege for women to hold them. These very assumptions are sexist.

Another problem Mednick noted was that, after the initial years of hardship, the kibbutz became very *pronatalist*, that is, in favor of having children, and guess who does that? With emphasis on reproduction, women automatically get into a traditional role, generating a more generalized division of labor along traditional lines.

Perhaps if such an experiment were undertaken today, our understanding of gender roles would be adequate to do a successful job of designing it.

In discussing changing gender roles and demands for equality of women and men, it is important to make a distinction between the notions "equal" and "identical" (what the Israelis call qualitative equality versus mechanical equality). If two people are equal, we mean that they are equal in the eyes of the law; their occupations and characteristics are equally valued. To be equal, however, these two people need not be identical. That is, they do not have to look exactly alike or behave exactly alike. For example, people with blue eyes and brown eyes receive equal treatment under the law, even though they are not identical — their appearance is different because of different eye color. And so it is for men and women being equal versus being identical. People often express the fear that if women become legally equal to men (for example through the Equal Rights Amendment), the romance will go out of sex because women will no longer be "different" — they will be identical to men. Notice that here the notions of "equal" and "identical" are confused. To grant women legal equality is not to make them identical to men. In our view, if society could totally remove role restrictions from women, then freedom and individual acceptance would be the ideal outcome, not that women must behave exactly (identically) as men do. For this would be a more subtle kind of role restriction, denying those qualities of woman that provide her uniqueness. Or, as Margaret Mead put it,

> If we once accept the premise that we can build a better world by using the different gifts of each sex, we shall have two kinds of freedom, freedom to use untapped gifts of each sex, and freedom to admit freely and cultivate in each sex their special superiorities. (1949, p. 358)

IN CONCLUSION

In this chapter, we have presented evidence to counter the argument that psychological gender differences are a result of biological forces. In viewing the aggressive Mundugumor women and the passive, nurturant Arapesh men, one cannot help but be impressed with the impact of culture in shaping the behavior of men and women. Yet we have also seen that the matter is not completely simple, that people cannot be whatever they want to be, that biological endowments combined with universal cultural experiences tend to produce phenomena like the universality of the lower status of the female role.

All this gives us food for thought in speculating about the future course of gender-role change in the United States, particularly the future

nature of the female role. In so doing, we need to ask two very fundamental, and very different, questions. First, in the absence of all shaping
of gender roles, what would females and males be like? And second, if we
accepted the ideology that men and women should be equal, and made
strong efforts at shaping them to be as similar (identical) as possible,
would we succeed? For the moment, we shall leave you to consider these
questions yourself. We shall offer our own speculations in the final chapter.

17

RETROSPECT AND PROSPECT

Standing on the ground of common sense and the constitution of the human mind, I deny that anyone knows, or can know, the nature of the two sexes, so long as they have only been seen in their present relation to one another . . . What is now called the nature of woman is an eminently artificial thing — the result of forced repression in some directions, unnatural stimulation in others.

JOHN STUART MILL

The great philosopher and feminist John Stuart Mill, quoted above, lived in an era in which there was no science of psychology. He believed that no one could understand the true nature of women and men. Over 100 years — and a great deal of psychological research — later, how can one respond to Mill?

Certainly we would not claim to know the "true nature" of woman any more than Mill did. But we would argue that that is not the right question. Rather than trying to establish the "true nature" of woman, we would do better to try to understand how women function psychologically now in our culture, how they function in some other cultures and other times, and what their potential for the future is.

This book has focused particularly on trying to understand how women function psychologically in our contemporary culture. To do this, we have reviewed the existing scientific theories and research. Often we were not able to provide definitive answers, but at least were able to provide some reasonable ideas that further research will continue to refine.

Several important themes have cropped up repeatedly in this book. One is gender similarities, the notion that women and men are more similar to each other than they are different. Another theme has been ambivalence, as seen in the conflict between achievement and femininity, between motherhood and career, and in ambivalence about sexuality. Finally, androgyny has emerged as an important mode of psychological functioning that may represent the ideal of the psychologically healthy individual of the future.

FUTURE RESEARCH

In 1974, in writing the first edition of this book, we commented that research on the psychology of women was in its infancy. However, coming away from the most recent (1978) convention of the American Psychological Association, we found that real progress had been made, and that research and theory were becoming increasingly sophisticated. There are now tests available to measure androgyny, and research is progressing in the investigation of exactly what the psychological consequences of being androgynous are. There are some fairly well-documented differences in the verbal and nonverbal communication styles of females and males, and research is proceeding to determine exactly what these differences mean. Feminist therapy is more than a twinkle in some feminist's eye, and is now widely practiced. And so the list goes.

Of course, this does not mean that we know everything there is to know about women. Far from it. There is much information that we do not yet have. The reader may want to spend some time thinking about what the most important questions for future research are. We will suggest a few that we think are important.

In this time of social change, we are all curious about child-rearing practices, and what sort of socialization procedures might be used to shape desirable characteristics in females. Much of the research that would be most appealing in this area would involve experimental manipulation of child-rearing procedures; such research would, unfortunately, generally be unethical. However, there are dozens of naturalistic experiments occurring now — communes, groups experimenting with alternative life styles — which all may be zealously performing the child-rearing practices that might be designed in an experiment. Certainly it would be fruitful to follow the development of children reared under such radically different conditions. The studies on children in the kibbutz are perhaps the best example (Maccoby and Feldman, 1972).

A great deal of research on the psychology of women has focused on high-achieving women, looking at their personality characteristics, common biographical themes, and so on. Such an approach has merit if one's goal is to improve women's achievements; studying high-achieving women may give suggestions as to how one "creates" a high-achieving female through child-rearing practices or other factors. The problem is that we concentrate 90 percent of the research on 1 percent of the population, and compound the problem by calling it the psychology of women, implying all women. While we need research on high-achieving women, we also need to redirect our efforts toward understanding the psychology of housewives, the psychology of secretaries, the psychology of mentally retarded women, the psychology of physically handicapped women, and many others. We are not suggesting that all studies must involve random sampling, but that we define groups other than high achievers, who are also of importance or interest. Of course, the study of all these groups of women is as important a task for psychology in general as it is for psychology of women.

With the growing popularity of androgyny, we need more research on it and its psychological consequences. In particular, more information is needed on the possible psychological costs of being androgynous so that they can be weighed against the many benefits.

We need more research on adjustment problems in women, particularly depression because it is so frequent. We need to know what causes depression and what can be done to prevent it (e.g., changing child-rearing practices, school policy, or family roles). Along with this, we need more work on psychotherapy for women's problems, and research on the effectiveness of these therapies. Related research should be directed toward the psychological aspects of women's health issues such as abortion and mastectomy.

As we have discussed in previous chapters, feminist scholars stress the importance of power relations between women and men. More psychological research is needed in this area. We need to know how men express power over women, and how women might more effectively begin to express power themselves. Psychologists Wendy McKenna and Florence Denmark (1979) did an interesting study that shows some of the possibilities for future research in this area. They attempted to find out whether women really could improve their perceived status by adopting some of the nonverbal communication patterns typical of males and high-status individuals. To do this, they made videotapes of a short skit involving two people who were described as working for the same company. One person asks for a favor, and the other at first refuses but then complies. In all possible combinations of men and women in the two roles, the researchers had one person exhibit high-status nonverbal behaviors (e.g., smiling infrequently, touching the person they are dealing with) and the other, low-status nonverbal behaviors. College students rated the job level of each of the videotaped men and women. Overall, the subjects thought that the person who showed high-status behaviors held the high-level job, regardless of the person's gender. Therefore, it seems that if women convey their competence nonverbally, they will be recognized as being competent and of high status. That is an encouraging finding. Unfortunately, there was also a suggestion that a man who showed low-status behaviors in the presence of a woman showing high-status behaviors was judged as having a lower-level job than when his partner was a man showing high-status behaviors. Therefore, men may lose prestige by working for high-status women, and male resentment may ensue. It is exactly this kind of information — about the positive and negative consequences of new patterns of behavior — that we need.

THE FUTURE OF THE FEMALE ROLE

How will the female role emerge in the United States from the present upheaval in gender roles? We shall structure our discussion of this question around two further questions that, while superficially similar, have quite different answers in our view: (1) How would males and females behave (what would be the nature of gender roles) in the absence of all forces demanding gender differences, whether in child-rearing practices or in social pressures, legal, economic, or otherwise? That is, if males and females were treated identically, would they behave identically, or would differences still emerge? If differences emerged, what would they be?; and (2) How would males and females behave if all social forces were directed toward making them behave identically — that is, if we systematically shaped males and females to behave as similarly as possible? (Note that this second hypothetical condition, unlike the first, might include differential treatment of females and males in order to bring about the desired similarity in behavior, such as encouraging aggressive behavior in girls while discouraging it in boys in order to bring both to some intermediate level of aggressive behavior, neither too aggressive nor too passive.)

Our feeling is that, under condition (1), there would be gender differences, and that under condition (2) there wouldn't be. While we have argued for the prevalence of gender similarities, we also hold that there are some gender differences that would emerge under condition (1); yet we are equally convinced that human beings are so malleable that even these differences could be eliminated by appropriate environmental manipulations.

What evidence do we have for these assertions? Our belief that gender differences would emerge in the absence of efforts at shaping them (condition 1) arises from two sources — the cross-cultural data and the biological data. The universality of the existence of gender roles cross-culturally is a strong argument that if things started from a state where no roles were expected, it would not be long until they reached an equilibrium in which there were differences, although the content of the differences might be quite different from those that now hold in the United States. Humans seem to have a universal tendency to create gender roles, although the precise content of the roles may vary. The biological data further persuade us that biological gender differences do create some psychological gender differences. Gender differences in physical strength surely will have some consequences, as will sex hormones, probably most importantly on aggressive behaviors. Biologically determined experiences, most notably pregnancy and breastfeeding, probably have consequences, particularly when the pregnancy/breastfeeding functions become generalized to include child-rearing.

On the other hand, the cross-cultural data also persuade us that such differences could be eliminated under appropriate environmental manipulations (condition 2). For example, among the Mundugumor observed by Mead, we have seen that females can be just aggressive as males, because the culture shapes them to be so. Certainly males could be assigned an equal role in care of infants, particularly when bottle feeding is so common, and the assignment would be a successful one. The hallmark of the human species is malleability, the ability to adapt, whether to diverse climatic conditions or to changes in gender roles.

Which course of action to take is ultimately not a scientific question, but rather a question of values — what we as a culture believe females and males should be like. Margaret Mead (1949) made an elegant analogy in this decision-making process to differences between people with good eyesight and people with poor eyesight. Certainly there are biological differences between them, one group being physiologically capable of seeing better than the other. But society holds that those with the inferior physiology should not be handicapped in their status in society, and so we provide them with eyeglasses to remedy their physiological deficiency, allowing them to function equally with those who have good vision. Does our value system also hold that females should function equally with males? If so, certainly our technology is adequate to overcome biological gender differences (for example, the use of machines to perform heavy lifting for females with inadequate physical strength, or the use of bottles to feed babies for males with inadequate mammary endowment), just as we give glasses to those with poor vision.

The question remains, what course of action will we, as a society, take? Will it be condition (1) or condition (2), or some alternative such as a modified version of status quo? We, of course, are not seers, and so we shall not make a prediction as to what course will be taken. What we do wish to do is to stimulate the reader to explore the consequences of the various alternatives.

In many ways, ours may be an optimal time for gender-role change for women. The de-emphasis on fertility and child-rearing may be critical. The nature of the female role is intimately tied to whether or not a society wants to reproduce at a high rate. With a strong emphasis on reproduction, maternal aspects of the female role are stressed. With the current de-emphasis on fertility, careers for women may become much more viable alternatives than they formerly were. Indeed, childlessness may become an option for women, freeing them for substantially different roles than housewife/mother (Hoffman, 1974b).

One problem to be faced is that we really have no adequate measure of social change. There has been a tendency to equate work outside the home with progress for women. Yet, as we saw in Chapter 16, working outside the home is the opposite of progress if it must be done in addition to all the housewife and mother tasks. The work of women, whether inside the home or outside the home, must be evaluated in terms of its contributions to society in general and to the growth of the individual (Dahlstrom, 1971). A much more complex and adequate measure of social change would result.

We need, then, to expand our notion of the meaning of equality — it means more than just women holding jobs outside the home, for example. Part of the expansion must include changes in the male role (Palme, 1972). The interest in gender roles sparked by the women's movement is also leading to an awareness that the male role has its problems (Chafetz, 1974). It, too, is restrictive, stressful, and unrealistic for some individuals. True equality requires modification of the male role, not only to make possible change in the female role, but because the male role itself is in need of revision.

But we must add one note of caution, and this is in regard to the values attached to gender roles. Cross-culturally (at least currently) it is a universal phenomenon that the male role is always more powerful, and the female role is always valued less. This devaluing of the female role surely has many consequences, among them psychological ones such as the higher frequency of psychiatric problems found in women. In our opinion it is imperative that, whatever the reallocation or modification of gender roles, the result be that the male role and the female role be valued equally.

While we are emphasizing the need for a higher valuing of the female role, it is also true that this higher valuing must come not only from without, but also from within. That is, institutional change aimed at raising the value of the female role — for example, treating child-rearing as a profession — and changing male attitudes are not enough. Women must also value themselves. This is an important goal of the many consciousness-raising groups formed by women across the country.

Whatever the reallocation of gender roles in the future, it is most important that equal respect and value be attached to both roles. In part, we are suggesting that gender roles in some form will probably continue, and that, rather than trying to eliminate them, we might more profitably concentrate on improving the valuation attached to the female role. Much as blacks have shifted from an emphasis on integration and assimilation into white culture to a proclamation that black is beautiful, so we hope women will come to believe that female is good. As Christabel Pankhurst, a turn-of-the-century British suffragette said,

> Remember the dignity
> of your womanhood.
> Do not appeal,
> do not beg,
> do not grovel.
> Take courage,
> join hands,
> stand beside us.

Bibliography

Abramowitz, S. I., et al. "Sex Bias in Psychotherapy: A Failure to Confirm." *American Journal of Psychiatry*, 133 (1976):706–709.

Abramowitz, S. I.; C. V. Abramowitz; C. Jackson; and B. Gomes. "The Politics of Clinical Judgment: What Nonliberal Examiners Infer about Women Who Do Not Stifle Themselves." *J. of Consulting and Clinical Psychology*, 41 (1973):385–391.

Adams, Kathryn A. and Audrey D. Landers. "Sex Difference in Dominance Behavior." *Sex Roles*, 4 (1978):215–224.

Adelson, J. "A Study of Minority Group Authoritarianism." In M. Sklare, ed., *The Jews: Social Patterns of an American Group*. Glencoe, Ill.: Free Press, 1958.

Adler, A. *Understanding Human Nature*. New York: Garden City Publishing Co., 1927.

Albin, Rochelle S. "Psychological Studies of Rape." *Signs*, 3 (1977):423–435.

Allport, G. *The Nature of Prejudice*. Reading, Mass.: Addison-Wesley, 1954.

———. *Personality*. New York: Holt, Rinehart & Winston, 1937.

Almquist, Elizabeth. "Women in the Labor Force." *Signs*, 2 (1977):843–853.

American Psychological Association. Task Force on Issues of Sexual Bias in Graduate Education. "Guidelines for Nonsexist Use of Language." *American Psychologist*, 30 (1975):682–684.

———. "Report of the Task Force on Sex Bias and Sex-Role Stereotyping in Psychotherapeutic Practice." *American Psychologist*, 30 (1975):1169–1175.

Amir, Menachem. *Patterns in Forcible Rape*. Chicago: University of Chicago Press, 1971.

Anastasi, Anne. *Differential Psychology*. 3d ed. New York: Macmillan, 1958.

———. "On the Formation of Psychological Traits." *American Psychologist*, 25 (1970):899–910.

Andrew, D. M., and D. G. Patterson. *Minnesota Clerical Test*, New York: Psychological Corporation, 1959.

In the bibliography we have followed the style of spelling out the first names of female authors. The purpose of this is not to discriminate against men, but rather to help readers become aware of the scientific contributions made by women.

Andrews, Eva, and Daniel Cappon. "Autism and Schizophrenia in a Child Guidance Clinic." *Canadian Psychiatric Association Journal*, 2 (1957): 1–25.

Angrist, Shirley S. "The Study of Sex Roles." *J. of Social Issues*, 25 (1969): 215–232.

Angrist, Shirley S.; Mark Lefton; Simon Dinitz; and Benjamin Pasamanick. *Women After Treatment: A Study of Former Mental Patients and Their Normal Neighbors*. New York: Irvington, 1968.

Anonymous: "When a Woman Is Attacked." In L. G. Schultz, ed., *Rape Victimology*. Springfield, Ill.: Charles C. Thomas, 1975.

Ardrey, R. *African Genesis*. New York: Dell, 1967.

Argyle, Michael, et al. "The Effects of Visibility on Interaction in a Dyad." *Human Relations*, 21 (1968):3–17.

Armon, Virginia. "Some Personality Variables in Overt Female Homosexuality," *J. of Projective Technique in Personality Assessment*, 24 (1960):292–309.

Asch, S. E. "Studies of Independence and Conformity: I. A Minority of One Against a Unanimous Majority." *Psychological Monographs*, 70 (1956): (9, Whole No. 416).

Asken, Michael J. "Psychoemotional Aspects of Mastectomy: A Review of Recent Literature." *American Journal of Psychiatry*, 132 (1975):56–59.

Astin, Helen S., and A. E. Bayer. "Sex Discrimination in Academe." *Educational Record*, 53 (1972):101–118.

Bailyn, Lotte. "Career and Family Orientations of Husbands and Wives in Relation to Marital Happiness." *Human Relations*, 23 (1970):97–113.

Bakan, D. *The Duality of Human Existence*. Chicago: Rand McNally, 1966.

Baker, H. J., and R. J. Stoller "Biological Forces Postulated as Having Role in Gender Identity." *Roche Reports: Frontiers of Hospital Psychiatry*, 4 (1967):3.

Baldwin, A. L. *Theories of Child Development*. New York: John Wiley & Sons, 1967.

Bamberger, Joan. "The Myth of Matriarchy: Why Men Rule in Primitive Society." In M. Z. Rosaldo and L. Lamphere, eds., *Woman, Culture, and Society*. Stanford: Stanford University Press, 1974.

Bandura, A. "Influence of Model's Reinforcement Contingencies on the Acquisition of Imitative Responses." *J. of Personality and Social Psychology*, 1 (1965):589–595.

Bandura, A., and R. H. Walters. *Social Learning and Personality Development*. New York: Holt, Rinehart & Winston, 1963.

Banks, W. Curtis. "White Preference in Blacks: A Paradigm in Search of a Phenomenon." *Psychological Bulletin*, 83 (1976):1179–1186.

Barbach, Lonnie G. *For Yourself: The Fulfillment of Female Sexuality*. Garden City, N. Y.: Anchor Press/Doubleday, 1975.

Bardwick, Judith M. "Her Body, the Battleground." *Psychology Today* 5, February 1972b:50–54.

———. *Psychology of Women: A Study of Bio-Cultural Conflicts.* New York: Harper & Row, 1971.

———, ed. *Readings on the Psychology of Women.* New York: Harper & Row, 1972a.

Barraclough, C. A., and R. A. Gorski. "Evidence That the Hypothalamus Is Responsible for Androgen-Induced Sterility in the Female Rat." *Endocrinology,* 68 (1961):68–79.

Barry, H.; Margaret K. Bacon; and I. L. Child. "A Cross-Cultural Survey of Some Sex Differences in Socialization." *J. of Abnormal and Social Psychology,* 55 (1957):327–332.

Bart, Pauline B. "Depression in Middle-Aged Women." In V. G. Gornick and B. K. Moran, eds., *Woman in Sexist Society.* New York: Basic Books, 1971.

Baruch, Grace K. "Sex-Role Stereotyping, the Motive to Avoid Success, and Parental Identification." *Sex Roles,* 1 (1975):303–309.

Baruch, Rhoda. "The Achievement Motive in Women: Implications for Career Development." *J. of Personality and Social Psychology,* 5 (1967):260–267.

Baughman, E. E. *Black Americans: A Psychological Analysis.* New York: Academic Press, 1971.

Baughman, E. E., and W. G. Dahlstrom. *Negro and White Children: A Psychological Study in the Rural South.* New York: Academic Press, 1968.

Baxter, James C. "Interpersonal Spacing in Natural Settings." *Sociometry,* 33 (1970):444–456.

Bayley, Nancy. *The California Infant Scale of Motor Development.* Berkeley: University of California Press, 1936.

Beach, F. A. "Evolutionary Changes in the Physiological Control of Mating Behavior in Mammals." *Psychological Review,* 54 (1947):5.

Beal, Frances M. "Double Jeopardy: To Be Black and Female." In R. Morgan, ed., *Sisterhood Is Powerful.* New York: Random House, 1970.

Beard, Mary. *Woman As Force in History.* New York: Macmillan, 1946.

Beauvoir, Simone de. *The Second Sex.* New York: Knopf, 1952.

Beck, Aaron T., and Ruth L. Greenberg. "Cognitive Therapy with Depressed Women." In V. Franks and V. Burtle, eds., *Women in Therapy.* New York: Brunner/Mazel, 1974.

Beckman, Linda J. "The Relative Rewards and Costs of Parenthood and Employment for Employed Women." *Psychology of Women Quarterly,* 2 (1978):215–234.

Bell, A. P. "Homosexualities: Their Range and Character." In *Nebraska Symposium on Motivation 1973.* Lincoln: University of Nebraska Press, 1974.

Bell, Robert R. *Premarital Sex in a Changing Society.* Englewood Cliffs, N.J.: Prentice-Hall, 1966.

Bell, R. Q. "Relations Between Behavior Manifestations in the Human Neonate." *Child Development,* 31 (1960):463–477.

Bell, R. Q.; G. M. Weller; and M. F. Waldrop. "Newborn and Preschooler: Organization of Behavior and Relations Between Periods." *Monographs of the Society for Research in Child Development*, 36 (1971):(1–2, Serial No. 142).

Belliveau, F., and Lyn Richter. *Understanding Human Sexual Inadequacy*. New York: Bantam Books, 1970.

Bem, Sandra L. "The Measurement of Psychological Androgyny." *J. of Consulting and Clinical Psychology*, 42 (1974):155–162.

———. "On the Utility of Alternative Procedures for Assessing Psychological Androgyny." *J. of Consulting and Clinical Psychology*, 45 (1977):196–205.

———. Sex-Role Adaptability: One Consequence of Psychological Androgyny," *J. of Personality and Social Psychology*, 31 (1975):634–643.

Bem, Sandra L., and D. J. Bem. "Case Study of Non-Conscious Ideology: Training the Woman To Know Her Place." In D. J. Bem, ed., *Beliefs, Attitudes, and Human Affairs*. Belmont, Calif.: Brooks/Cole, 1970.

Bem, Sandra L., and Ellen Lenney. "Sex-Typing and the Avoidance of Cross-Sex Behavior." *J. of Personality and Social Psychology*, 33 (1976): 48–54.

Bem, Sandra L.; W. Martyna; and C. Watson. "Sex Typing and Androgyny: Further Explorations of the Expressive Domain." *J. of Personality and Social Psychology*, 34 (1976):1016–1023.

Benedek, Therese F. "Sexual Functions in Women and Their Disturbance." In S. Arieti, *American Handbook of Psychiatry*. New York: Basic Books, 1959.

Benedek, Therese, and B. B. Rubenstein. "The Sexual Cycle in Women: The Relation Between Ovarian Function and Psychodynamic Processes." *Psychonomic Medicine Monographs*, 3 (1942):1–307.

Bentzen, F. "Sex Ratios in Learning and Behavior Disorders." *American Journal of Orthopsychiatry*, 33 (1963): 92–98.

Berg, Phyllis, and Janet S. Hyde. "Gender and Race Differences in Causal Attributions." Paper presented at American Psychological Association Meetings, September 1976.

Berman, Ellen; Sylvia Sacks; and H. Lief. "The Two-Professional Marriage: A New Conflict Syndrome." *J. of Marital and Sex Therapy*, 1 (1975): 242–253.

Bermant, G. "Behavior Therapy Approaches to Modification of Sexual Preferences: Biological Perspective and Critique." Paper presented at the California State Psychological Association. Reprinted in J. Bardwick, ed., *Readings on the Psychology of Women*. New York: Harper & Row, 1972.

Bernard, Jesse. *Marriage and Family Among Negroes*. New York: Prentice-Hall, 1966.

Berardo, F. "Widowhood Status in the United States: Perspective on a Neglected Aspect of the Family Life-Cycle." *Family Coordinator*, 17 (1968):191–203.

Berscheid, Ellen, et al. "Physical Attractiveness and Dating Choice: A Test of the Matching Hypothesis." *J. of Experimental Social Psychology,* 7 (1971):173–189.

Bettelheim, B. *Symbolic Wounds.* New York: Collier Books, 1962.

Bibring, Grete L.; T. F. Dwyer; D. S. Huntington; and A. F. Valenstein. "A Study of the Psychological Processes in Pregnancy and of the Earliest Mother-Child Relationship." *The Psychoanalytic Study of the Child, 16.* New York: International Universities Press, 1961.

Bird, Caroline. *Born Female.* New York: David McKay, 1968.

Birnbaum, Judith A. "Life Patterns and Self-Esteem in Gifted Family Oriented and Career Committed Women." In M. Mednick, L. W. Hoffman, and S. Tangri, eds., *Women and Achievement: Social and Motivational Analyses.* New York: Halsted Press, 1975.

Blair, G. E. "The Relationship of Selected Ego Functions and Academic Achievement of Negro Students." *Dissertation Abstracts,* 28 (1972): 3031A.

Blanchard, W. H. "The Group Process in Gang Rape." *J. of Social Psychology,* 49 (1959):259–266.

Blau, Zena Smith. *Old Age in a Changing Society.* New York: New Viewpoints, 1973.

Blaubergs, Maija S. "Changing the Sexist Language: The Theory Behind the Practice." *Psychology of Women Quarterly,* 2 (1978): 244–261.

Block, Jeanne H. "Another Look at Sex Differentiation in the Socialization Behaviors of Mothers and Fathers." In J. Sherman and F. Denmark, eds., *Psychology of Women: Future Directions of Research.* New York: Psych Dimensions, 1978.

———. "Conceptions of Sex Role: Some Cross-Cultural and Longitudinal Perspectives." *American Psychologist,* 28 (1973):512–526.

———. "Issues, Problems, and Pitfalls in Assessing Sex Differences: A Critical Review of *The Psychology of Sex Differences.*" *Merrill-Palmer Quarterly,* 22 (1976):283–308.

Block, M. A. *Alcoholism: Its Facets and Phases.* London: Oxford University Press, 1962.

Blumstein, Philip W., and Pepper Schwartz. "Bisexual Women." In J. P. Wiseman, ed., *The Social Psychology of Sex.* New York: Harper & Row, 1976.

Bock, E. W. "Farmer's Daughter Effect: The Case of the Negro Female Professionals." *Phylon,* 30 (1969):17–26.

Bock, E. Wilbur, and Irving Webber. "Suicide Among the Elderly: Isolating Widowhood and Mitigating Alternatives." *J. of Marriage and the Family,* 34 (1972):24–31.

Bock, R. D., and D. Kolakowski. "Further Evidence of Sex-Linked Major-Gene Influence on Human Spatial Visualizing Ability." *American Journal of Human Genetics,* 25 (1973):1–14.

Bodine, Ann. "Sex Differentiation in Language." In B. Thorne and N. Henley, eds., *Language and Sex: Difference and Dominance*. Rowley, Mass.: Newbury House, 1975.

Bohannon, Paul, ed. *Divorce and After*. Garden City, N.Y.: Doubleday, 1970.

Bonaparte, Marie. *Female Sexuality*. New York: Grove Press, 1965. First published by International Universities Press, 1953.

Bosselman, Beulah C. "Castration Anxiety and Phallus Envy: A Reformulation." *Psychiatric Quarterly*, 34 (1960):252–259.

Bouchard, T. J., and M. G. McGee. "Sex Differences in Human Spatial Ability: Not an X-linked Recessive Gene Effect." *Social Biology*, 24 (1977): 332–335.

Bradburn, W., and D. Caplovitz. *Reports on Happiness*. Chicago: Aldine, 1965.

Brecher, Ruth, and E. Brecher. *An Analysis of Human Sexual Response*. Boston: Little, Brown, 1966.

Brend, Ruth M. "Male-Female Intonation Patterns in American English." *Proceedings of the Seventh International Congress of Phonetic Sciences*, (1971):866–869. The Hague: Mouton, 1972. Reprinted in B. Thorne and Henley, eds., *Language and Sex: Difference and Dominance*. Rowley, Mass.: Newbury House, 1975.

Bridgette, R. E. "Self-Esteem in Negro and White Southern Adolescents." Unpublished Ph.D. dissertation, University of North Carolina at Chapel Hill, 1970.

Brien, Lois, and Cynthia Sheldon. "Gestalt Therapy and Women." In E. I. Rawlings and D. K. Carter, eds., *Psychotherapy for Women*. Springfield, Ill.: Charles C. Thomas, 1977.

Briffault, R. *The Mothers*. New York: Macmillan, 1927.

Brim, O. J. "Family Structure and Sex Role Learning in Children: A Further Analysis of Helen Koch's Data," *Sociometry*, 21 (1958):1–16.

———. "The Parent-Child Relation as a Social System: 1. Parent and Child Roles." *Child Development*, 28 (1957):343–364.

———. "Personality Development as Role Learning." In I. Iscoe and H. Stevenson, eds., *Personality Development in Children*. Austin: University of Texas Press, 1960.

Broderick, C. "Social Heterosexual Development Among Urban Negroes and Whites." *J. of Marriage and the Family* (May 1965), 200–203.

Brodsky, Annette. "A Decade of Feminist Influence on Psychotherapy." Presidential address to Division 35 of the American Psychological Association, Toronto, 1978.

———. "Therapeutic Aspects of Consciousness-Raising Groups." In E. I. Rawlings and D. K. Carter, eds., *Psychotherapy for Women*. Springfield, Ill.: Charles C. Thomas, 1977.

Brodsky, Carroll M. "Rape at Work." In M. J. Walker and S. L. Brodsky, eds., *Sexual Assault: The Victim and the Rapist*. Lexington, Mass.: D. C. Heath, 1976.

Broverman, Inge K.; D. M. Broverman; F. E. Clarkson; P. S. Rosenkrantz; and Susan R. Vogel. "Sex Role Stereotypes and Clinical Judgments of Mental Health." *J. of Consulting and Clinical Psychology*, 34 (1970):1–7.

Broverman, Inge K.; Susan R. Vogel; D. M. Broverman; F. E. Clarkson; and P. S. Rosenkrantz. "Sex Role Stereotypes: A Current Appraisal." *J. of Social Issues,* 28 (1972):59–78.

Brown, C. A.; R. Feldberg; E. M. Fox; and J. Kohen. "Divorce: Chance of a New Lifetime." *J. of Social Issues,* 32(1) (1976):119–133.

Brown, D. R. *Role and Status of Women in the Soviet Union.* New York: Teachers College Press, 1968.

Brownmiller, Susan. *Against Our Will: Men, Women, and Rape.* New York: Simon and Schuster, 1975.

Brussel, J. A. "Comment Following Menachem Amir, *Forcible Rape.*" *Sexual Behavior,* 1 (1971):8.

Buffery, A. W. H., and J. A. Gray. "Sex Differences in the Development of Spatial and Linguistic Skills." In C. Ounsted and D. C. Taylor, eds., *Gender Differences: Their Ontogeny and Significance.* Baltimore, Md.: Williams & Wilkins, 1972.

Bugental, Daphne E.; Leonore R. Love; and Robert M. Gianetto. "Perfidious Feminine Faces." *J. of Personality and Social Psychology,* 17 (1971): 314–318.

Burgess, Ann W., and Lynda L. Holmstrom. "Rape Trauma Syndrome." *American Journal of Psychiatry,* 131 (1974a):981–986.

———. *Rape: Victims of Crisis.* Bowie, Md.: Robert J. Brady Company, 1974b.

Cade, Toni, ed. *The Black Woman.* New York: New American Library, 1970.

Calahan, D.; I. H. Cislin; and H. M. Crossley. *American Drinking Practices: A National Study of Drinking Behavior and Attitudes.* New Haven, Conn.: College and University Press, 1969.

Campbell, A.; P. E. Converse; and W. L. Rodgers. *The Quality of American Life.* Ann Arbor, Mich.: ISR Social Science Archive, 1975.

Caplan, G. "Emotional Implications of Pregnancy and Influences on Family Relationships." In H. C. Stuart and D. G. Prugh, eds., *The Healthy Child.* Cambridge, Mass.: Harvard University Press, 1960.

Carlson, Rae. "Sex Differences in Ego Functioning." *J. of Consulting and Clinical Psychology,* 37 (1971b):267–277.

———. "Understanding Women: Implications for Personality Theory and Research." *J. of Social Issues,* 28 (2):1972.

———. "Where Is the Person in Personality Research?" *Psychological Bulletin,* 75 (1971a):203–219.

Carpenter, T. R., and T. V. Busse. "Development of Self-Concept in Negro and White Welfare Children." *Child Development,* 40 (1969):935–939.

Castillejo, Irene C. de. *Knowing Woman: A Feminine Psychology.* New York: G. P. Putnam's Sons, 1973.

Castle, C. S. "A Statistical Study of Eminent Women," *Archives of Psychology,* 27 (1913).

Census Bureau. *Current Population Reports* (1972):20, No. r39, p. 5.

————. *We the American Elderly*, 1973.

Chafetz, Janet S. *Masculine/Feminine or Human? An Overview of the Sociology of Sex Roles.* Itasca, Ill.: F. E. Peacock, 1974.

Cherry, Frances and Kay Deaux. "Fear of Success Versus Fear of Gender-Inappropriate Behavior." *Sex Roles,* 4 (1978):97–102.

Chesler, Phyllis. *Women and Madness.* Garden City, N.Y.: Doubleday, 1972.

Chess, S. "Diagnosis and Treatment of Hyperkinetic Children." *N. Y. State Journal of Medicine,* 60 (1960):2379.

Chisholm, Shirley. "Race, Revolution and Women." *The Black Scholar,* December 1971.

Chodorow, Nancy. "Family Structure and Feminine Personality." In M. Z. Rosaldo and L. Lamphere, eds., *Woman, Culture, and Society.* Stanford: Stanford University Press, 1974.

Christmas, June J. "Self-Concept and Attitudes." In K. S. Miller and R. M. Dreger, eds., *Comparative Studies of Blacks and Whites in the United States.* New York: Academic Press, 1973.

Clark, K. B., and Mamie P. Clark. "Racial Identification and Preferences in Negro Children." In T. M. Newcomb and E. L. Hartley eds., *Readings in Social Psychology.* New York: Holt, Rinehart & Winston, 1947.

Clay, W. L. "The Socio-Economic Status of Blacks." *Ebony,* (Sept. 1975):29.

Cohen, M. L.; R. Garofalo; R. Boucher; and T. Seghorn. "The Psychology of Rapists." *Seminars in Psychiatry,* 3 (1971):311.

Constantinople, Anne. "Masculinity-Femininity. An Exception to a Famous Dictum." *Psychological Bulletin,* 80 (1973):389–407.

Cooperstock, R. "Sex Differences in the Use of Mood-modifying Drugs: An Explanatory Model." *J. of Health and Social Behavior,* 12 (1971): 238–244.

————. "Women and Psychotropic Drugs." In A. MacLennan, ed., *Women: Their Use of Alcohol and Other Legal Drugs.* Toronto, Canada: Addiction Research Foundation of Ontario, 1976.

Cordaro, L., and J. R. Ison. "Psychology of the Scientist: X. Observer Bias in Classical Conditioning of the Planarian." *Psychological Reports,* 13 1963:787–789.

Cosentino, F., and A. B. Heilbrun. "Anxiety Correlates of Sex-Role Identity in College Students." *Psychological Reports,* 14 (1964):729–730.

Crandall, Virginia C. "Achievement Behavior in Young Children." In W. W. Hartup and Nancy L. Smothergill, eds., *The Young Child: Reviews of Research.* Washington, D.C.: National Association for the Education of Young Children, 1967.

————. "Sex Differences in Expectancy of Intellectual and Academic Reinforcement." In C. P. Smith, ed., *Achievement Related Motives in Children.* New York: Russell Sage Foundation, 1969.

————. "Expecting Sex Differences and Sex Differences in Expectancies: A Developmental Analysis." Paper presented at American Psychological Association Meetings, Toronto, August 1978.

Dahlstrom, E., ed. *The Changing Roles of Men and Women*. Boston: Beacon Press, 1971.

Dalton, Katharina. "The Influence of Mother's Menstruation on Her Child." *Proceedings of the Royal Society for Medicine*, 59 (1966):1014.

———. *The Premenstrual Syndrome*. Springfield, Ill.: Charles C. Thomas, 1964.

Dan, A. J., and S. Beekman. "Male Versus Female Representation in Psychological Research." *American Psychologist*, 27 (1972):1078.

D'Andrade, R. G. "Sex Differences and Cultural Institutions." In E. E. Maccoby, ed., *The Development of Sex Differences*. Stanford: Stanford University Press, 1966.

Davis, K. E. "Sex on Campus: Is There a Revolution?" *Medical Aspects of Human Sexuality*, (January 1971):128–142.

Davis, Elizabeth Gould. *The First Sex*. New York: G. P. Putnam's Sons, 1971.

Deaux, Kay. *The Behavior of Women and Men*. Monterey, Calif.: Brooks/ Cole, 1976.

Deaux, Kay, and T. Emswiller. "Explanations of Successful Performance on Sex-Linked Tasks: What Is Skill for the Male Is Luck for the Female." *Journal of Personality and Social Psychology*, 29 (1974):80–85.

Dellas, M., and E. L. Gaier. "The Self and Adolescent Identity in Women: Options and Implications." *Adolescence*, 10 (1975):399–407.

DeFries, John C. et al. "Parent-Offspring Resemblance for Specific Cognitive Abilities in Two Ethnic Groups." *Nature*, 261 (1976):131–133.

Delaney, Janice; Mary Jane Lupton; and Emily Toth. *The Curse: A Cultural History of Menstruation*. New York: E. P. Dutton, 1976.

Denmark, Florence L., and Helen M. Goodfield. "A Second Look at Adolescence Theories." *Sex Roles*, 4 (1978):375–380.

Deutsch, Helene. "The Psychology of Woman in Relation to the Functions of Reproduction." *International Journal of Psychoanalysis*, 6 (1924).

———. *The Psychology of Women*. New York: Grune & Stratton, 1944.

Diner, Helen. *Mothers and Amazons: The First Feminine History of Culture*. Original in German, 1930. U. S. edition by Julian Press, 1965.

Dobert, Margarete. "Tradition, Modernity, and Woman Power in Africa." In M. S. Mednick; L. W. Hoffman; and S. S. Tangri, eds., *Women: Psychological Perspectives on Achievement*. Washington, D.C.: Hemisphere, 1975.

Donelson, Elaine. "Becoming a Single Woman." In E. Donelson and J. Gullahorn, eds., *Women: A Psychological Perspective*. New York: John Wiley & Sons, 1977.

Dornbusch, S. M. "Afterword." In E. E. Maccoby, ed., *The Development of Sex Differences*. Stanford: Stanford University Press, 1966.

Dörner, G. "Prophylaxie und Therapie Angeborener Sexualdeviatonen." *Deutsche Medizinische Wochenschrift-Sonderdruck*, February 2, 1969.

Douvan, Elizabeth. "New Sources of Conflicts in Females at Adolescence and Early Adulthood." In J. Bardwick; E. Douvan; M. Horner; and D.

Gutman, eds., *Feminine Personality and Conflict*. Belmont, Calif.: Brooks/Cole, 1970.

Douvan, Elizabeth, and J. Adelson. *The Adolescent Experience*. New York: John Wiley & Sons, 1966.

Dowty, Nancy. "To Be a Woman in Israel." *School Review*, 80 (1972):319–332.

Dreger, Ralph M., et al. "Behavioral Classification Project." *J. of Consulting Psychology*, 28 (1964):1–13.

Dweck, Carol S., and N. D. Reppucci. "Learned Helplessness and Reinforcement Responsibility in Children." *J. of Personality and Social Psychology*, 25 (1973):109–116.

Eagly, Alice H. "Sex Differences in Influenceability." *Psychological Bulletin*, 85 (1978):86–116.

Edwards, D. A. "Early Androgen Stimulation and Aggressive Behavior in Male and Female Mice." *Physiology and Behavior*, 4 (1969):333–338.

Elder, Glenn H. "Appearance and Education in Marriage Mobility." *American Sociological Review*, 34 (1969):519–533.

Epstein, Cynthia F. "Black and Female: The Double Whammy." *Psychology Today*, 7(3) (August 1973b):57.

———. *Woman's Place: Options and Limits in Professional Careers*. Berkeley: University of California Press, 1970.

———. "Positive Effects of the Multiple Negative." *American Journal of Sociology*, 78 (1973a):912–935.

Erikson, E. H. *Childhood and Society*. New York: Norton, 1950.

———. "Identity and the Life Cycle." *Psychological Issues*, 1(1) (1959).

———. "Inner and Outer Space: Reflections on Womanhood." In R. J. Lifton, ed., *The Woman in America*, Boston: Beacon Press, 1964.

Eron, Leonard, et al. "The Convergence of Laboratory and Field Studies of the Development of Aggression." In J. de Wit and W. W. Hartup, eds., *Determinants and Origins of Aggressive Behavior*. The Hague: Mouton, 1974.

Ervin, Clinton V. "Psychologic Adjustment to Mastectomy." *Medical Aspects of Human Sexuality*, 7(2) (February 1973):42–65.

Fabrikant, B. "The Psychotherapist and the Female Patient: Perceptions, Misperceptions and Change." In V. Franks and V. Burtle, eds., *Women in Therapy*. New York: Brunner/Mazel, 1974.

Faulk, M. "Men Who Assault Their Wives." *Medicine, Science, and Law*, 14 (1974):180–183. Reprinted in Maria Roy, ed., *Battered Women*. New York: Van Nostrand, 1977.

Feather, N. T. "Attribution of Responsibility and Valence of Success and Failure in Relation to Initial Confidence and Perceived Locus of Control." *J. of Personality and Social Psychology*, 13 (1969):129–144.

Feild, Hubert S. "Attitudes Toward Rape: A Comparative Analysis of Police, Rapists, Crisis Counselors, and Citizens. *J. of Personality and Social Psychology*, 36 (1978):156–179.

Feshbach, Seymour, and Neal Malamuth. "Sex and Aggression: Proving the Link." *Psychology Today*, 12(6) (November 1978):110.

Fidell, L. S. "Empirical Verification of Sex Discrimination in Hiring Practices in Psychology." *American Psychologist*, 25 (1970):1094–1098.

Field, M. G., and Karin I. Flynn. "Worker, Mother, Housewife: Soviet Woman Today." In D. R. Brown, ed., *Role and Status of Women in the Soviet Union*. New York: Teachers College Press, 1968.

Fisher, S. *Understanding the Female Orgasm*. New York: Basic Books, 1973.

Fisher, S., and H. Osofsky. "Sexual Responsiveness in Women: Psychological Correlates," *Archives of General Psychiatry*, 17 (1967):214–226.

Fishman, Pamela M. "Interaction: The Work Women Do." *Social Problems*, 25 (1978):397–405.

Fogarty, M. P.; Rhona Rapoport; and R. Rapoport. *Sex, Career and Family*. Beverly Hills, Calif.: Sage Publications, 1971.

Ford, C. S., and F. A. Beach. *Patterns of Sexual Behavior*. New York: Harper & Row, 1951.

Forssman, H., and I. Thuwe. "One Hundred and Twenty Children Born after Application for Therapeutic Abortion Refused." *Acta Psychiat. Scand.*, 42 (1966):71–88.

Franck, Kate, and L. Rosen. "A Projective Test of Masculinity and Femininity," *J. of Consulting Psychology*, 13 (1949):247–256.

Frank, R. T. "The Hormonal Causes of Premenstrual Tension." *Archives of Neurological Psychiatry*, 26 (1931):1053.

Franks, Violet, and Vasanti Burtle. *Women in Therapy*. New York: Brunner/ Mazel, 1974.

Freedman, J. L.; J. M. Carlsmith; and D. O. Sears. *Social Psychology*. Englewood Cliffs, N.J.: Prentice-Hall, 1970.

Freedman, M. J. "Homosexuality Among Women and Psychological Adjustment," *Ladder*, 12 (1968):2–3.

French, E. G. "Some Characteristics of the Achievement Motive in Women," *J. of Abnormal and Social Psychology*, 68 (1964):119–128.

Freud, S. *The Interpretation of Dreams*. Trans. by J. Strachey. New York: Basic Books, 1955.

———. *New Introductory Lectures in Psychoanalysis*. New York: W. W. Norton, 1933.

———. "Some Psychical Consequences of the Anatomical Distinction Between the Sexes." In *Collected Papers*, vol. V, trans. under the supervision of J. Riviere. London: Hogarth Press, 1948, 186–197.

Frieze, Irene H.; Jacquelynne E. Parsons; Paula B. Johnson; Diane N. Ruble; and Gail L. Zellman. *Women and Sex Roles: A Social Psychological Perspective*. New York: W. W. Norton, 1978.

Frieze, Irene H., and S. J. Ramsey. "Nonverbal Maintenance of Traditional Sex Roles." *Journal of Social Issues*, 32(3) (1976):133–141.

Frodi, Ann; Jacqueline Macaulay; and Pauline R. Thome. "Are Women Always

Less Aggressive Than Men? A Review of the Experimental Literature." *Psychological Bulletin*, 84 (1977):634–660.

Furstenberg, F. "Birth Control Experience Among Pregnant Adolescents: The Process of Planned Parenthood." *Social Problems*, 19 (1971):192–203.

Gagnon, John H. *Human Sexualities.* Glenview, Ill.: Scott, Foresman, 1977.

Gainer, W. L. "Ability of the WISC Subtests to Discriminate Between Boys and Girls of Average Intelligence." *California Journal of Educational Research*, 13 (1962):9–16.

Gall, M. D. "The Relationship Between Masculinity-Femininity and Manifest Anxiety." *J. of Clinical Psychology*, 25 (1969):294–295.

Gayford, J. S. "Wife Battering: A Preliminary Survey of 100 Cases." *British Medical Journal* (January 25, 1975):196.

Gebhard, P. H.; W. B. Pomeroy; C. E. Martin; and Cornelia V. Christenson. *Pregnancy: Birth and Abortion.* New York: John Wiley & Sons, 1958.

Gelles, Richard. *The Violent Home: A Study of Physical Aggression Between Husbands and Wives.* New York: Sage Publications, 1974.

Gilley, Hoyt M., and Stephen S. Collier. "Sex Differences in the Use of Hostile Verbs." *J. of Psychology*, 76 (1970):33–37.

Goffman, Erving. "Genderisms." *Psychology Today*, 11(3) (1977):60.

———. *Interaction Ritual: Essays on Face-to-Face Behavior.* Garden City, N.Y.: Anchor Books, 1967.

Goldberg, P. "Are Some Women Prejudiced Against Women?" *Transaction*, 5 (April 1968):28–30.

Goldberg, Susan, and M. Lewis. "Play Behavior in the Year-Old Infant: Early Sex Differences." *Child Development*, 40 (1969):21–31.

Goleman, Daniel. "Jason and Medea's Love Story." *Psychology Today*, 9(11) (1976):84.

———. "Special Abilities of the Sexes: Do They Begin in the Brain?" *Psychology Today*, 12(6) (1978):48.

Golub, Sharon. "The Effect of Premenstrual Anxiety and Depression on Cognitive Function." *J. of Personality and Social Psychology*, 34 (1976): 99–104.

Gomberg, Edith S. "Women and Alcoholism." In V. Franks and V. Burtle, eds., *Women in Therapy.* New York: Brunner/Mazel, 1974.

Gomes, Beverly, and Stephen I. Abramowitz. "Sex-Related Patient and Therapist Effects on Clinical Judgment." *Sex Roles*, 2 (1976):1–14.

Gordon, E. M. "Acceptance of Pregnancy Before and Since Oral Contraception." *Obstetrics and Gynecology*, 29 (1967):144–146.

Gordon, R. E., and Katherine K. Gordon. "Factors in Postpartum Emotional Adjustment." *American Journal of Orthopsychiatry*, 37 (1967):359–360..

Gordon, R. E.; E. E. Kapostins; and Katherine K. Gordon. "Factors in Postpartum Emotional Adjustment." *Obstetrics and Gynecology*, 25 (1965): 158–166.

Gottschalk, L. A.; S. Kaplan; Goldine D. Gleser; and Carolyn M. Winget

"Variations in Magnitude of Emotion: A Method Applied to Anxiety and Hostility During Phases of the Menstrual Cycle." *Psychosomatic Medicine*, 24 (1962):300–311.

Gough, H. G. "A Cross-Cultural Analysis of the CPI Femininity Scale." *J. of Consulting Psychology*, 30 (1966):136–141.

————. "Identifying Psychological Femininity." *Educational and Psychological Measurement*, 12 (1952):427–439.

————. *Manual for the California Psychological Inventory*. Palo Alto, Calif.: Consulting Psychologists Press, 1957 (rev. ed. 1964).

Gove, W. R., and Jeannette F. Tudor. "Adult Sex Roles and Mental Illness." *American Journal of Sociology*, 78 (1973):812–835.

Graham, P. A. "Women in Academe." *Science*, 169 (1970):1284–1290.

Gray, S. W. "Masculinity-Femininity in Relation to Anxiety and Social Acceptance." *Child Development*, 28 (1957):203–214.

Greenblatt, R. "Metabolic and Psychosomatic Disorders in Menopausal Women." *Geriatrics*, 10 (1955):165.

Grier, W. H., and P. M. Cobbs. *Black Rage*. New York: Basic Books, 1968.

Gurin, G.; J. Veroff; and S. Feld. *Americans View Their Mental Health*. New York: Basic Books, 1960.

Haavio-Mannila, Elina. "Sex Differentiation in Role Expectations and Performance." *J. of Marriage and the Family*, 29 (1967):568–578.

Hacker, Helen M. "Women as a Minority Group." *Social Forces*, 30 (1951): 60–69.

Hall, C. S., and G. Lindzey. *Theories of Personality*. 2d ed. New York: John Wiley & Sons, 1970.

Hall, Judith A. "Gender Effects in Decoding Nonverbal Cues." *Psychological Bulletin*, 85 (1978):845–857.

Hamilton, Eleanor. "Emotional Aspects of Pregnancy: An Intensive Study of Fourteen Normal Primiparae." Unpublished doctoral dissertation, Columbia University, 1955.

Hampson, J. L. "Determinants of Psychosexual Orientation." In F. A. Beach, ed., *Sex and Behavior*. New York: John Wiley & Sons, 1965.

Hampson, J. L., and J. G. Hampson. "The Ontogenesis of Sexual Behavior in Man." In W. C. Young, ed., *Sex and Internal Secretions, Vol. II.* Baltimore: Williams & Wilkins, 1961.

Harding, M. Esther. *Woman's Mysteries Ancient and Modern: A Psychological Interpretation of the Feminine Principle As Portrayed in Myth, Story, and Dreams*. New York: G. P. Putnam's Sons, 1971.

Harford, T. C.; C. H. Willis; and H. L. Deabler. "Personality Correlates of Masculinity-Femininity." *Psychological Reports*, 21 (1967):881–884.

Hariton, E. Barbara. "The Sexual Fantasies of Women." *Psychology Today*, 6 (March 1973):39–44.

Harris, Gloria G., and Susan M. Osborn. *Assertiveness Training for Women*. Springfield, Ill.: Charles C. Thomas, 1974.

Harris, G. W. and S. Levine. "Sexual Differentiation of the Brain and Its Experimental Control." *J. of Physiology,* 181 (1965):379–400.

Harris, S. "Influence of Subject and Experimenter Sex in Psychological Research." *J. of Consulting and Clinical Psychology,* 37 (1971):291–294.

Hartlage, L. "Sex-Linked Inheritance of Spatial Ability." *Perceptual and Motor Skills,* 31 (1970):610.

Hartley, Ruth E. "Children's Concepts of Male and Female Roles." *Merrill-Palmer Quarterly,* 6 (1959–60):83–91.

———. "Some Implications of Current Changes in Sex Role Patterns." *Merrill-Palmer Quarterly,* 3 (1960):153–164.

———. "Sex Role Pressures and Socialization of the Male Child." *Psychological Reports,* 5 (1959):457–468.

Hartnagel, T. F. "Father Absence and Self-Conception Among Lower Class White and Negro Boys." *Social Problems,* 18 (1970):152–163.

Havens, Elizabeth. "Women, Work and Wedlock: A Note on Female Marital Patterns in the United States." *American Journal of Sociology,* 78 (1973):975–981.

Hays, H. R. *The Dangerous Sex: The Myth of Feminine Evil.* New York: G. P. Putnam's Sons, 1964.

Hedblom, J. H. "The Female Homosexual: Social and Attitudinal Dimensions." In J. A. McCaffrey, ed., *The Homosexual Dialectic.* Englewood Cliffs, N.J.: Prentice-Hall, 1972.

Heilbrun, A. B. "Measurement of Masculine and Feminine Sex Role Identities as Independent Dimensions." *J. of Consulting and Clinical Psychology,* 44 (1976):183–190.

Heiman, Julia R. "The Physiology of Erotica: Women's Sexual Arousal." *Psychology Today,* 8(11) (April 1975):90–94.

Heiman, Julia; Leslie LoPiccolo; and Joseph LoPiccolo. *Becoming Orgasmic: A Sexual Growth Program for Women.* Englewood Cliffs, N.J.: Prentice-Hall, 1976.

Helson, Ravenna. "Personality of Women with Imaginative and Artistic Interests. The Role of Masculinity, Originality, and Other Characteristics in Their Creativity." *J. of Personality,* 34 (1966):1–25.

———. "Sex Differences in Creative Style." *J. of Personality,* 35 (1967):214–233.

———. "Women Mathematicians and the Creative Personality." *J. of Consulting and Clinical Psychology,* 36 (1971):210–220.

Henley, Nancy. "Power, Sex, and Nonverbal Communication." In B. Thorne and N. Henley, eds., *Language and Sex: Difference and Dominance.* Rowley, Mass.: Newbury House, 1975.

———. "Status and Sex: Some Touching Observations." *Bulletin of the Psychonomic Society,* 2 (1973):92–93.

Henley, Nancy, and Jo Freeman. "The Sexual Politics of Interpersonal Behavior." In J. Freeman, ed., *Women: A Feminist Perspective.* Palo Alto, Calif.: Mayfield Publishing Co., 1975.

Henton, C. L. "The Effect of Socioeconomic and Emotional Factors on the Onset of Menarche Among Negro and White Girls." *J. of Genetic Psychology*, 98 (1961):255–264.

Hersey, R. B. "Emotional Cycles in Man." *J. of Mental Science*, 77 (1931): 151–169.

Hoffman, Lois W. "Early Childhood Experiences and Women's Achievement Motives." *J. of Social Issues*, 28(2) (1972):129–155.

———. "Effects of Maternal Employment on the Child: A Review of the Research." *Developmental Psychology*, 10 (1974a):204–228.

———. "The Employment of Women, Education, and Fertility." *Merrill-Palmer Quarterly*, 20 (1974b):99–119.

Hoffman, Martin L. "Sex Differences in Empathy and Related Behaviors." *Psychological Bulletin*, 84 (1977):712–722.

Holmstrom, Lynda L. *The Two-Career Family*. Cambridge, Mass.: Schenkman, 1972.

Holroyd, Jean C., and Annette M. Brodsky. "Psychologists' Attitudes and Practices Regarding Erotic and Nonerotic Physical Contact with Patients." *American Psychologist*, 34 (1977):843–849.

Holter, Harriet. "Sex Roles and Social Change." *Acta Sociologica*, 14 (1971): 2–12.

———. *Sex Roles and Social Structure*. Oslo: Universitet-forlaget, 1970.

Hooke, J. F., and P. A. Marks. "MMPI Characteristics of Pregnancy." *J. of Clinical Psychology*, 18 (1962):316–317.

Hopkins, J. H. "The Lesbian Personality." *British Journal of Psychiatry*, 115 (1969):1433–1436.

Horner, Matina S. "Fail: Bright Women." *Psychology Today*, 3(6) (1969):36.

———. "Femininity and Achievement: A Basic Inconsistency." In J. Bardwick; E. Douvan; M. Horner; and D. Gutman, eds., *Feminine Personality and Conflict*. Belmont, Calif.: Brooks/Cole, 1970a.

———. "The Motive to Avoid Success and Changing Aspirations of College Women." In *Women on Campus: 1970, A Symposium*. Ann Arbor, Mich.: Center for the Continuing Education of Women, 1970b.

———. "Toward an Understanding of Achievement-Related Conflicts in Women." *J. of Social Issues*, 28(2) (1972):157–175.

Horney, Karen. "The Flight from Womanhood." *International Journal of Psychoanalysis*, 7 (1926):324–339.

———. "On the Genesis of the Castration Complex in Women." *International Journal of Psychoanalysis*, 5 (1924):50–65.

House, W. C. "Actual and Perceived Differences in Male and Female Expectancies and Minimal Goal Levels as a Function of Competition." *J. of Personality*, 42 (1974):493–509.

Howard, Ephraim M., and Joyce L. Howard. "Women in Institutions: Treatment in Prisons and Mental Hospitals." In V. Franks and V. Burtle, eds., *Women in Therapy*. New York: Brunner/Mazel, 1974.

Huang, Lucy J. "A Re-evaluation of the Primary Role of the Communist Chinese Woman: the Homemaker or the Worker." *Marriage and Family Living*, (May 1963):162–168.

Humphreys, L. *Tearoom Trade: Impersonal Sex in Public Places*. Chicago: Aldine, 1970.

Hunt, M. *Sexual Behavior in the 1970s*. Chicago: Playboy Press, 1974.

Huston-Stein, Aletha, and Ann Higgins-Trenk. "The Development of Females from Childhood Through Adulthood: Career and Feminine Role Orientations." In P. D. Baltes, ed., *Life-Span Development and Behavior*, Vol. I. New York: Academic Press, 1978.

Hyde, Janet S. *Understanding Human Sexuality*. New York: McGraw-Hill, 1979.

Hyde, Janet S.; Eva R. Geiringer; and Wendy M. Yen. "On the Empirical Relation Between Spatial Ability and Sex Differences in Other Aspects of Cognitive Performance." *Multivariate Behavioral Research*, 10 (1975):289–310.

Hyde, Janet S., and Diane E. Phillis. "Androgyny Across the Lifespan." *Developmental Psychology*, 15 (1979):334–336.

Hyde, Janet S.; B. G. Rosenberg; and JoAnn Behrman. "Tomboyism." *Psychology of Women Quarterly*, 2 (1977):73–75.

Hyde, Janet S., and John R. Schuck. "The Development of Sex Differences in Aggression." Paper presented at American Psychological Association Meetings, San Francisco, 1977.

Hyman, H. H., and J. S. Reed. "'Black Matriarchy' Reconsidered: Evidence from Secondary Analysis of Sample Survey." *Public Opinion Quarterly*, 33 (1969):346–354.

Ivey, M. E., and Judith M. Bardwick. "Patterns of Affective Fluctuation in the Menstrual Cycle." *Psychosomatic Medicine*, 30 (1968):336–345.

Izard, C. E., and S. Caplan. "Sex Differences in Emotional Responses to Erotic Literature." *J. of Consulting and Clinical Psychology*, 42 (1974):468.

Jacklin, Carol N.; Eleanor E. Maccoby; and A. E. Dick. "Barrier Behavior and Toy Preference: Sex Differences and Their Absence in the Year-Old Child." *Child Development*, 44 (1973):196–200.

Jackson, Jacquelyne J. "Black Women in Racist Society." In B. Brown, B. Kramer, and C. Willie, eds., *Racism and Mental Health*. Pittsburgh: University of Pittsburgh Press, 1972.

———. "Family Organization and Technology." In K. S. Miller and R. M. Dreger, eds., *Comparative Studies of Blacks and Whites in the United States*. New York: Seminar Press, 1973.

Jakubowski, Patricia A. "Assertive Behavior and Clinical Problems of Women." In E. I. Rawlings and D. K. Carter, eds., *Psychotherapy for Women*. Springfield, Ill.: Charles C. Thomas, 1977.

Jakubowski-Spector, Patricia. "Facilitating the Growth of Women Through Assertive Training." *The Counseling Psychologist*, 4 (1973):75.

Jamison, Kay R.; D. K. Wellisch; and R. O. Pasnau. "Psychosocial Aspects of

Mastectomy: I. The Woman's Perspective." *American Journal of Psychiatry*, 135 (1978):432–436.

Janowsky, D. S., et al. "Premenstrual-Menstrual Increases in Psychiatric Hospital Admission Rates." *American Journal of Obstetrics and Gynecology*, 103 (1969):189–192.

Janowsky, D. S.; W. E. Fann; and J. M. Davis. "Monoamines and Ovarian Hormone Linked Sexual and Emotional Changes: A Review." *Archives of Sexual Behavior*, 1 (1971):205–218.

Jokl, E. *Medical Sociology and Cultural Anthropology of Sport and Physical Education*. Springfield, Ill.: Charles C. Thomas, 1964.

Jones, E. E.; D. E. Kanouse; H. H. Kelley; R. E. Nisbett; S. Valins; and B. Weiner. *Attribution: Perceiving the Causes of Behavior*. Morristown, N.J.: General Learning Press, 1971.

Jones, Mary C. "Personality Antecedents and Correlates of Drinking Patterns in Women." *J. of Consulting and Clinical Psychology*, 36 (1971):61–69.

Jourard, Sidney M. "An Exploratory Study of Body-Accessibility." *British Journal of Social and Clinical Psychology*, 5 (1966):221–231.

Jung, C. G., ed., *Man and His Symbols*. Garden City, N.Y.: Doubleday, 1964.

Kagan, J. *Understanding Children*. New York: Harcourt Brace Jovanovich, 1971.

Kagan, J., and H. A. Moss. *Birth to Maturity*. New York: John Wiley & Sons, 1962.

Kane, F. J.; M. A. Lipton; and J. A. Ewing. "Hormonal Influences in Female Sexual Response." *Archives of General Psychiatry*, 20 (1969):202–209.

Kanin, Eugene J. "Selected Dyadic Aspects of Male Sex Aggression." *J. of Sex Research*, 5 (1969):12–28.

Kanin, Eugene J., and Stanley R. Parcell. "Sexual Aggression: A Second Look at the Offended Female." *Archives of Sexual Behavior*, 6 (1977):67–76.

Kanter, Rosabeth Moss. "Women in Organizations: Sex Roles, Group Dynamics, and Change Strategies." In A. Sargent, ed., *Beyond Sex Roles*. St. Paul, Minn.: West, 1977.

Kantor, H. I.; Carmen M. Michael; S. H. Boulas; H. Shore; and H. W. Ludvigson. "The Administration of Estrogens to Older Women; a Psychometric Evaluation." Seventh International Congress of Gerontology Proceedings, June 1966.

Kaplan, Alexandra G. "Androgyny as a Model of Mental Health for Women: From Theory to Therapy." In A. G. Kaplan and J. P. Bean, eds., *Beyond Sex-Role Stereotypes: Readings Toward a Psychology of Androgyny*. Boston: Little, Brown, 1976.

———. "Clarifying the Concept of Androgyny: Implications for Therapy." *Psychology of Women Quarterly*, 3 (1979):223–230.

Kaplan, Helen S., and C. J. Sager. "Sexual Patterns at Different Ages." *Medical Aspects of Human Sexuality*, (June 1971):10–23.

Karabenick, S. A., and Joan M. Marshall. "Performance of Females as a Function of Fear of Success, Fear of Failure, Type of Opponent, and Performance-Contingent Feedback." *J. of Personality*, 42 (1974):220–237.

Katchadourian, H. A., and D. T. Lunde. *Fundamentals of Human Sexuality*. New York: Holt, Rinehart & Winston, 1972.

Kegel, A. H. "Sexual Functions of the Pubbococcygeus Muscle." *Western Journal of Surgery*, 60 (1952):521–524.

Kenyon, F. E. "Studies in Female Homosexuality—Psychological Test Results," *J. of Consulting and Clinical Psychology*, 32 (1968):510–513.

Key, Mary Ritchie. *Male/Female Language*. Metuchen, N.J.: Scarecrow Press, 1975.

Kincaid, Marylou B. "Changes in Sex-Role Attitudes and Self-Actualization of Adult Women Following a Consciousness-Raising Group." *Sex Roles*, 3 (1977):329–336.

Kinsey, A. C.; W. B. Pomeroy; and C. E. Martin. *Sexual Behavior in the Human Male*. Philadelphia: Saunders, 1948.

Kinsey, A. C.; W. B. Pomeroy; C. E. Martin; and P. H. Gebhard. *Sexual Behavior in the Human Female*. Philadelphia: Saunders, 1953.

Kinsey, Barry A. *The Female Alcoholic: A Social Psychological Study*. Springfield, Ill.: Charles C. Thomas, 1966.

Kirkpatrick, J. J. "Occupational Aspirations, Opportunities, and Barriers." In K. S. Miller and R. M. Dreger, eds., *Comparative Studies of Blacks and Whites in the United States*. New York: Seminar Press, 1973.

Kirsh, Barbara. "Consciousness-Raising Groups as Therapy for Women." In V. Franks and V. Burtle, eds., *Women in Therapy*. New York: Brunner/Mazel, 1974.

Klaus, M. A., et al. "Maternal Attachment: Importance of the First Postpartum Days." *New England Journal of Medicine*, 286 (1972):460–463.

Knop, C. A. "The Dynamics of Newly Born Babies." *J. of Pediatrics*, 29 (1946):721–728.

Koch, Helen L. "Sissiness and Tomboyishness in Relation to Sibling Characteristics." *J. of Genetic Psychology*, 88 (1956):231–244.

Kohlberg, L. "A Cognitive-Developmental Analysis of Children's Sex-Role Concepts and Attitudes." In E. E. Maccoby, ed., *The Development of Sex Differences*. Stanford: Stanford University Press, 1966.

———. "Stage and Sequence: The Cognitive-Developmental Approach to Socialization." In D. A. Goslin, ed., *Handbook of Socialization Theory and Research*. Chicago: Rand McNally, 1969.

Komarovsky, Mirra. "Cultural Contradictions and Sex Roles." *American Journal of Sociology*, 52 (1946):184–189.

———. "Cultural Contradictions and Sex Roles: The Masculine Case." *American Journal of Sociology*, 78 (1973):873–884.

Konopka, Gisela. *Young Girls: A Portrait of Adolescence*. Englewood Cliffs, N.J.: Spectrum Books, 1975.

Kramer, Cheris. "Folk-Linguistics: Wishy-washy Mommy Talk." *Psychology Today*, (June 1974a):82–89.

————. "Women's Speech: Separate But Unequal?" *Quarterly Journal of Speech* (February, 1974b):14–24.

————. "Stereotypes of Women's Speech: The Word from Cartoons." *J. of Popular Culture*, (1976).

Kramer, Cheris; Barrie Thorne; and Nancy Henley. "Perspectives on Language and Communication." *Signs*, 3 (1978):638–651.

Kronhausen, Phyllis, and E. Kronhausen. *The Sexually Responsive Woman.* New York: Grove Press, 1964.

Kukla, A. "Attributional Determinants of Achievement-Related Behavior." *J. of Personality and Social Psychology*, 21 (1972):166–174.

Kuvlesky, W., and A. Obordo. "A Racial Comparison of Teenage Girls' Projection for Marriage and Procreation." *J. of Marriage and the Family*, 34 (February 1972):75–84.

Ladner, Joyce A. *Tomorrow's Tomorrow: The Black Woman.* Garden City, N.Y.: Doubleday, 1971.

Lakoff, Robin. "Language and Woman's Place." *Language and Society*, 2 (1973):45–79. Reprinted in paperback by Harper & Row, 1975.

Lanson, Lucienne. *From Woman to Woman.* New York: Knopf, 1975.

Lazarus, Arnold A. "Women in Behavior Therapy." In V. Franks and V. Burtle, eds., *Women in Therapy.* New York: Brunner/Mazel, 1974.

Lederer, W. *The Fear of Women.* New York: Harcourt Brace Jovanovich, 1968.

Lenney, Ellen. "Women's Self-Confidence in Achievement Settings." *Psychological Bulletin*, 84 (1977):1–13.

Lerner, Gerda. *Black Women in White America: A Documentary History.* New York: Pantheon, 1972.

Levin, Robert J., and Amy Levin. "Sexual Pleasure: The Surprising Preferences of 100,000 Women." *Redbook*, 145 (September 1975):51. And "The Redbook Report on Premarital and Extramarital Sex." *Redbook*, 145(6) (October 1975):38.

Levy, Jere. "Lateral Specialization of the Human Brain: Behavioral Manifestation and Possible Evolutionary Basis." In J. A. Kiger, ed., *The Biology of Behavior.* Corvalis: Oregon University Press, 1972.

Levy-Agresti, Jere, and R. W. Sperry. "Differential Perceptual Capacities in Major and Minor Hemispheres." *Proceedings of the National Academy of Science*, 61 (1968):1151.

Lewin, K. "Self-Hatred Among Jews." *Contemporary Jewish Record*, 4 (1941): 219–232.

Lewis, M. "State as an Infant-Environment Interaction: Analysis of Mother-Infant Interaction as a Function of Sex." *Merrill-Palmer Quarterly*, 18 (1972):95–121.

Lewis, M.; W. Meyers; J. Kagan; and R. Grossberg. "Attention to Visual Patterns in Infants." Paper presented at the Symposium on Studies of Attention in Infants. American Psychological Association, Philadelphia, 1963.

Lipman-Blumen, Jean. "How Ideology Shapes Women's Lives." *Scientific American*, 226(1) (1972):34–42.

Ljung, B. "The Adolescent Spurt in Mental Growth." *Stockholm Studies in Educational Psychology*, 8 (1965).

Loney, J. "Background Factors, Sexual Experiences and Attitudes Toward Treatment in Two 'Normal' Homosexual Samples." *J. of Consulting and Clinical Psychology*, 38 (1972):57–65.

Longstaff, H. P. "Practice Effects on the Minnesota Vocational Test for Clerical Workers." *J. of Applied Psychology*, 38 (1954):18–20.

LoPiccolo, Joseph, and Charles Lobitz. "The Role of Masturbation in the Treatment of Sexual Dysfunction." *Archives of Sexual Behavior*, 2 (1972):163–171.

Lopata, Helen Z. "Social Relations of Black and White Widowed Women in a Northern Metropolis." *American Journal of Sociology*, (1973): 1003–1010.

Loraine, J. A.; D. A. Adampopoulos; K. E. Kirkhan; A. A. Ismail; and G. A. Dove. "Patterns of Hormone Excretion in Male and Female Homosexuals." *Nature*, 234 (1971):552–554.

Lott, Bernice. "Behavioral Concordance with Sex Role Ideology Related to Play Areas. Creativity, and Parental Sex Typing of Children." *J. of Personality and Social Psychology*, 36 (1978):1087–1100.

Luria, Zella. "Recent Women College Graduates: A Study of Rising Expectations." *American Journal of Orthopsychiatry*, 44 (1974):312–326.

Maccoby, Eleanor E. "The Meaning of Being Female." *Contemporary Psychology*, 17 (1972):369–372.

———. "Sex Differences in Intellectual Functioning." In E. E. Maccoby, ed., *The Development of Sex Differences*. Stanford: Stanford University Press, 1966.

Maccoby, Eleanor E., and S. Shirley Feldman. "Mother-Attachment and Stranger Reactions in the Third Year of Life." *Monographs of the Society for Research in Child Development*, 37(1) (1972):1–86.

Maccoby, Eleanor E., and Carol N. Jacklin. *The Psychology of Sex Differences*. Stanford: Stanford University Press, 1974.

———. "Stress, Activity and Proximity Seeking: Sex Differences in the Year-Old Child." *Child Development*, 44 (1973):34–42.

Machotka, P., and A. S. Ferber. "Delineation of Family Roles," *American Journal of Orthopsychiatry*, 37 (1967):409–410.

Macdonald, Nancy E., and Janet S. Hyde. "Fear of Success, Need Achievement, and Fear of Failure: A Factor-Analytic Study." *Sex Roles*, (1979).

Mack, Thomas M., et al. "Estrogens and Endometrial Cancer in a Retirement Community." *New England Journal of Medicine*, 294 (1976):1262–1267.

MacKinnon, D. W. "The Nature and Nurture of Creative Talent." *American Psychologist*, 17 (1962):484–495.

Malina, R. M. "Biological Substrata." In K. S. Miller and R. M. Dreger, eds., *Comparative Studies of Blacks and Whites in the United States*. New York: Seminar Press, 1973.

Mandel, William. *Soviet Women*. Garden City, N.Y.: Anchor, 1975.

Marcus, Dale E., and Willis F. Overton. "The Development of Cognitive Gender Constancy and Sex Preferences." *Child Development*, 49 (1978):434–444.

Marini, Margaret M. "Sex Differences in the Determination of Adolescent Aspirations: A Review of Research." *Sex Roles*, 4 (1978):723–754.

Marmor, J., ed. *Sexual Inversion: The Multiple Roots of Homosexuality*. New York: Basic Books, 1965.

Martin, Del. *Battered Wives*. San Francisco: Glide Publications, 1976.

Martin, Del, and Phyllis Lyon. *Lesbian/Woman*. San Francisco: Glide Publications, 1972.

Martyna, Wendy. "Beyond the He/Man Approach: The Case for Linguistic Change." *Signs*, (1979).

Marx, Jean L. "Estrogen Drugs: Do They Increase the Risk of Cancer?" *Science*, 191 (1976):838.

Masters, W. H., and Virginia E. Johnson. *Human Sexual Inadequacy*. Boston: Little, Brown, 1970.

———. *Human Sexual Response*. Boston: Little, Brown, 1966.

Mayo, Peter. "Sex Differences and Psychopathology." In B. Lloyd and J. Archer, eds., *Exploring Sex Differences*. New York: Academic Press, 1976.

McArthur, Leslie, and Beth G. Resko. "The Portrayal of Men and Women in American Television Commercials." *J. of Social Psychology*, 97 (1975):209–220.

McCary, J. L. *Human Sexuality*. 2d ed. New York: Van Nostrand, 1973.

McClelland, D. C.; J. W. Atkinson; R. A. Clark; and E. L. Lowell. *The Achievement Motive*. New York: Appleton-Century-Crofts, 1953.

McClintock, M. K. "Menstrual Synchrony and Suppression," *Nature*, 229 (1971):244–245.

McConnell-Ginet, Sally. "Intonation in a Woman's World." *Signs*, 3 (1978): 541–559.

McGinnis, M. *Single: The Woman's View*. Old Tappan, N.J.: Fleming H. Revell, 1974.

McGraw-Hill Book Company. *Guidelines for Equal Treatment of the Sexes in McGraw-Hill Book Company Publications*. New York: McGraw-Hill, 1974.

McKenna, Wendy, and Florence L. Denmark. "Gender and Nonverbal Behavior as Cues to Status and Power." *Annals of the New York Academy of Sciences*, in press.

McKenna, Wendy, and Suzanne J. Kessler. "Experimental Design as a Source of Sex Bias in Social Psychology." *Sex Roles*, 3 (1977):117–128.

McKinlay, Sonja M., and Margot Jeffreys. "The Menopausal Syndrome." *British Journal of Preventive and Social Medicine*, 28(2) (1974):108.

McMahan, I. D. "Sex Differences in Causal Attributions Following Success and Failure." Paper presented at Eastern Psychological Association Meetings, April 1971.

———. "Sex Differences in Expectancy of Success As a Function of Task." Paper presented at Eastern Psychological Association Meetings, April 1972.

McMillan, Julie R., et al. "Women's Language: Uncertainty or Interpersonal Sensitivity and Emotionality?" *Sex Roles*, 3 (1977):545–560.

Mead, Margaret. "Cultural Determinants of Sexual Behavior." In W. C. Young, ed., *Sex and Internal Secretions*, Vol. II. Baltimore: Williams & Wilkins, 1961.

———. *Culture and Commitment: A Study of the Generation Gap.* Garden City, N.Y.: Doubleday, 1969.

———. *Sex and Temperament in Three Primitive Societies.* New York: William Morrow, 1935.

———. *Male and Female.* New York: William Morrow, 1949.

Mead, Margaret, and Frances B. Kaplan, eds. *American Women: The Report of the President's Commission on the Status of Women.* New York: Charles Scribner's, 1965.

Mednick, Martha T. S. "Social Change and Sex-Role Inertia: The Case of the Kibbutz." In M. T. S. Mednick, S. G. Tangri, and L. W. Hoffman, eds., *Women and Achievement: Social and Motivational Analyses.* New York: Halsted Press, 1975.

Mehrabian, Albert. "Verbal and Nonverbal Interaction of Strangers in a Waiting Situation." *J. of Experimental Research in Personality,* 5 (1971):127–138.

Messer, S. B., and M. Lewis. "Social Class and Sex Differences in the Attachment and Play Behaviors of the Year-Old Infant." *Merrill-Palmer Quarterly,* 18 (1972):295–306.

Meyer, J. W., and Barbara I. Sobieszek. "Effects of a Child's Sex on Adult Interpretations of Its Behavior." *Developmental Psychology,* 6 (1972):42–48.

Miele, J. "Sex Differences in Intelligence: The Relationship of Sex to Intelligence As Measured by the Wechsler Adult Intelligence Scale and the Wechsler Intelligence Scale for Children." *Dissertation Abstracts,* 18 (1958):2213.

Mill, J. S. "The Subjection of Women," 1869. Reprinted in *Three Essays by J. S. Mill.* London: Oxford University Press, 1966.

Miller, Casey, and Kate Swift. *Words and Women.* Garden City, N.Y.: Anchor Press/Doubleday, 1976.

Millett, Kate. *Sexual Politics.* Garden City, N.Y.: Doubleday, 1969.

Mischel, W. "A Social-Learning View of Sex Differences in Behavior. In E. E. Maccoby, ed., *The Development of Sex Differences.* Stanford: Stanford University Press, 1966.

Monahan, Lynn; Deanna Kuhn; and Phillip Shaver. "Intrapsychic Versus

Cultural Explanations of the 'Fear of Success' Motive." *J. of Personality and Social Psychology,* 29 (1974):60–64.

Money, J. "Nativism Versus Culturalism in Gender-Identity Differentiation." Paper presented at American Association for the Advancement of Science Symposium in Sex Role Learning in Childhood and Adolescence, Washington, D.C., December 1972.

———. "Sex Hormones and Other Variables in Human Eroticism." In W. C. Young, ed., *Sex and Internal Secretions, Vol. 2.* Baltimore: Williams & Wilkins, 1961.

———. "Sexual Dimorphism and Homosexual Gender Identity." *Psychological Bulletin,* 73 (1970):425–440.

Money, J., and Anke Ehrhardt. *Man & Woman, Boy & Girl.* Baltimore: The Johns Hopkins University Press, 1972.

———. "Prenatal Hormonal Exposure: Possible Effects on Behavior in Man." In R. P. Michael, ed., *Endocrinology and Human Behavior,* London: Oxford University Press, 1968.

Money, J.; J. L. Hampson; and J. G. Hampson. "An Examination of Some Basic Sexual Concepts: The Evidence of Human Hermaphroditism." *Bulletin of the Johns Hopkins Hospital,* 97 (1955):301–319.

Montagu, A. *The Natural Superiority of Women.* New York: P. F. Collier, 1964; first published 1952.

Moos, R. "Psychological Aspects of Oral Contraceptives." *Archives of General Psychiatry,* 30 (1968):853–867.

Moss, H. A. "Sex, Age and State as Determinants of Mother-Infant Interaction." *Merrill-Palmer Quarterly,* 13 (1967):19–36.

Moulton, Janice R.; George M. Robinson; and Cherin Elias. "Psychology in Action: Sex Bias in Language Use: "Neutral" Pronouns That Aren't." *American Psychologist,* 33 (1978):1032–1036.

Mulvihill, D. J., et al. *Crimes of Violence, a Staff Report to the National Commission on the Causes and Prevention of Violence.* Washington, D.C.: U.S. Government Printing Office, 1969, Vol. 11.

Murdock, G. P. "Comparative Data on the Division of Labor by Sex." *Social Forces,* 15 (1937):4.

Murray, Saundra R., and Martha T. S. Mednick. "Black Women's Achievement Orientation: Motivational and Cognitive Factors." *Psychology of Women Quarterly,* 1 (1977):247–259.

Murty, Lakshmi. "Transition for Whom? Adolescence Theories with Androcentric Bias." *Sex Roles,* 4 (1978): 369–374.

Mussen, P. H. "Long-Term Consequents of Masculinity of Interests in Adolescence." *J. of Consulting Psychology,* 26 (1962):435–440.

Neugarten, Bernice L. "A New Look at Menopause." In C. Tavris, ed., *The Female Experience.* Del Mar, Calif.: CRM, 1973.

Neugarten, Bernice L., and Ruth J. Kraines. "Menopausal Symptoms in Women of Various Ages." *Psychosomatic Medicine,* 27 (1965):266.

Newton, Niles. "Interrelationships Between Various Aspects of Female Reproductive Behavior: A Review." In J. Zubin and J. Money, eds., *Contemporary Sexual Behavior: Critical Issues in the 1970s*. Baltimore: Johns Hopkins University Press, 1973.

———. "Trebly Sensuous Woman." *Psychology Today*, 5 (July 1971):18.

Nobers, D. R. "The Effects of Father Absence and Mother's Characteristics on the Identification of Adolescent White and Negro Males." *Dissertation Abstracts*, (1968):1508-B–1509-B.

Oakes, Merilee. "Pills, Periods, and Personality." Unpublished doctoral dissertation, University of Michigan, 1970.

Oakley, Anne. *The Sociology of Housework*. Bath, England: Pitman, 1974.

Oberstone, Andrea K., and Harriet Sukoneck. "Psychological Adjustment and Life Style of Single Lesbians and Single Heterosexual Women." *Psychology of Women Quarterly*, 1 (1976):172–188.

O'Leary, Virginia. *Toward Understanding Women*. Monterey, Calif.: Brooks/Cole, 1977.

Orloff, Kossia. "The Trap of 'Androgyny.'" *Regionalism and the Female Imagination*, 4(ii) (1978):1–3.

Osofsky, Joy D., and Howard J. Osofsky. "The Psychological Reactions of Patients to Legalized Abortions." *American Journal of Orthopsychiatry*, 42 (1972):48–60.

Paige, Karen E. "Effects of Oral Contraceptives on Affective Fluctuations Associated with the Menstrual Cycle." *Psychosomatic Medicine*, 33 (1971):515–537.

———. "Women Learn to Sing the Menstrual Blues." *Psychology Today*, 7(4) (September 1973):41.

Palme, O. "The Emancipation of Men." *J. of Social Issues*, 28(2) (1972): 237–246.

Paloma, Margaret M., and T. N. Garland. "The Married Professional Woman: A Study in the Tolerance of Domestication." *J. of Marriage and the Family*, 33 (1971):531–540.

Papanek, Hanna. "Men, Women, and Work: Reflections on the Two-Person Career." *American Journal of Sociology*, 78 (1973):852–872.

Parkes, C. M. "The First Year of Bereavement." *Psychiatry*, 33(4) (1970): 444–467.

Parlee, Mary B. "The Premenstrual Syndrome." *Psychological Bulletin*, 80 (1973):454–465.

———. "The Rhythms in Men's Lives." *Psychology Today*, (1978):82–91.

Parsons, T. "Age and Sex in the Social Structure in the United States," *American Sociological Review*, 7 (1942):604–606.

Parsons, T., and R. F. Bales. *Family, Socialization and Interaction Process*. Glencoe, Ill.: The Free Press, 1955.

Peplau, Letitia Anne; Susan Cochran; Karen Rook; and Christine Padesky. "Loving Women: Attachment and Autonomy in Lesbian Relationships." *J. of Social Issues*, 34(3) (1978):7–27.

Perls, Fritz, S. *Gestalt Therapy Verbatim*. Moab, Utah: Real People Press, 1969.

Persky, H.; K. D. Smith; and G. K. Basu. "Relation of Psychologic Measures of Aggression and Hostility to Testosterone Production in Man." *Psychosomatic Medicine*, 33 (1971):265–277.

Persky, Harold, et al. "Plasma Testosterone Level and Sexual Behavior of Couples." *Archives of Sexual Behavior*, 1 (1978):157–173.

Pheterson, G. I.; S. B. Kiesler; and P. A. Goldberg. "Evaluation of the Performance of Women as a Function of Their Sex, Achievement, and Personal History." *J. of Personality and Social Psychology*, 19 (1971): 114–118.

Phillips, Derek, and Bernard Segal. "Sexual Status and Psychiatric Symptoms." *American Sociological Review*, 34 (1969):58–72.

Phoenix, C. H.; R. W. Goy; A. A. Gerall; and W. C. Young. "Organizing Action of Prenatally Administered Testosterone Propionate on the Tissues Mediating Mating Behavior in the Female Guinea Pig." *Endocrinology*, 65 (1959):369–382.

Piaget, J. *The Construction of Reality in the Child*. New York: Basic Books, 1954.

Pizzey, Erin. *Scream Quietly or the Neighbors Will Hear*. London: If Books, 1974.

Pleck, Joseph H. "Masculinity-Femininity: Current and Alternate Paradigms." *Sex Roles*, 1 (1975):161–178.

Polster, Miriam. "Women in Therapy: A Gestalt Therapist's View." In V. Franks and V. Burtle, eds., *Women in Therapy*. New York: Brunner/Mazel, 1974.

Porter, Natalie P.; Florence L. Geis; and Joyce J. Walstedt. "Are Women Invisible as Leaders?" Paper presented at American Psychological Association Meetings, Toronto, August 1978.

Powell, Barbara. "The Empty Nest, Employment, and Psychiatric Symptoms in College-Educated Women." *Psychology of Women Quarterly*, 2 (1977):35–43.

Psathas, G. "Toward a Theory of Occupational Choice for Women." *Sociology and Social Research*, 52 (1968):253–265.

Puryear, G. R., and Martha S. Mednick. "Black Militancy, Affective Attachment, and Fear of Success in Black College Women." *J. of Consulting and Clinical Psychology*, 42 (1974):263–266.

Rabin, A. I. "The Sexes: Ideology and Reality in the Israeli Kibbutz." In G. H. Seward and R. C. Williamson, eds., *Sex Roles in Changing Society*. New York: Random House, 1970.

Radloff, Lenore. "Sex Differences in Depression: The Effects of Occupation and Marital Status." *Sex Roles*, 1 (1975):249–265.

Radloff, Lenore G., and Megan K. Monroe. "Sex Differences in Helplessness —with Implication for Depression." In L. S. Hansen and R. S. Rapoza, eds., *Career Development and Counseling of Women*. Springfield, Ill.: Charles C. Thomas, 1978.

Ramey, Estelle. "Men's Cycles." *Ms.*, (Spring 1972):8–14.

Rauh, J. L.; D. A. Schumsky; and M. T. Witt. "Heights, Weights, and Obesity in Urban School Children." *Child Development*, 38 (1967): 515–530.

Rawlings, Edna T., and Dianne K. Carter. "Feminist and Nonsexist Psychotherapy." In E. I. Rawlings and D. K. Carter, eds., *Psychotherapy for Women*. Springfield, Ill.: Charles C. Thomas, 1977.

Rebecca, Meda; Robert Hefner; and Barbara Oleshansky. "A Model of Sex-Role Transcendence." *J. of Social Issues*, 32(3) (1976):197–206.

Rees, L. "Psychosomatic Aspects of the Premenstrual Tension Syndrome." *J. of Mental Science*, 99 (1953):62–73.

Reinisch, June M. "Fetal Hormones, the Brain, and Human Sex Differences: A Heuristic, Integrative Review of the Recent Literature." *Archives of Sexual Behavior*, 3 (1974):51–90.

Reiss, I. L. "Sociological Studies of Sexual Standards." In G. Winokur, ed., *Determinants of Human Sexual Behavior*. Springfield, Ill.: Charles C. Thomas, 1963.

Rhodes, Barbara. "The Changing Role of the Black Woman." In R. Staples, ed., *The Black Family*. Belmont, Calif.: Wadsworth Publishing Co., 1971.

Riffaterre, Birgitte B. "Determination of Pregnancy Depression and Its Relation to Marital Status and Group Affiliation in a Single Ethnic Group." *Dissertation Abstracts*, 25 (1965):53–90.

Romm, M. E. "Sexuality and Homosexuality in Women." In J. Marmor, ed., *Sexual Inversion: The Multiple Roots of Homosexuality*. New York: Basic Books, 1965.

Rosaldo, Michelle Z. "Woman, Culture, and Society: A Theoretical Overview." In M. Z. Rosaldo and L. Lamphere, eds., *Woman, Culture, and Society*. Stanford: Stanford University Press, 1974.

Rosaldo, Michelle Z., and Louise Lamphere. *Woman, Culture, and Society*. Stanford: Stanford University Press, 1974.

Rosen, D. H. *Lesbianism: A Study of Female Homosexuality*. Springfield, Ill.: Charles C. Thomas, 1974.

Rosenberg, B. G. "Social Roles and Social Control: Changing Concepts of Masculinity-Femininity." In J. P. Scott and S. F. Scott, eds., *Social Control and Social Change*. Chicago: University of Chicago Press, 1971.

Rosenberg, B. G., and B. Sutton-Smith. "Family Interaction Effects on Masculinity-Femininity." *J. of Personality and Social Psychology*, 8 (1968):117–120.

———. "Family Structure and Sex Role Variations." *Nebraska Symposium on Motivation*, 1973. Lincoln: University of Nebraska Press, 1974.

———. "Ordinal Position and Sex Role Identification." *Genetic Psychology Monographs*, 70 (1964):297–328.

———. *Sex and Identity*. New York: Holt, Rinehart & Winston, 1972.

Rosenberg, Florence R., and Roberta G. Simmons. "Sex Differences in the Self-Concept in Adolescence." *Sex Roles*, 1 (1975):147–159.

Rosenberg, Morris. *Society and the Adolescent Self-Image*. Princeton, N.J.: Princeton University Press, 1965.

Rosenblatt, Paul C., and Michael R. Cunningham. "Sex Differences in Cross-Cultural Perspective." In B. Lloyd and J. Archer, eds., *Exploring Sex Differences*. New York: Academic Press, 1976.

Rosenkrantz, P. S., et al. "Sex-Role Stereotypes and Self-Concepts in College Students." *J. of Consulting and Clinical Psychology*, 32 (1968):287–295.

Rosenthal, R. *Experimenter Effects in Behavioral Research*. New York: Appleton-Century-Crofts, 1966.

Rosner, M. "Women in the Kibbutz: Changing Status and Concepts." *Asian and African Studies*, 3 (1967):35–68.

Rossi, Alice S. "Women in Science: Why So Few?" *Science*, 148 (1965): 1196–1202.

Roth, M. "The Phenomenology of Depressive States." *Canadian Psychiatric Association Journal*, 4(Supplement) (1959):532–554.

Roy, Maria, ed. *Battered Women*. New York: Van Nostrand, 1977a.

––––––. "A Current Survey of 150 Cases." In M. Roy, ed., *Battered Women*. New York: Van Nostrand, 1977b.

Rubin, Lillian. *Women of a Certain Age*. New York: Harper & Row, 1979.

Ruble, Diane N. "Premenstrual Symptoms: A Reinterpretation." *Science*, 197 (1977):291–292.

Rumenick, Donna K.; Deborah R. Capasso; and Clyde Hendrick. "Experimenter Sex Effects in Behavioral Research." *Psychological Bulletin*, 84 (1977):852–87.

Russell, Diana. *The Politics of Rape: The Victim's Perspective*. New York: Stein and Day, 1975.

Saghir, M., and E. Robins. *Male and Female Homosexuality*. Baltimore: Williams & Wilkins, 1973.

––––––. "Male and Female Homosexuality: Natural History." *Comprehensive Psychiatry*, 12 (1971):503–510.

Salhanick, H. A., and R. H. Margulis. "Hormonal Physiology of the Ovary." In J. J. Gold, ed., *Textbook of Gynecologic Endocrinology*. New York: Harper & Row, 1968.

Sayers, Dorothy. *Unpopular Opinions*. London: Victor Gollancz, 1946.

Scanzoni, Letha, and John Scanzoni. *Men, Women, and Change*. New York: McGraw-Hill, 1976.

Schafer, Siegrid. "Sociosexual Behavior in Male and Female Homosexuals: A Study in Sex Differences." *Archives of Sexual Behavior*, 6 (1977):355–364.

Schaller, G. B. *The Deer and the Tiger*. Chicago: University of Chicago Press, 1967.

Schmidt, G., and V. Sigusch. "Sex Differences in Responses to Psychosexual Stimulation by Films and Slides." *J. of Sex Research*, 6 (1970):268–283.

Schneidler, Gwendolyn G., and D. G. Patterson. "Sex Differences in Clerical Aptitude." *J. of Educational Psychology*, 33 (1942):303–309.

Schuckit, M. "The Woman Alcoholic: A Literature Review." *Psychiatry in Medicine*, 3 (1972):37–44.

Schuckit, M., et al. "Alcoholism I.: Two Types of Alcoholism in Women." *Archives of Environmental Health*, 18 (1969):301–306.

Schultz, Ardelle P. "Radical Feminism: A Treatment Modality for Addicted Women." In E. I. Rawlings and D. K. Carter, eds., *Psychotherapy for Women*. Springfield, Ill.: Charles C. Thomas, 1977.

Schulz, Murial R. "The Semantic Derogation of Woman." In B. Thorne and N. Henley, eds., *Language and Sex: Differences and Dominance*. Rowley, Mass.: Newbury House, 1975.

Sclare, A. B. "The Female Alcoholic." *British Journal of Addictions*, 65 (1970): 99–107.

Scott, Eileen; R. Illsley; and M. E. Biles. "A Psychological Investigation of Primigravidae, III. Some Aspects of Maternal Behavior." *J. of Obstetrics and Gynaecology of the British Empire*, 63 (1956):494.

Scott, Foresman and Company. *Guidelines for Improving the Image of Women in Textbooks*. Glenview, Ill.: Scott, Foresman, 1972.

Scottish Council for Research in Education. *The Intelligence of a Representative Group of Scottish Children*. London: University of London Press, 1939.

———. *The Trend of Scottish Intelligence*. London: University of London Press, 1949.

Sears, R. R. "Development of Gender Role." In F. A. Beach, ed., *Sex and Behavior*. New York: John Wiley & Sons, 1965.

———. Relation of Early Socialization Experiences to Self-Concepts and Gender Role in Middle Childhood." *Child Development*, 41 (1970): 267–289.

Seavy, Carol A.; Phyllis A. Katz; and Sue R. Zalk. "Baby X: The Effects of Gender Labels on Adult Responses to Infants." *Sex Roles*, 1 (1975): 103–110.

Seligman, Martin E. P. *Helplessness: On Depression, Development and Death*. San Francisco: Freeman, 1975.

Selkin, J. "Rape." *Psychology Today*, 8(8) (1975):70.

Serbin, Lisa A. et al. "A Comparison of Teacher Response to the Pre-academic and Problem Behavior of Boys and Girls." *Child Development*, 44 (1973):796–804.

Shainess, Natalie. "The Equitable Therapy of Women in Psychoanalysis." In E. I. Rawlings and D. K. Carter, eds., *Psychotherapy for Women*. Springfield, Ill.: Charles C. Thomas, 1977.

Shapiro, Johanna. "Socialization of Sex Roles in the Counseling Setting: Differential Counselor Behavioral and Attitudinal Responses to Typical and Atypical Female Sex Roles." *Sex Roles*, 3 (1977):173–184.

Shaver, Phillip. "Questions Concerning Fear of Success and Its Conceptual Relatives." *Sex Roles*, 2 (1976):305–320.

Sherfey, Mary Jane. "The Evolution and Nature of Female Sexuality in Relation to Psychoanalytic Theory." *J. of the American Psychoanalytic Association*, 14 (1966):28–128.

Sherman, Julia A. *On the Psychology of Women: A Survey of Empirical Studies*. Springfield, Ill.: Charles C. Thomas, 1971.

———. "Problem of Sex Differences in Space Perception and Aspects of Intellectual Functioning." *Psychological Review*, 74 (1967):290–299.

———. *Sex-Related Cognitive Differences*. Springfield, Ill.: Charles C. Thomas, 1978.

Shope, David F. *Interpersonal Sexuality*. Philadelphia: Saunders, 1975.

Shusterman, Lisa R. "The Psychosocial Factors of the Abortion Experience: A Critical Review." *Psychology of Women Quarterly*, 1 (1976):79–106.

Shuttleworth, Margaret. "A Biosocial and Developmental Theory of Male and Female Sexuality," *Marriage and Family Living*, 22 (1959):163–170.

Shuy, Roger W. "Sex as a Factor in Sociolinguistic Research." Paper presented at Anthropological Society of Washington, 1969. Available from Educational Resources Information Clearinghouse, No. ED027522.

Siegel, A.; L. Stolz; E. Hitchcok; and J. Adamson. "Dependence and Independence in Children." In F. Nye and L. Hoffman, eds., *The Employed Mother in America*. Chicago: Rand McNally, 1963.

Siegelman, M. "Adjustment of Homosexual and Heterosexual Women." *British Journal of Psychiatry*, 120 (1972):477–481.

Simon, J. G., and N. T. Feather. "Causal Attributions for Success and Failure at University Examinations." *J. of Educational Psychology*, 64 (1973):46–56.

Simon, Rita J.; Shirley M. Clark; and Kathleen Galway. "The Woman Ph.D.: A Recent Profile." *Social Problems*, 15 (1967):221–236.

Simpson, G. E., and J. M. Yinger. *Racial and Cultural Minorities*. 3d ed. New York: Harper & Row, 1965.

Singer, R. N. *Motor Learning and Human Performance*. New York: Macmillan, 1968.

Slater, P. "Parental Role Differentiation." *American J. of Sociology*, 67 (1961):296–311.

Sommer, Barbara. "The Effect of Menstruation on Cognitive and Perceptual-Motor Behavior: A Review." *Psychosomatic Medicine*, 35 (1973):515–534.

———. "Menstrual Cycle Changes and Intellectual Performance." *Psychosomatic Medicine*, 34 (1972):263–269.

Spence, Janet T., and Robert L. Helmreich. *Masculinity and Femininity*. Austin: University of Texas Press, 1978.

Spence, Janet T.; R. Helmreich; and J. Stapp. "Ratings of Self and Peers on Sex-Role Attributes and Their Relation to Self-Esteem." *J. of Personality and Social Psychology*, 1975.

Spiro, M. E. *Kibbutz: Venture in Utopia*. Cambridge, Mass.: Harvard University Press, 1956.

Spivack, G., and J. Spotts. "The Devereux Child Behavior Scale: Symptoms Behaviors in Latency Age Children." *American Journal of Mental Retardation*, 67 (1965):839–853.

Spreitzer, Elmer, and Lawrence Riley. "Factors Associated with Singlehood." *J. of Marriage and the Family*, 36 (1974):533–542.

Spreitzer, Elmer; Eldon E. Snyder; and David Larson. "Age, Marital Status, and Labor Force Participation as Related to Life Satisfaction." *Sex Roles*, 1 (1975):235–247.

Stafford, R. "Sex Differences in Spatial Visualization As Evidence of Sex-Linked Inheritance." *Perceptual and Motor Skills*, 13 (1961):428.

Staines, G. L.; Carol Tavris; and Toby E. Jayaratne. "The Queen Bee Syndrome." *Psychology Today*, 7(8) (January 1974):55.

Stark, Rodney, and James McEvoy. "Middle-Class Violence." *Psychology Today*, 30 (November 1970):52.

Stein, Aletha H. "The Influence of Social Reinforcement on the Achievement Behavior of Fourth-Grade Boys and Girls." *Child Development*, 40 (1969):727–736.

Stein, Aletha H., and Margaret M. Bailey. "The Socialization of Achievement Orientation in Females." *Psychological Bulletin*, 80 (1973):345–366.

Stein, L. S., et al. "A Comparison of Female and Male Neurotic Depressives." *J. of Clinical Psychology*, 32 (1976):19–21.

Steinman, Ann, and P. J. Fox. "Attitudes Towards Women's Family Role Among Black and White Undergraduates." *The Family Coordinator*, 19 (1970):363–367.

Steinmetz, Suzanne K. "Wifebeating, Husbandbeating — A Comparison of the Use of Physical Violence Between Spouses to Resolve Marital Rights." In M. Roy, ed., *Battered Women*. New York: Van Nostrand, 1977.

Stephens, W. N. "A Cross-Cultural Study of Menstrual Taboos." *Genetic Psychology Monographs*, 64 (1961):385–416.

Stewart, M.; F. Pitts; A. Craig; and W. Dieruf. "The Hyperactive Child Syndrome." *American Journal of Orthopsychiatry*, 36 (1966):861.

Stiller, R. "Why Girls Get Pregnant." *Sexology* (October 1966):162–165.

Stricker, G. "Implications of Research for Psychotherapeutic Treatment of Women." *American Psychologist*, 32 (1977):14–22.

Strodtbeck, F. L., and R. D. Mann. "Sex Differentiation in Jury Deliberation." *Sociometry*, 19 (1956):3–11.

Strodtbeck, F. L.; Rita M. James; and Charles Hawkins. "Social Status in Jury Deliberations." *American Sociological Review*, 22 (1957):713–719.

Sullerot, Evelyne. *Woman, Society, and Change*. New York: McGraw-Hill, 1971.

Summerhayes, Diana L., and Robert W. Suchner. "Power Implications of Touch in Male-Female Relationships." *Sex Roles*, 4 (1978):103–110.

Sutherland, H., and I. Stewart. "A Critical Analysis of the Premenstrual Syndrome." *Lancet*, 1 (1965):1180–1183.

Sutton-Smith, B., and B. G. Rosenberg. *The Sibling*. New York: Holt, Kinehart & Winston, 1970.

Swacker, Marjorie. "The Sex of the Speaker as a Sociolinguistic Variable." In B. Thorne and N. Henley, eds., *Language and Sex: Difference and Dominance*. Rowley, Mass.: Newbury House, 1975.

Szasz, T. S. "Legal and Moral Aspects of Homosexuality." In J. Marmor, ed., *Sexual Inversion: The Multiple Roots of Homosexuality*. New York: Basic Books, 1965.

Taleisnik, S.; L. Caligaris; and J. J. Astrada. "Sex Difference in Hypothalamo-Hypophysial Function." In C. H. Sawyer and R. A. Gorski, eds., *Steroid Hormones and Brain Function*. Berkeley: University of California Press, 1971.

Tangri, Sandra A. "Determinants of Occupational Role-Innovation Among College Women," *J. of Social Issues*, 28 (1972):177.

Tavris, Carol. "Masculinity." *Psychology Today*, 19(8) (January 1977):34.

Taylor, H. P. "Nausea and Vomiting of Pregnancy: Hyperemesis Gravidarum." In W. S. Kroger, ed., *Psychosomatic Obstetrics, Gynecology, and Endocrinology*. Springfield, Ill.: Charles C. Thomas, 1962.

————. "Teen-Age Sex: Letting the Pendulum Swing." *Time*, (August 21, 1972):34–38.

Terman, L. M. "Correlates of Orgasm Adequacy in a Group of 556 Wives." *J. of Psychology*, 32 (1951):115–172.

Terman, L. M., and Melita H. Oden. *The Gifted Child Grows Up*. Stanford: Stanford University Press, 1947.

Thorne, Barrie, and Nancy Henley. "Difference and Dominance: An Overview of Language, Gender, and Society." In B. Thorne and N. Henley, eds., *Language and Sex: Difference and Dominance*. Rowley, Mass.: Newbury House, 1975.

Thorpe, C. B. "Status, Race, and Aspiration: A Study of the Desire of High-School Students to Enter a Professional or a Technical Occupation." *Dissertation Abstracts*, 29 (1969):10-A, 3672 (Abstr.).

Tresemer, D. "Fear of Success: Popular, But Unproven," *Psychology Today*, 7(10) (1974):82.

Turner, C. D., and J. T. Bagnara. *General Endocrinology*. 5th ed. Philadelphia: Saunders, 1971.

Tyler, Leona E. *The Psychology of Human Differences*. New York: Appleton-Century-Crofts, 1965.

Unger, Rhoda. "The Rediscovery of Gender." *American Psychologist*, (1979), in press.

U. S. Department of Commerce. *Some Demographic Aspects of Aging in the U. S. Growth of the Population 65 Years and Over*. Washington, D.C.: U. S. Government Printing Office.

U. S. Department of Labor. *20 Facts on Women Workers*. Washington, D.C.: U. S. Department of Labor, 1978.

U. S. Public Health Service, Center for Disease Control. Comparative Risks of Three Methods of Midtrimester Abortion. *Morbidity and Mortality Weekly Report*, November 26, 1976:370.

von Franz, M.-L. "The Process of Individuation." In C. G. Jung, ed., *Man and His Symbols*. New York: G. P. Putnam's Sons, 1964.

Waber, Deborah P. "Biological Substrates of Field Dependence: Implications of the Sex Difference." *Psychological Bulletin*, 84 (1977):1076–1087.

Walters, Cathryn; J. T. Shurley; and O. A. Parsons. "Differences in Male and Female Responses to Underwater Sensory Deprivation: An Exploratory Study." *J. of Nervous and Mental Disease*, 135 (1962):302–310.

Webb, A. P. "Sex-Role Preferences and Adjustment in Early Adolescents." *Child Development*, 34 (1963):609–618.

Weideger, Paula. *Menstruation and Menopause*. New York: Knopf, 1976.

Weil, M. W. "An Analysis of the Factors Influencing Married Women's Actual or Planned Work Participation." *American Sociological Review*, 26 (1961):91–96.

Weinberg, Martin S., and Colin Williams. *Male Homosexuals: Their Problems and Adaptations*. New York: Oxford University Press, 1974.

Weiner, B., and A. Kukla. "An Attributional Analysis of Achievement Motivation." *J. of Personality and Social Psychology*, 15 (1970):1–20.

Weis, Kurt, and Sandra S. Borges. "Victimology and Rape: The Case of the Legitimate Victim." *Issues in Criminology*, 8(2) (1973):71–115.

Weiss, Noel S., et al. "Increasing Incidence of Endometrial Cancer in the United States." *New England Journal of Medicine*, 294 (1976):1259–1261.

Weiss, R. S. "The Emotional Impact of Marital Separation." *J. of Social Issues*, 32(1) (1976):135–145.

Weissman, Myrna M., and E. S. Paykel. *The Depressed Woman*. Chicago: University of Chicago Press, 1974.

Weisstein, Naomi. "Psychology Constructs the Female, or the Fantasy Life of the Male Psychologist." In M. H. Garskof, ed., *Roles Women Play: Readings Toward Women's Liberation*. Belmont, Calif.: Brooks/Cole, 1971.

Weitz, Shirley. "Sex Differences in Nonverbal Communication." *Sex Roles*, 2 (1976):175–184.

Weitzman, Lenore J.; Deborah Eifles; Elizabeth Hokada; and Catherine Ross. "Sex Role Socialization in Picture Books for Pre-School Children." *American Journal of Sociology*, 72 (1972):1125–1150.

Wendland, M. M. "Self-Concept in Southern Negro and White Adolescents as Related to Rural-Urban Residence." Unpublished Ph.D. dissertation, University of North Carolina at Chapel Hill, 1967.

Werry, J. S., and H. C. Quay. "The Prevalence of Behavior Symptoms in Younger Elementary School Children." *American Journal of Orthopsychiatry*, 41 (1971):136–143.

Weston, P. J., and Martha T. Mednick. "Race, Social Class, and the Motive to Avoid Success in Women." *J. of Cross-Cultural Psychology*, 1 (1970):285–291.

White, M. S. "Psychological and Social Barriers to Women in Science." *Science*, 170 (1970):413–416.

Whorf, B. L. *Language, Thought, and Reality*. Cambridge, Mass.: MIT Press, 1956.

Wilbur, C. B. "Clinical Aspects of Female Homosexuality. In J. Marmor, ed., *Sexual Inversion: The Multiple Roots of Homosexuality*. New York: Basic Books, 1965.

Williams, D. E. "Self-Concept and Verbal Mental Ability in Negro Pre-School Children." *Dissertation Abstracts*, 29 (1969):3475-B.

Williams, John E., and J. Kenneth Morland. "Comment on Banks's 'White Preference in Blacks: A Paradigm in Search of a Phenomenon.'" *Psychological Bulletin*, 86 (1979):28–32.

Willis, Frank N. "Initial Speaking Distance as a Function of the Speakers' Relationship." *Psychonomic Science*, 5 (1966):221–222.

Willis, J. *Addicts: Drugs and Alcohol Re-examined*. London: Pitman, 1973.

Wilsnack, Sharon C. "Femininity by the Bottle." *Psychology Today*, 6(11) (April 1973):39.

Winokur, G.; P. J. Clayton; and T. Reich. *Manic Depressive Illness*. St. Louis, Mo.: C. V. Mosby, 1969.

Witkin, H. A. "Origins of Cognitive Style." In C. Sheerer, ed., *Cognition: Theory, Research, Promise*. New York: Harper & Row, 1964.

Witkin, H. A.; H. B. Lewis; M. Hertzman; K. Machover; P. B. Meissner; and S. Wapner. *Personality Through Perception*. New York: Harper & Row, 1954.

Wittig, Michele A., and Paul Skolnick. "Status Versus Warmth as Determinants of Sex Differences in Personal Space." *Sex Roles*, 4 (1978): 493–503.

Wolff, Charlotte. *Love Between Women*. New York: Harper & Row, 1971.

Wolpe, Joseph, and A. A. Lazarus. *Behavior Therapy Techniques: A Guide to the Treatment of Neuroses*. New York: Pergamon Press, 1966.

Women on Words and Images. *Dick and Jane As Victims: Sex Stereotyping in Children's Readers*. Princeton, N. J.: Women on Words and Images, 1972.

Woudenberg, Roger A. "The Relationship of Sexual Attitudes, Attitudes Toward Women, and Racial Attitudes in White Males." *Sex Roles*, 3 (1977):101–110.

Yen, Wendy M. "Sex-Linked Major-Gene Influences on Selected Types of Spatial Performance." *Behavior Genetics*, 5 (1975):281–298.

Young, W. C.; R. Goy; and C. Phoenix. "Hormones and Sexual Behavior." *Science*, 143 (1964):212–218.

Zelditch, M. "Role Differentiation in the Nuclear Family. A Comparative Study." In T. Parsons and R. F. Bales, eds., *Family, Socialization and Interaction Process*. Glencoe, Ill.: Free Press, 1955.

Zimbardo, P. G., and Wendy Meadow. "Sexism Springs Eternal — In *The Reader's Digest*." Paper presented at Western Psychological Association Meetings, April 1974.

Zimmerman, Don H., and Candace West. "Sex Roles, Interruptions and Silences in Conversation." In B. Thorne and N. Henley, eds., *Language and Sex: Difference and Dominance*. Rowley, Mass.: Newbury House, 1975.

Zimmerman, E., and Mary B. Parlee. "Behavioral Changes Associated with the Menstrual Cycle: An Experimental Investigation." *J. of Applied Social Psychology*, 3 (1973):335–344.

Zuckerman, M., and L. Wheeler. "To Dispel Fantasies About the Fantasy-Based Measure of Fear of Success." *Psychology Bulletin*, 82 (1975): 932–946.

Index